Resource Kit

Microsoft

WINDOWS
MEDIA®
RESOURCE KIT

Tricia Gill, Bill Birney, and the
Microsoft® Windows Media® Team

PUBLISHED BY
Microsoft Press
A Division of Microsoft Corporation
One Microsoft Way
Redmond, Washington 98052-6399

Library of Congress Cataloging-in-Publication Data
Gill, Tricia.
    Microsoft Windows Media Resource Kit / members of the Microsoft Windows Media
Team, Tricia Gill, Bill Birney.
        p. cm.
    Includes index.
    ISBN 0-7356-1807-0
    1. Interactive multimedia. 2. Microsoft Windows (Computer file). I. Birney, Bill, 1950-
II. Title.

QA76.76.I59G53 2003
006.7--dc21   2003043649

Printed and bound in the United States of America.

1 2 3 4 5 6 7 8 9   QWT   8 7 6 5 4 3

Distributed in Canada by H.B. Fenn and Company Ltd.

A CIP catalogue record for this book is available from the British Library.

Microsoft Press books are available through booksellers and distributors worldwide. For further information about international editions, contact your local Microsoft Corporation office or contact Microsoft Press International directly at fax (425) 936-7329. Visit our Web site at www.microsoft.com/mspress. Send comments to *rkinput@microsoft.com*.

Acquisitions Editor: Alex Blanton
Project Editor: Aileen Wrothwell

Body Part No. X08-95161

To Gordon, for your continuous encouragement
and complete confidence in me.
—Tricia

To Joanne, Rachel, and Pat, for being there
and understanding.
—Bill

Contents at a Glance

Table of Contents

Foreword

The digital media revolution that began a decade ago with a handful of enthusiasts has become a full-blown phenomenon. The proliferation of top-tier entertainment content combined with the growing availability of broadband access has a new generation of users flocking to the Internet for digital movies and music. Our research indicates that six out of ten U.S. households use digital media each month, including downloading or streaming audio or video.

The corporate demand for digital media is growing just as fast. Enterprise customers are augmenting traditional means of corporate communication with live CEO broadcasts and "enterprise TV"; classroom training is being repackaged into Web-based interactive video training sessions that employees can attend from their desktops; and distance learning opportunities mean that employees can receive the training they need without the associated travel costs.

Several years ago, we embarked upon a mission to develop new technologies that would enable content providers, Internet Service Providers (ISPs), content delivery networks (CDNs), enterprises, and consumers to enjoy the best digital media experience available today. Windows Media 9 Series is the culmination of many years of work by a team of world-class professionals who have been dedicated to achieving this goal. From Fast Streaming, which can deliver an instant-on, always-on streaming experience, to the new professional-level audio and video codecs, Windows Media 9 Series delivers better sound quality and clearer video more reliably than ever before.

New dynamic content programming capabilities in Windows Media 9 Series, such as server-side playlists, enable content providers to change broadcast programming on the fly, or to insert advertisements in real time. This capability is of enormous value to advertisers who demand an experience much like you find on television: full-fidelity video with seamless playback.

Improved video-compression technology in Windows Media 9 Series helps lower bandwidth costs by 20 percent. The Windows Media Audio 9 Professional codec is the first technology to enable Web-based delivery of six-channel discrete surround sound, and the new Windows Media Video codec provides high-definition TV-like video quality in the same space as today's standard-definition DVD compression. And securing intellectual property is easy using built-in digital rights management (DRM) technology.

The open architecture of Windows Media 9 Series enables application developers to deliver exciting new products and services built upon Windows Media Technologies, using a state-of-the-art plug-in model for Windows Media Player, Windows Media Services, and Windows Media Encoder.

A vastly improved software development kit will allow developers to easily incorporate digital media into their applications and solutions, using the programming languages with which they are already familiar. Overall, the flexibility and extensibility of Windows Media 9 Series will provide the foundation for an entire new generation of client-side and server-side digital media solutions.

Understanding all that Windows Media 9 Series has to offer is the first step toward participating in the phenomenon that is digital media. This book, the *Windows Media Resource Kit*, uses an innovative, scenario-based approach to take you step-by-step through all the key features of Windows Media 9 Series. We have included detailed roadmaps for deploying Windows Media 9 Series in the enterprise and over the Internet. Along the way, we offer best practices, tips, and tools that will get your content streaming in no time.

So sit back, relax, and prepare to be amazed. I think you'll find that Windows Media 9 Series is packed with innovations that increase productivity and deliver the highest-quality entertainment while enabling you to operate your digital media system at lower costs than ever before.

Will Poole
Senior Vice President, Windows Client
Microsoft Corporation

Introduction

If you've ever clicked a link on a Web site that took you to a news story or movie trailer, or listened to a song snippet before ordering a CD from an online music store, then you've probably experienced streaming media. Streaming media is a new and continuously evolving medium that gets more interesting every day.

This book is a roadmap for setting up a streaming media system using Microsoft Windows Media 9 Series. What is Windows Media 9 Series? It's a suite of tools that enables you to create, encode, distribute, and play high-quality audio and video content over the Internet.

Streaming media isn't only for national retail chains with a large online presence. Nor is it only for Fortune 500 companies with global interests and extensive information technology (IT) departments. Rather, streaming media is for anyone who has an interest in making their music or movies available to others on the World Wide Web. So if you are thinking about using Windows Media 9 Series to create a streaming media system for a garage band or starting an Internet-only radio station, read on.

In this book, we'll address three distinct scenarios in three different market segments, and we'll explain from beginning to end how to implement these scenarios in your own environment. These scenarios were chosen based on our research into the most common streaming media implementations. While it would not be possible in a book of this size to cover all the nuances of each scenario, we do offer best practices where possible and offer suggestions for alternatives when it makes sense to do so.

Having explained what this book is, let's take a moment to describe what the book is not intended to be. This book is neither a troubleshooting guide nor an in-depth examination of Windows Media tools and features. It does not attempt to compare Windows Media 9 Series to other products on the market today. While this book does contain a chapter on the basics of streaming media, it does not purport to educate you on the history or science of the medium.

Who Should Read This Book?

The *Windows Media Resource Kit* is intended for anyone who wants to learn about streaming media in general and Windows Media 9 Series in particular. It is also meant for business decision makers who are looking for a streaming solution either inside corporate walls or over the Internet. This book is also written for content producers who are looking for ways to put their audio and video on the World Wide Web. And finally, this book is written for IT professionals who are tasked with implementing a streaming media infrastructure in the commercial or enterprise market.

How to Use this Book

The *Windows Media Resource Kit* is broken into four main parts and some appendixes. The first section introduces general concepts and serves as a primer for both streaming media and Windows Media 9 Series. Each of the sections that follow describes the implementation of a specific scenario. If you're new to streaming media, we recommend that you read the sections in order because each builds in complexity upon the the previous scenario. If you already know the basics and are familiar with Windows Media 9 Series, a quick scan of part I might be all you need before you skip directly to the part that most closely matches what you are trying to do. The appendixes and CD also provide reference material that you might find helpful.

How this Book is Organized

The book begins with a review of streaming media basics. These basics hold true regardless of the technology being used to stream digital media. In the first chapter of part I, we'll cover the differences between streaming content and downloading it, discuss the four phases of streaming, learn best practices for creating compelling audio and video content, understand how to calculate the optimal bit rate for your content, and explain the importance of codecs.

Chapters 2, 3, and 4 take those concepts and show how they apply to the Windows Media 9 Series platform. We'll introduce the three main components of the Windows Media platform, which enable you to compress, distribute, and play back digital media content. We'll also dig deeper into some of the features of each of these components in order to illustrate the breadth of tools available for ensuring that your streaming media implementation is just what you need it to be.

Parts II, III, and IV introduce real-life scenarios that can be put into practice in order to achieve different goals. In these scenarios, we walk you through the implementation process from envisioning the streaming media solution to planning for it, deploying it, and testing it. Along the way we discuss hardware and software needs, network considerations, fine-tuning, and scaling. We'll also discuss tools such as vision statements, business plans, topology maps, and so on that you might use to mark completion of each phase of the implementation.

How to Use the Companion CD

The CD that is provided with this book contains numerous white papers that supplement the material presented here. We've also included demos of Windows Media 9 Series in action and some useful tools, such as Windows Media Load Simulator 9 Series, that are referenced throughout the book. You'll also find Windows Media Player 9 Series and Windows Media Encoder 9 Series with its companion utilities.

System Requirements

The companion CD requires the following:

- Microsoft Internet Explorer 6.0

- Microsoft Producer for PowerPoint 2002. Microsoft Producer has the following minimum system requirements:

  - Microsoft Windows 2000 with Service Pack 1 or Microsoft Windows XP operating system.

  - 400 megahertz (MHz) processor. A processor speed of 600 MHz or higher is recommended when capturing from a digital video device.

  - 128 megabytes (MB) of RAM.

  - 2 gigabytes (GB) of free hard disk space.

  - An audio capture device to capture audio.

  - A video (DV or analog) capture device to capture video.

  - Microsoft Windows Media Player 7.1 or later. Windows Media Player 9 Series is recommended.

  - An Internet or network connection to publish a presentation to a Web site, intranet site, e-service provider, or shared network location.

Acknowledgements

While our names are on the cover, this book really is the result of months of collaboration among many talented and enthusiastic people. We offer our deepest thanks and appreciation to all of them.

A special thanks goes to Robert van Schooneveld who not only reviewed the entire book while out-waiting a power outage in the middle of winter, but continuously checked in to offer his assistance and encouragement, wrote scripts and code samples whenever requested, and spent many an afternoon on the phone fleshing out scenario details that were both compelling and realistic.

Many thanks also to Michael Wagner of Approach, Inc. Michael focused his enormous talents on the enterprise section of this book and sought to infuse us with his vast knowledge gained from many years in the streaming media business. He demonstrated great patience with all of our questions and brought credibility to the material that we could not have achieved without him.

We were fortunate to have drawn upon the expertise of many partners and third-party contributors. We offer our thanks to Gary Price and Tony Greenberg of Ramprate; Steve Lerner, of Speedera; Geoff Brousseau, of Playstream; and Michael (Chi Hung) Chiu and Kevin Headley. We also appreciate the assistance of our in-house experts at MS Studios, Jim Balazic and Mark Beauchamp.

It has been a pleasure to work the talented and professional people that made up our project team. Terrence Dorsey, our editor, guided us patiently and persistently, using wisdom gained from previous book projects. Paul Johnson, our artist, tackled our enormous list of art requests without hesitation. Harry Goodwin, John Green, Travis Wilson, and Keith Gabbert pulled together our companion CD into the cohesive package that it is today. Greg Lovitt painstakingly converted our text and graphics into a print-ready package, despite our occasional complaints about fonts and formats. Kari Rosenthal Annand, our indexer, carefully read through our material to create an index that was both comprehensive and concise. Starr Andersen put other projects aside in order to lend her subject expertise and writing talents to chapter 23. Our management, Gail McClellan and Tom Woolums, gave us their support and encouragement, allowing us the time and resources we needed to tackle a project of this size. We also extend a thank you to Microsoft Press, especially Alex Blanton and Aileen Wrothwell, for their gentle guidance and support.

We are also grateful for the crucial contributions of Alexandre Ferreira, Chris Knowlton, Matt Lichtenberg, Marc Melkonian, Michael Patten, Joe Powell, Andrea Pruneda, Dave Roth, Jim Travis, Justine Vick, Jennifer Winters, David Workman, and Lan Ye.

And finally, we are grateful to all the members of the Windows Media team for embracing this project. We are continually awed by their talents.

Microsoft Press Support Information

Every effort has been made to ensure the accuracy of the book and the contents of this companion CD. Microsoft Press provides corrections for books through the World Wide Web at:

http://www.microsoft.com/mspress/support

To connect directly to the Microsoft Press Knowledge Base and enter a query regarding a question or issue that you may have, go to:

http://www.microsoft.com/mspress/support/search.asp

If you have comments, questions, or ideas regarding the book or this CD-ROM, or questions that are not answered by querying the Knowledge Base, please send them to Microsoft Press via e-mail to:

mspinput@microsoft.com

or via postal mail to:

Microsoft Press
Attn: Microsoft Windows Media Resource Kit Editor
One Microsoft Way
Redmond, WA 98052-6399

Please note that product support is not offered through the above addresses.

Part I

Getting Started with Streaming Media

As the popularity of streaming media grows, content producers, businesses, and others are looking for ways to easily put their audio and video on the Web. This part takes a brief look at audio and video fundamentals, describes the process of capturing, encoding, distributing, and playing streamed audio and video, and introduces you to the latest Windows Media tools that will enable you to stream content over the Internet.

1

Understanding Streaming Media Concepts

Streaming media has become enormously popular in the last few years, and this popularity can be attributed to many factors. One obvious factor is that surfing the World Wide Web has become a popular pastime for a growing number of users. Surfing is possible because advances in technology have made broadband access more commonplace in households, schools, and businesses. While the "World Wide Wait" is not quite a faint memory, many users now have options for speeding up the flow of data that they didn't have before.

Content providers, such as news organizations and record labels, have recognized the potentially vast audience on the Internet and have incorporated audio and video into their Web sites in the form of news stories, music videos, movie trailers, and interviews with artists and performers. Companies, both large and small, have found that streaming audio and video from their internal Web sites is one way to reduce travel costs because employers can conduct training sessions or virtual company meetings where employees never have to leave their desks. Universities are now offering distance learning courses as a way to reach more students, such as those who cannot attend on-site classes due to family or work responsibilities. And parents are now able to keep grandparents up to date on the growth and progress of their grandchildren despite differences in geography.

So now that you understand how streaming audio and video are being used today, let's take a look at what streaming is and demystify the process of getting digital media content out of your camera or VCR and onto users' desktops.

Streaming Versus Download

It's important to understand the difference between streaming content and downloading it. When you download a file, you click a link on a Web page that corresponds to a file on a Web server somewhere, watch the little papers fly across the screen, and wait for a confirmation that the download is complete. When the download is complete, a copy of the original file has been safely stored somewhere on your computer's hard disk. The original file remains on the Web server, where it is available for others to copy. This act of copying is similar to copying a file locally from a floppy disk to your hard disk drive.

When you download a digital media file, such as a song or video, the process is the same. You click a hyperlink on a Web page that points to a file on a Web server. Your browser initiates the process of copying the file from the server. After the file has been copied to your hard disk, you can open and play it using a player application such as Windows Media Player.

The main advantage of downloading is that the file you download can be of any type: music file, text file, bitmap, and so on. And you can play the file over and over because, once downloaded, it resides on your computer's hard disk. A disadvantage is that downloading files takes time, and you have to wait for all of the data to be copied from the server to your hard disk before you can play or view the file. Why? Because the application you will use to view the file cannot access it until the download is complete.

But what if you could skip the download process and simply play the data in real time as it is being received by your computer? Instead of waiting for an entire video to be copied, for example, your player application could play it as soon as the first chunk of video arrives. This is the concept of streaming. Content is played as it is received from a server over a network, and it is not saved to your hard disk.

With streaming media, you get instant gratification—there is no download wait. Streaming a prerecorded audio or video file is like playing a CD or tape. You have all the same playback controls, like play, pause, stop, and rewind. The only thing you don't have is the physical media, such as CD or tape. You can choose what you want to listen to and when you want to listen to it.

Streaming also enables you to do live broadcasting, just like a radio or television station, except the broadcast is over the Internet.

But streaming does have disadvantages. Real-time playback of audio and video is highly dependent on the bit rate of the content and the bandwidth available on the network that is being used to deliver the stream.

Bandwidth and Bit Rate

In order for streaming to work properly, the player application must play the audio and video content at a steady and continuous rate. If the stream isn't continuous, the picture and sound will either stop or play back unevenly. This uneven playback occurs when the content is streamed at a bit rate that is higher than the bandwidth of the network.

The amount of time needed to download the file is directly related to the size of the file, the available bandwidth of the network, and the speed of your modem or network interface card. Network bandwidth can be compared to a water pipe. If you connect to the Internet using a modem and telephone line, the size of your pipe is very narrow—only a limited quantity of data can get through in a given amount of time. If you think of a file as being like a tank of water, then you understand that a very large tank of water takes a long time to go through a small pipe. Similarly, a large file can take several minutes to download from the Internet, through your telephone line, and onto your computer's hard disk, as shown in figure 1.1. Furthermore, if the files you download are large, such as a 60-minute video, you can quickly run out of hard disk space.

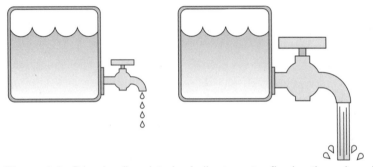

Figure 1.1   Downloading data is similar to water flowing through a pipe.

If bandwidth is the size of the pipe, then the bit rate is the amount of water—or data per second—that can travel through the pipe. Bit rate is most often measured in kilobits per second (Kbps). When preparing content for streaming over the Internet— a process called encoding—it is important to consider the amount of bandwidth that is available to the people who will be playing the stream, and then to select a bit rate that is appropriate for that bandwidth. For example, a person with a 28.8 modem can potentially receive 28,800 bits per second or 28.8 Kbps. But it's much more likely that they will receive less.

Why? Network overhead.

Network overhead is the other traffic that is always present on a network, filling up part of the available pipe. So if you are connecting to the Internet over a modem with a connection speed of 28.8 Kbps, then expect to do no better than 20 Kbps, maybe less. Similarly, a 56-Kbps modem probably won't deliver more than 33 Kbps, and so on.

The following table illustrates the different kinds of network connections that are available today and the maximum bandwidth associated with each.

Connection	Bandwidth
Dial-up	28.8 to 56 Kbps
ISDN	64 to 128 Kbps
DSL or Cable	128 to 768 Kbps
T-1	1.5 megabits per second (Mbps)
T-3	45 Mbps
DS-3	45 Mbps

Live Versus On-demand

Two delivery options are possible when streaming: live broadcast and on-demand. When to use each option depends primarily on the event itself, but there are other factors to consider as well.

Obviously, a live broadcast is necessary when an event of great importance takes place and viewers want to see and hear the event as it occurs. Examples might be a presidential election, a farewell performance by a beloved singer, breaking news, or a high-profile sporting event. If you intend to stream events such as these, you must ensure that you have the infrastructure to support it. This infrastructure includes encoders to compress the content, enough bandwidth to accommodate all the concurrent stream requests, multiple servers to distribute the load and to provide redundancy in case one or more servers go down, and, on networks where it is possible, routers that have been configured to support a special kind of broadcast called "multicast."

Streaming on demand is the appropriate choice for all the other times when the message is not time-critical. Streaming on demand enables you to re-broadcast a live event to those users who may have missed it the first time. They request the stream when they have the time to watch it, and they control the playback by rewinding, fast forwarding, pausing, and so on, to meet their needs. On-demand streaming potentially has lower bandwidth requirements because you are not required to service hundreds (or thousands) of concurrent streams.

Tools of the Trade

All the content that you will stream originates from some source. That source might be a file, a video stored on VHS tape or DVD, a live event recorded through an analog or digital camera, a television broadcast, and so on. While you can acquire content in a variety of ways, getting that content from the source and onto user's desktops requires three specific tools:

- An encoder

- A media server

- A player

The encoder compresses the content so it can traverse the network. Compression is necessary because audio and video in its native state is too large to fit within available network bandwidth.

The media server delivers the content to the player application that requests it. Usually, the player requests the stream from a page on a Web server. The Web server then sends a message to the media server to deliver the stream. You're probably wondering what the difference is between a Web server and a media server. Stay tuned. We'll get to that in a moment.

The player is the window through which the end user—the person requesting the stream—listens to your music or watches your video. It contains various controls that are similar to what you'll find on a VCR, including fast forward, rewind, pause, play, stop, and lots of other features as well. When watching an on-demand stream (a stream that was recorded earlier), viewers can use these controls to start and stop the stream at will or to repeat favorite sections of it. During a live broadcast, such as a concert or company meeting, such interaction is not possible because the event is being streamed as it happens.

Phases of Streaming Media

Before we go much further into the technical details, it's important to point out the four phases of streaming. We've already alluded to two of them, but here they are, in order, along with a brief description of each.

- Capturing: Pulling audio and video onto your computer from your camera, DVD player, or VCR and, when necessary, converting it to a digital form. In the case of on-demand streaming, the digitized content is saved to a file. For live streaming, it is not.

- Encoding: Compressing the content using specific codecs and settings so that it takes up less bandwidth when being streamed.

- Distribution: Delivering the compressed digital media over the network or onto storage media such as CD-ROM, DVD, or floppy disk.

- Playback: Decompressing the audio and video for viewing in a player application.

To help you understand the process, let's say you want to make a movie that currently resides on VHS tape available for streaming on the Internet.

Capturing

The capture phase is where you pull audio and video from its source and onto the computer using a capture card. If the source is analog, such as on a VHS videotape, then the capture card will convert the analog data to a digital form before depositing it on the computer. The digitizing process converts the audio and video to a stream of zeros and ones, or bits. Because data is being changed from one form to another, you will incur a slight quality loss during the process.

If you are using a digital device, such as a digital video camera, you would still run the audio and video through a capture card that is suitable for digital devices in order to get the data onto your computer. But since the data is already in a digital form, no conversion is necessary, and no degradation in quality occurs.

Many capture cards include a simple capture program that allows you to save the digitized media as an uncompressed AVI file, which is a standard video file format. If you are streaming a live event, saving the content into a file is not necessary because you move directly to the encode phase.

Encoding

Encoders come in two varieties: hardware and software. Their main purpose is to compress the content so it can be streamed over a network such as a local area network (LAN) or the Internet. After compression, the data is encoded into a streaming media format, such as Windows Media Video (WMV) or Windows Media Audio (WMA). Encoders use codecs (compressor/decompressors), which are algorithms that calculate and apply the amount of compression that is necessary based on the quality of the content and the intended transfer bit rate. Compressing is important because without it, content would never be suitable for streaming. For example, say the movie on a VHS tape is two hours long. Streaming it in its native state would require about 105 Mbps, which would choke a typical dial-up modem or broadband connection.

This book focuses on software encoders, specifically Windows Media Encoder 9 Series, which is introduced in chapter 2.

Distribution

With your movie digitized to a file on your computer, you can now distribute it in many ways. For example, you could put it in an e-mail message, burn it onto a CD, put it on a Web server for downloading, or stream it over the Internet.

Streaming content over the Internet requires a streaming media server. A streaming media server is different from a Web server in many ways.

First, a Web server delivers data as quickly as possible to the client computer and then moves on to service the next request. The Web server delivers this data in chunks in order to get it to the intended destination with minimal delay. In contrast, a streaming media server must maintain a constant connection with the client in order to send data at predictable rates. Maintaining a predictable rate is important because it reduces the potential for playback glitches and buffering delays that can disrupt the flow of content and negatively affect the end user experience. The streaming media server can also regulate the data being sent to the client based on feedback it receives from the player and log client data, which you can then use to understand trends, identify bottlenecks, or trouble-shoot performance issues on your server. Web servers do not provide this kind of func-tionality.

Second, Web servers cannot use the User Datagram Protocol (UDP), which is a connectionless protocol and the preferred protocol for streaming. If the client requests content from a Web server, the delivery of the stream is more likely to be interrupted by periods of silence because the player must collect and temporarily store or buffer data from the server.

Third, Web servers do not support live or multicast streaming. Live streaming can be extremely useful when you want to distribute important news to employees of your company, for example, as a live presentation happens. Multicast streaming is a one-to-many distribution method that saves bandwidth because only one stream is distributed to many clients. (See chapter 22 for more information about multicast streaming.)

Finally, Web servers cannot stream content at multiple bit rates, which can be useful when you need to stream content to a number of clients who are accessing your server at various connection speeds.

Although there are several streaming media servers on the market today, this book focuses on Windows Media Services 9 Series, which is part of Windows Server 2003, and is discussed further in chapter 3.

Playback

The final phase is where you view the movie or listen to music on your computer. To play back a streamed file, you either enter the location of the content in your player applica-tion or click a link on a Web page. The player then contacts the server to start the stream.

The player application we will use in each scenario described in this book is Win-dows Media Player 9 Series, the third piece of the Windows Media 9 Series platform.

Calculating Bit Rates

Now that you understand bandwidth and bit rate and are familiar with how they figure into the streaming media phases, let's talk about how to calculate them for both audio and video.

Bit Rates for Audio

When capturing audio and converting it to a digital form, you take discrete measurements of the audio signal at different points in time. These measurements are called samples. The more samples you take, the higher your sampling rate. Higher sampling rates usually mean better audio quality because the digitized version will more closely match the original. To put this in context, the sampling rate for a compact disc is 44,100 samples per second. This is denoted as 44.1 kilohertz (KHz).

Before we start calculating bit rate, however, there are two additional concepts to consider when thinking about audio: bit depth and channels. Bit depth refers to the number of bits that are used to store data about a particular sample. A greater bit depth means that more data is available about each sample, and more data leads to higher quality. CDs have a bit depth of 16 bits.

Channels, the final concept in the audio equation, are the number of discreet signals in an audio file or stream. Stereo, for example, has two channels, while mono has one. This is important because the number of channels figures into the size of your audio file.

Now for the audio bit rate calculations:

```
Samples per second * bit depth per sample * number of channels =
total bits per second (bps)

Total bits per second / 1024 bits per kilobit =
total Kbps
```

The bit rate of a CD, which in technical terms is uncompressed pulse code modulation (PCM) audio, would be as follows:

```
44,100 * 16 * 2 = 1,411,200 bps

1,411,200 / 1024 = 1,378 Kbps
```

According to our calculations, an uncompressed CD audio file would stream at 1,378 Kbps, while a typical 28.8 or 56 Kbps dial-up modem can stream up to approximately 32 Kbps. The dial-up modem would bog down before you hear a single note. Obviously, this kind of user experience is unacceptable.

Bit Rates for Video

To create the perception of motion, the brain automatically adds or fills in missing information. It does this first through a concept known as persistence of vision, where a visual stimulus continues to be registered by the brain for a very short time after the stimulus ends. Secondly, it takes advantage of what is known as the phi function. According to the phi function, when two adjacent lights alternately flash on and off, the brain interprets the flashing as a single light shifting back and forth. This is because we tend to fill in gaps between closely spaced objects of vision.

Motion pictures take advantage of these two phenomena to suggest the appearance of movement. Video content, for example, is a collection of static images rendered so quickly that the images appear to be in motion. Flip-page animations are also based on this concept. By making a series of drawings on separate pages and flipping them quickly with your thumb, you can make a picture seem to move.

In video, the images are called frames, and the speed at which they are displayed is measured in frames per second (fps). The higher the fps, the smoother the motion appears. Generally, the minimum fps needed to display smooth motion is about 30 fps. For high-motion content, you'll need 60 fps.

> **Note**   The 30 fps quoted above represents the National Television System Committee (NTSC) standard. Phase Alternating Line (PAL) is the European standard and uses 25 fps.

NTSC, PAL, and SECAM

The number of lines in a frame and the number of frames broadcast per second are determined by three main television broadcast standards. The standards are in place to ensure that broadcast signals are compatible with the television sets made to receive them. Most countries or regions use one of three standards. Each standard, however, is incompatible with the others.

- NTSC is used by many countries or regions in North and South America and Asia. It specifies 525 horizontal lines per frame, and uses a frame rate of 30 fps.

- PAL is used in most European countries or regions (except France and Russia). It specifies 625 lines per frame, and uses a frame rate of 25 fps. PAL also uses a wider channel and wider video bandwidth than NTSC.

- Sequential Couleur Avec Memoire (SECAM) was implemented in France in the early 1960s. It specifies 625 lines per frame, and uses a frame rate of 25 fps. Like PAL, SECAM also uses a wider channel and wider video bandwidth than NTSC.

Both the NTSC and PAL standards use interlaced video signals.

Each frame of video is composed of between 525 and 625 horizontal lines. Broadcast television uses a variation called interlaced frames in which every frame is composed of two fields. Each field contains every other line of the television frame, or half the image. One field contains the odd lines, the other the even lines. When displaying video, an NTSC television draws one field every 1/60th of a second, and PAL televisions display one field every 1/50th of a second. When video is converted to a digital format by using a capture card, the two interlaced fields are combined into a complete frame and rendered at 30 fps or 60 fields per second. This process is called deinterlacing and is explained further in chapter 2.

As you can see, the frames per second calculation is of primary importance and contributes directly to the bit rate required to stream video. Of equal importance is image resolution. If you think of image resolution as the number of pixels that combine to create a picture, then you understand that the more pixels you use, the better your image quality will be. But high-resolution video also creates large files, takes up more bandwidth, and requires more system resources to encode and render.

To determine the bit rate of uncompressed video, use these formulas:

```
Video resolution * video frame rate = Total pixels per second

Total pixels per second * [12 bits per pixel (based on the YUV pixel
format, which is more efficient for streaming)] = total bps

Total bps / 1024 = total Kbps

Total Kbps / 1024 = total Mbps
```

Let's say you want to figure the bit rate of the VHS movie that we discussed earlier. Its resolution is 640 × 480, and its frame rate is 30 frames per second.

```
640 * 480 * 30 = 9,216,000 pixels per second

9,216,000 pixels * 12 bits per pixel = 110,592,000 bps

110,592,000 bits / 1024 = 108,000 Kbps

108,000 Kbps / 1024 = 105 Mbps
```

You're not going to have much luck streaming 105 Mbps over any Internet connection that's available today. Add to that the audio bit rate that we calculated earlier so you can have a video signal with an accompanying sound track, and we're talking about a lot of bits! Enter the encoder.

Encoders, you'll recall, compress digitized audio and video and encode them into formats suitable for streaming. How much compression is applied depends on your desired audio and video quality and the bandwidth available to you. In broadband scenarios, you can go with higher resolutions because you have the bandwidth to accommodate them.

But in dial-up scenarios, you must make tradeoffs in order to deliver lower-bit-rate content at an acceptable level of quality. Once you know how much bandwidth you have to work with, you can use your encoder to compress the content sufficiently to fit within that bandwidth.

Pixel Formats

There are different methods for representing color and intensity information in a video image. The video format that a file uses to store this information is also known as the pixel format. When you convert a file to Windows Media Format, some pixel formats are recommended over others in order to maintain high content quality. The two major types of pixel formats are RGB and YUV.

Color video is comprised of three primary colors: red, green, and blue. When encoding using the RGB pixel format, 8 bits are allocated to each of the red, green, and blue values of every pixel for a total of 24 bits per pixel. The human eye is not capable of discerning all of the subtle variations in color, so bits are being expended when there really is no benefit to doing so.

The YUV pixel format is a color-encoding scheme that divides the spectrum of color into luminance (the black-and-white component of a video signal that controls the light intensity) and chrominance (the color component of the video signal). The human eye is less sensitive to color variations than to intensity variations, so YUV allows the encoding of luminance (Y) information at full bandwidth and chrominance (UV) information at half bandwidth. This means that 16 bits or fewer are allocated per pixel rather than the 24 bits allocated by the RGB pixel format, making YUV a more efficient pixel format for streaming.

Different YUV formats use different sampling techniques. These techniques vary in both the direction of the sampling and the frequency. They also differ in the ratio of luminance-to-chrominance sampling of a video signal. For example, when encoding using the YUY2 (4:2:2) sampling method, for every four pixels, each pixel is sampled for its luminance value. Two of the pixels are then sampled for their blue value, and the other two are sampled for their red value. Another scheme is 4:2:0, in which two bits are sampled for their blue value and none are sampled for the red value. This method uses less bandwidth and requires less storage space, but produces a slightly lower-quality video signal.

(continued)

Pixel Formats *(continued)*

The following list contains the recommended pixel formats (in order of preference) for encoding:

IYUV/I420 (planar 4:2:0 or 4:1:1).

YV12 (planar 4:2:0 or 4:1:1).

YUY2 (packed 4:2:2).

UYVY (packed 4:2:2)

YVYU (packed 4:2:2)

RGB 24

RGB 32

RGB 15/16

YVU9 (planar 16:1:1)

RGB 8

Creating the Best Audio and Video

The quality of the audio and video you stream largely depends on the quality of your source. If your video source is fuzzy or choppy, for example, your video stream will be as well. So before you stream your first video, it's important to make sure that you have the right equipment and an environment that is conducive to creating content that is the best that it can be.

This section provides best practices for creating audio and video. These best practices can be divided into two categories: the physical environment where the audio or video will be recorded, and the tools that will be used to record and edit it.

Ideally, the physical environment is a studio that has been soundproofed and equipped with state-of-the-art filming or recording equipment. But in practice, the environment is often a conference room in a busy office building or a spare bedroom in your home. You can create high-quality content at either of these locales by implementing as many of the best practices below as your schedule and budget will allow.

Audio Best Practices

Record your audio in a room that is void of ambient noise. This kind of noise can be caused by air conditioning systems, street traffic from outside the building, or other computers. You can reduce the noise significantly by:

■   Hanging curtains or tapestries on the walls to soften hard surfaces.

■   Turning off the heating, ventilation, and air conditioning system in the room.

- Turning off computers, fans, or other machines.

- Using an interior room that is isolated from street noise.

If using a microphone, point the microphone at the source. When the microphone is not aimed properly, the source could sound distant or muffled, making it difficult to understand. Keep hands and objects away from the microphone to reduce or eliminate microphone noise.

Many audio editing tools, ranging from simple to sophisticated, are available today. Some are professional-grade hardware tools that provide graphical depictions of the audio waveform. Others are software tools that enable you to cut and paste portions of the audio, add effects, or filter out hisses, pops, and other background noises. When setting up your audio source and the audio settings on your computer, keep these tips in mind:

- Sample the audio waveform at a rate that is at least twice the highest frequency component in the analog signal. For example, the human ear can hear sound up to a frequency of approximately 20 KHz. To accurately capture all the sound a human can hear, you would sample the analog audio waveform at a rate of at least 40 KHz.

- Capture audio using a high-quality card with digital input. A consumer-grade card is less expensive, but can pick up noise from the disk drives or computer peripherals. If you must capture audio from an analog source, balanced audio connections are better than RCA.

- If going from a balanced output to an unbalanced input on a sound card, make sure you use an audio adapter to isolate and match the input and output.

- Adjust the line input audio level in your system so that it is as high as possible, but without distortion. Some audio cards include an audio meter, which can show you when your recording level is too high or too low. If too high, indicated by the red area on the sound meter, digital distortion can result. If the level is too low, indicated by the yellow area of the meter, noise in the audio system will become more audible. To determine whether you have an audio meter, double-click the Volume icon in your system tray to display your audio mixer properties.

Video Best Practices

Selecting the right background can significantly improve the quality of your encoded video. A background that is continuously changing requires more bits to encode and results in a larger file or higher bandwidth requirements. If the bandwidth isn't available, then compromises in frame rate or image quality become necessary. When the background remains unchanged, fewer bits are needed because redundant data is not encoded. This results in better video quality without the higher bandwidth demands. Always try to use a solid, unchanging background, such as a professional photo studio backdrop.

Provide enough lighting for your subject so that the recorded image will have sharp edges, low contrast, and rich color. Diffuse the light, if possible, with a diffusion sheet or reflective umbrella to soften the light source, remove heavy contrasts, and reduce harsh shadows. Add light to the background if necessary, and focus a backlight at the back of the subject to help separate the subject from the background and improve edge definition.

Bright colors in a person's clothing can give the effect of bleeding into surrounding objects. Avoid white, orange, and fire-engine red. Stripes can also be distracting as they appear to move or crawl, especially when a person moves. For best results, choose colors that compliment the subject's skin tones and contrast with the background and other overlapping objects.

When setting up your video source and the video settings on your computer, keep these tips in mind:

- Adjust your video monitor using SMPTE color bars like the ones shown in figure 1.2. Adjust your computer monitor to match, using a high-resolution bitmap of the SMPTE bars. Don't adjust color levels with an uncalibrated computer monitor under fluorescent lights.

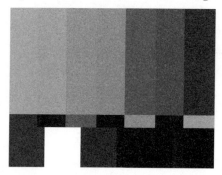

Figure 1.2   Adjust your monitor using SMPTE color bars.

- Adjust the brightness, contrast, saturation, and hue on your capture card so that it matches those on the video monitor.

- Start with a high-quality source. The following is a list of possible sources, in the order from best to worst:

  ❑ Serial digital interface (SDI) video. Used for digital video cameras and camcorders. Because the content stays in a digital format throughout the capturing and encoding processes, this results in the least amount of data translation, and results in the best-quality video.

❑   Component video. Used when sourcing from DVDs. With this source, the video signals are separated, for example, into the RGB or Y/R-y/ B-y format. Results in good video quality.

❑   S-Video. Used for S-VHS, DVD, or Hi-8 camcorders. The video signal is divided into luminance and chrominance. Results in good video quality.

❑   DV video. Used with DV devices, such as MiniDV digital camcorders connected through an IEEE 1394 video port. Results in good video quality.

❑   Composite video. Used for analog cameras, camcorders, cable TV, and VCRs. Composite video should only be used as a source as a last resort. With composite video, luminance and chrominance components are mixed, which makes it difficult to get good video quality.

2

Capturing and Encoding Content with Windows Media Encoder

In chapter 1 you learned about the four phases of streaming: capturing, encoding, distributing, and playing back. This chapter and the two that follow will take the concepts introduced in chapter 1 and apply them to Microsoft Windows Media 9 Series, the latest streaming media platform from Microsoft.

Windows Media 9 Series is a set of technologies that enables you to deliver rich digital media across all types of networks and devices. The technologies include:

- Windows Media Encoder 9 Series. Used in conjunction with the Windows Media 9 Audio and Video codecs to compress content. Windows Media Encoder and the codecs are explained in this chapter.

- Windows Media Services 9 Series. Used to distribute content over internal and external networks. Windows Media Services is explained in chapter 3.

- Windows Media Player 9 Series. Used to decode and render the content on personal computers and other consumer electronic devices. Windows Media Player is explained in chapter 4.

- Digital Rights Management (DRM). Used by content owners to set usage policies. DRM is introduced here in chapter 2.

- Windows Media 9 Series Software Development Kits. Used to build tailored applications and services.

Understanding Windows Media File Formats

You're probably already familiar with two standard Windows digital file formats, AVI and WAV. These are video and audio file formats, respectively, that provide the highest-quality playback when played from a CD or your computer's hard disk. But these file formats are not suitable for streaming because they are often uncompressed or have little compression applied, and are simply too large to traverse common network bandwidths.

Windows Media Format is the digital media format used for streaming. It is also suitable for local playback from CD or DVD, your computer's hard disk, set-top boxes, and portable devices. Windows Media Format is composed of Windows Media Audio and Video codecs, an optional integrated digital rights management (DRM) system, and a file container called Advanced Systems Format (ASF). It is a format that enables you to deliver audio and video data over a network while maintaining a quality level that is close to that of the content source.

Audio and video content is converted to Windows Media Format during the encoding process. Once encoded, these audio and video files or streams are indicated by the file name extensions listed in the table below.

Extension	File type	Description
.wma	Windows Media Audio	Files that include audio and can be played back using the Windows Media Audio codec.
.wmv	Windows Media Video	Files that include both audio and video (or video only) and can be played back using the Windows Media Audio and Windows Media Video codecs.
.asf	Advanced Systems Format	Content encoded with earlier versions of the Windows Media codecs. This content can be played back using both the Windows Media Audio and Windows Media Video codecs.

Understanding ASF

Advanced Systems Format (ASF) is an extensible file format designed primarily for storing synchronized digital media streams. The format supports data delivery over a wide variety of networks and protocols, while still proving suitable for local playback. ASF is the container format for Windows Media Audio and Windows Media Video-based content.

Understanding   ASF   *(continued)*

The ASF file container can store the following elements in a single file: audio, video, attributes (such as the file's title and author), and index and script commands (such as URLs and closed captioning). The file container supports files as large as 17 million terabytes.

In previous versions of Windows Media, files containing audio and video were indicated by the .asf file name extension. Although the .wma and .wmv file name extensions are now used, it is still possible to stream .asf files or to change the .asf file name extension to .wma (for audio-only files) or .wmv (for video-only or audio and video files).

Some tools and services that were created for use with earlier versions of Windows Media Technologies require the .asf extension to accept the content. You can simply rename any .wma or .wmv file with the .asf extension to use them with those tools. (However, it is recommended that you use the most current tool or service, when possible.)

Capturing Content

You might recall from chapter 1 that capturing content is the process of pulling content from a source—such as VCR, DVD, or camera—and running it through the computer where it will be compressed and converted into the Windows Media Format. Capturing is accomplished through the use of an audio or video capture card.

Two kinds of capture cards are available: analog and digital. The kind of card that is right for you depends on whether the source of your content is analog or digital. When using a digital camera, for example, you would use a digital capture card. This card enables you to capture the content from the source and transfer it to the computer without digitizing the data along the way. Digitizing is not necessary because, coming from a digital camera, the data is already in digital form. In contrast, analog cards take content from an analog device and digitize it before passing it on to the computer for encoding.

The capture process works like this:

1. Install the capture card in your computer. The card fits into one of the available expansion slots at the back of your computer. Numerous capture cards are available today in all price ranges. Some cards specialize in audio capture, while others are intended for video capture. When choosing your capture card, make sure it includes Video for Windows or Windows Driver Model (WDM) drivers, or look for the Windows Media 9 Series logo. A list of supported capture cards is provided on the Partner Center page of the Windows Media 9 Series Web site (http://www.microsoft.com/windowsmedia).

2. Connect your device to the input ports on your capture card. You'll need to connect both the audio and video sources to your card. Audio ports are fairly straightforward, but video ports can be a little confusing. Your card might contain several different kinds of video ports, such as those described in the accompanying sidebar.

Video and Audio Connections

A variety of connection and plug types are used to attach audio and video sources to your computer. Here are a few examples:

Video Connections

Composite video: Video intensity (luminance), color (chrominance), and synchronization components of an analog video signal are combined using a television standard, such as NTSC, in a single composite video signal. Composite ports typically use either RCA or BNC connectors, as shown in figure 2.1.

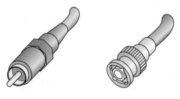

RCA   BNC

Figure 2.1   RCA and BNC connectors.

S-video: Before being combined into a composite signal, the luminance and chrominance signals can be used to transfer video between devices through an S-video port. Because the components have not been combined, the picture quality is better. However, in order to display the video, it must at some point be converted to a composite signal. S-video ports are available on devices such as S-VHS and Hi-8 camcorders and players, and many DVD players, and use special S-video connectors as shown in figure 2.2.

Figure 2.2   An S-video connector.

Video and Audio Connections   *(continued)*

Component video: Before video is processed into luminance and chrominance signals, it is in the form of three component signals: red, green, and blue (RGB). Component video ports provide the best quality analog video because the video has gone through the least amount of processing. You typically connect component video with three BNC or RCA connectors (see figure 2.1).

Serial digital interface (SDI): An SDI port carries a digital video signal coded using the CCIR-601 international standard for digital video transport. CCIR-601 is the predominant standard for high-quality uncompressed digital video. SDI ports are found on professional digital camcorders and videotape recorders, and use a BNC connector.

IEEE 1394: A computer bus standard that supports high-speed data transfer rates. IEEE 1394 ports are often used to transfer compressed digital video between consumer camcorders and computers, using the MiniDV video format. IEEE 1394 connectors, as shown in figure 2.3, are used on the ports.

Figure 2.3   An IEEE 1394 connector.

Audio Connections

Analog audio: The basic non-digital signal conveys audio electrically using changes in voltage to reproduce sound waves. Most devices that use sound have analog audio ports. Analog audio uses many different types of connectors, typically RCA, TRS, and XLR (see figure 2.4).

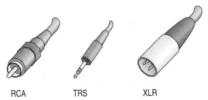

RCA   TRS   XLR

Figure 2.4   RCA, TRS, and XLR connectors.

SPDIF: An uncompressed, high-quality digital audio format used primarily in consumer devices. Most SPDIF ports use RCA or TRS (see figure 2.4) connectors with a heavy coaxial cable to reject external electrical interference.

AES/EBU: An uncompressed, high-quality digital audio format used primarily in professional devices. Most AES/EBU ports use XLR connectors (see figure 2.4).

3. Optimize your computer by:

    ■   Defragmenting your hard disk.

    ■   Turning off network and file sharing.

    ■   Closing all other programs, especially if a program accesses the hard disk.

4. Use Windows Media Encoder or the capture card software to capture the content. Use the capture card software when you want to save the content to an AVI file first. Capturing to AVI enables you to create a high-quality archive of uncompressed content that you can encode from later. It also enables you to edit the video using a variety of third-party editing tools before encoding the final cut.

    If broadcasting a live stream or converting directly to Windows Media Format, bypass the capture card software and use the encoder to capture the content.

    When you are capturing audio and video, keep these tips in mind:

■   Avoid converting pixel formats; instead, capture to the YUY2 or YUV12 pixel format. The YUY2 (4:2:2) pixel format enables you to avoid pixel format conversions during encoding. The Windows Media Video 9 codec is primarily a 4:2:0 pixel format, except that if you choose to maintain the interlacing in your content (a new feature with Windows Media Encoder 9 Series), then a 4:1:1 pixel format is used. Because the YUY2 format is a superset of both 4:2:0 and 4:1:1 pixel formats, the content can be converted to either format without any data loss. (See chapter 1 for more information about pixel formats.)

■   Crop your video to eliminate letterbox bars; this can greatly reduce the bandwidth requirement.

■   If your audio source has a 48 KHz sampling rate, then capture at that rate to a file, then either use a 48 KHz codec profile or re-sample before you encode. If you switch the sampling rate during encoding (for example, if your source is 48 KHz and you capture to a 44.1 KHz file), you use the operating system's re-sampler which yields poorer quality.

■   The resolution of your source content depends on the medium from which it originated. Professional-grade NTSC content is 720 × 480 pixels. Consumer-grade NTSC content is 640 × 480 pixels, and content from a DVD is 720 × 480. If you need to change the resolution of your video before streaming it, use a third-party tool to resize it, and then set the encoder output size to be the same as the input size. Attempting to resize and digitize the video at the same time could result in quality degradation.

Once your content has been captured to your computer, you are ready to encode. With Windows Media 9 Series, you have several options for encoding your content:

- Windows Media Encoder 9 Series. Windows Media Encoder is a powerful tool that encapsulates all of the latest encoding features, including the latest audio and video codecs, into a single user interface. Windows Media Encoder can compress audio and video sources for live or on-demand streaming. Windows Media Encoder is the encoding tool used throughout this book.

- Windows Media Encoding Script. This command-line tool provides much of the functionality of the full-featured encoder and is installed automatically as a separate utility when you install Windows Media Encoder.

- Alternative encoding solutions that are built on top of the Windows Media porting kits. These solutions include hardware encoders from companies such as Optibase, Tandberg Television, and Texas Instruments, as well as software encoders from companies such as Accom, Adobe, Avid, Discreet, and Sonic Foundry. While these third-party solutions are beyond the scope of this book, you can find more information about them at the Microsoft Web site (http://www.microsoft.com/windowsmedia).

Encoding Content with Windows Media Encoder

Windows Media Encoder 9 Series is the tool for compressing audio and video content into Windows Media Format so that is suitable for streaming over the Internet, downloading onto users' computers, or playing back on hardware devices. Using the encoder consists of three basic steps:

1.   Choosing a source. For example, you can capture content from devices such as a VCR or video camera, or you can convert files from one format or bit rate into Windows Media Format.

2.   Choosing your target destination and audio and video quality settings. Are you targeting a download-and-play scenario? Do you plan to stream the content? Or are you creating a high-quality archive? The encoder includes many pre-defined destination, video, and audio settings (profiles) that enable you to easily target your content for delivery to a variety of destinations, including set-top boxes, personal digital assistants (PDA), CD and DVD, and, of course, the Internet. The encoder also has a number of features that enable you to adjust and refine the predefined profiles to ensure that your encoded content meets your needs.

3. Selecting the distribution method. You can encode content to a file or broadcast it live, either directly from the encoder or from a Windows Media server.

Windows Media Encoder is available for download to any licensed user of Microsoft Windows.

Enhancements to Windows Media Encoder 9 Series

The encoder has evolved significantly over the past several years and now includes a rich set of features that gives you more control and flexibility at unmatched levels of audio and video quality.

Device Control

It's now possible to control the functions of your device—play, pause, stop, fast-forward, rewind, and eject—directly from the encoder. Device control is available for digital video cameras that are connected to an IEEE 1394 digital video port and videotape recorders (VTR) that are connected through a COM port and support the Sony RS422 protocol. You can also set up edit decision lists (EDLs) to specify the discrete segments of your content that you want to encode. Once the EDL is in place, encoding can proceed with minimal intervention on your part.

Multichannel Audio Sourcing

The encoder now enables you to encode multichannel audio for surround sound playback in six (5.1 audio) or eight (7.1 audio) channels. The format is specifically designed for CD, DVD, high-definition television (HDTV), and digital cinema audio programs.

Live DRM

You can control the use of your encoded content by protecting it with digital rights management (DRM) technology during the encoding process. You can use DRM either when encoding to a file or when broadcasting the stream. While content is being encoded it is encrypted with a key. A license is then required in order for users to play the content. This license contains the key to unlock the content and the rights that govern its use. For example, the license determines the number of times a user can play the content or when the playback period expires.

Push Distribution

From the encoder, initiate a connection with a remote Windows Media server to stream content. This is useful if the encoder is behind a firewall or if you, as the encoder user, want to control the stream.

Multiple Destinations

Optimize content for streaming or download-and-play scenarios. Or extend your reach to portable devices, set-top boxes, or physical format delivery (such as CDs or DVDs). In addition, support for interlaced content enables you to get better playback on televisions by preserving the odd and even fields of an interlaced frame. Nonsquare pixel support preserves the true resolution of DV and MPEG-2 content without distortion.

Improved MBR Streaming

Create the right file for any audience with MBR audio, multiple language support, and scalable video resolution that enables a different frame size for every bit rate in the MBR stream.

Scalable Video Resolution

When streaming over the Internet, content providers never know what connection speeds their audience will be using. And the possible range can be anywhere from 56 Kbps to 10 Mbps. While you can encode content at different rates and then provide links that allow users to choose the connection that fits them best, many users won't know their connection speed. Asking them to choose could result in a poor user experience. Moreover, connection speeds are dynamic and subject to change as a result of network congestion and many other factors.

To ensure an optimal user experience, the encoder, in conjunction with Windows Media Services, enables you to stream MBR content that is encoded at different bit rates and resolutions. This means you can encode one stream containing multiple rates that are optimized for each connection speed. The following table lists the common resolutions and bit rates for dial-up, DSL, and broadband users.

Resolution	Bit rate	Target audience
176 × 144	29 Kbps	Dial-up users
320 × 240	100 Kbps	DSL users
640 × 480	500 Kbps	Corporate LAN and cable modem users

Throughout the broadcast, the server can dynamically measure throughput to a given player to ensure that the best possible stream is delivered to each user, as shown in figure 2.5. The process of selecting the appropriate stream is handled by the server and the Player and is invisible to the user.

Figure 2.5   Content encoded at different resolutions and delivered as an MBR stream.

Multiple Languages

Use the encoder to encode audio in different languages, and then use Windows Media Stream Editor, a utility installed with the encoder, to combine the languages into one Windows Media file. Users can choose the language they want to listen to during playback. When combining audio streams, make sure the bit rates, codecs, encoding mode, and audio format are the same for all streams.

Helpful Utilities

Installed with the encoder are several additional utilities that allow you to trim portions of your encoded video, or add scripts, markers, and attributes (Windows Media File Editor); create and edit encoding profiles (Windows Media Profile Editor); split streams into separate files or combine streams from multiple source files (Windows Media Stream Editor); or perform encoding tasks from the command line (Windows Media Encoding Script). With the exception of Windows Media Encoding Script, each of these utilities is launched from the **Start** menu. Windows Media Encoding Script is launched from the command line by navigating to the directory where the Encoding Script is located, and typing "cscript.exe wmcmd.vbs" followed by the appropriate encoding command.

Upgrade Considerations

If you have used earlier versions of Windows Media Encoder, you'll be glad to know that upgrading to Windows Media Encoder 9 Series is easy. Simply download the encoder from the Windows Media page at the Microsoft Web site (http://www.microsoft.com/windowsmedia), and follow the instructions in the setup wizard.

If Windows Media Encoder 7 or 7.1 is resident on your computer, it will be overwritten during the installation process. Existing configuration files (files with the .wme file name extension) will be preserved.

Configuration files from version 4 of the encoder can be used with Windows Media Encoder 9 Series, but they must be renamed to use the .wme file name extension. (Version 4 files used the .asd file name extension.) You should modify these version 4 configuration files to use HTTP because the MSBD protocol is no longer supported.

All custom profiles will be preserved during the installation process. System profiles that have been updated for Windows Media Encoder 9 Series will replace earlier system profiles; system profiles that were not updated will be left intact. New Windows Media 9 Series screen capture profiles will be installed in the existing %systemroot% Program Files\Windows Media Components\Encoder\Profiles folder. New Windows Media 9 Series system profiles are stored in the %systemroot%Program Files\Windows Media Components\Encoder\Settings folder. All profiles have a .prx extension.

Understanding Codecs

We demonstrated in chapter 1 how quickly audio and video can consume bandwidth when converted to a digital format. You might recall that an uncompressed movie streamed at 30 frames per second with a resolution of 640 × 480 pixels would require 105 Mbps. Add to that 1 Mbps for audio and 4 Mbps for network overhead, and you have an unrealistic number, no matter how much bandwidth you have available.

The only way to stream this content over common Internet bandwidths is to compress the content to a reasonable size. You can compress content by applying compression algorithms to the data, taking into account the desired output quality and available bandwidth. Before the content is played, it is decompressed using decompression algorithms. These compression and decompression algorithms are called codecs, and the same codec that compresses the content during the encoding process must decompress the content during playback.

Codecs can be divided into two categories: lossy and lossless. Lossy compression methods discard redundant information, thereby changing enough of the original data that it is not possible to recreate the original during playback. Lossless compression methods use a kind of shorthand to represent redundant information. Because all of the redundant information is preserved, the original content can be recreated during playback.

Because all information is preserved during compression, lossless compression methods produce the highest-quality sound or video. But only lossy methods are capable of compressing data enough to achieve the low bit rates necessary for streaming on the Internet. Most of the Windows Media Audio and Video codecs are lossy.

Codecs are designed with a particular type of content in mind, such as video, applications video (screen images), music, or voice content. Because of this specialization, a codec rarely works efficiently for any type of media other than that for which it was designed. A codec that works well for music, for example, can produce good-quality speech, but probably will not compress the speech content to its absolute minimum size. For this reason, speech and music usually are handled by different codecs.

If you have used previous versions of Windows Media Encoder, you are already familiar with the audio, video, and screen codecs. All of them have been updated for Windows Media 9 Series to improve quality and efficiency, and are explained below.

Windows Media Audio 9 Codec

The Windows Media Audio 9 codec is the most popular codec for creating Windows Media Audio (WMA) files when only audio is used. The decoding portion of the codec (or bit stream syntax) was frozen more than four years ago, and only the encoding portion has been improved since then. Maintaining backward compatibility has been critical to support the consumer electronics manufacturers who choose to build devices that play WMA, and the Windows Media Audio 9 codec represents the third generation of backward-compatible improvements. You can play most audio content encoded with the Windows Media Audio 9 codec in Windows Media Player 6.4 and later.

In the Windows Media Audio 9 codec, five encoding modes are supported. The one-pass constant-bit-rate (CBR) encoding mode has been improved with rate control and masking algorithms. These algorithms enable the codec to intelligently predict which frequencies are inaudible. Those that are deemed inaudible are not encoded, therefore preserving bits in order to reduce file size. The Windows Media Audio 9 codec also includes new two-pass and variable-bit-rate (VBR) modes that further enhance quality over the one-pass mode.

For any of the codecs, one-pass CBR encoding is applicable to live encoding and transmission, while two-pass CBR is recommended for off-line encoding applications, such as on-demand streaming. The VBR modes are appropriate when the compressed clips will be downloaded and then played on the user's device, since the bit rate fluctuations are higher and require longer buffering delays. There is also a peak-constrained VBR encoding mode, which also requires two encoding passes, that is meant for playback on devices with a constrained reading speed. The Windows Media Audio 9 codec supports all of these encoding modes.

Note that content encoded using VBR encoding with the Windows Media Audio 9 codec may have glitches or silence during playback in Windows Media Player version 6.4. For Windows Media Player version 7.1 and later, content encoded with the Windows Media Audio 9 codec does not require the user to download the codec.

The Windows Media Audio 9 codec also supports a large list of encoding settings for mono and stereo audio, with bit rates ranging from 5 Kbps to 320 Kbps, and sampling rates ranging from 8 KHz to 48 KHz. At the typical CD sampling rate (44.1 KHz), most users select bit rates between 48 Kbps to 192 Kbps to achieve CD-like quality, depending on their sensitivity to compression artifacts and bandwidth availability.

Windows Media Audio 9 Professional Codec

The Windows Media Audio 9 Professional codec is the first Windows Media codec for audio that supports high-resolution (up to 24 bits per audio sample, and sampling rates of up to 96 KHz), and multiple channels (up to 8 discrete channels) for typical 5.1 or 7.1 speaker configurations in high-end home systems or commercial digital theaters.

This codec is designed for encoding multi-channel music and movie sound tracks at Internet broadband rates. Windows Media Audio 9 Professional codec can encode 5.1 channels at as low as 128 Kbps, although 192 Kbps provides excellent quality while leaving plenty of bandwidth for encoding video for broadband delivery.

As with the Windows Media Audio 9 codec, the Windows Media Audio 9 Professional codec supports five encoding modes: one-pass CBR, two-pass CBR, one-pass quality-based VBR, two-pass bit-rate-based VBR, and two-pass peak-constrained VBR. In addition, Windows Media Audio 9 Professional allows near-lossless compression at its highest-quality VBR setting.

For more information about encoding 5.1 audio content, see the CD at the back of this book.

Windows Media Audio 9 Voice

Windows Media Audio 9 Voice is a brand new codec that compresses mono-only audio at very low bit rates, which is useful for transmitting digital media through low-bit-rate modem or ISDN connections. The supported bit rates range from 4 to 20 Kbps and from

8 to 22 KHz, respectively. At this time, Windows Media Audio 9 Voice only supports one-pass CBR encoding mode.

When encoding audio at very low bit rates, some codecs will generally produce better quality on music, while others will produce better quality on speech. Windows Media Audio 9 Voice is a unique hybrid codec that uses an automatic classifier to detect voice and music, and applies the appropriate coding mode for each segment. When the content contains audio and speech, the mode selected depends on the dominant type of audio. The encoder also provides a manual mode so you can select the desired mode for any given segment of your audio.

Windows Media Audio 9 Lossless

Windows Media Audio 9 Lossless can compress a wide variety of audio sources, from CD resolution and sampling rates up to 24-bit, 96 KHz, 5.1 channel audio.

The Windows Media Audio 9 Lossless codec is integrated into the CD Copy function of Windows Media Player 9 Series and can achieve compression ratios of about 2:1 for stereo content. Multi-channel, high-resolution audio clips can often be compressed losslessly with higher ratios.

Windows Media Video 9 Codec

The Windows Media Video 9 codec enables you to encode high-quality video for delivery over a full range of bandwidths, and supports all five encoding modes.

Windows Media Video 9 achieves 15 to 50 percent compression improvements over version 8, and the improvements tend to be greater at higher bit rates. With the compression efficiency of Windows Media Video 9, you can achieve broadcast-quality BT.601 video at about 2 Mbps, and high-quality, high-definition video (720p, for example) at high-end broadcast or DVD rates (4 to 6 Mbps). All the broadcast formats are supported, including the high-definition 720p and 1080i variants.

The decoder portion of the Windows Media Video 9 codec also includes a frame interpolation feature. Frame interpolation, also known as video smoothing, is the process of creating intermediate video frames based on the data in two consecutive frames of encoded video. In effect, frame interpolation increases the frame rate of encoded video at the time of decoding. You can use frame interpolation to improve the smoothness of playback for video streams with low frame rates.

Because frame interpolation is a decoding feature, it does not involve any special encoding options and adds no overhead to the content. You can enable video smoothing using the Windows Media Format SDK or from the Video Acceleration Settings in Windows Media Player.

Windows Media Video 9 Screen Codec

The Windows Media Video 9 Screen codec is designed for capturing moving images of a computer desktop for the purposes of creating a demonstration. The entire desktop can be coded and transmitted at rates as low as 28 Kbps, although when there are images embedded in the desktop application, the bit rate is usually around 100 Kbps. Windows Media Video 9 Screen is much improved over earlier versions of the codec in both image quality and CPU usage, and it now supports one-pass VBR and one-pass CBR encoding.

MPEG-4 Compatibility

Does Microsoft support MPEG-4 video in Windows Media 9 Series? With the ISO MPEG-4 codec, Microsoft supports the video portion of the MPEG-4 standard. The ISO MPEG-4 codec is compliant with the video simple profile and interoperates with MPEG-4 video codecs developed independently by other companies.

Although Windows Media 9 Series only installs the ISO MPEG-4 decoder, it is possible to use the encoder portion of the codec when you import an MPEG-4 profile from an earlier version of the encoder or when the codec is already resident on your computer. It is recommended, however, that you use Windows Media Video 9 instead. Windows Media Video 9 is not compliant with the MPEG-4 standard, but does provide better video quality for a given bit rate.

Encoding Modes

Using Windows Media Encoder, you can encode audio and video content at either a constant bit rate (CBR) or a variable bit rate (VBR). The mode to use depends on the scenario you are targeting.

Choosing the Right Codec

With so many codecs to choose from, how do you decide which is best for your encoding needs? Because codecs are designed with a particular type of content in mind, any single codec rarely works efficiently for all typse of media. A codec that works well for music, for example, can produce good-quality speech, but probably will not compress the speech content to its absolute minimum size. For this reason, speech and music usually are handled by different codecs.

(continued)

Choosing the Right Codec   *(continued)*

Windows Media Encoder 9 Series attempts to choose the best codec for you based on the information you provide when setting up your session. This information includes the destination of the encoded content, the encoding mode (CBR or VBR), the bit rate, and so on. But you can always change the selected codec by clicking the **Edit** button on the **Compression** tab of the **Properties** dialog box.

Which audio codec should you use? For typical stereo broadcast and Internet broadband applications, use the Windows Media Audio 9 codec. If the audio or film contains a high-resolution or multi-channel track, then use Windows Media Audio 9 Professional. Use Windows Media Audio 9 Voice for low-bit-rate delivery over dial-up modem or ISDN, and use Windows Media Audio 9 Lossless when you want to minimize compression artifacts.

Which video codec is best? In the vast majority of cases, including broadband applications, use the Windows Media Video 9 codec. The Windows Media Video 9 Screen codec is intended for more limited scenarios, such as when you want to encode mouse movements for computer application training.

Constant Bit Rate Encoding

CBR encoding is designed to work most effectively in a streaming scenario. As its name implies, this mode encodes content at a fairly constant bit rate. The amount of bit rate fluctuation is constrained by the buffer size specified during encoding (typically five seconds). The same bit rate is applied to all of the content being encoded, regardless of complexity. This is ideal for streaming because you can ensure that your stream stays within the required bandwidth limits.

The drawback of CBR encoding is that the quality of the encoded stream fluctuates because some pieces of content are more difficult to compress than others. A "talking head" video—just a person talking, such as a reporter during a newscast—is relatively simple to compress because there isn't a lot of movement and the scene doesn't change. A car race, however, is fast moving and requires more bits to encode each scene. In CBR encoding, the same number of bits would be applied to both types of content, which could mean that the talking head gets more bits than it really needs and the car race doesn't get enough. Generally, these quality fluctuations are more pronounced at lower bit rates.

With CBR encoding, you can do one- or two-pass encoding. With one-pass encoding, the content passes through the encoder once, and compression is applied as the content is encountered. With two-pass encoding, the content is analyzed during the first pass, and then encoded in the second pass based on the data gathered during the first pass. Two-pass encoding can result in better quality because the encoder can allocate the bits more effectively within the window specified by the buffer. However, two-pass encoding takes longer because the encoder goes through all of the content twice. Two-pass encoding is not available for live broadcasts or when sourcing from devices unless you have enabled device control.

Variable Bit Rate Encoding

VBR encoding is most suited to scenarios in which preserving the quality of the source is more important than restricting the bandwidth or file size. For example, use VBR encoding when you are archiving content, or when you plan to distribute the content for downloading and playing either locally or on a device that has a constrained reading speed, such as a CD or DVD player. (You can also use the peak VBR encoding mode when you plan to stream the content.)

With VBR encoding, the bit rate fluctuates over the course of the stream, according to the complexity of the content. This is most advantageous when encoding content that is a mix of simple and complex data, such as video that switches between slow and fast motion. With VBR encoding, fewer bits are automatically allocated to less complex portions of the content, leaving enough bits available to encode more complicated portions. This means that content that has consistent complexity (for example, a "talking head" news story) would not benefit from VBR encoding.

When used on mixed content, VBR encoding produces a much better encoded output given the same file size when compared to CBR encoding. In some cases, you can end up with a VBR-encoded file that has the same quality as a CBR-encoded file, but with only half the file size.

There are three VBR encoding modes:

- Quality-based VBR encoding

- Bit rate-based VBR encoding

- Peak bit rate-based VBR encoding

Quality-based VBR Encoding

This is the preferred method when you want to guarantee the quality of your encoded content, such as when you are archiving content. With quality-based VBR encoding, you specify a desired quality level (from 0 to 100). Then, during encoding, the bit rate fluctuates according to the complexity of the stream—a higher bit rate is used for intense detail or high motion, and a lower bit rate is used for simpler content.

The advantage of quality-based VBR encoding is that quality remains consistent across all streams for which you specify the same quality setting. The disadvantage is that you cannot predict the file size or bandwidth requirements of the encoded content before encoding. Quality-based VBR encoding uses one-pass encoding. It is recommended that you use quality settings of 91 and above with this mode.

Bit Rate-based VBR Encoding

This mode enables you to achieve the highest possible quality level while staying within a predictable average bandwidth. Use this mode when you are planning to create files that can be downloaded before being played, or to control the size of the output file.

With bit rate-based VBR encoding, you specify the desired average bit rate. At any point, the bit rate may exceed the average bit rate but the overall bit rate does not exceed the average bit rate. Bit rate-based VBR encoding uses two-pass encoding. In the first pass, the data complexities are analyzed. Then, in the second pass, the quality level is set to achieve the average bit rate. Bit rate-based VBR encoding is not suitable for live broadcasts.

Peak Bit Rate-based VBR Encoding

This option is best when the content will be played back on a device that has a constrained reading speed, such as a CD or DVD player. This mode is similar to bit rate-based VBR encoding, except that you also specify the peak bit rate. The encoder then determines the image quality that can be achieved without exceeding the peak bit rate. The bit rate does fluctuate during encoding, but does not exceed the specified peak bit rate. This enables content to be played in low-bit-rate streaming scenarios or on devices with limited computing power. Peak bit rate-based VBR encoding uses two-pass encoding.

Choosing the right encoding mode can be confusing. The choice really depends on the method with which you will distribute your content, as shown in the following table:

Encoding mode	When to use
One-pass CBR	Use for live broadcasts, when streaming to earlier versions of the Player or to devices, or for progressive downloads from a Web server.
Two-pass CBR	Use for on-demand streaming of files.
Quality-based VBR	Use for content you want to archive.
Bit rate-based VBR	Use when you plan to have users download your files for local playback on a computer.
Peak bit rate-based VBR	Use when you plan to distribute your content on CDs or DVDs.

Optimizing Video

Standard motion picture film is shot at 24 fps. Before it can be broadcast on television, it must be converted to videotape and put through a telecine process (see figure 2.6) where frames are added that convert it to the 29.97 or 30 fps required by the NTSC standard. This process is also known as the 3:2 pulldown because two fields from two consecutive frames are combined to create a third frame of video.

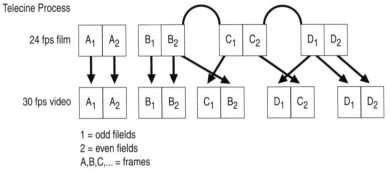

Telecine Process

24 fps film A_1 A_2 B_1 B_2 C_1 C_2 D_1 D_2

30 fps video A_1 A_2 B_1 B_2 C_1 B_2 D_1 C_2 D_1 D_2

1 = odd filelds
2 = even fields
A,B,C,... = frames

Figure 2.6   The telecine process.

A video frame can be either interlaced or progressive. An interlaced video frame contains two fields per frame captured at different instants in time, as shown in figure 2.7. The first field contains the odd lines, and the second contains the even lines. When the video is being rendered, the lines of one field are displayed first, and then the lines of the second field are displayed. In contrast, with a progressive video frame, the lines in each frame are painted sequentially. Interlaced content is common because the NTSC and PAL standards use interlaced video signals.

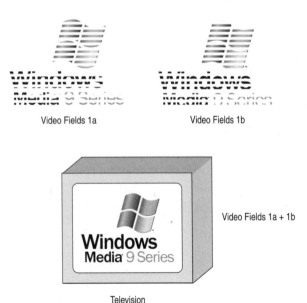

Video Fields 1a   Video Fields 1b

Video Fields 1a + 1b

Television

Figure 2.7   Video signals are interlaced to create a single frame.

Displaying video that has been telecined or interlaced on a computer monitor can result in flickering or streaking because computer monitors use a progressive display format, where lines of a frame are painted one after another in quick succession. The only way to eliminate this flickering and streaking is to remove the telecine or interlacing effects. There are hardware solutions for doing this, or you can use the Windows Media Encoder deinterlace and inverse telecine filters.

The Windows Media Encoder filters enable you to handle telecined and interlaced content effectively by removing the extra frames from the telecine process or deinterlacing the content before it is encoded. A built-in interlace filter enables you to retain the interlacing of your source video when you intend for your content to be played back on an interlaced display.

The filter that you apply depends on the source of your content and your playback intentions. The following filters are available in Windows Media Encoder 9 Series.

Normal Deinterlacing

Default deinterlacing filter that blends the even and odd fields of an interlaced frame to create a progressive frame.

Half-size Deinterlacing

Blends the even and odd fields into one frame. Used when the number of lines specified for the output video is half (or less) than those of the input video. For example, this filter is used when the resolution of the input video is 640 × 480 pixels and the output is 320 × 240 pixels.

Half-size, Double Frame Rate Deinterlacing

Produces a progressive frame from each field of the video sequence in order to preserve the full motion of the interlaced frames. Used when the number of lines specified for the output video is half (or less) than those of the input video, and the output frame rate is twice as high. Because of the amount of processing required, this filter has higher performance and bit rate requirements.

Interlacing

Preserves the interlaced frames during the encoding process so content can be played back effectively on interlaced devices such as televisions and set-top boxes. If your source video is mixed (progressive and interlaced) and you select this option, the output video will also be mixed.

Maintaining interlacing in source video when encoding at a low frame rate (for example, 15 fps) can introduce undesirable artifacts in the encoded content. Therefore, if you are encoding at a low frame rate, it is recommended that you deinterlace the video, even if the content is intended for display on an interlaced device.

Inverse Telecine

Detects and removes frames that were added during the telecine process. Also removes artifacts that resulted from telecine pattern breaks introduced during the video editing process. Should only be used when content originated on film.

Optimizing Your Encoding System

Encoding requires a great deal of CPU resources. You can minimize the CPU demands, especially when capturing screens or encoding a live broadcast, by following a few simple guidelines:

- A fast computer. Using a fast computer is especially important if you plan to capture and compress content in real time. A computer with two or more processors is your best bet to ensure that enough horsepower is available to process audio and video samples in real time. The encoder can use up to four processors for video and two for audio. As a general rule, if you find that you continually reach or exceed 80 percent of the CPU load (as indicated on the **General** tab of the **Monitor** panel), you may want to consider upgrading your computer.

- Supported audio and video cards. For a complete list of supported cards, see the Partner Center page of the Windows Media 9 Series Web site.

- Microsoft Windows XP Professional. Windows XP Professional takes full advantage of a multiprocessor computer by automatically spawning separate threads to enable processes to run different parts of their programs on different processors simultaneously. This parsing of the work enables you to perform high-end encoding tasks without maximizing your CPU usage.

- Check network bandwidth. It is rare that you will achieve 100 percent throughput when sending content over a network. For optimal results, ensure that your network can accommodate the aggregate bandwidth required by your broadcast session plus the overhead for HTTP.

- High-performance hard disks. For archiving or file conversion, use a high-performance hard disk, such as SCSI hard disks operating at 15,000 rotations per minute, in conjunction with a RAID 0 configuration. Using a high-performance hard disk and a RAID array can help to offload performance requirements from the main CPU, freeing up more processing power for encoding. In addition, it is useful to use the hard disk array only for encoding purposes.

- Keep the encoder on a dedicated computer. If you are streaming content from a server running Windows Media Services, it is recommended that you run the encoder on a separate computer from the Windows Media server.

- Turn off video preview and postview. The **Input** and **Output** areas in the main encoder window show you what your content looks like before and after it is encoded. Turning off these displays improves encoding performance. Or, to achieve a minor performance improvement, you can reduce the views.

■ Store captured content temporarily. If you are encoding to a file while sourcing from devices, store the content to a hard disk temporarily. In addition, use a different hard disk than the one dedicated to encoding.

■ Disable hardware acceleration. By disabling hardware acceleration, you lower the video quality and frame rate of the display, thus simplifying the encoding process. To disable hardware acceleration, open **Control Panel**, click **Appearance and Themes**, and click **Display**. On the **Display Properties** page, click **Settings**, click **Advanced**, and then click the **Troubleshoot** tab. Move the slider to the left toward **None**.

■ Use an NTFS volume. The FAT32 file system has a file size limit of 4 GB, so an NTFS volume is a better choice for storing content.

■ Optimize your computer. To optimize your computer, defragment your hard drive, turn off network and file sharing, close unused applications, and disable any services that you aren't using in order to free up system resources.

When you are capturing video of the computer screen, keep the following recommendations in mind:

■ Use a lower frame rate, such as 5 fps. The higher the fps, the more memory required to process the data.

■ Set your monitor to use a lower display size. For example, capturing at a 1024 × 768 resolution yields more data than capturing at 640 × 480.

■ Use a fast video card and set your color display to 16-bit or 8-bit color. Or, to further improve the CPU usage set the encoder to run in 256-color mode. Keep in mind that running in 256 colors can introduce a palette change when switching between programs that have different color schemes. The encoder does not support palette changes for real-time screen capture. Therefore, you should use 16-bit colors or capture to an AVI file first, then use the encoder to convert the file to Windows Media Format.

■ Avoid multiple scene changes, such as opening and closing windows in rapid succession during the capture.

■ Capture screens or regions only from the primary monitor when using a dual-monitor scenario.

■ Set up the output frame size to be the same as the source. Do not use the encoder to resize the source video.

■ Use a solid background on your desktop. Using complex designs, pictures, gradient shading, or multiple colors requires more CPU resources because there is more data to capture.

Video Optimization

Similar to choosing a codec or encoding mode, choosing the kind of optimization to apply to your content depends on the content itself and how it will be played back.

TV Sources

Your source was shot with TV cameras, then it is interlaced. Maintain the interlacing during encoding when you intend for the content to be played on a television, such as when using a set-top box.

When the content will be played back on a computer, either maintain interlacing and allow the decoder to deinterlace the frames during playback or apply a more sophisticated deinterlacing filter prior to encoding.

Film Sources

If your source was shot on film and then converted to video, it is telecined. Apply the inverse telecine filter to eliminate the extra frames and set your frame rate in the encoder to 24 fps. Inverse telecine is intended for NTSC content only. Do not use this filter for PAL content.

Unknown Sources

If you are uncertain of the origin, use the encoder to detect the format.

Mixed Sources

If your content is a mix of film and video, then it is telecined and interlaced. Maintain the interlacing during encoding when you intend for the content to be played on a television, such as when using a set-top box.

When the content will be played back on a computer, either maintain interlacing and allow the decoder to deinterlace the frames during playback or apply a more sophisticated deinterlacing filter prior to encoding.

Note that these recommendations apply only when you are encoding interlaced or mixed content of the typical 480i (NTSC), 576i (PAL), or 1080i formats without cropping any video lines (resolutions such as 640 × 480, 720 × 480, 320 × 480, 720 × 576, 360 × 576, and so on). Otherwise, you should always deinterlace before encoding.

Best Practices for Encoding

Encoding is a complex task, involving tradeoffs between delivery bit rate, frames per second, buffer size, video quality, and other factors. The encoder includes many predefined destination, video, and audio settings (profiles) that have already taken this balance into consideration. You can easily encode content using a predefined profile. However, if you want to customize the settings, use the following information to decide which changes will provide the best results in your scenario.

- Use a frame size that can be streamed efficiently and played back over common Internet bandwidths. Lowering the screen resolution decreases the amount of data to capture. A resolution of 320 × 240 pixels is adequate for streaming over the Internet.

- Use a frame rate that is appropriate for the content. For example, if you are encoding screens, use a low frame rate, such as 5 fps. On the other hand, when sourcing from high-motion content, use 30 fps. There is often a tradeoff between image quality and frame rate.

    Ideally, you would increase the frame rate to keep pace with the image quality. But as you increase the resolution and frame rate, you also increase the demands on your encoding computer. If your computer can't meet those demands it will start to drop frames. In that case, you should decide which setting is more important, and adjust the other accordingly. For example, if maintaining the frame rate is more important, then decrease the image quality setting.

- Adjust image quality, depending on the content. You can adjust the image quality to be smoother or more clear. Increasing the clarity can affect the frame rate, depending on the video. For example, if your video contains a lot of motion, increasing the clarity may decrease the frame rate. In addition, increasing the clarity results in a higher bit rate requirement and may also necessitate increasing the buffer size.

- Use a larger buffer in order to avoid intermittent buffering delays. The bit rate and quality of content will fluctuate within the confines of the buffer size. Using a larger buffer allows the codec more content over which to normalize the quality level. This can result in better quality, but the user must wait longer for the video to start, as a player waits to play until its buffer is filled.

    Typically, the buffer delay matches the time, in seconds, of the buffer size set in the encoder. However, if you plan to stream from a Windows Media server, you can set a larger buffer size in the encoder. A feature in Windows Media Services, called Fast Start, enables a player to fill its buffer faster than real time, assuming there is sufficient bandwidth. This means that the initial buffer delay may be much shorter. For example, when a user attempts to play back 56-Kbps encoded content on a DSL or cable modem, the start-up delay may be only a second or two, even if the buffer size set during encoding was much longer.

- Increase the distance between key frames. A key frame (also known as an I-frame) is an element in a video file that contains all of the data needed to display a single frame of video. The intermittent frames that occur between key frames only include data for changes, or deltas, from the previous key frame.

For low-motion content, such as a speaker at a podium, a setting of 20 seconds is typically appropriate because very little is changing within the scene. For higher-bit-rate content, such as a sporting event where the entire frame changes very quickly, you should lower the key frame distance so key frames are generated more frequently. The encoder will generate a key frame automatically before the time interval specified if there is enough change within the scene to warrant it.

- Use a high bit rate. A higher bit rate achieves better image quality. If the bit rate setting is too low, the codec will drop frames to produce a higher-quality image, although this may not be visible to the viewer. (Note that if you are encoding low-motion video, the actual bit rate may be significantly lower than the expected bit rate.)

- Use the appropriate codec. For example, when your audio source is voice or primarily voice, use the Windows Media Audio 9 Voice codec. For a screen capture session, use the Windows Media Video 9 Screen codec.

- Use two-pass encoding when possible. You will typically achieve higher quality with two-pass encoding, because the encoder has the opportunity to analyze the content during the first pass. Two-pass encoding is a function of the codec and is used in conjunction with CBR and VBR encoding modes.

- When encoding high-bit-rate on-demand content, capture to an uncompressed AVI file first. Capturing an uncompressed frame is much less CPU intensive, and you can use a two-pass VBR encoding mode (bit rate-based or peak bit rate-based) to achieve higher quality. When encoding content into an uncompressed file, you need plenty of available hard drive space to accommodate the large file size.

- Only use the deinterlace and inverse telecine filters when necessary. Deinterlacing content or removing extra frames with the inverse telecine filter consumes CPU resources and can cause quality degradation when used inappropriately, such as applying the inverse telecine filter to content that was not previously telecined.

- Consider the Player versions that your users will use to view your content. Content encoded with the Windows Media 9 Series codecs (except for the Windows Media Audio 9 codec) is not supported in Windows Media Player version 6.4. Content encoded with the Windows Media Audio 9 codec may have glitches or silence during playback in Windows Media Player version 6.4.

Encoding Feature Requirements

The following table provides information about the Windows Media Encoder features that have specific Windows Media Player, operating system, or codec requirements.

Encoder Feature	Player Version	Operating System	Codecs
Interlaced output video	Windows Media Player 9 Series	Windows XP	Windows Media Video 9 .
Nonsquare pixel output	Windows Media Player 9 Series		
Multiple-resolution MBR content	Windows Media Player 9 Series		
MBR audio	Windows Media Player 9 Series		
DRM support	Windows Media Player 6.4 and later		
Multichannel audio	Windows Media Player 9 Series	Windows XP	Windows Media Audio 9 Professional or Windows Media Audio 9 Lossless
High-resolution audio (24-bit, 96 kHz)[1]	Windows Media Player 9 Series	Windows XP	Windows Media Audio 9 Professional
Dynamic range control	Windows Media Player 9 Series	Windows XP Professional	Windows Media Audio 9
CBR encoding (one-or two-pass)	Windows Media Player 6.4 or later		See the following table
Quality-based VBR	Windows Media Player 7.1 or later		See the following table
Bit rate-based VBR	Windows Media Player 7.1 or later		See the following table
Peak bit rate-based VBR	Windows Media Player 7.1 or later		See the following table

[1] Earlier players or operating systems will render 16-bit, 48-kHz content

Understanding the Buffer

"Buffering" is a dirty word in the streaming media business. While buffering is a necessary evil in streaming, it is often confused with the concept of delay.

Buffering refers to the time during which Windows Media Player receives and stores data("filling the buffer"), but before it can start rendering the content. The Fast Start and Fast Cache features of Windows Media Services greatly improve the end-user experience by minimizing the time it takes to fill the Player buffer.

"Delay" refers to amount of time it takes for a frame to be captured, encoded, and then rendered on the Player. Current technology does not allow you to stream content in real time with less than a 2-second delay. But there are a few adjustments you can make to the encoder, server, and Player to reduce the amount of delay by a few seconds end-to-end.

- On the server running Windows Media Services, select the appropriate broadcast publishing point, click the **Properties** tab, click **Networking**, right-click **Enable buffering**, and then click **Disable**.

- In Windows Media Player, click the **Tools** menu, and then click **Options**. Click the **Performance** tab, click **Buffer**, and then type the number of seconds to use for buffering.

- In Windows Media Encoder, click **Properties**, click the **Compression** tab, and then click **Edit**. Click the tab containing the bit rate for which you will adjust the buffer, such as 282 Kbps. In **Buffer size**, type the number of seconds to use for buffering. This number indicates the amount of time content will be stored before encoding begins. It also represents the amount of time that the Player will lag behind the encoder during a broadcast.

Note that these adjustments could lower playback quality and performance.

Note that content encoded with the Windows Media Audio and Video 9 codecs (except for the Windows Media Audio 9 codec) is not supported in Windows Media Player version 6.4. For Windows Media Player version 7.1 and Windows Media Player for Windows XP, content encoded with any of the codecs requires users to download the codec before playback. Content encoded using VBR encoding with the Windows Media Audio 9 codec may have glitches or silence during playback in Windows Media Player version 6.4. For Windows Media Player version 7.1 and Windows Media Player for Windows XP, content encoded with the Windows Media Audio 9 codec does not require a user to download the codec.

The following table lists the supported encoding methods for the codecs that are included with the encoder.

Codec	One-pass CBR	Two-pass CBR	Quality-based VBR	Bit rate-based VBR	Peak bit rate-based VBR
Windows Media Audio 9 Professional	Yes	Yes	Yes	Yes	Yes
Windows Media Audio 9 Lossless	No	No	Yes	No	No
Windows Media Audio 9	Yes	Yes	Yes[1]	Yes[1]	Yes[1]
Windows Media Audio 9 Voice	Yes	No	No	No	No
Windows Media Video 9	Yes	Yes	Yes	Yes	Yes
Windows Media Video 8.1	Yes	Yes	Yes	Yes	Yes
Windows Media Video 7	Yes	Yes	Yes	Yes	Yes
Windows Media Video 9 Screen	Yes	No	Yes	No	No

[1] Some glitches or silence may occur during playback in Windows Media Player version 6.4.

Protecting Content with Digital Rights Management

As the availability of online music, books, films, and other types of digital media has increased, so have the concerns of content owners, artists, and publishers who own the copyrights to the material. In response to these concerns, Microsoft developed DRM technology to be used in conjunction with Windows Media Encoder and Windows Media Player.

DRM enables content owners to package their Windows Media-based files by encrypting the content with a key. The key is a piece of data that locks and unlocks the content. To play the encrypted file or stream, the user needs to obtain a separate license that contains this key. The license enables content owners to set rights determining how users can use the protected content. For example, a content owner could set an expiration date for the license or allow users to play the content a given number of times, after which the user would need to acquire a new license. Licenses are typically issued by a license provider, who provides a licensing service for one or more content owners. Licenses are bound to the computer to which they were issued, and so cannot be copied or shared.

The DRM process is described in the following download scenario. A content owner encodes source content to create a Windows Media file, protects it using DRM, then distributes the protected file to users on a Web site. A user downloads the file and then plays it using a player that supports DRM. The player, detecting that the file is protected, connects to the license provider's Web site to acquire a license. Once the user has agreed to the terms of the license, the license is issued. The user can then play the content according to the terms of the license.

Figure 2.8 shows the basic DRM process.

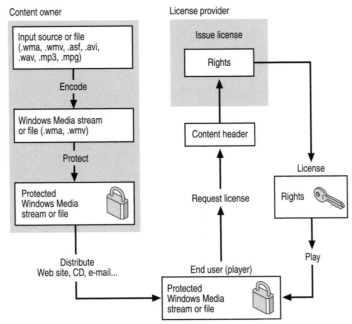

Figure 2.8 Encrypting, licensing, and playing a protected file.

In previous releases of Windows Media Technologies, the process of encrypting content required the use of the Microsoft Windows Media Rights Manager SDK, and was performed after the content had already been encoded into a Windows Media file. In Windows Media 9 Series, real-time DRM is available with Windows Media Encoder and the Windows Media Encoder SDK; that is, you can protect and encode content in the same process. Now, in addition to developers using the Windows Media SDKs, users of Windows Media Encoder can also protect their content.

However, protecting content is only the first half of the DRM process; licenses must also be issued. License providers use the Windows Media Rights Manager SDK to create a licensing service, and Windows Media Encoder users can use one of these services to issue licenses for their content.

Encoding and Protecting Content

Once you have a DRM profile, you are ready to protect your content. Using Windows Media Encoder 9 Series, you can protect files or streams as a step during the encoding process.

Figure 2.9. shows how you select the DRM profile for protecting your content during the encoding session.

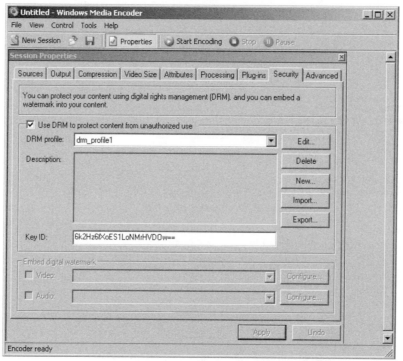

Figure 2.9   Protecting content with DRM during the encoding process.

Once you have configured the encoding session and selected a DRM profile, you can apply the settings you specified and start encoding. During this process, the key to lock the content is created, the content is encrypted with that key, and DRM-specific information is added to the content header.

At this time, a key ID is also generated. The key ID is used in the encryption algorithm, along with other secret values, to generate the key. The key ID is stored in the content header and is extracted later by the license provider to generate the correct license. While you can specify a key ID, it is recommended you let Windows Media Encoder generate a unique value each time you encode.

Playing Protected Content

After content has been encoded and protected, the user can begin to play it by using player software that supports DRM, such as Windows Media Player 9 Series. When the player detects that the content is protected, it searches the computer for a license. If one is not found, the player opens the URL to the license provider's service to request a license. The licensing service issues a license as described in the next section. Then the user can play the content according to the rights that are specified in the license.

Depending on whether the license allows it, the user can transfer protected files to portable devices that support DRM. The license for a particular protected file may allow a limited number of transfers, or it may disallow playback on portable devices altogether.

Generating and Issuing Licenses

When a user tries to play protected content, the player sends a license request to the license provider's service. This license request includes the content header, which contains the key ID. The license provider uses the key ID and the rights specified by the content owner to generate the license for the content.

A license contains the following information:

- The key to unlock the protected file or stream.

- The rights and conditions of the license.

- Priority of the license with respect to other licenses for the same content.

- Custom attributes (name-value pairs), which might include the date the license was generated or a description of the license.

Once the user has met the requirements for the license (for example, providing payment or registration information), the license is issued.

Licenses can be issued silently or non-silently. Issuing the license silently makes sense when you have no need for the user to provide any information in order to acquire the license. The license can be issued in the background while the user is completing the transaction, such as purchasing or downloading a song. The user might notice a slight delay before being able to play the downloaded file.

Issuing a license non-silently is best when you need information from the user before issuing the license, or if you want the user to be aware of the license acquisition process. This also ensures that users see the terms of the license before they proceed with downloading their content.

3

Distributing Content with Windows Media Services

Windows Media Services 9 Series is the distribution component of the Windows Media 9 Series platform. It is a streaming media server that works in conjunction with Windows Media Encoder and Windows Media Player to deliver live or on-demand audio and video content to clients over an intranet or the Internet. The clients might be other computers or devices that play back the content using a player, such as Windows Media Player, or they might be other computers running Windows Media Services (called Windows Media servers) that are proxying, caching, or redistributing your content. Clients can also be custom applications that have been developed using the Windows Media Format Software Development Kit (SDK).

Content Distribution Methods

Windows Media Services can deliver a live stream, such as a broadcast of a live event, or existing content, such as a digital media file. In the case of live content, Windows Media Services gets the stream from Windows Media Encoder before sending it on to clients. There are two ways in which this can be done: push distribution and pull distribution.

In the push method of distribution (which is a new addition to Windows Media 9 Series), the encoder initiates contact with the Windows Media server and then *pushes* the live content to a broadcast publishing point on that server.

In pull distribution, the Windows Media server or Windows Media Player contacts the encoder to request or *pull* the stream. While both options ultimately deliver live content to Windows Media Player, each is designed for a different scenario.

Push Distribution

Pushing a stream from the encoder is ideal when the encoder is behind a firewall. Some firewalls don't support connections that are initiated externally, so push distribution enables the encoder administrator to control the broadcast directly from the encoder.

For example, say you have just received last-minute notice that the president of your company wants to deliver important information to company employees in a live address. The Windows Media server is located outside your company firewall and the server administrator is not currently available. You, as the encoder administrator, have administrative rights on the Windows Media server and can configure the encoding session, set up a broadcast publishing point on the Windows Media server, and start the broadcast without ever leaving the Windows Media Encoder user interface. The stream is pushed through the firewall using HTTP, as shown in figure 3.1.

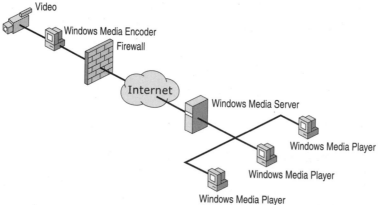

Figure 3.1   The encoder pushes the stream to a Windows Media server.

Using push distribution is also a good idea when you are initiating a broadcast to a server that is controlled by a third party, such as a content delivery network (CDN). In this case, you might have breaking news that you need to broadcast right away. Using push, you can initiate the stream when it's necessary to do so without having to locate the server administrator in order to start the stream.

Pull Distribution

Pulling a stream from an encoder is useful in several scenarios. First, if there are multiple distribution servers, all connecting at different times, each server can initiate the connection with the encoder when it is ready to stream. Next, pulling from a server is useful if it is important to minimize bandwidth usage between the server and the encoder. For example, the server administrator can add a publishing point and configure it to start automatically, which means that the server does not initiate the connection with the encoder until the first client connects. This eliminates unnecessary bandwidth use between the server and the encoder.

Pulling from the server is also useful when the server is behind a firewall. For example, you might set up the encoder on a public network because you are streaming events at a conference. You need to get the stream to a distribution server inside the protected network so it can be delivered to clients on the corporate LAN. In this case, the server administrator can pull the stream from the encoder through the firewall using HTTP, as shown in figure 3.2.

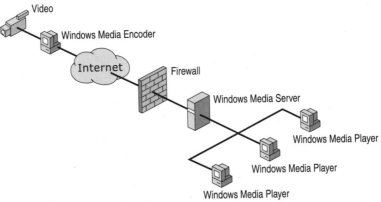

Figure 3.2 Windows Media Services pulls the stream from Windows Media Encoder.

Finally, pulling from the encoder is necessary when you want to authorize clients to connect directly to the encoder to receive the stream, as shown in figure 3.3. Windows Media Encoder supports up to five concurrent connections. When you are enabling clients to pull the stream, you can restrict access to specific IP addresses or to groups of IP addresses.

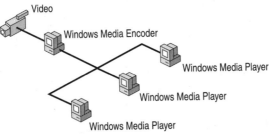

Figure 3.3 Client computers pull the stream directly from the encoder

Fast Streaming

If you've clicked an audio or video link on the Internet, then you've probably experienced the buffering that occurs while your Player collects enough data to render the stream. You've probably also experienced some rebuffering or choppy playback when you clicked your Player's fast forward or rewind controls. This buffering and rebuffering occurs because the Player has used up the data in its buffer and is waiting for the buffer to be refilled with additional content from the server. This kind of playback experience can be extremely frustrating.

Windows Media Services now addresses these playback interruptions through a set of features called Fast Streaming. The Fast Streaming feature, when combined with Windows Media Player 9 Series, virtually eliminates annoying buffering delays and playback interruptions by taking advantage of networking resources, such as available bandwidth and network signaling to deliver content to the Player quickly. Furthermore, Fast Streaming provides redundancy and automatic restoration of dropped connections to ensure an uninterrupted viewing experience. Fast Streaming is possible because of the following four components:

Fast Start

When Windows Media Services receives a stream request, it takes advantage of available bandwidth to fill the Windows Media Player buffer at a bit rate that exceeds that of the requested stream. This enables the Player to start rendering the stream more quickly. After the initial buffer requirement is fulfilled, the server streams the content at the requested bit rate. Buffering the content in this way enables end users to fast forward and rewind content without additional delay and rebuffering. Fast Start is supported in Windows Media Player for Windows XP and Windows Media Player 9 Series.

Fast Cache

This feature enables Windows Media Player to *cache* streamed content thus making it available later without having to stream it again. This saves network bandwidth on subsequent requests. Fast Cache also enhances the Player's ability to play back the content faster or slower than real time and makes the Player resistant to playback errors due to lost packets or other network issues. Fast Cache is not supported when streaming with UDP.

Fast Recovery

Fast Recovery makes use of forward error correction (FEC) to stream content to a Player that has unreliable network connections. In an environment that is subject to latency problems, such as satellite wireless networks, FEC enables the server to send data packets containing redundant data to Players. The Player then uses this redundant data to correct missing or corrupted data packets during playback. With the help of FEC, the Player can usually recover lost or damaged data packets without having to request that the server resend the data. FEC and Fast Recovery can only be used with clients such as Windows Media Player 9 Series that connect to your server using the RTSP protocol in conjunction with UDP (RTSPU).

Fast Reconnect

Fast Reconnect minimizes the impact to Windows Media Player during a temporary network outage by enabling the Player to reconnect to the server automatically and restart streaming. If the Player was connected to an on-demand publishing point, playback starts at the point at which the connection was lost. If the content includes video, the Player estimates the approximate video frame at which the connection was lost. If the content is indexed, this estimate is more accurate. For a connection to a broadcast publishing point, the Player reconnects to the broadcast in progress. Depending on the content and whether Fast Cache is enabled, there may be a gap in the broadcast. Fast Reconnect is available to any client that connects using the default MMS, HTTP, or RTSP protocols.

Unicast and Multicast Streaming

The terms unicast and multicast refer to how Windows Media Player receives data from a Windows Media server. In a unicast stream, each Player establishes a one-to-one connection with the server in order to receive a single stream. In making the request, the Player provides its IP address, and the server then directs the stream to that IP address.

Unicast Streaming

A unicast stream can be live or on-demand, and is sent only to the Player that requested it. When the stream is on-demand, the user can control the stream using typical playback controls, such as pause, fast forward, and rewind. The user also has control over when an on-demand stream starts and stops. In a broadcast, the experience is very similar to watching broadcast television. You can tune in and out during the broadcast but have no control over its playback.

Unicast streaming is the most common form of streaming, especially over wide area networks (WANs). However, unicast streaming does have high bandwidth requirements, especially when delivering concurrent streams. If too many streams are being delivered at one time, your available bandwidth will be consumed, and additional users who then attempt to connect will be denied.

Understanding IPv6

Internet Protocol version 6 (IPv6) is a new suite of standard protocols for the network layer of the Internet. IPv6 is designed to solve many of the problems of the current version of IP (known as IPv4) with regard to address depletion, security, auto-configuration, extensibility, and other issues. IPv6 features include the following:

- A new header format, designed to keep header overhead to a minimum by placing non-essential and optional fields after the IPv6 header, and streamlining header processing at intermediate routers.

- Large address space, increasing the address size from 32 bits to 128 bits to support a larger addressing hierarchy and a greater number of addressable nodes.

- Efficient and hierarchical addressing and routing infrastructure, designed to support multiple levels of Internet service providers.

- Stateless and stateful address configuration, enabling hosts to automatically communicate without manual configuration.

- Built-in security, with requirements to support IP Security (IPSec), which provides a standards-based solution for network security needs and promotes interoperability between different IPv6 implementations.

- Better support for Quality of Service (QoS), with new fields in the header to define how traffic is handled and identified.

- Extensibility by enabling additional headers after the IPv6 header, which are only constrained by the size of the IPv6 packet.

IPv6 is expected to be available in Windows Server 2003, but may not be installed by default. You can install it through the Network Connections dialog box on your server. See Windows Server Help and Support for more information. Windows Media Services 9 Series also supports IPv6.

Multicast Streaming

A multicast stream is a one-to-many method of data transmission. In a multicast stream, the server sends one stream to a standard, Class D multicast IP address range (224.0.0.1 to 239.255.255.255). A client subscribes to the multicast by requesting it from an upstream router. That router, in turn, requests the stream from another, and the process is repeated until the request reaches the last router in the chain. That router receives the multicast stream, and then sends it downstream to everyone who requested it.

The benefit of multicast streaming is that only one stream travels the network between the server and the clients, which greatly reduces the amount of network traffic, especially during important broadcasts. No Player ever has a direct connection to the server in a multicast stream, so there is no playback control. The drawback of this scenario is that many networks are not currently configured for multicast streaming. Consequently, most multicast streaming occurs today within LANs. Multicast streaming is not available for on-demand scenarios.

> **Note** Multicast streaming from a broadcast publishing point is only available in Windows Media Services in Windows Server 2003, Enterprise Edition and Datacenter Edition. If you are running Windows Media Services in Windows Server 2003, Standard Edition, this feature is not supported.

Publishing Points

A publishing point represents a directory structure on your server where streaming content is stored. By default, all content is stored in the \WMPub\WMRoot directory on your server. You might add a subdirectory to that path called Company Meetings and store all of your company meeting streams in that directory. Your publishing point might then be named Company Meetings and would point to the directory structure you created. For a unicast stream, clients either connect to the publishing point directly to request the stream, or request it using a link on a Web page. The Web page then redirects the client to the publishing point to receive the stream.

You receive a multicast stream by clicking an announcement file. The announcement file contains information about the stream, including the stream format and content location. The stream format is what enables the Player to decode and play the stream.

Windows Media Services 9 Series supports two kinds of publishing points: on demand and broadcast.

On-Demand Publishing Points

An on-demand publishing point is used to stream content from a file, directory, or playlist. The stream from an on-demand publishing point doesn't start until the client connects to it. Once the stream is started, the end user can actively participate in the playback by pausing, rewinding, and fast forwarding it. An on-demand publishing point can also be used to stream content from an encoder or another server. An on-demand publishing point always delivers content as a unicast stream.

Broadcast Publishing Points

A broadcast publishing point is normally used to stream live content from a file, encoder, remote server, or other broadcast publishing point. Receiving a stream from a broadcast publishing point is similar to watching broadcast television in that the user can view the stream but has no control over when it starts or stops. Additionally, the user cannot fast forward, rewind, or pause the stream.

Although a broadcast publishing point can stream from a file or playlist, it will treat the content as a broadcast stream and will not allow users to pause, fast forward, or rewind. Broadcast publishing points can deliver content as a unicast or multicast stream.

During installation of Windows Media Services 9 Series, default on-demand and broadcast publishing points are created for you. These publishing points are pre-configured and point to sample content that you can stream. You will need to start the broadcast publishing point before you can stream the sample content, however, and set your publishing points to allow new connections. In addition to streaming sample content from these publishing points, you can use them to stream the content you create or copy their configuration and customize as appropriate.

There is no limit to the number of publishing points you can have, and you can easily create them using wizards that not only walk you through the creation of publishing points, but also assist with creating announcement files and playlists, should you choose to do so.

> **Note** The implementation of publishing points in Windows Media 9 Series is different from earlier versions. For a detailed description of the changes, see the paper *Upgrading to Windows Media Services 9 Series* on the CD provided with this book.

Streaming Media Protocols

A protocol is a set of rules and procedures that determine how data is transferred between devices or computer programs. Protocols contain important information to ensure data is delivered properly. Depending on the protocol, this information can include the IP addresses of the sending and receiving computers, port numbers, error-checking methods, end-of-file indicators, and so on.

There is not one protocol that suits all purposes. Rather, protocols have different tasks depending on their position in the Open System Interconnection (OSI) model. According to this model, protocols are implemented in seven layers. The lower layers define how to connect devices to one another. The upper layers specify rules for conducting communications or interpreting applications. The higher they are in the stack, the more sophisticated the tasks and their associated protocols become. Figure 3.4 shows the seven layers of the OSI model.

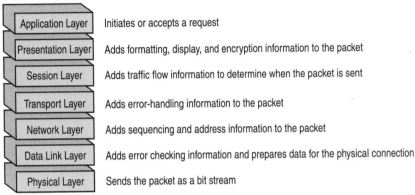

Figure 3.4 The seven layers of the OSI protocol model.

When streaming, you will use protocols from the network, transport, and application layers. Some protocols are standard Internet protocols that you are probably already familiar with, and others are streaming protocols that might be new to you.

Standard Internet Protocols

A few of the protocols used by Windows Media 9 Series for streaming are standards of networking and the Internet. They should be familiar to anyone who has worked on networking computers or building Web sites. These protocols include TCP/IP, UDP, HTTP, RTP, and IPv6.

Transmission Control Protocol/Internet Protocol (TCP/IP)

At the root of the standard Internet protocols is the Transmission Control Protocol/ Internet Protocol (TCP/IP) suite. TCP/IP is an industry standard and includes a collection of protocols that work together to provide reliable data communications across both LANs and WANs. One example of a WAN is the Internet.

The IP portion of TCP/IP is a network-layer protocol responsible for specifying the format and address of packets on the network. IP is often combined with TCP in order to establish a connection between the host and destination and to guarantee that packets reach their destination as intended.

TCP is a transport-layer protocol that guarantees delivery of data and guarantees that packets will be delivered in the same order that they were sent. One way that TCP is able to provide these guarantees is by requiring a receipt from the destination verifying that the packets were received. While retaining the integrity of data delivery, this receipt exchange also generates traffic, which adds to the network overhead and can slow down delivery of the data.

User Datagram Protocol (UDP)

Like TCP, User Datagram Protocol (UDP) is a transport-layer protocol. UDP is the preferred protocol for streaming because it provides for one-to-one or one-to-many communications on a connectionless basis. Because it is connectionless, no delivery receipts are required. Instead, the UDP protocol relies upon other applications or upper-layer protocols to make sure the packets arrive intact. This enables UDP to transmit data very quickly.

Hypertext Transfer Protocol (HTTP)

Hypertext Transfer Protocol (HTTP) is an application-layer communication protocol that Web browsers and Web servers use to exchange information. HTTP relies heavily on the transport capability of TCP for traffic control.

Real-Time Protocol (RTP)

Real-Time Protocol (RTP) has some properties of a transport-layer protocol and is used for transmitting real-time data such as audio and video. RTP does not guarantee real-time delivery of data, but provides control mechanisms such as time stamps for the sending and receiving applications to support streaming data. Typically, RTP runs on top of the UDP protocol.

Streaming Media Protocols

Windows Media 9 Series uses two streaming protocols in conjunction with the standard Internet protocols described above: the Real-Time Streaming Protocol (RTSP) and the Microsoft Media Server (MMS) protocol.

Real-Time Streaming Protocol (RTSP)

RTSP is an application-layer protocol that controls the real-time delivery of data, including audio and video content. RTSP supports two-way communication, which enables users to fast forward, rewind, and pause the playback of on-demand streams.

RTSP works with RTP to format packets of multimedia content and negotiate the most efficient transport-layer protocol (either UDP or TCP) to use when delivering the stream. Server administrators can also specify whether to use UDP or TCP for transferring packets. This decision is based on numerous factors, including firewall configuration and the speed of UDP versus the quality of TCP. RTSP is intended for unicast transmissions between servers and clients or between origin and distribution servers.

Microsoft Media Server (MMS) Protocol

MMS is a proprietary application-layer protocol developed by Microsoft to deliver unicast streams. It enables two-way communication so users can fast forward, rewind, and pause the playback of unicast, on-demand streams. Like RTSP, MMS can use either UDP or TCP to carry media packets across the network. MMS is intended for unicast streaming between servers and clients. Note that, with Windows Media 9 Series, MMS is no longer supported for server-to-server communication.

MMS was developed for use with earlier versions of Windows Media Services and represents the "rollover" protocol. When you create the URL that clients will use to connect to your content, use MMS. MMS enables Windows Media Player to negotiate (or roll over) to the optimal protocol for the connection automatically.

Media Stream Broadcast Distribution (MSBD) Protocol

Media Stream Broadcast Distribution (MSBD) protocol was used in earlier versions of Windows Media Technologies, but is no longer supported. Any Windows Media metafiles that currently specify MSBD should be changed to use MMS. Also, if your Windows Media Services 9 Series server is sourcing from a version 4.1 server, you'll need to change the source URL to use MMS. See the online help for Windows Media Services for more information.

Protocol Rollover

Protocol rollover is the process that Windows Media Player uses to negotiate the best connection protocol for receiving a stream. Protocol rollover is enabled by default in Windows Media Player 9 Series and is supported through control protocol plug-ins in Windows Media Services 9 Series. By enabling multiple protocol plug-ins (including the WMS HTTP Server Control plug-in) on your Windows Media server, you can support a variety of client versions, client connection through firewalls, and clients that are connecting through different types of networks.

The request for a Windows Media stream usually begins with a user clicking a link on a Web page. This link is the announcement that contains a URL to your content. By default, the announcement uses the MMS protocol to ensure that protocol rollover will occur if necessary. Most of the time, the first connection attempt between a client and server is successful and no further action is taken. If that connection request is not successful, protocol rollover occurs, and the client attempts to connect to the server using another supported protocol. The client experiences a very small, usually unnoticeable period of latency during each protocol rollover attempt. In addition, when a client attempts to establish a new connection to the server, preference is given to the protocol that the client used in the previous connection.

It is recommended that you use protocol rollover to ensure that your clients have the optimal streaming experience. If clients connect to your stream using a URL with an mms:// prefix, any necessary protocol rollover will occur automatically.

Be aware that users can disable streaming protocols in the property settings of Windows Media Player. If a user disables a protocol, then it is disabled for rollover only. For example, if HTTP is disabled, then URLs will not roll over to HTTP. The logic used with protocol rollover differs depending on the type of client connecting to the server.

- When Windows Media Player 9 Series or a Player that uses the Windows Media Player 9 Series ActiveX control attempts to connect to the server using a URL with an mms:// prefix, the server automatically uses RTSP.

- If Fast Cache is enabled on the server (the default condition for all new publishing points), the server tries to connect to the client using RTSP with TCP-based transport (RTSPT) first.

- If the Player does not support that protocol, then the server attempts to connect using RTSP with UDP-based transport (RTSPU).

- If that connection is also not successful, the server will attempt to connect using the HTTP protocol if the WMS HTTP Server Control Protocol plug-in is enabled.

- If Fast Cache is not enabled, the server first tries to connect to the client using RTSPU, then RTSPT, and finally HTTP.

Earlier versions of Windows Media Player, such as Windows Media Player for Windows XP, do not support the RTSP protocol. However, the MMS protocol provides protocol rollover support for those players. Thus, when an earlier version of the Player attempts to connect to the server using a URL with an mms:// prefix, the server automatically negotiates the best protocol for the Player.

- The server first tries to connect to the client using MMS with UDP-based transport (MMSU).

- If that protocol is not supported, then the server attempts to connect using MMS with TCP-based transport (MMST).

- If that connection is also not successful, the server will attempt to connect using the HTTP protocol if the WMS HTTP Server Control Protocol plug-in is enabled.

Protocol rollover is not used when a distribution server attempts to connect to an origin server. Distribution servers cannot use a URL with an mms:// prefix to request a connection to the origin server. If the distribution server attempts to connect using RTSP, that request is translated as RTSPU. If TCP-based transport is preferred or required, then the URL must use an rtspt:// prefix. If the servers must connect using HTTP, then the URL must use an http:// prefix.

Ports and Firewalls

A firewall is a piece of hardware or software that controls which data packets either enter or leave a network. To control the flow of traffic, numbered ports in the firewall are either opened or closed to certain types of packets. The firewall typically considers the destination port, the source IP address, and the destination IP address associated with each packet. Some firewalls also look at the protocol. If the firewall is configured to accept the specified protocol through the targeted port, the packet is allowed through.

When allocating ports for Windows Media streams, open all of the UDP and TCP ports that correspond to the protocols you want to support, as shown in the following table.

If you want to use...	Then open...
MMST	TCP port 1755
MMSU	UDP port 1755, and TCP port 1755
RTSPT	TCP port 554
RTSPU	UDP port 5005, and TCP port 554
HTTP	TCP port 80

Port range restrictions potentially affect all remote procedure call (RPC) and Distributed Component Object Model (DCOM) applications sharing the system, not just Windows Media Services. If the port range is not broad enough, other services such as Internet Information Services (IIS) will fail with random errors. The port range must be able to accommodate all services in the system that use RPC, COM, and DCOM.

> **Note** To enable IP Multicasting you must allow packets to be sent through your firewall to this standard, Class D multicast IP address range 224.0.0.1 to 239.255.255.255.

Announcement Files and Playlists

While it is possible for Windows Media Player to connect directly to a server or encoder to receive a stream, generally it connects to content by using a link in an e-mail message or on a Web page. These links are metafiles that tell the Player how to connect to a Windows Media server to receive content.

Windows Media playlist files are Extensible Markup Language (XML) documents with .wsx or .asx file name extensions. You can create playlist files by using the Windows Media Services 9 Series Playlist Editor, Windows Media Player, or any text editor.

> **Note**   See appendix A for more information about constructing server-side playlists using SMIL elements and attributes.

Announcement Files

Known as redirector files, these files contain instructions and references that direct Windows Media Player to the server that is distributing your stream. The announcement contains the URL of the content and information about the content, including author, title, and copyright. The .asx and .wvx files refer to Windows Media streams that contain both audio and video. The .wax extension is reserved for streams containing audio only.

Windows Media Services 9 Series uses two different types of announcement file: unicast announcements and multicast announcements. The multicast announcement is slightly different because it also includes a multicast information file (a Windows Media metafile with an .nsc extension), which contains information the Player needs to decode a multicast stream. This information includes:

- Multicast IP address

- Multicast port

- Time-to-live value

- Default error correction span

- Multicast logging URL

- Unicast rollover URL

- Stream formats used by the content being delivered

Two wizards are available in Windows Media Services 9 Series that can help you create an announcement file. One wizard creates a unicast announcement, and the other creates a multicast announcement. The wizards can also help you create a Web page that has Windows Media Player embedded into it, and they can provide the code to embed a Player ActiveX control in your own Web page. (For more information about embedding Windows Media Player in a Web page, see chapter 4.)

Playlists

Playlists provide a means of organizing different pieces of digital media content into a single stream. They are a set of instructions that specify what to play and the order in which to play it. These instructions can be carried out either on the client side or the server side.

Client-side playlists are Windows Media metafiles with an .asx file name extension. You can use Windows Media Player to create a client-side playlist that includes a selection of your favorite songs. You can then set the playlist to loop or shuffle to suit your preferences. A client-side playlist might also be a script that resides on a Web server.

In a server-side playlist, you use Windows Media Services 9 Series to stream a sequence of content, such as digital media files, encoder URLs, advertisements, and even content from other servers to users from a publishing point. Using server-side playlists, you can create your sequence of content and manage it from the server, even while clients are receiving the content. A server-side playlist has a .wsx file name extension. Server-side playlists are based on the Synchronized Multimedia Integration Language (SMIL) 2.0 language specification.

Best Practices for Streaming with Windows Media Services

For best results when streaming audio and video from Windows Media Services 9 Series, follow these guidelines.

Running Windows Media Services on a Separate Computer

Streaming audio and video in real time can require a lot of CPU resources. Sharing these resources with other services, such as IIS, can cause disruption in the smooth and constant streaming of data that is required for optimal performance, especially during high-traffic periods. Running the two services on the same server can also cause conflicts because both services attempt to bind to port 80 by default.

If you must run both services on the same server, you can avoid port conflicts either by assigning Windows Media Services to a different port or by creating separate IP addresses for each service, and then using port 80 on each IP address.

Assigning Windows Media Services to a different port is not advisable when you intend to stream using HTTP. While HTTP is not the most efficient protocol for streaming, it does enable you to stream through firewalls. Changing the default port to something other than 80 could prevent you from reaching clients through firewalls.

Creating separate IP addresses for each service is the preferred approach when you must run IIS and Windows Media Services on the same server. When a server has more than one IP address it is considered to be *multi-homed*. You can create a multi-homed server in two ways:

■   Assigning multiple IP addresses to a single network card

■   Assigning a single IP address to each network card that is installed in the server.

Once you've added the IP addresses, you must enable HTTP streaming for those addresses that are associated with Windows Media Services.

With IIS 6.0, HTTP requests are handled by the Http.sys listener utility. By default, Http.sys will monitor all requests coming in on port 80 for all IP addresses bound to the computer (except for the loopback address, 127.0.0.1). For Windows Media Services to bind to port 80 for streaming content, you must limit the Http.sys listener to specific IP addresses so that Windows Media Services can monitor the rest. Enabling the HTTP Server Control Protocol plug-in without configuring the Http.sys listener results in the error shown in figure 3.5.

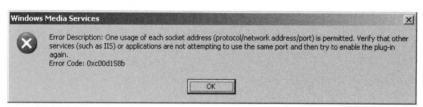

Figure 3.5   Error message indicating a port conflict on your server.

Follow these steps to configure the HTTP.sys listener:

1.   From a command prompt, type these commands to stop the relevant services:

```
net stop wmserver
net stop iisadmin/w3svc
net stop http
```

2.   Run the WMSHttpSysCfg.exe utility (located at %systemroot%\system32 \windowsmedia\server\admin\mmc\WMSHttpSysCfg.exe).

3.   Add the IP addresses that you want Http.sys to monitor. The addresses that Http.sys does not monitor will be used by Windows Media Services.

4.   Click **OK** to close the dialog box.

5.   At the command prompt, restart the services that you stopped in step 1 by running these commands.

```
net start http
net start iisadmin
net start wmserver
```

Now configure the WMS HTTP Server Control Protocol:

1. Start the Windows Media Services MMC snap-in.

2. Click the **Properties** tab.

3. In **Category**, click **Control protocol**.

4. In **Plug-in**, right-click **WMS HTTP Server Control Protocol**, and then click **Disable** (if it is not already disabled or if it is in an error state).

5. In **Plug-in**, right-click **WMS HTTP Control Protocol**, and then click **Properties**.

6. Click **Allow selected IP addresses to use this protocol**.

7. Select the IP addresses that you want to use to deliver content over port 80.

> **Note** Do not select the same IP addresses that you added to the Http.sys listener in step 3, otherwise the plug-in might go into an error state when it is enabled.

8. Click **Use default port (80)**, and then click **OK**.

9. Right-click **WMS HTTP Server Control Protocol**, and then click **Enable**.

Running Windows Media Encoder on a Separate Computer

Capturing and compressing content is a CPU-intensive process, and maintaining connections with clients during the streaming process is memory intensive. Performing both tasks on the same computer could overburden your server, especially when the content you are encoding is complex, or when your server is experiencing a lot of traffic. When the server is overburdened, frames or even clients might be dropped or clients might from the stream. For best results on both the encoding and streaming ends of the process, keep Windows Media Encoder and Windows Media Services on different computers.

Verifying that You Can Connect to the Server

Choose an audio or video clip that you have encoded (or choose one that is included with Windows Media Services, such as content_clip1.wmv), and attempt to connect to it. For example:

- Can you connect to content_clip1.wmv from the local server?

- Can you connect to content_clip1.wmv from a computer plugged into the same hub?

- Can you connect to content_clip1.wmv from a computer on the same subnet?

- Can you connect to content_clip1.wmv from a computer on a different subnet (different side of the router)?

- Can you connect to content_clip1.wmv from a computer on the other side of the firewall?

Running Windows Media Load Simulator to Test Stability and Capacity

Windows Media Load Simulator is a tool that enables you to simulate client load on your Windows Media server. This is an effective way to test real-world scenarios without exposing your server to actual clients. You can use the information gleaned from the load tests to set limits on your server and alter the configuration of publishing points, authentication or authorization plug-ins, and so on.

Windows Media Load Simulator 9 Series is available from the Downloads page of the Windows Media 9 Series Web site and on the CD provided with this book.

Making Sure Affinity is Set if Using Network Load Balancing

When using a bank of load-balanced servers, there is no guarantee that a client will be directed to the same media server each time it connects. This could potentially cause packet resend requests, logging errors, or connection problems. To avoid these problems, set affinity on the Network Load Balancing service. Setting affinity ensures that over the course of a session, a connected client will always be connected to the same media server. See the Network Load Balancing online Help for more information.

Enhancements to Windows Media Services

Windows Media Services is an optional component in Windows Server 2003 family of operating systems. Being an optional component, Windows Media Services is not installed by default, but is easy to add by using the **Add/Remove Windows Components** feature in **Control Panel**. You should be aware that an expanded set of features is available for Windows Media Services in the Enterprise and Datacenter editions of Windows Server 2003, as the following table explains.

Feature	Windows Server 2003, Standard Edition	Windows Server 2003, Enterprise Edition	Windows Server 2003, Datacenter Edition
Advertising server support	✓	✓	✓
Cache/proxy server support		✓	✓
Unicast content delivery	✓	✓	✓
Multicast content delivery		✓	✓
Control protocol support (MMS, HTTP, RTSP)	✓	✓	✓
Wireless streaming optimizations		✓	✓
Authorization methods (NTFS, ACL, IP Address)	✓	✓	✓
Internet authentication (Digest)		✓	✓
Intranet authentication (Negotiate authentication, Anonymous access)	✓	✓	✓
Playlist parser support (SMIL 2.0, Directory)	✓	✓	✓
Media parser support (Windows Media, MP3)	✓	✓	✓
Custom plug-in support		✓	✓
Event notification (WMI, SNMP)	✓	✓	✓
Event-based scripting support		✓	✓
Fast Cache	✓	✓	✓
Fast Start	✓	✓	✓
Fast Streaming	✓	✓	✓
Fast Reconnect	✓	✓	✓
Fast Recovery		✓	✓
RTSP streaming	✓	✓	✓
Internet Protocol version 6 (IPv6) support	✓	✓	✓
Server based content repacketization	✓	✓	✓

Cache and Proxy Solutions

Cache and proxy servers are servers that run Windows Media Services and include a third-party cache/proxy plug-in. Because a single server can perform both caching and proxying, they are usually indicated as cache/proxy servers. Cache/proxy servers act as "middle men" to receive content from an origin server and pass it along to the clients that requested it.

Why are cache/proxy servers important? Because an Internet site that draws customers from around the country or across the globe cannot always service all requests from a central location. Bandwidth can be consumed rapidly with all requests feeding in to one server or server cluster, and data can be lost or bogged down when it has to travel long distances, especially over slower network segments.

As indicated by its name, a cache/proxy server has two functions: caching and proxying. Let's begin with caching.

Cache Servers

Caching is a way of temporarily storing frequently requested on-demand content in a place where it is easily accessible. For example, each time a user visits a favorite Web page, a copy of that Web page is saved on the user's computer where it can be retrieved and displayed quickly. This is an efficient way of delivering data because it greatly reduces access time, which enables you to get the content to the user who requested it without delay.

Caching is also effective for streaming, especially for large enterprises with satellite offices, content delivery networks (CDNs), or Internet retailers with a national or international Web presence. These types of organizations usually maintain multiple servers that are scattered about the country or around the world. The location of these servers depends on where the users are. For example, a U.S. shipping company based in Los Angeles might have offices in New York, New Orleans, San Francisco, and Seattle. While the company does maintain a bank of Windows Media servers in the Los Angeles headquarters, it doesn't make sense for employees in New York or New Orleans to access those servers when they need information. The distance from point A to point B is far enough that users might experience *latency* when attempting to access the content. And if multiple users are accessing the content at the same time then much of the interoffice bandwidth will be consumed.

Instead, our shipping company would place a server or set of servers in each of these locations, as close to the users as possible. These servers are often called "edge servers" because they are on the edge of the company's network. Some data from the origin servers in Los Angeles, such as line-of-business applications, would then be replicated to the edge servers. Other data, such as a corporate training video, would be cached. The caching process might work like this:

1. A user at a remote location requests content from the closest edge server.

2. The edge server checks its cache to determine whether the requested content is there. If it is, and if it's up to date, the content is delivered to the user. If it isn't, the edge server contacts the origin server to request the content.

3. The origin server delivers the content to the edge server.

4. The edge server delivers the requested content to the user and saves a copy in its cache. The next user who requests the content will receive it from the cache, and no additional connections to the origin server are required. The content remains in the cache until its expiration date.

Proxy Servers

The other half of the cache/proxy story is the proxy server. A proxy server is used to request content from an origin server and deliver it to a client computer. The process is very similar to caching, except that the content can be live or on-demand, and no files are cached. When a client computer requests a live stream from the proxy server, the proxy determines whether it is already proxying the live content. If not, it contacts the origin server to request the stream and then proxies the stream to the client that requested it. When additional clients request the stream, the proxy server can split the stream for each client. In this way, there is only one connection between the cache/proxy server and the origin server.

Windows Media Services does not offer a cache/proxy solution out-of-the-box. Rather, it supports caching and proxying content through the use of third-party plug-ins. Developers can build custom cache/proxy solutions by using the Windows Media Services SDK.

Network Service Account

Windows Media Services runs under the Network Service user account. This is a change from Windows Media Services version 4.1 in Windows 2000 Server. In that version, Windows Media Services created its own administrator account with administrator rights and permissions to access system resources.

The Network Service account is a predefined local account that first appeared in the Windows XP operating system. Services that are running under the Network Service account can access network resources by using the credentials of the computer account. The Network Service account has minimal privileges on the local computer. This prevents someone from using the account to gain access to protected resources on your system. The Network Service account does not have a password associated with it.

Because Windows Media Services uses the Network Service account credentials to respond to authentication requests from other resources, the Network Service account must have the appropriate permissions in the access control lists (ACLs) of any files, folders, data sources, or other items to which Windows Media Services will read and write data. For example, if you are going to write log file information to a network location that is different from the default location, you must grant the appropriate permissions to the Network Service account for that location for Windows Media Services to write log files successfully. The Network Service account has the appropriate permissions for the default folder, WMRoot.

Plug-in Architecture

Windows Media Services 9 Series is completely customizable. This customization is possible because of the plug-in architecture. A plug-in is an auxiliary software component that extends or enhances the features of other software, in this case the server. Many of the features of Windows Media Services are implemented through plug-ins, and you can enable or disable those plug-ins to establish the feature set that you want to use.

Plug-ins enable you to perform a wide range of tasks, including protocol handling, data parsing, authentication, authorization, and archiving. You can apply a plug-in to either an entire Windows Media server or to a specific publishing point on the server by enabling the plug-in at the appropriate level. You can also modify the plug-in settings for each server or publishing point you are managing.

Windows Media Services plug-ins are divided into categories by function. Each category contains several types of plug-ins. The table at the end of this chapter describes the plug-in categories.

Third-party or custom plug-ins, such as cache/proxy solutions discussed earlier, also extend the functionality of Windows Media Services. These plug-ins enable you to implement customized streaming solutions such as multiple streaming formats, customized logging applications, and specialized data storage. A list of third-party plug-ins for Windows Media Services is available on the Windows Media Partner Center page at the Microsoft Web site (http://www.microsoft.com/windowsmedia).

Plug-in category	Description
Archiving	Used to archive content that is being streamed from a broadcast publishing point to a file.
Authentication	Used to validate client credentials before any content is sent to the client.
Authorization	Used to grant or deny client access to content.
Cache/proxy management	Used to control cache and proxy policies on your computer.
Control protocol	Used to control the data sent between clients and servers.
Data source	Used to receive data from an encoder, file system, or network source.
Event notification	Used to control and customize how the server responds to internal events.
Logging	Used to record server and client activity.
Media parser	Used to allow the server to translate different digital media file types or real-time streams.
Multicast streaming	Used to control the delivery of content through multicast transmission. This plug-in must be configured for each publishing point that is going to use multicast delivery.
Playlist parser	Used to allow the server to translate different playlist types.
Playlist transforms	Used to change the manner in which content is streamed from a playlist or directory.
Unicast streaming	Used to control the delivery of content through unicast transmission.

4

Playing Content with Windows Media Player

Windows Media Player is the client software that enables end users to play back audio and video on their desktop computers and handheld devices. Windows Media Player is capable of playing music and video from a variety of sources including CDs, DVDs, and files (for example, WMA, WMV, and MP3), as well as on-demand content that is downloaded from a Web site or streamed from a Windows Media server.

Windows Media Player also reads and performs commands contained in Windows Media metafiles, such as playlists and announcement files that have .wsx and .asx file name extensions.

For most digital media, users can control the playback of audio and video using the standard controls that are included with the Player. These controls include **Fast Forward**, **Rewind**, **Seek**, **Play**, **Pause**, **Stop**, **Previous**, **Next**, and **Mute**. Figure 4.1 shows the controls from the default Player skin.

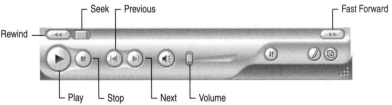

Figure 4.1 Playback controls in Windows Media Player.

There are times when users can't control the playback of a stream. These include:

■ When the stream is live. The concept is similar to that of broadcast television. When you tune into your favorite show, you are able to turn the television on and off, change channels, or adjust the volume. If you tune in after the show has started, then you can watch it from that point forward, but cannot rewind it to play the part that you missed. The experience is the same with tuning into a live stream. You can use the Player to connect to and disconnect from the stream and adjust the volume, but that is the extent of your interaction with the broadcast.

■   When the content is not indexed. Indexing is performed during the encoding stage. This is where key frames are referenced in an on-demand file. The player then uses these reference points for seeking within the file.

■   When a legacy player is receiving content from a server-side playlist. The ability to fast-forward, skip, rewind, and pause while playing content from a server-side playlist is only supported by Windows Media Player 9 Series or a player that uses the Windows Media Player 9 Series ActiveX control.

Customizing the Player

End users can customize many features of Windows Media Player to suit their mood or personality. For example, the Player includes a number of interchangeable skins that completely change the look of the Player, much like changing the face plate on a cellular phone. Additional skins are available on the Web today, and more will be added in the future. Figure 4.2 shows an example of Windows XP, which is one of the pre-installed skins.

Figure 4.2   Windows XP is a pre-installed skin.

When changing the skin, you are still able to use all of the playback controls, but you might need to do a little experimenting in order to find them.

Other kinds of customization include:

■ Turning captions and subtitles on and off. Captions and subtitles are strings of information that might be added to your content during the encoding process. If caption and subtitle information is included, it will be displayed in the video playback area of the Player. This feature is available on the **Play** menu.

■ Creating playlists. Playlists provide a means of organizing different pieces of digital media content into a single stream. They are a set of instructions that specify what to play and the order in which to play it. You can create a playlist of your favorite songs or videos and set it to play back in a specific or random sequence.

■ Adding features through plug-ins. Windows Media Player 9 Series has an extensible object model that enables you to enhance the feature set through the use of plug-ins. Plug-ins enable you to add visualizations, add audio or video effects, and more. You must be a member of the administrator or power users group on your computer to add plug-ins to the Player. To download plug-ins, click **Tools**, click **Plug-ins**, and then click **Download Plug-ins**.

Protecting Your Privacy

As described earlier, Windows Media Player 9 Series provides a variety of customization options. Some of these options, including **Media Guide**, **Radio Tuner**, and license acquisition and retrieval, require that information about your computer be sent across the Internet. While no personal information is ever collected, you might want to understand what information is transmitted and why. Knowing this will enable you to make informed decisions about what customizations to allow.

Privacy Settings

One of the primary functions of Windows Media Player is to play back content that is delivered over a network. To provide this service, it is necessary for Windows Media Player to communicate with a Windows Media server.

During playback of the streamed media, Windows Media Player will send the streaming media server a log. The log includes such details as: connection time, operating system version, Player version, Player identification number (or Player ID), date, protocol, and so on. The purpose of the Player ID is to allow content providers to identify your connection. If a unique Player ID is sent, content providers will be able to correlate the information in the logs over several sessions.

In order to protect your privacy, Windows Media Player sends an anonymous Player ID by default. But some content providers will require you to send them a unique Player

ID in order to access their content or services. You can send a unique Player ID by clicking **Tools**, clicking **Options**, clicking the **Privacy** tab, and then selecting the **Send Unique Player ID to Content Providers** check box.

Other options on the **Privacy** tab enable you to specify whether information about your CDs, DVDs, and music files can be retrieved from the Internet, whether automatic license acquisition is allowed for protected content, and whether you want to participate in the Customer Experience Improvement Program. All of these options require an exhange of information—usually by installing cookies or logging an IP address—over the Internet.

Media Library

By default, Windows Media Player does not allow Web pages to access your digital media files or **Media Library**. But Web pages may attempt access in order to offer you similar content, advertise sales, or recommend music or video services, such as subscriptions.

Before the Player shares information from your files and **Media Library**, it displays a message notifying you that the Web page is seeking read or full access to your files and **Media Library**. If you grant the Web page read access, it can scan the contents of your files and **Media Library**. Full access allows the item to scan and change media information in your files and **Media Library**. This can include adding, removing, and changing media information, such as a track name, in **Media Library** and your digital media files.

If you grant a Web page read or full access to **Media Library** when prompted, you only grant access for that single instance. In other words, when you open the Web page again, you will be prompted to grant access again.

WindowsMedia.com

WindowsMedia.com is a Web site operated by Microsoft and is used by Windows Media Player. The **Media Guide** and the **Radio Tuner** features are Web pages provided by WindowsMedia.com. All the CD audio data, DVD data, radio presets, and the information in the Info Center View pane come directly from WindowsMedia.com. Other services provided by WindowsMedia.com include Player updates and download support for codecs, skins, and visualizations.

Like most Web sites, WindowsMedia.com maintains a log of all requests that are sent to it along with the sender's IP address. The log will include your WindowsMedia.com cookie if cookies are enabled for the site.

A cookie is sent to WindowsMedia.com whenever Windows Media Player communicates with the WindowsMedia.com service (for example, when you click **Media Guide** or **Radio Tuner**, or when the Player requests supplemental CD or DVD information). The cookie allows WindowsMedia.com to personalize your WindowsMedia.com experience (for example, your radio presets are stored in this cookie). The cookie also contains a unique identifier, which allows WindowsMedia.com to generate anonymous visitor statistics. This identifier is not the same as the Player ID described earlier and does not contain any personally identifiable information.

Streaming media servers you connect with may also establish cookies on your computer. What data is stored in these cookies and how that data is used is determined by the content provider.

Understanding Cookies

A cookie is a small text file that is placed on your hard disk by a Web server. Cookies are uniquely assigned to you, and can only be read by a Web server in the domain that issued the cookie to you. Cookies cannot be used to run programs or deliver viruses to your computer.

A cookie is often used to personalize your visit to a Web site. For example, to facilitate a purchase the cookie could contain information such as your current selection, as well as personally identifiable information such as your name or e-mail address. To help Web sites track individual visitors, cookies often contain a unique identifier. It is up to the Web site that created the cookie to disclose to you what information is stored in the cookie and how that information is used.

It is possible to block the creation and transfer of cookies using Internet Explorer. If you decide to block one or more cookies, the Web sites that use them may not function correctly. For example, if the WindowsMedia.com cookie is blocked, you may lose some features like the ability to set **Radio Tuner** presets.

To prevent all cookies from being stored on your computer, open Internet Explorer, click the **Tools** menu, click **Internet Options**, and then click the **Privacy** tab. Move the slider up to **Block All Cookies**. With this setting, Web sites will not be able to store cookies on your computer.

Blocking all cookies is an extreme action to take. The next two Internet Explorer privacy levels, **High** and **Medium High**, may be more suitable. In addition, it is possible to block a cookie for a specific site using the **Edit** menu. See Internet Explorer online Help for more information.

Digital Rights Management

Content providers use digital rights management (DRM) technology to protect the integrity of their content so their intellectual property, including copyright, is not misappropriated. Microsoft and other companies offer software, such as Windows Media Player, that can play content secured with DRM.

License Acquisition

To play secure content, a license for the digital media content must be resident on your computer. The license is a file that contains a non-traceable ID. By default, Windows Media Player will attempt to acquire a license when you try to play the secure content if one was not issued to you by the content provider when you downloaded the content. If the content provider requires a fee or some type of registration, they will prompt you for this information; otherwise the license will be acquired silently. It is the responsibility of the content provider to inform you how any information they collect from you is used.

If you do not want licenses to be acquired automatically, you can disable this feature in Windows Media Player. From the **Tools** menu, click **Options**, click the **Privacy** tab, and then clear the **Acquire licenses automatically for protected content** check box.

License Restore Service

Microsoft has worked with partners (such as record labels, handheld device manufacturers, video distributors, and many others) to develop a service that enables you to move and restore your digital media licenses (for legitimate purposes only) between your own computers. This service is not available for moving licenses between computers that belong to different users. The restore service allows for a limited number of license transactions. When you restore your licenses, you are sending information to Microsoft that uniquely identifies your computer. Microsoft stores this information in a database and keeps track of the number of times you attempt to restore your licenses. Microsoft does not share this information with other companies.

To use the restore service from Windows Media Player, click the **Tools** menu, click **License Management**, and then click **Restore Now**.

Revocation Lists

If the security of the playback software is compromised, owners of secure content may request that Microsoft revoke the software's right to copy, display, or play secure content. Revocation does not alter the revoked software's ability to play unprotected content. A list of revoked software is sent to your computer whenever you acquire a license. Microsoft will not retrieve any personally identifiable information, or any other information, from your computer by downloading such revocation lists. The only way to avoid receiving revocation lists is to not acquire licenses for secure content.

Security Upgrades

Owners of secure content may also require you to upgrade some of the DRM components on your computer before accessing their content. When you attempt to play such content, Windows Media Player will notify you that a DRM upgrade is required, and then will ask for your consent before the DRM upgrade is downloaded (third-party playback software may do the same). If you decline the upgrade, you will not be able to access content that requires the DRM upgrade; however, you will still be able to access unprotected content and secure content that does not require the upgrade.

If you accept the upgrade, Windows Media Player will connect to an Internet site operated by Microsoft and will send a unique identifier along with a Windows Media Player security file. This unique identifier does not contain any personal identifiable information. Microsoft will then replace the security file with a customized version of the file that contains your unique identifier. This helps prevent security breaches that could affect you and other users of secure content.

Codec Updates

Codecs are updated periodically to improve performance or add enhancements. Once updated, the codecs are stored on a codec server where your Player can retrieve them automatically. But the automatic update of codecs is not always desirable for a variety of reasons, such as when company policy prohibits software downloads or when a group of users has standardized on a specific codec for playback. In these cases, you can turn off the automatic download from the **Tools** menu by clicking **Options**, clicking the **Player** tab, and then clearing the **Download codecs automatically** check box. You must have administrative privileges to change this setting.

Other Player Settings

Windows Media Player provides a few additional settings that you can use to personalize your Windows Media experience.

Usage History

In order to make it easier for you to find frequently played content, the Player keeps a list of local files and Web-based content you have accessed recently. This information is displayed in various places such as when you click **File**, click **Open**, and click **Open URL**. If you share acomputer, you may not want others to see this information.

To clear this information, and to prevent it from being saved and displayed, open Windows Media Player. From the **Tools** menu, click **Options**, click the **Privacy** tab, and clear the **Save file or URL history in the Player** check box.

Subscription Services

Windows Media Player includes a **Premium Services** button that takes you to a page that displays a list of available subscription services. When you click one of the sign-up links, no personally identifiable information is sent by Windows Media Player to the service. The service, on the other hand, may ask you for personal information as part of signing up for the service. It is the responsibility of the service to disclose to you what information they collect from you and how that information is used.

Enhancements to Windows Media Player 9 Series

Windows Media Player has a new object model that provides full support for Fast Streaming, multichannel audio, RTSP, and the latest codecs. Windows Media Player 9 Series is available for download from the Windows Media page of the Microsoft Web site (http://www.microsoft.com/windowsmedia).

In addition to its new object model, Windows Media Player has many new features that provide you greater control over the playback of your audio and video content. Some of these new features, such as Fast Streaming, were mentioned in earlier chapters, but are revisited here to help you understand them from the Player perspective. Other new features are described below.

Fast Streaming

Fast Streaming is a collection of features that enable the server and Player to work together to deliver an uninterrupted viewing experience. They do this by delivering content through a combination of streaming, downloading, and caching using these four components:

- Fast Start. The Player receives the beginning portion of the content at a bit rate that is faster than the requested bit rate given the maximum bandwidth available. Delivering the content in this way reduces the amount of time required to fill the buffer and the amount of time the user has to wait before playing content.

- Fast Cache. As the stream continues, the server makes use of any additional available bandwidth to send data to the Player buffer, which allows the Player to better withstand network bandwidth fluctuations.

- Fast Recovery. The server uses forward error correction to reduce packet corruption and interruption when delivering content to clients over wireless and satellite networks.

- Fast Reconnect. Enables the Player to reconnect to the server automatically when a connection is lost because of adverse network conditions.

Fast Streaming can be enabled and configured on the Windows Media server and through playlist and announcement files that are accessed by the Player. For example, when using Fast Reconnect, a server administrator might specify in an announcement file that the Player should attempt to reconnect to the server three times if a connection is lost. The code would look like this:

```
<asx version = "3.0">
    <entry>
            <ref href = mms://media_server_01/Execs?wmreconnect=3"/>
```

The Player would receive these instructions when accessing the announcement file and carry them out if a connection is lost.

No Fast Streaming configuration is necessary on the Player side. If you are using Windows Media Player 9 Series, then you can take advantage of the features automatically. Windows Media Player for Windows XP has limited support; earlier versions of the Player do not support Fast Streaming.

Adjusting the Playback Speed

Windows Media Player 9 Series enables you to adjust the playback speed of your content. Adjusting the speed can be useful when you need to slow the content down in order to understand a difficult concept, or if are having trouble deciphering the lyrics of a song. It can also be useful when you want to watch a video, but can't spend the full playback time to do it. Changing the playback speed has no effect on the audio pitch.

This feature is available from the **View** menu. Click **Enhancements**, click **Play Speed Settings**, and then click **Slow**, **Normal**, or **Fast**.

Controlling the Audio Dynamic Range

Used in conjunction with the Windows Media Audio 9 Lossless or Windows Media Audio 9 Professional codecs, Quiet Mode enables you to control the difference between the loudest and softest sounds in your audio in order to avoid wide volume swings. This is useful in a movie, for example, that has quiet conversation followed by loud action scenes.

You can turn on Quiet Mode from the **View** menu by clicking **Enhancements**, clicking **Quiet Mode**, and then selecting your Quiet Mode options.

Smart Jukebox

Smart Jukebox is a collection of features that enable you to easily manage your digital audio collection. These features include Audio CD Burning with Volume Leveling, Auto Folder Monitoring, Auto Find, Auto Ratings, Auto Info, and the Advanced Tag Editor.

Audio CD Burning with Volume Leveling

Volume leveling, also known as normalization, is the process of automatically increasing or decreasing the average volume of a file to a specified level when it is played back. The goal of volume leveling is to make all files play at roughly the same volume level so you do not have to adjust the volume level manually for each file. The Player adds volume leveling values to Windows Media files or MP3 files when you copy tracks from an audio CD to **Media Library**, copy files from **Media Library** to an audio CD, play a file on your computer from start to finish without interruption (for example, without pausing, fast-forwarding, rewinding, or seeking), or add files to **Media Library** by searching your computer.

In Windows 2000 and Windows XP, the **Media Library** database is associated with individual users, so any volume leveling you perform will only affect your files. The exception is when you or another user selects the **By searching computer** option to locate media files. Then all writeable media files, regardless of the user who created them, will have the volume leveling applied. Read-only files will not be affected.

Auto Folder Monitoring

Specify which folders you want Windows Media Player to monitor. Any time the Player detects a change to the digital media in that folder, it will update **Media Library** accordingly. For example, if new media is added to a folder, it will be added to **Media Library**. If a media file is deleted, it will be removed from **Media Library**. And if a media file changes, it will be updated in **Media Library**. All of this is automatic.

Auto Find

Locate all digital media files on your computer so they can be included in **Media Library**. Once links to the files are included in **Media Library**, you can add them to playlists, edit their metadata, rate them, and perform other functions from one convenient location.

Auto Ratings

All of the content in **Media Library** is assigned a rating of three stars. Content that is played more often is assigned additional stars. You can use this information as criteria for setting up auto playlists. You can also assign your own ratings to all content.

Auto Info

Automatically correct or add album details (tags) to your MP3 and WMA files, including information such as artist or album name, year, composer, or track number. The Player attempts to update any missing media information in your music files by sending data about the files to a database operated by WindowsMedia.com.

Advanced Tag Editor

Add album, artist, track, genre, language, and other information to a media file. This information is displayed when you play back the content. You can also add synchronized lyrics by specifying the time at which they should be displayed. Advanced Tag Editor is accessible by right-clicking a media file in **Media Library** and then clicking **Advanced Tag Editor**.

Auto Playlists

While an ordinary playlist specifies one or more media items to be played in a sequence, an auto playlist specifies rules that are executed each time the playlist is played. Because the playlist does not contain specific items, the music or video that is played can be different with every execution of the playlist. For example, one of your rules might be to play five songs from a particular genre. Or you might set up your auto playlist to play only those songs or videos that you haven't played in the last month. You can also use other criteria when creating your playlist rules, such as album title, artist, encoding date, bit rate, or rating.

All of the songs or videos referenced in your auto playlist must reside in **Media Library**. You may also set limits on the number of items played, the duration of the playlist, or the playlist size.

Windows Media Player 9 Series includes sample auto playlists, which are located in the \My Documents\My Music\Sample Playlists directory. All auto playlist files are plain-text XML files with a .wpl file name extension. To create an auto playlist, click **Media Library**, click **Playlists**, and then click **New Auto Playlist**.

Embedding the Player in a Web Page

The core functionality of Windows Media Player is contained within a software library called an ActiveX control. As with earlier versions of Windows Media Player, you can embed the Player ActiveX control in a Web page in order to add streaming capabilities to your Web site. By embedding the control in an HTML page, you can use Internet Explorer or Netscape Navigator to craft visually complex graphical environments that take advantage of a rich and dynamic event model. Using the Player control, you can completely sculpt the Web site user's audio and video experience.

The Windows Media Player 9 Series control adds new functionality and updates and extends existing functionality from the previous version. New and updated features include:

- Support for Internet Explorer 5.01 and later, Netscape Navigator 4.7, Netscape Navigator 6.2, and Netscape Navigator 7. Support for the Java 2 Runtime Engine (J2RE) version 1.3.x is also provided.

- Enhanced and updated **Media Library** support. The Windows Media Player 9 Series ActiveX control provides greater access to metadata in a user's **Media Library**. For example, you can determine how many times a user plays a particular song or content by a particular artist, and then use that information to offer that user related products or services. (See Protecting Your Privacy for information about allowing Web pages to access your Media Library.)

- Language selection. New properties and methods enable you to take advantage of multiple language tracks. For example, you can automatically provide your audio stream in the language that is appropriate for each user.

- Time compression and expansion, which enables users to slow down or speed up content while still preserving pitch. This enables users to review material such as newscasts or informational videos more quickly, or to slow down playback to understand details more clearly.

- Invisible user interface (UI) mode. The "invisible" value for the **Player.ui-Mode** property gives you the ability to embed the control in a Web page without displaying the Player interface to Web site visitors. This mode is particularly advantageous in audio-only scenarios such as Internet radio.

- Support for SMPTE time code. SMPTE time code is the industry-standard way of identifying individual video frames.

- Enhancements to closed captioning support. The **ClosedCaption** object exposes new methods and properties for working with languages and styles in Synchronized Accessible Media Interchange (SAMI) files. For example, you can automatically provide captions in the language that is appropriate for each user.

Note that the Windows Media Player 9 Series control has the same CLSID as the Windows Media Player 7.1 control (6BF52A52-394A-11D3-B153-00C04F79FAA6). If you already embedded the Windows Media Player 7.1 control in your Web pages, you do not have to modify the number in your Web page code to take advantage of the Windows Media Player 9 Series control.

A number of changes have been made in the Windows Media Player 9 Series ActiveX control to address security and privacy issues. As a means of implementing these changes without altering the code in the version 6.4 control, a wrapper was created to map the functionality of the 6.4 control to the Windows Media Player 9 Series control.

The wrapper is installed automatically upon installation of Windows Media Player 9 Series. The wrapper provides you with the benefits of the latest Windows Media Player 9 Series control, such as security and privacy improvements, without requiring that you make significant changes to your existing Web page code.

Because the mapping between version 6.4 and 9 Series Players is not precise, the behavior of the 9 Series ActiveX control when embedded in a Web page differs in some cases from version 6.4. Additionally, some version 6.4 features are no longer supported in Web pages, including ActiveMovie and NetShow compatibility features.

It is recommended that you test your Web pages after the Player upgrade to ensure they perform as expected. For complete details about how your embedded Player will be affected once Windows Media Player 9 Series is installed, see the Windows Media Player 9 Series SDK.

Deploying Windows Media Player Across an Intranet

It is the policy in some large organizations to deploy Windows Media Player uniformly to every computer on the intranet. Often these organizations want to specify exactly which features are enabled and what skin or branding is applied. There are two ways to centrally administer the deployment and use of Windows Media Player over an intranet: the Enterprise Deployment Pack and Group Policy.

Deploying Windows Media Player with Enterprise Deployment Pack

With Windows Media Player version 7.1 came the introduction of the Enterprise Deployment Pack. The Enterprise Deployment Pack enabled network administrators to centrally manage the deployment of the Player over the intranet. Using the Enterprise Deployment Pack, network administrators could:

- Deploy specific skins that hide unwanted Player features.

- Specify preset proxy settings.

- Specify supported streaming protocols.

- Turn off automatic updating of features and automatic download of codecs.

- Silently install the Player on every desktop by using a software distribution system, such as Microsoft System Management Server or Application Bookshelf.

The Enterprise Deployment Pack is being updated for Windows Media Player 9 Series and is expected to be available from the Windows Media 9 Series page of the Microsoft Web site (http://www.microsoft.com/windowsmedia).

Deploying Windows Media Player with Group Policy

The Microsoft Active Directory Group Policy feature in Windows 2000 and Windows Server 2003 is a powerful administration tool that enables an administrator to define the availabilities and behaviors of various components on a user's desktop. Not only can you define how the desktop looks, but what applications are available to the users in your organization. For example, using Group Policy to administer Windows Media Player, you could lock a skin, prevent codec download, and specify supported protocols. Specific Group Policy settings include:

- Preventing shortcut creation.

- Preventing automatic updates.

- Hiding the **Privacy**, **Network**, and **Security** tabs.

- Locking skins.

- Preventing codec downloads.

- Specifying streaming protocols.

- Configuring protocols.

You manage the group policy settings for your organization through the Group Policy Object Editor. The Group Policy Object Editor is a standalone MMC snap-in that you can add from the **File** menu of MMC. Figure 4.3 shows the Group Policy settings that have been set for the networking features of Windows Media Player.

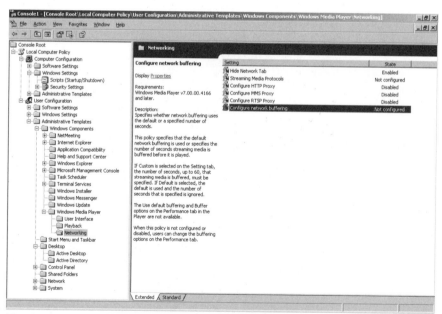

Figure 4.3   Group Policy settings for Windows Media Player

Computer administration using Group Policy Object Editor is explained in detail in Windows Help and Support.

Part II

Small-Scale Internet Streaming

This part describes how to deploy Windows Media Technologies in a small company that is just establishing a streaming presence on the Internet. This scenario represents the most basic installation of a streaming media infrastructure, and is the conceptual foundation on which all other scenarios in this book are built. The phases of this scenario are relevant to any small business, garage band, or extended family that wants to stream music or video across the Internet.

Because no streaming media system can be implemented overnight, we'll see firsthand how the scenario is planned and deployed by using a phased approach. This approach is applicable regardless of the size or complexity of the streaming media implementation and will be used again and expanded upon in subsequent parts of this book.

5

Envisioning the Streaming Media Site

Envisioning is the first of the four-phase process that we use to design and build a streaming media system. In this chapter, we introduce a scenario about a fictional small company that wants to add streaming media to its Web site. We'll walk through the steps that this company takes to identify goals for the site and brainstorm ideas for achieving them. We'll also discuss what we want the end-user experience to be for this site. We'll close this phase of the process by producing a preliminary project schedule and a list of tasks that will move us into the next phase.

The Scenario

Coho Winery is, for the purpose of this scenario, a small family-owned winery located in lush farm country east of the Cascade Mountain range. The winery has been a family business for generations and has relied exclusively on wine sales, tourism, and the occasional art exhibit or concert series for its revenue. Most of the tourism is a result of word-of-mouth, but the winery has advertised in local and national publications. It also provides brochures to the local chamber of commerce for handing out to prospective visitors.

The winery owners have decided to grow the tourism side of the business in the hopes that they will sell more wine and increase their revenue stream. Increased revenue will help them to cover the rising costs of maintaining the winery and enable them to expand their Art Series to include marquee acts that they are currently unable to afford. The winery owners believe that the Internet is one obvious solution for reaching more people, so they have recently designed a Web site that they host themselves. The Web site contains a history of the winery, photos of the vineyards and neighboring countryside, descriptions of some of the award-winning Coho wines, reviews from wine critics, and a program of recent and planned Arts Series events. Figure 5.1. shows the current Coho Winery Web site.

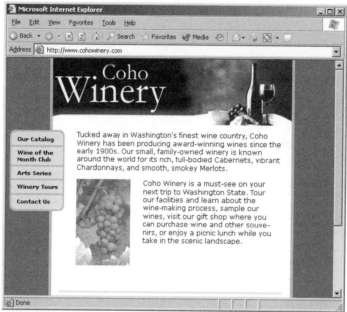

Figure 5.1   The current Coho Winery Web site.

The Web site has been experiencing a better-than-expected level of traffic, and the owners are now ready to expand it by offering streaming media in an attempt to entice more visitors to the winery. As part of its regular tour, the winery shows a brief video that details the winery's history and wine-making process. The owners want to put portions of that video on their Web site, along with clips of recent wine-tasting events, and a voice-over that explains all of the products and services that the winery has to offer. The owners will eventually want to sell wine and souvenirs on their Web site, but those plans are outside the scope of this book.

The winery currently uses frame relay to connect to the Internet through their Internet Service Provider (ISP), and they experience a maximum throughput of 1.5 megabits per second (Mbps).

Developing the Vision

With their vision in mind, the winery owners set about determining its feasibility. While it is easy to say that you want to add streaming media to a site, you must consider the cost and scale of such an endeavor. Successful streaming can be achieved across a wide range of scale and budget. The first step in determining the feasibility of a streaming media site is to set goals that are achievable given the constraints of your particular situation.

Goals

The winery's goals for adding streaming media to its site are three-fold:

- To increase customer traffic on the winery Web site.

- To entice visitors to visit the winery where they will purchase wine and souvenirs.

- To build enough customer interest that the winery can expand its programs, including adding an online store to its Web site.

All of these goals can be summarized in one word: growth. The winery wants to achieve growth in its revenue stream, growth in its customer base, and growth in the products and services it offers. The first two goals are directly related to adding streamed audio and video. If the first video is done well, for example, it will encourage users to watch others or to read the related articles and information that is available on the site. This, in turn, could lead to an increase in sales of wine and souvenirs.

The third goal, to expand its product and service offerings, is really an outgrowth of the first two. It can be achieved in many ways, including through the use of streaming media.

Now that they have determined their goals, the winery owners can start thinking about how to achieve them. One effective method for doing this is brainstorming.

Brainstorming

The brainstorming process can be very quick or be spread over a number of days. It can be a formal process with specific deliverables or an informal conversation in the hallway. How you go about it and how long it takes really isn't important as long as you leave the process with an understanding and agreement among all interested parties as to how you will proceed toward achieving your goals.

In the brainstorming process, the winery owners and staff meet to develop ideas for what the streaming media system should be both now and in the future. They realize that each member of the staff will have a different perspective and might have ideas that the owners have not considered. They also want to make sure that none of the plans conflict with one another or with the overall goals.

In the end, the winery team agreed to these basic tenets:

Content

The winery is in the business of making wine, not video, yet they want their streaming audio and video to be of good quality. Purchasing professional-grade equipment is not possible given their budget constraints, and learning to use such equipment would require more time than they are willing to invest. The winery has a library of videos that they use for internal training, promotion, and educational purposes. All of the videos were produced professionally for them and are stored on DVD. The winery decides to use these videos for the on-demand content they will stream.

Distribution

The winery does not anticipate streaming any live broadcasts now or in the near future. The owners have one Web server on which they host their site. While they can put videos on it temporarily, they are concerned about the amount of buffering time that users will encounter when trying to download the videos, and they fear that users will move on before the download is complete. The winery owners also want to retain control over their copyrighted property. They realize they can't do that if the videos are being downloaded instead of streamed.

Playback

After conducting some research, the winery team has learned that many users who connect to the Coho Winery Web site do so over 28.8 or 56 Kbps dial-up modems. However, the winery often plays host to corporate events, such as holiday parties or executive retreats. Corporations usually have high-speed lines available to them. Because of the variety of ways that customers might access the Coho Winery site, any video that is produced would have to play well over a range of connection speeds.

Administration

Once audio and video are added to their site, the winery owners want to monitor the number of streams requested, the duration of each request, the amount of bandwidth being used, and other statistics in order to ensure their server is keeping up with the load. The results will also help determine their return on investment. If the response is good, the winery will consider adding videos, rotating audio and video depending on the the season, and including advertisements with their streams.

Schedule

The winery would like to have their system in place within three months in order to take advantage of the summer tourist traffic.

Assigning Action Items

After brainstorming is complete, it's time to assign action items. Depending on the size of your implementation and the status of your existing infrastructure, action items can include research, planning, and ordering or reallocating equipment. This is not the time to assign implementation tasks. Those tasks will be identified later after the plan is complete.

At the Coho Winery, the winery owners are committed to their plan but have to be realistic about the amount of money they can spend and the amount of time they can invest in putting a streaming site into production. They do not want to invest a lot of time or money until they know the benefit is worth the cost. So, once again, they call a meeting to discuss the vision and begin researching the cost of a streaming solution.

The team envisions posting up to three videos on their Web site in the next year. The first, a shorter version of the video shown on the tour will be used as a test case. If usage statistics indicate that the video receives a sufficient number of stream requests, the team will proceed with posting the other two. Otherwise, the team will keep the one video on the site, monitor usage and sales trends, and re-evaluate whether to refresh the site with updated video content.

Because the winery team wants to stream a shorter version of the existing tour video, they decide to go back to the production company that produced the original to request an estimate for creating an edited version. They'll also request estimates for editing two additional videos: one featuring the wine-making process and one highlighting the Art Series events. The team will provide a description of the work to the production company for estimating purposes. The description includes the quantity of videos requested, the timeline, the purpose, and a brief summary of the content. This summary is provided by the sales and marketing department.

The sales team has specific ideas about what information the first video should contain. They compile a list of talking points for the audio portion and images that should be used in the video portion. The sales team will work closely with the production company to create each video with the appropriate message.

The winery Webmaster agrees to collect usage statistics on the current site in order to estimate the amount of bandwidth needed for streaming. Knowing that Windows Media Player can be embedded in the existing Web page or launched in a separate window, she will investigate the merits of each implementation and experiment with the existing Web page to determine the best approach for the winery site.

The IT specialist will evaluate the current systems against the requirements of Windows Media 9 Series and create a specification, including a network topology, for the system that the winery will integrate into its current network. With usage and bandwidth calculations from the Webmaster, he'll assess whether the current Internet connection is sufficient for the anticipated load. The IT specialist will use all of the information presented in the specification to make upgrade or hardware purchase recommendations.

Developing a Preliminary Schedule

An implementation schedule is a must-have in any deployment scenario because it forces you to target an implementation date and enables you to determine whether the amount of time allotted is sufficient given the work that is required. As with other deliverables discussed in this section, the level of detail required for your schedule depends on your situation. It can be a high-level schedule where only major milestones are reflected, or a more detailed list of phases and associated tasks. What's important is that everyone involved with the project understands and commits to the schedule you establish.

During the brainstorming process, the winery team agreed that their Web site should be streaming the first audio and video in time for the summer tourist traffic. They estimate that the process should take approximately eight weeks and break the tasks into three phases: planning, developing, and implementing. The tasks within each of those phases are as follows:

- Planning
    - ❑ Prepare request for video editing proposal.
    - ❑ Conduct research.
    - ❑ Design system architecture.
    - ❑ Produce project specification.
    - ❑ Evaluate proposal and award contract.

- Developing
    - ❑ Procure hardware and software.
    - ❑ Install hardware and software.
    - ❑ Receive completed content.
    - ❑ Configure server and encoder.
    - ❑ Conduct pilot test.

- Implementing
    - ❑ Complete end-to-end testing.
    - ❑ Encode all content and post on server.
    - ❑ Go live.

Once their tasks are defined, the team can estimate the amount of time needed for each. Then they use a scheduling tool, such as Microsoft Project, to lay out the tasks on a calendar in order to identify any overlaps or resource allocation problems that will prevent tasks from being completed on time. Figure 5.2 shows the schedule that the winery team produced.

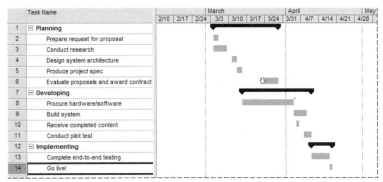

Figure 5.2 Coho Winery streaming media Web site development schedule.

Within each of the tasks listed in this schedule are numerous sub-tasks that will be divided among the winery team members. We'll discuss each of those tasks in detail in the next chapter.

In this chapter we discussed the importance of envisioning as a step toward implementing a streaming media site on the Internet. We used a fictional scenario to illustrate the steps in the envisioning phase: developing the vision, setting goals, brainstorming, assigning action items, and creating a schedule. In our scenario, team members evaluated their Coho Winery site as it stands today and described how they would expect it to look in the future both from a content perspective and technologically.

In chapter 6, we move into the planning phase where the Coho Winery team members will complete their research, refine their goals, and work together to create an implementation plan.

6

Planning the Streaming Media Site

Every deployment needs a plan, regardless of the size of the deployment. The plan can be as complex as detailed specifications and network diagrams or as simple as a drawing on a cocktail napkin. What's important is the process. By thinking about what you want—given your schedule, budget, hardware, or other constraints—you can design a system that meets your needs while avoiding escalating costs and unforeseen delays along the way.

The plans discussed in this chapter are appropriate for a small Internet streaming scenario, such as the site of our fictional company, the Coho Winery. They provide examples of the types of information any deployment needs, and a way to organize the information and get the process rolling. Even if your deployment is comparatively simple, you should go through a similar thought process to make sure you have considered every angle, understand the risks, and know exactly what you have to do to make your vision a reality.

The original objective of the Coho Winery deployment was to create a streaming media system using Windows Media 9 Series that will enhance the existing Web site with streaming audio and video. The topics that follow describe their planning process.

The Sales Team Plan

The sales team is most concerned with getting the right message into the minds of customers so those customers will visit the winery and spend their money on wine, souvenirs, and special programs. Their task is to determine the focus of each video and develop talking points that can be integrated into the audio portion of the content.

The sales team agrees that a maximum of three videos should be produced for the first phase of streaming. All three videos already exist in the winery library and will be edited for online delivery. The videos, in priority order, are:

■ **History of the winery.** Includes photos of the early days when the winery was getting started, interviews with winery owners, tours of the vineyards and buildings, and a display of some of Coho Winery's award-winning wines.

■ **Wine-making process.** Shows how wine is made today at the winery and includes a tour of the Coho facilities.

■ **Special events.** Showcases the Arts Series events that have taken place recently. Includes images of wine tasting parties and corporate retreats.

Because they don't expect most users to sit through a long video, the sales team determines that each video should last from three to five minutes, and that there should be little duplication among the three.

The sales team puts this information and the schedule produced in chapter 5 into a request for proposal that they then submit to the production company that developed the original video.

The IT Plan

Most of the responsibility for planning and implementing streaming media at the Coho Winery falls on the IT department. The IT department has full control over the winery's computers, Web site, and network. In the previous chapter, the IT department was given responsibility for calculating current usage patterns, evaluating existing systems, and making recommendations for streaming media integration.

Network and Hardware

The winery currently uses frame relay to connect to the Internet, and has 1.5 Mbps of total bandwidth available. Analysis of the current IIS logs showed an average of 120 connections during any given one-hour period. Using this average, IT estimated that 50 percent of those hitting the Web site might choose to watch the videos. If 60 users watch a video during the course of one hour, and each video is five minutes long, then the server would experience approximately 10 concurrent connections. Assuming that all 10 concurrent connections are over a 56 Kbps modem, IT calculated that users would consume a maximum of 560 Kbps (10 x 56,000) of bandwidth. Realistically, that number would be about 30 percent lower, or approximately 400 Kbps, because of network overhead. IT then considered that half the connections might be 56 Kbps and the other half might be 100 Kbps broadband lines. This bumped the total throughput to a maximum of 780 Kbps.

Based on these figures, IT is aware that increased traffic could eventually saturate the existing connection. Upgrading to a fractional T3 connection could buy them extra bandwidth and enable them to stream higher-bit-rate content, but at a considerable cost. IT recommends monitoring actual traffic patterns over several months after the on-demand videos are in place to determine whether an upgrade to a fractional T3 connection is necessary and financially feasible.

The winery decided to host its Web site on the Windows Server 2003 platform, but had to do some research to decide which version of Windows Server was right for them. Because the winery was primarily interested in hosting a small Web site and then streaming from it, IT recommended Windows Server 2003, Standard Edition. This choice meant that they had to forego certain streaming features such as multicast distribution, cache/proxy support, digest authentication, and custom plug-in support. But because they are a small company with only one server, they found that IIS 6.0, Active Directory, and the Windows Media Services features in Windows Server 2003, Standard Edition, to be a comfortable fit.

Because the winery has only the one server, they choose to use it for hosting their Web site and streaming on-demand content. The server has a 1.2 GHz processor, 1 GB of memory, and uses a RAID 5 array for content storage. The server also contains a 100-Mbps Ethernet card. IT recommends adding a second 100-Mbps Ethernet card for the server to handle back-end connections to the encoder and internal network.

The encoder will run on a 900 MHz single-processor computer running Windows XP Professional. Because the winery intends to do on-demand streaming exclusively, the 900-MHz computer will be adequate for the job. The computer does not have an audio or video capture card currently, so IT recommends purchasing an inexpensive one for capturing the audio and video from DVD.

The server is connected to the encoding computer using a crossover cable. The crossover cable connects the network cards of the two computers and is used in lieu of a hub. A crossover cable is necessary because the send and receive lines in an Ethernet cable are crossed, and the cable ensures that the send wires are matched up with the receive wires on the other end.

Based on the existing equipment and additional recommendations, IT produces the site topology shown in figure 6.1 for streaming audio and video from the Coho Winery Web site:

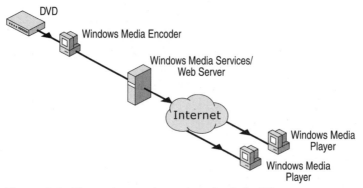

Figure 6.1   Planned network topology for Coho Winery.

Content Creation

The content creation process fits into four categories: planning, pre-production, post production, and encoding. We've already talked about planning. In production, you shoot the scene on film or videotape and record the audio. In post-production, you mix the audio, edit the video, add special effects, and so on. Because the production tasks are being handled by the production company that originally produced the videos for the Coho Winery, we do not describe them here. Rather, we focus on the encoding tasks, where the Coho Winery Webmaster captures the audio and video and encodes them into Windows Media Format.

The Coho Winery Webmaster will encode all content that is provided by the production company. The encoding task will be relatively small because the current plan calls for a total of three videos to be produced. Depending on the response, additional videos might be added to the site, but those plans are at least a year away.

While awaiting the new content from the production company and a capture card for the encoding workstation, the Webmaster downloads and experiments with Windows Media Encoder 9 Series by encoding AVI files that she's acquired from various sources. She knows that she wants to use multiple-bit-rate (MBR) encoding in order to adequately deliver video to customers with high- and low-bandwidth connections. And she wants to understand the encoding settings in order to create an appropriate encoding *profile* for all streamed content on the Web site. A profile is a collection of settings tailored to the type of content being encoded, the audience, and the intended distribution (file or broadcast). The properties stored in a profile include: the audio and video quality, connection speed for the intended audience, available bandwidth, and appropriate codecs. Using profiles enables you to standardize the encoding settings that you use thus ensuring that encoding results are always the same.

Playback

The Webmaster's other action item was to investigate whether to embed Windows Media Player in the winery Web site or to launch a separate Player window when users click the video link. Benefits to embedding the Player include:

- The ability to wrap winery branding around the Player.

- The ability to control the user's video playback.

Winery management is in favor of putting branding on their site, and they want to keep their customers focused on the winery Web page rather than sending them out to a separate window to watch the videos because they know that any time you send users away from your site you run the risk of losing them. They also like being able to control the size of the Player so it blends effectively with their site design.

The main drawback of embedding the Player is that some older browsers might not support it. As you might recall from chapter 4, the core functionality of Windows Media Player has been included in an ActiveX control that can be embedded in Web pages. ActiveX controls are programs that cannot run by themselves, but must be used by another program, such as a browser. In the winery case, if a customer's browser does not support ActiveX controls, then that customer will not be able to watch any of the winery videos. The winery has no information about which browsers their customers are using and must decide whether the benefits of embedding the Player outweigh the risk of some users not being able to view the content.

The Webmaster determines that the problem can be solved by adding some code to the winery Web page that will check for ActiveX compatibility and, if necessary, then point users to a Web site where they can download the Player control. She can also create an announcement file with an .asx extension that launches a stand-alone Player, if necessary. This solution tips the scale, and winery management agrees to embed the Player in the winery Web page.

Risks

One final step in preparing an implementation plan is to identify potential risks associated with the streaming media implementation. Risks are a part of any business decision, and it's important to be aware of them. The risks you identify at the beginning of the process might be resolved as you progress, or may be replaced with other risks that you discover along the way. It's important to reassess your installation periodically to ensure that risks have been considered and to develop mitigation plans where necessary.

The Coho Winery identified the following risks associated with their Windows Media 9 Series implementation. The team will revisit these risks in the next chapter as they prepare a mitigation plan for each of them.

Risk	Implication
The server goes down.	The Web server and streaming media server reside on the same computer. If the server goes down, then the entire site is un-available until the server is back online. Coho Winery does not have a backup server.
Customers have an older Player that is incompatible with the latest streaming technology.	The latest Windows Media encoding technology is supported by Windows Media Player 7.1, XP, and 9 Series. Customers running any other version of the Player will have limited success when attempting to view the winery video content.
Content that resides on the Web server could potentially be hacked or acquired illegally	By default, content is stored in *%systemdrive%*\WMPub\WMRoot. When stored in this location, content is safe from unauthorized access. But if content is stored in the WWWroot directory, a user could acquire the content and save it to a computer where it could be propagated or replayed indefinitely.
Requests saturate the allocated bandwidth.	Clients currently receiving a stream encounter buffering delays or jitters in playback because the server is experiencing a higher volume of requests than it is capable of delivering.

Writing the Site Specification

The site specification is a compilation of all the research and decisions that have been made in the envisioning and planning stages. It is the blueprint for how the implementation should proceed. The site specification does not have to be large or complex. It could be a bullet list of decisions in an e-mail message or a formal document that is routed for approval. The form and content are up to you. But it's important to create some type of site specification at the end of the planning stage because it allows everyone involved in the process to review the decisions that have been made. It also provides a point of reference when questions arise during the actual implementation of the project. The site specification can take on greater importance in large deployments where multiple people and departments are involved.

A typical site specification includes these topics:

- Vision

- Goals

- Research

- Recommendations

- Site Topology

- ■ Risks

- ■ Schedule

- ■ Summary

As part of the envisioning and planning stages, the Coho Winery team collected all of this information. Assembling it into a single document is easy, and the result is a comprehensive plan that the team can review and approve before moving forward.

Once the plan is approved, the team proceeds to the developing stage where the hardware, software, and content are integrated and streaming begins. We address those tasks in the next chapter.

In this chapter we followed the Coho Winery team through the planning stage of their streaming media implementation. The most time-consuming portion of this phase was conducting the research that would lead them to recommendations and decisions about their site. Once those recommendations and decisions were made, they were compiled, along with a topology and schedule, into a site specification that will be used as the blueprint for developing the site.

In the next chapter we build the system and stream the first video.

7

Developing the Streaming Media Site

In chapter 6 we created a site specification and topology. In this chapter we use the site specification as a guide toward configuring all hardware and software, embedding Windows Media Player in a Web page, and encoding and streaming the first test video.

Once you have all of your equipment in place, developing the site can be accomplished rather quickly. It really only consists of four steps and, depending on the complexity of your site, can be ready in a week or less. The four steps are:

- Setting up the audio and video source

- Setting up the encoder

- Setting up the server

- Embedding Windows Media Player in the Web page

In the pages that follow, each of these steps is explained in detail.

Setting up the Source

You can capture your audio and video content from a variety of sources, including VCR, Digital Betacam, analog or digital camera, DVD, file, or even cable TV.

When encoding from a device, such as VCR or camera, you must have a capture card installed in your computer. Depending on your device and the ports available on your capture card, you might use composite, S-video, SDI, or IEEE 1394 connectors to hook the device and capture card together. (See chapter 2 for a description of each of these connectors.) The only time you do not need a capture card is when you are encoding application windows using the Windows Media Screen codec or when converting existing files to Windows Media Format.

Some capture cards are able to capture both audio and video. Other cards do one or the other. It doesn't matter how many capture cards you have as long as they are compatible with Windows Media Encoder. You can tell Windows Media Encoder which cards you want to use for each audio and video source. Windows Media Encoder supports many different capture cards, and all supported cards are listed on the Hardware Providers page of the Windows Media Web site (http://www.microsoft.com/windowsmedia).

Capture cards are usually installed in the PCI slots in your computer. To install the card, you must remove the outer case of your computer and insert the card into one of the available PCI slots. You'll also need to install the software that accompanies the capture card. See the documentation provided with your capture device for hardware and software installation details.

Once your capture cards are installed and your device is in place, use cables to connect the audio and video inputs on the card to the audio and video outputs, such as S-video or composite, on your device as shown in figure 7.1.

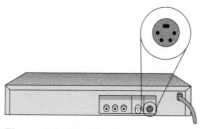

Figure 7.1 The S-video port on a video device.

Coho Winery intends to capture pre-recorded audio and video content from DVD. This content was professionally produced and requires no further editing or post-production work before it can be encoded. The DVD player is the device that will connect to the capture card.

The Webmaster begins by installing an Osprey 210 capture card in her encoding computer. She chose the Osprey 210 because it offers a variety of analog inputs, but any card that supports the Video for Windows (VFW) or Windows Driver Model (WDM) drivers will suffice.

Next the Webmaster uses BNC connectors to connect the **S-video out** port on the DVD player to the **S-video** port on the capture card. Using S-video is preferable to the composite format because the luminance and chrominance signals are passed directly to the capture card without having to undergo a conversion process the way composite video does. This conversion process for composite video combines the luminance and chrominance signals to produce video that is NTSC compliant. However, it also introduces artifacts into the video that ultimately degrade the quality. Using S-video to bypass the whole conversion process results in a cleaner video source, which then produces a higher-quality video stream.

Once the hardware is connected, the Webmaster is ready to install and configure the encoder.

Setting up the Encoder

Encoding is the process of compressing content and converting it to Windows Media Format so it can be streamed over the Internet or an intranet. Windows Media Encoder 9 Series is the tool that provides the compression and conversion function of the streaming media process.

The encoder is included on the CD at the back of this book and is available for download from the Windows Media 9 Series page of the Microsoft Web site. As part of the installation, you will receive all of the Windows Media 9 Series Audio and Video codecs and four utilities, including Windows Media Encoding Script, Windows Media File Editor, Windows Media Profile Editor, and Windows Media Stream Editor. With the exception of Windows Media Encoding Script, these utilities are launched individually from the **Start** menu. Windows Media Encoding Script is a command-line utility. A brief description of all utilities is provided in chapter 2.

To install the encoder, follow these steps:

1. Download the encoder from the Windows Media 9 Series page at http://www.microsoft.com/windowsmedia. If you choose to open the installation package, then the Setup Wizard will start automatically. If you choose to download the installation package, then you'll have to start the setup wizard manually.

2. Accept the license agreement.

3. Accept the default installation location or specify a different one.

4. Click **Install**.

The encoder is installed with a number of quick-start templates that enable you to start encoding with minimal setup time. Quick-starts are designed for the most common encoding scenarios, such as capturing a live stream for local playback, and are completely configured except for a destination or output file name, and sometimes a source file name. The encoder also includes numerous profiles that are designed to achieve optimal results in all the typical encoding scenarios, such as when encoding for Pocket PC devices or for streaming from a Windows Media server. Profiles offer more flexibility than quick-starts and require more configuration from the user before encoding can begin. You can also customize these profiles to suit your specific needs.

When Windows Media Encoder is fully installed, you're ready to start encoding.

Configuring an Encoding Session

It's always a good idea to run some encoding tests on your content to determine the profiles that work best for you given your distribution method, the connection speeds of your audience, and the quality of your audio and video. You might recall from chapter 6 that the Webmaster at the Coho Winery experimented with many of the profiles to determine which ones met her needs for the on-demand winery videos. Encoding and re-encoding from the same source has no effect on the source content, which Coho Winery has safely stored on DVD. But you should always have a backup of your source content in case your encoded version gets damaged or lost. That backup could also be an additional DVD or high-quality archive, such as an uncompressed AVI file.

If you haven't encoded before or are unfamiliar with the latest encoding profiles, choosing the right profile might be a daunting task. The choice is actually straightforward when you consider the following questions.

What Is the Resolution of the Output Video?

Think of the height and width of the output video as a collection of pixels used to display the image. Pixels are used to indicate both the width and height of an image, and are usually communicated as $x \times y$, meaning x pixels wide by y pixels high. For example, the number of pixels used to display a typical computer desktop is 1024×768 pixels.

The larger the image, the more pixels needed to display it, and the more bits needed to encode it. The more bits you use, the more bandwidth you will need to stream the encoded file. You can offset the larger image size somewhat by lowering the quality level of the encoding. But if you've gone to the trouble to increase the output size, it doesn't really make sense to degrade the quality of the image that will be shown at that larger size.

The optimal output resolution really depends on what your content is and how it is being distributed. In many streaming scenarios, such as executive broadcasts or distance learning, 320×240 is a good resolution because it provides an image that is large enough to be viewed easily at a quality level that can be streamed without frame dropping or rebuffering delays, especially at higher connection speeds. Figure 7.2 shows an example of an image that is 320×240 pixels and was encoded with one-pass CBR using a video smoothness setting of 60. Video smoothness ranges from 0 to 100. 0 indicates smoother video and 100 yields clearer images. This image is streaming 29.97 fps at a bit rate of 273 Kbps.

If your users are connecting at dial-up rates, such as 28.8 or 56 Kbps, then consider using a smaller resolution such as 160×120. This is the type of user who would be viewing streaming video from the Coho site. Figure 7.3 shows an example of an image that is 160×120 pixels and was encoded with one-pass CBR using a video smoothness setting of 50. This image is streaming 15 fps at a bit rate of 52 Kbps.

Figure 7.2   Streaming a 320 x 240 image at 273 Kbps.

Figure 7.3   Streaming a 160 x 120 image at 52 Kbps.

At what Speeds are Users Connecting to Your Site?

If your users are connecting over a range of connection speeds, you might want to consider encoding a single piece of content at multiple bit rates. A good rule of thumb is to group low and high bit rates into two separate MBR streams. For example, 28.8, 56K, and ISDN connections would be served by one MBR stream, while LAN, DSL, cable, and other broadband connections would be served by a second MBR stream. Grouping the MBR streams in this way requires extra storage space because the file is as large as the aggregate streams. Grouping also enables you to save CPU power during the encoding process because the codecs don't have to calculate the compression ratios for a large range of connection speeds.

New to Windows Media Encoder 9 Series is the ability to customize the output resolution of each stream in an MBR file. Now, when configuring the encoding session you can specify the resolution that's ideal for each bit rate in your profile. The higher bit rates would have a larger resolution, such as 320 × 240, and the lower bit rates would have something smaller, such as 160 × 120. Customizing the image size in this way enables you to better serve all of your audiences without having to encode content multiple times. MBR encoding is appropriate only when delivering live or on-demand content in a unicast stream.

Because visitors to the Coho Winery Web site have connection speeds ranging from 28.8 to 100 Kbps, all content will be encoded at multiple bit rates. The Webmaster has decided to create one MBR file that includes all narrowband bit rates such as 24, 37, 49, and 57 Kbps. Because the audio will consist primarily of voice-over, all audio will be encoded at voice quality, which is approximately 4 Kbps.

After the content is in place and the Webmaster has had time to review the client usage logs, she will decide whether to encode an additional MBR stream that is made up of higher bit rates to reach those users with broadband access.

Did Your Content Originate on Film or Videotape?

This question determines the kind of filter to apply to your content during the encoding process. Inverse telecine filters can remove extra frames that were inserted when the original content (which was shot on film) was processed for transfer to videotape. The deinterlace filter can blend the even and odd fields of an interlaced frame to create a progressive frame when the source content originated on videotape.

When determining which filter to use for your content, remember these rules of thumb:

- Any content that was recorded with television or video cameras is interlaced. Interlaced content requires the deinterlace filter in order to blend the odd and even fields and remove editing artifacts so the content can be displayed effectively on a progressive-scan display, such as a computer screen. The Coho Winery content originated on videotape before being put through an editing process. Therefore, the Webmaster will use the deinterlace filter when encoding winery content.

- Content that was shot on film and then converted to videotape is put through a telecine process in order to boost the number of frames per second from 24 to 30. This is also known as the 3:2 pulldown method. Freshly telecined content has an interlaced, coherent 3:2 pattern. Any video editing that is performed after the film has been telecined can break the coherent 3:2 pattern. These pattern breaks are called incoherencies. When content that was shot on film is converted to video and subsequently edited, you should use the inverse telecine filter to repair the incoherencies that were introduced during the editing process.

- Content that was shot on videotape and is intended for playback on interlaced devices, such as televisions, should retain its interlacing during the encoding process. This is not done by default. Rather, you must specify that you want to retain the interlaced format when setting up your encoding session and make sure you use the Windows Media Video 9 codec. If your source video is mixed (progressive and interlaced) and you choose to retain interlacing, the output video will also be mixed.

Should You Use VBR or CBR Encoding?

If your content is to be streamed, use CBR encoding. CBR encoding enables you to accurately estimate the size of the encoded video and set the bit rate at which the content will be encoded. This bit rate remains constant throughout the entire clip. In order to maintain the constant bit rate, the quality of the clip will fluctuate depending on the complexity of the material being encoded. For example, if you have encoded a clip that includes high motion and static images, the images might be clear while the motion appears blurred. This is because more bits are needed to encode the motion than are available at the specified bit rate.

The Coho Winery content consists of crowd scenes, landscape shots, and workers involved in the wine-making process. It contains relatively low motion and will be streamed from a Windows Media server. For these reasons, and because the winery is sourcing from DVD, most content could be encoded using one-pass CBR. But there is a second alternative. The winery can capture the content and, using a capture card utility, save it as an uncompressed AVI file first. Then, using the AVI file as the source, the Winery Webmaster could convert the content to WMV by using two-pass CBR.

You might recall that the Webmaster experimented with encoding AVI files in the previous chapter. She also experimented with encoding directly from DVD to Windows Media Format. After capturing to AVI, she used two-pass CBR encoding. When encoding directly to WMV, she used one-pass CBR. She found that capturing to AVI first and then using two-pass CBR resulted in better quality video. This better quality can be achieved with two-pass CBR because the encoder reads through the content first in order to collect data about its complexity, and then allocates bits more precisely during the second pass based on the information gathered. Liking this quality difference, the Webmaster decided that all winery content would be captured to AVI first and then encoded into the Windows Media Format using two-pass CBR.

But VBR encoding is compelling as well. The winery can foresee creating promotional CDs or DVDs containing higher-quality video content, screen savers, and demo tracks from artists participating in the Art Series events. VBR encoding is perfectly suited to this kind of content that is delivered on physical media.

In VBR encoding, the bit rate fluctuates to match the complexity of the content being encoded. For example, an automobile race would be encoded at a higher bit rate than a reporter delivering a newscast. When content is encoded for CD or DVD delivery, you can use a special VBR mode that constrains the amount of variation in the bit rate according to the reading speed of the playback device. In this mode, called peak bit-rate-based VBR, the encoder reads through the content twice to determine the image quality that can be achieved without exceeding the peak bit rate. While the bit rate does fluctuate during encoding, it does not exceed the specified peak bit rate. This is the mode the winery will use to encode content for the promotional CDs. This is also the mode that you should use if you must stream VBR content because you allow for some bit rate fluctuation in order to improve quality but set a limit on how much fluctuation can occur. See chapter 2 for more information about the CBR and VBR encoding modes.

Should You Encode Using Push or Pull?

This question is relevant when you are broadcasting a live stream from an encoder. When setting up the encoder for a live stream, you have the option to either *push* the stream from the encoder to the server or use the server to *pull* the stream from the encoder. Pushing a stream from the encoder is useful if the encoder is behind a firewall or if you want to initiate the connection from the encoder to a remote server.

Some companies don't allow connections across a firewall to be initiated externally. In these instances, it is useful to have the encoder initiate the connection from inside the firewall and push data out to the Windows Media server.

Here are some scenarios where pulling is best:

■   When there are multiple distribution servers, all connecting at different times. Each server can initiate the connection with the encoder when the server is ready to stream.

■   When it is important to minimize bandwidth usage between the server and the encoder. For example, you can configure your publishing point to start automatically upon client request, which means that the server does not initiate the connection with the encoder until the first client connects.

■   When the server is behind a firewall.

The push and pull options are only available for live broadcasts. Since the Coho Winery content is on-demand only, they will encode to file, and then use the file as a source when creating a publishing point on the server.

Using the New Session Wizard

Once you've considered all of the questions above, you are ready to run the New Session Wizard to configure your encoding session. Four wizards are available, depending on whether you're broadcasting live, capturing content from a device, converting content to Windows Media Format, or capturing screen images. Figure 7.4 shows the opening screen where you choose your session configuration option.

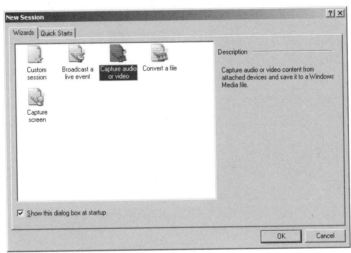

Figure 7.4   The New Session Wizards.

You can also create a custom session, which allows you to set all of the encoding properties without the assistance of a wizard.

The Coho Winery Webmaster chooses the **Convert a file** option and proceeds through the wizard. The first step is to choose the input and output file options, as shown in figure 7.5.

The next step is to choose the method of distribution for the encoded content. The method you choose determines the settings that are available to you. For example, choosing **Windows Media hardware profiles** would enable you to use peak-constrained VBR, but **Pocket PC** would not. In figure 7.6, the Coho Webmaster chooses **Windows Media server** because she intends to stream the content over the Internet to desktop computers.

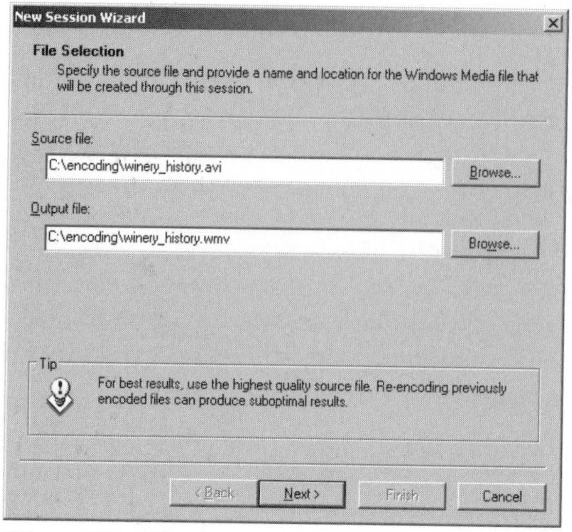

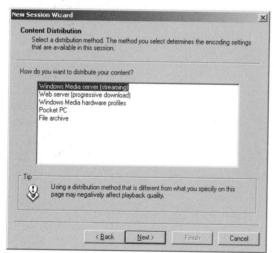

Figure 7.5 Choose your input and output files.

Figure 7.6 Choose the method to use for distributing your content.

Once the file names and distribution method have been determined, it's time to select the compression settings. Coho Winery, you'll recall, is encoding an MBR stream for narrowband users. The Webmaster will choose the bit rates for the MBR stream from the dialog box shown in figure 7.7.

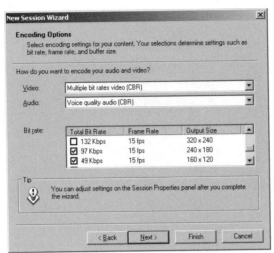

Figure 7.7   Choose the audio and video profiles and bit rates for your content.

The final step in the configuration is to enter metadata about the content. This metadata is optional, but can include title, author, copyright, rating, and description. The Coho Winery Webmaster provides the information shown in figure 7.8. Figure 7.9 shows Windows Media Encoder after session configuration is complete.

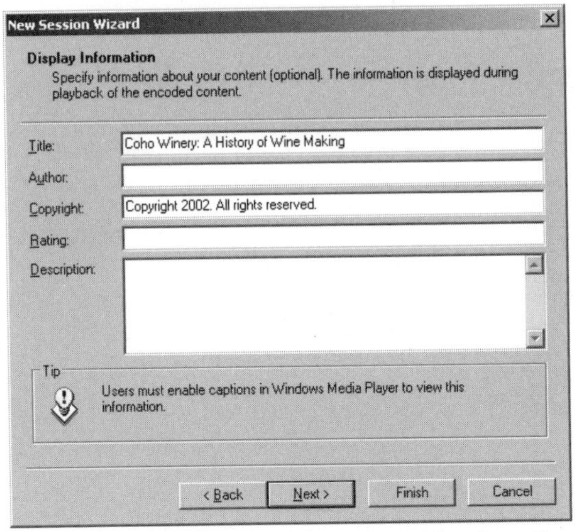

Figure 7.8   Entering display information is optional.

Figure 7.9   Encoder control panel.

Encoding Sample Content

After configuring your session, encode some test content. You can encode it to file and play it back locally, encode a broadcast and use your Windows Media Player to connect directly to the encoder to play it back, or stream it using your Windows Media server. If you are encoding content to a file, you can save the file to either a local hard drive or to the %systemdrive%\WMPub\WMRoot folder on your Windows Media server. If broadcasting live, you can either push the content to your server or use the server to pull it directly from the encoder.

Encoding some test content enables you to get a feel for how the encoder works, how the various features interact, and how changing settings affects the encoded output. For example, if you are using VBR encoding, consider adjusting the quality level with each subsequent encoding test and observe how the size of your encoded file changes. It's also a good idea, if you're planning to encode MBR files, to experiment with the range of bit rates and output sizes you use in each MBR stream in order to find the optimal combination of encoding efficiency and CPU performance.

Setting up the Server

Windows Media Services 9 Series provides the distribution function of the streaming media process. It runs on the Windows Server 2003 family of operating systems. So if you are currently running a previous version of Windows and have decided to move to the Windows Server 2003 platform, then you need to decide whether to upgrade your existing configuration using the upgrade wizard or to use a new installation. Each option has its benefits.

If you choose to upgrade, many of your Windows settings are configured automatically in the new environment. You will still have to do some configuration by hand, and you will need to enable features that were not previously available. The upgrade process is usually faster than a clean install because you don't have to reinstall other applications. The main drawback of an upgrade is that you might encounter some compatibility problems with drivers or other utilities that currently reside on your computer. Complete instructions for upgrading are provided in the white paper entitled "Upgrading to Windows Media Services 9 Series," which is included on the CD at the back of this book.

A clean installation enables you to remove all data fragments and unused files that might be resident on the computer, and you can be sure that all of the settings are configured exactly as you need them to be. A clean installation takes longer, but usually results in less troubleshooting at the end of the process.

Whether to perform an upgrade or a new installation depends entirely on your situation. Regardless of the route you take, always back up your existing system so you can restore it in the unlikely event that the upgrade is unsuccessful. Also, familiarize yourself with the new features of Windows before the upgrade so you can anticipate the changes you'll need to make—this will minimize site downtime or disruption in service for your viewers.

Because it is an optional component, Windows Media Services is not installed by default. It is easy to add, however, using the **Add/Remove Windows Components** feature of Windows **Control Panel**. To install Windows Media Services 9 Series, follow these steps:

1. Open **Control Panel**.

2. Click **Add or Remove Programs**.

3. Click **Add/Remove Windows Components**.

4. In the **Windows Components** dialog box, check the box next to **Windows Media Services**.

5. Click **Details**.

6. Check the box next to each subcomponent you want to include with your installation. At a minimum, you'll want to select **Windows Media Services**.

The following optional components can also be installed:

■ Select **Windows Media Services snap-in** if you intend to administer the server from the Microsoft Management Console.

■ Select **Windows Media Services Administrator for the Web** if
you intend to administer your server from a remote location.

■ Select **Multicast and Advertisement Logging Agent** if you intend
to use the logging and multicast features and want to log client data for
them. Install this component on a Web server where Windows Media
Services is not installed (see chapter 23 for more information).

7. Click **OK**, and then click **Next** to continue with the Windows Components
Wizard.

Note   If you have an older version of Windows Media Services installed,
it will be upgraded for you automatically and you will not have to choose
it during setup.

Once Windows Media Services 9 Series is installed, consider the following questions in order to configure your server appropriately for your streaming scenario:

Will Content Be Broadcast Live or Available for On-demand Streaming?

The answer to this question determines the kind of publishing point to configure. Wizards are available to walk you through the configuration of both types of publishing points.
The main difference in configuring the two is that a broadcast publishing point enables
you to decide whether to deliver the content as unicast or multicast. Content from an on-
demand publishing point is always delivered as a unicast stream.

Will You Stream VBR Content?

While streaming VBR content is not recommended, you can stream bit-rate-based VBR
content when the Fast Cache and Fast Start features are enabled on your Windows Media
server. These features enable the server to take advantage of the lower points of bandwidth usage to fill the Player buffer with content in order to accommodate bit rate fluctuations during the stream. But VBR streaming is only supported by Windows Media Player
9 Series, Windows Media Player for Windows XP, and Windows Media Player 7.1. Users with earlier versions of the Player might experience glitches or periods of silence during
the stream.

How Will You Determine the Access Privileges for Users?

Client access to your server and content is handled by two types of plug-ins. The authentication plug-ins specify how user credentials are to be obtained, and the authorization plug-ins use the information from the authentication plug-in to grant clients access to your content. Windows Media Services 9 Series includes three authentication and three authorization plug-ins.

Authentication Plug-ins

The three authentication plug-ins are:

- WMS Anonymous User Authentication

- WMS Digest Authentication

- WMS Negotiate Authentication

WMS Anonymous User Authentication enables users to access content without being prompted for a user name and password. This plug-in assigns the default Windows user account credentials to unauthenticated users who are attempting to access content. This account is established during setup and consists of a user name and password. The user name is WMUS_*computername*, where *computername* is the name of the server on which Windows Media Services is running. The password is randomly generated, but can be changed. This account has read permissions already established on the %systemdrive%\ WMPub\WMRoot directory, which is the default directory for Windows Media content. If you, like the Coho Winery, have no need to restrict the content on your site and are not interested in knowing who is connecting, then Anonymous User Authentication is the plug-in to use. It is enabled by default.

The WMS Digest Authentication and WMS Negotiate Authentication plug-ins rely on a user name and password being provided by the user in order to authenticate and grant access to the server. They are more secure authentication mechanisms than Anonymous User Authentication. WMS Negotiate Authentication is an appropriate choice when the server and Player are on the same domain. WMS Digest Authentication is appropriate when users are connecting to your site from a network, such as the Internet, and you want them to provide a user name and password before accessing the content. Digest is only available in Windows Media Services 9 Series in Windows Server 2003, Enterprise Edition or Windows Server 2003, Datacenter Edition.

Authorization Plug-ins

The three authorization plug-ins enable you to enforce access to your content either through access control lists or IP address. Each plug-in can be enabled at the server level, publishing point level, or both. The plug-ins are:

- WMS NTFS ACL Authorization

- WMS IP Address Authorization

- WMS Publishing Points ACL Authorization

The WMS NTFS ACL Authorization plug-in enforces access control policies that you set on files or directories in an NTFS file system and is useful when you want to set different access control policies for your content. Once this plug-in is enabled, each piece of content streamed from the publishing point or server must be authorized for the user account specified by the authentication plug-in. This means that if you are streaming content from a playlist, the user account must be authorized for every item listed in the playlist.

The WMS Publishing Points ACL Authorization plug-in also uses ACLs to enforce user access but applies them to all content in a publishing point or all publishing points on a server. This plug-in is enabled at the server level with the following access permissions by default:

- **Everyone**. The Everyone group has read permissions only.

- **BUILTIN\Administrators**. The Administrators group has full permissions.

The WMS IP Address Authorization plug-in allows you use specific IP addresses or a range of IP addresses as a means of granting or denying access to your content. This plug-in is useful when you want to grant access only to users on an intranet, for example. This plug-in is not enabled by default.

The Coho Winery Webmaster accepts the program defaults, which means that she'll use both NTFS ACL Authorization and Publishing Point ACL Authorization plug-ins at the server level. No additional configuration is necessary.

HTTP Basic Authentication

The HTTP Basic Authentication protocol is not supported in Windows Media Services 9 Series. Basic Authentication sends user credentials over the network without the use of encryption.

If you are using Basic Authentication in conjunction with Secure Sockets Layer (SSL) on your Web server, you can still use HTTP Basic Authentication with Windows Media 9 Series components. SSL provides a layer of encryption to help protect the end user credentials even when HTTP Basic Authentication is used.

If you are not using SSL on your Web server, then make sure Basic Authentication is disabled. Otherwise, even if other authentication methods are enabled, the Player could stop responding and give you an error message stating that access is denied.

Should You Use HTTP Streaming?

Coho Winery is streaming from a server that also has IIS installed. This is not a problem for them, however, because they are neither streaming through a firewall nor to other servers containing earlier versions of Windows Media Services. Because of this, they can use either the MMS or RTSP protocols for all streams.

But you can use HTTP streaming when Windows Media Services 9 Series and IIS coexist on the same computer. The HTTP Server Control Protocol is not enabled by default because Windows Media Services and IIS would each attempt to bind to port 80 for content delivery, resulting in a port conflict. If you must use HTTP streaming, then you have two choices: either change the port to which Windows Media Services is assigned or assign separate IP addresses to Windows Media Services and IIS so both can use port 80.

Changing the port to which Windows Media Services is assigned is the simplest solution. To do so, follow these steps:

1. From the MMC snap-in, select the server for which you will enable HTTP streaming.

2. Click the **Properties** tab.

3. In **Category**, click **Control protocol**.

4. In **Plug-in**, right-click **WMS HTTP Control Protocol**, and then click **Properties**.

5. In **Port selection**, click **Use other port**, and then type the number of the port (between 1 and 65535) that Windows Media Services should use for streaming (see figure 7.10). Make sure the port that you choose has been opened on your firewall.

6. Click **OK**.

7. Right-click **WMS HTTP Control Protocol** again, and then click **Enable**.

As an alternative to changing the port number, you can assign additional IP addresses to the server, enabling each service to have its own IP address and still use port 80. The simplest way to accomplish this is to install multiple network interface cards on your server. However, if this solution is not possible, you can create multiple IP addresses on a single network interface card and assign separate port 80 addresses to them. You must then configure Windows Media Services and your Web service to bind to separate IP address/ port 80 combinations. See chapter 3 for instructions.

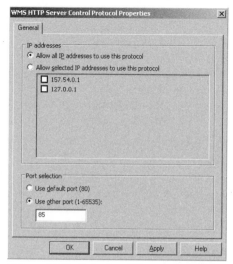

Figure 7.10   Select a different port for streaming.

Should You Log Client Data?

Windows Media Services stores information about the clients that view streams in information logs. This information can be used to determine a variety of things, including which stream is watched most often, how long a client receives a stream, the IP address of the client receiving a stream, and the Internet Service Provider (ISP) a client is using. You can also use log data to track usage patterns, estimate a timeline for adding resources to your system, keep track of historical data, and respond to client issues that are reported in the log using event codes.

Coho Winery is very interested in tracking the usage of their streaming media system. Coho wants to know, for example, which streams are most requested, whether clients connect successfully, if clients watch the entire stream, and how many clients connect at any one time. These statistics will not only help Coho to justify their investment in a streaming site, but also determine their plans moving forward. Should they add more videos? If the existing videos aren't being viewed, the winery staff might want to consider the reasons why. It could be that their content is not compelling enough to draw customers in. Perhaps there are technical difficulties that are preventing clients from connecting. Lack of traffic could also indicate that streaming media isn't a good fit for the winery business.

Windows Media Services collects this kind of information using the WMS Client Logging plug-in. This plug-in collects and saves data about clients that receive content as a unicast stream. The log collects numerous statistics about everything from the file that is being streamed to what protocol is being used and more. All of the statistics are stored in a space-delimited text file that adheres to the World Wide Web Consortium (W3C) standard for log files. By default, log files created by the WMS Client Logging plug-in are saved to the folder %systemroot%\System32\LogFiles\WMS. Because they are text files, you can read them with any text editing program such as Microsoft Notepad. You can also arrange the data in rows and columns by opening the file in Microsoft Excel.

WMS Client Logging is not enabled by default. Should you decide to use WMS Client Logging, you will need to enable it first. To enable the logging plug-in, follow these steps:

1. Click the publishing point for which logging will be enabled. (You can also enable logging at the server level.)

2. Click the **Properties** tab.

3. In **Category**, click **Logging**.

4. In **Plug-in**, right-click **WMS Client Logging**, and then click **Enable**.

How Will You Manage Server Overload?

One way is to use an additional server or servers to share the load when the number of connections grows. In our scenario, however, we've chosen to use only one streaming media server that doubles as a Web server. In this case, you manage server overload through the use of limits. At this point, what limits to set is really a best guess on your part based on existing knowledge of usage patterns. If you don't have existing data about the amount of traffic on your site, then you should stick with the program defaults until all testing is complete. We'll discuss load testing and setting limits in chapter 8.

Using limits, which can be customized for the server or individual publishing points, you can control the number of Player connections allowed, specify the maximum bandwidth allowed for Players and distribution servers, limit the number of distribution servers that can connect to your origin server, and so on.

Configuring Publishing Points

We introduced publishing points in chapter 3. Windows Media Services uses publishing points to translate a client request for content into a physical path on the server hosting the content. After a client successfully connects to a publishing point, your Windows Media server manages the connection and streams the content.

Two default publishing points—one for broadcast content and one for on-demand content—are provided during setup. These are preconfigured with sample content, playlists, and program defaults. You can rename these publishing points or save them with a new name to customize the configuration. You can also create new publishing points from scratch by using the publishing point wizards.

When configuring your publishing point, the wizard will ask you to provide the following information:

- **Content source (encoder, file, directory, or playlist) and associated details.** Because Coho Winery is streaming files that were encoded from DVD, the Webmaster chooses the directory option as shown in figure 7.11.

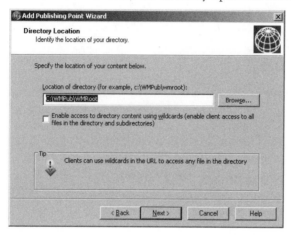

Figure 7.11   Provide the name and location of the content source.

- **Publishing point name and type (on-demand or broadcast).** Coho Winery will stream on-demand content only and is creating a single publishing point for all content. This is the simplest way to set up the structure and is easy to maintain. All of the content for the publishing point will be stored in the same directory. WMPub\WMRoot is the default directory for content in Windows Media Services. If the streaming media site is successful, and the winery team decides to add more videos, they will revisit the directory structure. At that time, they may decide to create separate directories for different kinds of content, such as audio-only content, high-bit-rate content, or some other differentiating factor. Having separate directories in this way makes for easier maintenance and administration, but is not necessary at this early stage.

  The name that the Coho Winery Webmaster assigns to the publishing point is related to the content that will be streamed, as shown in figure 7.12.

- **Distribution method (unicast or multicast).** When streaming on-demand content, unicast delivery is the only distribution method available, and the choice is made automatically. If the Coho Winery were to stream live content, the Webmaster would have to choose between unicast and multicast delivery. However, since they stream to clients over the Internet, and because most Internet networks don't yet support multicast distribution, any live Coho Winery content would also be streamed using unicast delivery.

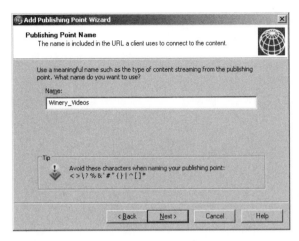

Figure 7.12   Provide a publishing point name that describes the content.

- **Logging preference.** As mentioned earlier, the Coho Winery team does want to collect and review client connection and usage data. When the Webmaster selects the client logging option (see figure 7.13), the WMS Client Logging plug-in is enabled for them so no further configuration of the plug-in is required (unless she wants to change the log location, change the log cycle, or make other adjustments).

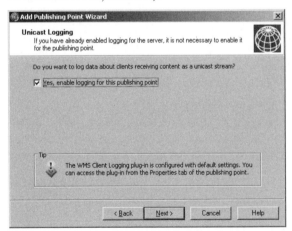

Figure 7.13   Enabling the client logging feature.

Announcing the Content

Your next task is to create the announcement file that will point Windows Media Player to your content. An announcement file is a redirector file with an .asx file name extension. Redirector files are used to transfer the request for content from the browser to Windows Media Player. Because browsers communicate using HTTP, they do not recognize popular streaming protocols and will attempt to download rather than play the referenced content. Once the redirector file sends the content request to Windows Media Player, the Player communicates directly with the Windows Media server to determine the appropriate protocol for delivering the stream. You can post the .asx file on your Web page or put it in an e-mail message to the users you want to target.

During the planning process, the Coho Webmaster decided that she would encode all winery content at multiple bit rates in order to serve a variety of customers: both dial-up and broadband. Even though she encoded the content at multiple bit rates, she still only needs one announcement file to post on the Coho Winery Web site. Using MBR streaming in this way also eliminates the need for users to choose the stream that is appropriate for them—a decision that some users are not comfortable making.

Creating the announcement file is a wizard-based process. The wizard will ask you for the following information:

- **URL of the content.** The URL should be specified using either the MMS or RTSP protocols (for example, mms://coho01/Winery_Videos). If you use MMS, the Player and server will automatically negotiate and roll over to the most suitable protocol based on the Player version and network conditions. While RTSP can also roll over to the most appropriate protocol, earlier versions of Windows Media Player do not support RTSP and will return an error when the stream request is received.

- **The name and location of the .asx file on your server.** By default, the .asx file takes the name of your publishing point and is placed in the folder %systemdrive%\inetpub\wwwroot. The Coho .asx file, for example, can be found at c:\inetpub\wwwroot\Winery_Videos.asx.

- **The name and location of your multicast information file if your content is to be multicast.** The multicast information file contains stream format details that the Player needs to decode the stream. This file will be generated for you by the announcement wizard. Like the announcement file, the multicast information file, which has an .nsc file name extension, is placed in the folder %systemdrive%\inetpub\wwwroot by default.

- **Optional metadata about the content.** This data includes title, author, and copyright. Because this data is displayed in the captioning area of Windows Media Player when users view the stream, Coho Winery includes a title and copyright, as shown in figure 7.14.

Additional metadata entries are possible. If you want a company logo or banner to be displayed in the Player, you can provide the location of that banner in the **Banner** field. **LogURL** is used for posting client logs to a Web server. If you have additional metadata that you want to provide, such as the date the content was produced, the company that edited it, and so on, you can add these attributes easily. These attributes will not be displayed in the Player but can be extracted by using search tools or other programs that are built using the Windows Media Format SDK.

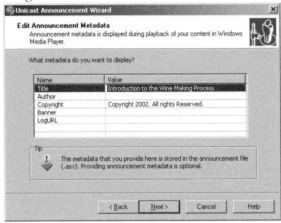

Figure 7.14   Entering optional metadata for a file or stream.

Testing the Stream

The final step for configuring the Windows Media server is to test the stream. Testing the stream enables you to verify that the content is encoded and delivered as expected, and that it plays back correctly. If the playback quality is not what you expect, you might need to encode the content again, or adjust your server settings until the content streams satisfactorily.

When you complete the Unicast Announcement Wizard, you are given the option to test the stream as shown in figure 7.15.

Figure 7.15   Testing the stream from the announcement wizard.

You can also test the stream from the **Source** tab of the Windows Media Services MMC snap-in by clicking the **Test** button at the bottom of the screen, shown highlighted by a square in figure 7.16.

Figure 7.16   Select the test button to test your stream.

Embedding the Player in a Web Page

Embedding Windows Media Player in a Web page can be beneficial for several reasons. It enables you to make use of corporate branding, control the size of the Player so you can be sure that it integrates with your site design, and control the amount of interactivity users have with the Player. For example, you can decide whether to include the rewind, fast forward, and pause buttons.

Both Internet Explorer and Netscape Navigator support embedding the Windows Media Player ActiveX control. However, the method for embedding the control is unique for each browser. Netscape Navigator does not directly support embedding of ActiveX controls, so the Player install program includes a Java applet that will host the Player ActiveX control when it is used with Navigator version 4.7 and later.

Unless you know for sure what browsers your viewers will be using when they visit your site, you'll probably want to add some code to your Web page that will detect the browser being used and then choose the appropriate embedding technique. You don't have to worry about confusing the browser with extra code because browsers only pay attention to the code they understand. If, for example, a customer connects to your site with Internet Explorer, the browser will execute the code that Internet Explorer understands and will ignore the code intended for Netscape browsers. The reverse is true as well.

Users of either browser must install Windows Media Player before viewing pages that embed the control. If Windows Media Player is installed after Netscape Navigator, the Player applet and an accompanying dynamic link library (DLL) are added to the appropriate Netscape directories automatically. In this case, no further setup is required by your users in order to view your pages in Navigator. You should instruct users who have installed Windows Media Player before Navigator to run the Player installation program again after Navigator has been installed.

Using the Player Control with Internet Explorer

To embed the Player control in a Web page for use with Internet Explorer, you use the OBJECT element with the ID and CLASSID attributes. You can use the HEIGHT and WIDTH attributes to specify the dimensions of the Player. Here is an example of the code used to embed the Player in a page that is viewed by Internet Explorer:

```
<OBJECT ID='Player' height='200' width='200'
     CLASSID='CLSID:6BF52A52-394A-11d3-B153-00C04F79FAA6'></OBJECT>
```

Internet Explorer uses the PARAM element to define specific startup conditions for the control. The PARAM element is embedded within the OBJECT element, and has two attributes: NAME and VALUE. Both attributes must be set. Here is an example of how the PARAM element is used:

```
{{
     document.writeln("<OBJECT ID='WMPEmbed' height='240' width='320'
          CLASSID='CLSID:6BF52A52-394A-11d3-B153-00C04F79FAA6'>");
     document.writeln("<PARAM NAME='autoStart' VALUE='FALSE'/>");
```

The following table describes some common name attributes that can be used with the PARAM element. For a full description of all of the available attributes, see the Windows Media Player SDK.

Parameter Name	Value	Description
autoStart	True or False.	Specifies whether the media item begins playing automatically Default is "true."
UIMode	Invisible, none, mini, full, or custom.	Specifies which controls are shown in the user interface. Default is full, meaning all controls are displayed.
URL	Any fully qualified URL.	Specifies the name and location of the clip.

Using the Player Control with Netscape Navigator

To embed the Player control in a Web page so that it displays correctly in Netscape Navigator, use the APPLET element with NAME and CODE attributes. You can use the HEIGHT and WIDTH attributes to specify the dimensions of the Player. Here is an example of the code used to embed the Player control for Netscape Navigator:

```
<APPLET NAME="Player" CODE="WMPNS.WMP" HEIGHT="200" WIDTH="200">
</APPLET>
```

To enable your Web pages to be viewed by both browsers, use the following SCRIPT element in the BODY element of your page at the location where the Player is to appear:

```
<SCRIPT>
if (navigator.appName == "Netscape")
{
    document.writeln("<APPLET NAME='Player' HEIGHT='200'
        WIDTH='200' CODE='WMPNS.WMP'>");
    document.writeln("<PARAM NAME='URL' VALUE='video.wmv'/>");
    document.writeln("</APPLET>");
}
else
{
    document.writeln("<OBJECT ID='Player''HEIGHT='200' WIDTH='200'
        CLASSID='CLSID:6BF52A52-394A-11d3-B153-00C04F79FAA6'>");
    document.writeln("<PARAM NAME='URL' VALUE='video.wmv'/>");
    document.writeln("</OBJECT>");
}
</SCRIPT>
```

> **Note**   All the Player control functionality available in Internet Explorer is also available in Navigator except for the defaultFrame property. In Navigator, each URL-type script command received displays the URL in a new browser window, regardless of the value of defaultFrame.

Building the Web Page

The Coho Winery Webmaster embeds the Player in the winery Web page and includes code for both Internet Explorer and Netscape Navigator. She specifies the height and width of the Player to make sure it appears correctly. She also uses the UI mode parameter, setting the value to "none" so no user controls are visible on the page.

Figure 7.17. shows the completed Coho Winery Web site with an embedded Player.

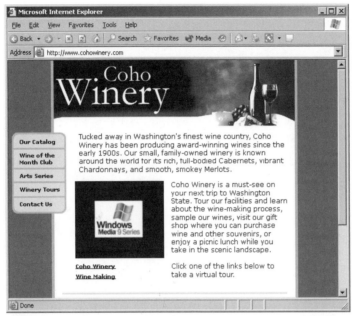

Figure 7.17   The Coho Winery Web site with an embedded Player control.

The HTML looks like this:

```
<HTML>
<HEAD>
<TITLE>Coho  Winery</TITLE>
</HEAD>
<BODY>

<script  language="JavaScript">
if (navigator.appName  ==  "Netscape")
{
    document.writeln("<APPLET  NAME='WMPEmbed''MAYSCRIPT
        HEIGHT='240'  WIDTH='320'  CODE='WMPNS.WMP'>");
    document.writeln("<PARAM  NAME='autoStart''VALUE='False'/>");
    document.writeln("<PARAM  NAME='URL''
        VALUE='http://ncwms/test.asx'/>");
    document.writeln("<PARAM  NAME='uiMode''VALUE='MINI'/>");
    document.writeln("</APPLET>");
}
else
{
    document.writeln("<OBJECT  ID='WMPEmbed''height='240'  width='320'
        CLASSID='CLSID:6BF52A52-394A-11d3-B153-00C04F79FAA6'>");
```

(continued)

```
          document.writeln("<PARAM NAME='autoStart''VALUE='FALSE'/>");
          document.writeln("<PARAM NAME='URL''
              VALUE='http://ncwms/test.asx'/>");
          document.writeln("<PARAM NAME='uiMode''VALUE='MINI'/>");
          document.writeln("</OBJECT>");
    }
    </script>

    <form align=center ID="Form1">
    <INPUT   TYPE="BUTTON""NAME="BtnPlay""VALUE="Play""
          OnClick="Player_Start()""ID="BtnPlay">
    <INPUT   TYPE="BUTTON""NAME="BtnStop""VALUE="Stop""
          OnClick="Player_Stop()""ID="BtnStop">
    <INPUT   TYPE="BUTTON""NAME="BtnPause""VALUE="Pause""
          OnClick="Player_Pause()""ID="BtnPause">
    </form>

    <SCRIPT>
    <!--
        function Player_Start ()
        {
            if (navigator.appName == "Netscape")
            {
                document.WMPEmbed.getControls().play();
            }
            else
            {
                document.WMPEmbed.controls.play();
            }
        }

        function Player_Stop ()
        {
            if (navigator.appName == "Netscape")
            {
                document.WMPEmbed.getControls().stop();
            }
            else
            {
                document.WMPEmbed.controls.stop();
            }
        }

        function Player_Pause ()
        {
            if (navigator.appName == "Netscape")
            {
                // 2 == Paused
```

```
            if (document.WMPEmbed.getPlayState() == 2)
                  document.WMPEmbed.getControls().play();
        else
                  document.WMPEmbed.getControls().pause();
    }
    else
    {
        // 2 == Paused
        if (document.WMPEmbed.playState == 2)
              document.WMPEmbed.Controls.Play();
        else
              document.WMPEmbed.Controls.Pause();
    }
}
//-->
</SCRIPT>
</BODY>
</HTML>
```

Reviewing the Mitigation Plan

The final step in the implementation phase is to revisit your mitigation plan. By now you may have elimintated some of the items in the plan or found new items to add. You may also have discovered solutions for some of the issues raised. Revisit the plan periodically to keep it up to date and to avoid unwanted surprises.

Here is the plan put together by the Coho Winery team. You'll notice that they've added a resolution column to the original plan.

Risk	Implication	Resolution
The server goes down.	The Web server and streaming media server reside on the same computer. If the server goes down, then the entire site is unavailable until the server is back online. Coho Winery does not have a backup server.	Back up all content regularly. Repair server as quickly as possible to get it back into service.
Customers have an older Player that is incompatible with the latest streaming technology.	The latest Windows Media encoding technology is supported by Windows Media Player 7.1, XP, and 9 Series. Customers running any other version of the Player will have limited success when attempting to view the winery video content.	Consider encoding the content with an earlier version of the Windows Media Video codec, such as Windows Media Video 8.1. Consider telling customers that they must have Windows Media Player 7.1 or later to view the content.

(continued)

135

(continued)

Risk	Implication	Resolution
Content that resides on the Web server could potentially be hacked or acquired illegally.	By default, content is stored in %systemdrive%\WMPub\WMRoot. When stored in this location, content is safe from unauthorized access. But if content is stored in the WWWroot directory, a user could acquire the content illegally and save it to the local machine where it could be propagated or replayed indefinitely.	Use the default Windows Media content directory, WMRoot.
Requests saturate the allocated bandwidth.	Clients currently receiving a stream encounter buffering delays or jitters in playback because the server is experiencing a higher volume of requests than it is capable of delivering.	Consider lowering the bit rate of the encoded content. Consider changing the limits on the server by allowing fewer concurrent connections or lowering the total allocated bandwidth. Consider increasing the Internet connection from T3 to OC3.

In this chapter we set up all of the components of the streaming media platform including Windows Media Encoder, Windows Media Services, and Windows Media Player. We also embedded the Player in a Web page and added code to ensure that both Internet Explorer and Netscape Navigator users would be able to view the content.

Now that your platform is in place, encode some test content, stream it from your server, and play it through the embedded Player on your Web site.

In the next chapter, we'll talk more about testing and stressing the platform in order to simulate real world usage patterns. This testing phase is the final phase before your site goes live.

8

Testing the Site Implementation

In the last chapter we experimented with encoding and streaming test content. In this chapter we take that experimentation one step further. The testing we do here is not a test of the content quality, but rather a real-world simulation of the usage patterns that you might encounter on your site. The goal of this testing is to stress your streaming media implementation in order to determine its capacity and stability. Pushing your implementation to its breaking point is a valuable exercise in a controlled environment. It enables you to put safeguards in place that should prevent problems once your site is live, and to ensure a positive experience for all users who visit your site.

By now you should have completed the following tasks:

- Designated an encoding computer and a Windows Media server.

- Installed all audio and video capture cards in your encoding computer.

- Added NICs as necessary and connected your encoding computer and server to your internal network.

- Configured Windows Media Encoder and connected your encoding computer to a content source, such as a VCR, camera, or DVD player.

- Configured Windows Media Services with one or more on-demand publishing points, and configured all plug-in properties.

- Created one or more announcement files and posted them on your Web page.

- Embedded Windows Media Player 9 Series in your Web page.

Setting up the Client Computer

The next task is to set up a client computer in order to view the test streams and simulate the client load. You'll need a computer running Microsoft Windows 98 Second Edition, Windows 2000, Windows ME, Windows XP Home Edition, Windows XP Professional, or Windows Server 2003. For optimal testing, Windows Media Player should not be running on the same computer as Windows Media Encoder or Windows Media Services.

Once your client computer is configured, you'll need to connect it to your internal network for testing. You should also install Windows Media Load Simulator 9 Series, which is available on the Windows Media 9 Series Web site (http://www.microsoft.com/windowsmedia) or on the CD provided with this book.

As its name suggests, Windows Media Load Simulator simulates the effects of hundreds of clients connecting to and receiving unicast streams from the Windows Media server. Its purpose is to determine the maximum capacity of your server by initiating a large number of client requests for streams—enough to potentially overwhelm your site or system resources. Windows Media Load Simulator requests and streams the content, but doesn't actually render it on the client end. This preserves CPU resources and memory on the client and enables one computer to simulate the load of a hundred or more.

The maximum number of client requests that can be simulated on a single client computer depends on the hardware configuration of that computer and the average bit rate of the simulated streams. Typically, a single client computer can simulate a few hundred concurrent client connections. Add client computers if you need to simulate additional client connections, but be sure to install Windows Media Load Simulator on each of them. Each instance of Windows Media Load Simulator would then connect to the same Windows Media server. For example, if you want to determine whether your Windows Media server can handle 1,000 client requests for unicast content, you could run Windows Media Load Simulator 9 Series on five client computers and configure each instance to simulate 200 clients. You might also want to use different network segments to avoid saturating your network during the test.

The peak usage and stress testing described above should always be done offline using a closed LAN. Because Windows Media Load Simulator creates the same server and network load that you get from an equivalent number of real clients, running a stress test over an active network could consume all available bandwidth and block real end users from gaining access to servers. By running peak usage tests over a closed LAN, you avoid disruption to end users on a network or the Internet, and you are free to run the bit rate up as high as necessary to completely test all servers and local network hardware.

Enabling Windows Media Services for Load Testing

Before your server can be put through a load test using Windows Media Load Simulator, you must create a file called WMLoad.asf and place it in the folder %SystemDrive%

\WMPub\WMRoot or in the directory you've specified as the default on your Windows Media server. While the format of the file needs to be streamable and recognizable by Windows Media Services, the actual content of this file is of little importance. It is the existence of the file that serves as a security measure to prevent unauthorized users from using Windows Media Load Simulator to launch a "denial of service" attack against your server. If WMLoad.asf is not present in your content directory, Windows Media Load Simulator will not run.

> **Caution**   You must remove the WMLoad.asf file from the content directory once testing is complete and before putting the server into service.

You can create the WMLoad.asf file using Windows Media Encoder, or by renaming one of the existing ASF files in the WMPub\WMRoot folder to WMLoad.asf. To further protect your server during load simulation testing, associate an access control list (ACL) with the WMLoad.asf file. In this way, users attempting to run Windows Media Load Simulator would have to provide a user name and password before being allowed to proceed. (You must enable WMS Negotiate Authentication on your Windows Media server in order for this to work.)

To set access permissions for WMLoad.asf, follow these steps:

1. From Windows Explorer, navigate to the %systemdrive%\WMPub \WMRoot directory, or to the directory you specified as the default. This is the directory where WMLoad.asf should be.

2. Right-click **WMLoad.asf**, and then click **Properties**.

3. Click the **Security** tab, and then click **Add**.

4. Type the domain (if applicable) and user names of the people who will have access to WMLoad.asf.

5. Select each user that you have added and verify that read permissions are allowed. Read permissions should be granted by default.

6. Click **OK**.

Test #1: On-demand Streaming

Your testing phase should simulate all of the possible scenarios that you will be supporting in your streaming environment. Because this section of the book has focused on on-demand streaming, we limit our discussion to on-demand testing. Recommended tests for live broadcasts, including multicast and unicast delivery, are provided in other sections of this book.

You should plan to use several files during the testing phase. Ideally, these files should be encoded at various bit rates and contain different kinds of content, such as high-motion, voice-overs, and even audio only. The Coho Winery Webmaster decided to encode five test files. The tests she runs on these files will accomplish the following tasks:

- Confirm that the encoder, server, and Player are communicating as expected.

- Simulate a large request for streams.

- Simulate authentication in a high-demand environment.

- Analyze test results and make configuration changes, if necessary.

Encoding the Test Files

To encode the five files for the load simulation test, the Coho Winery Webmaster followed these steps:

1. Open Windows Media Encoder 9 Series. In the **New Session** dialog box, click the **Convert a file** wizard. In the wizard:

   - Enter c:\encoding\test1.avi as the name and path for the first input file.

   - Enter c:\encoding\test1.wmv as the name and path for the first output file.

   - Select **Windows Media server** as the content distribution method.

   - Select **Multiple bit rates** for video and audio, and select the 28, 43, and 58 Kbps check boxes for the first file. For the other four test files, she'll use different bit rates, such as 109 Kbps, 148 Kbps, 282 Kbps, and higher and make sure that each file contains at least two or three bit rates.

> **Note**   Even though Coho Winery is encoding from file, it's a good idea to test device capture on live broadcast as well, just to see how performance is affected on the encoder, server, and player.

2. Encode 30 to 60 seconds of the video source. As the encoder ran, she kept an eye on **CPU Load** in the **Monitor** panel. When monitoring the CPU load, especially during device capture or live broadcast, watch for a load that con-

sistently exceeds 60 to 70 percent. When this happens, the quality of the encoded video could be affected. You can decrease the CPU load by closing other applications, especially background programs such as screen savers. You can also close or reduce the size of the video input panel on your encoder or encode single rather than multiple-bit-rate streams. If CPU load is still high, you will have to lower the encoding bit rate.

3. Open the file in Windows Media Player to check the playback. She then went back and encoded the remaining four test files.

4. Copy all of the files to the Windows Media server. The Webmaster copied the files to the %systemdrive%\WMPub\WMRoot folder on her Windows Media server. This folder is the default location for all Windows Media content and also contains additional sample files that you can use for testing.

Configuring the Server for Testing

Once your test content is in the default content directory, \WMPub\WMRoot, you can configure your server for the load simulation. To configure your server, follow these steps:

1. Open the Windows Media Services snap-in for MMC. Your server is listed in the console tree on the left side of the screen. Figure 8.1. shows the MMC as configured for the Coho Winery site. Coho01 is the server.

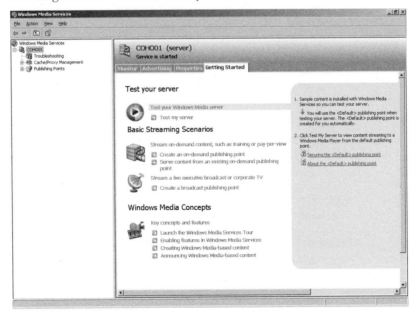

Figure 8.1 Coho Winery server in the Windows Media Services console tree.

2. Expand the **Publishing Points** node and select the default on-demand publishing point. Click the **Source** tab in the details pane to verify that your source files are listed.

3. By default, the <Default> publishing point is set to deny new connections as a security measure. Click the **Allow New Unicast Connections** button on the row below the list (shown in figure 8.2).

Figure 8.2 The **Allow New Unicast Connections** button.

4. With the publishing point node highlighted, click the **Properties** tab, right-click the **Logging** plug-in, and then click **Enable**. Although the Coho Winery Webmaster will not use this log during her test, she turns on logging because it increases the load on the server and gives a more accurate picture of server performance in a live environment.

5. Create five users, and name them User1, User2, User3, User4, and User5. Give them read access to the server that will be tested with Windows Media Load Simulator. Because Coho Winery has only one server, the Webmaster ensures that each user account has read access on Coho01. These users will attempt to authenticate during the test, which places an additional load on the server.

6. Open Windows Media Performance Monitor. The performance monitor gives you a good view of the health of your server and the streams it is sending to the clients. You can view the performance of the server or individual publishing points, and you can customize the view by adding or removing individual performance counters. To open Windows Media Performance Monitor, click your server in the console tree, click the **Monitor** tab, and then click the **View Performance Monitor** button at the bottom of the screen (as shown in figure 8.3).

Figure 8.3 The **View Performance Monitor** button.

Streaming the Test Files

The server is now ready for the test, so it's time to prepare the client computer or computers that will be used to simulate multiple client requests for streams. This preparation is simple: just make sure the client can connect to the server and receive the stream.

1. On each client computer that will be used in the test, open Windows Media Player 9 Series.

> **Note**   If you expect that some of your users will be using earlier versions of the Player, you might want to repeat this test with those versions. Since you encoded your test files with the Windows Media 9 Series codecs, the Player will first attempt to download the codecs before playing the content. Alternatively, you could re-encode one or more of your test files to use an earlier codec.

2. Open and stream one of the test files. Click **File**, and then click **Open**. In the **Open URL** dialog box, type the URL of the file (for example, mms:// Coho01/test1.wmv). If the file streams correctly, go on to the next step. If there is a problem, retrace your steps to resolve it. Here are some troubleshooting suggestions:

   - **File or path not found.** Make sure the file is in the default root folder, and the file name and path are correct in the URL. Make sure the publishing point is accepting new connections.

   - **Server not found.** There are many reasons why the Player might not find a server, including a mistyped URL or a problem with the network cable.

   - **Access denied.** Authorization and authentication have been added to the server or publishing point, and the user who is logged on to the client computer does not have access.

   - **Codec.** The Player attempted to stream a file for which there was no codec installed. It attempted to download the codec, unless the download codec feature was disabled, but could not locate the codec site to install it.

Configuring Windows Media Load Simulator

Before opening Windows Media Load Simulator, make sure you log on to the client computer using the same user name that you used during the installation process. This is important because Windows Media Load Simulator installation makes some changes in the Windows Media Player configuration file that are individualized for each user.

> **Warning** If you do not log as the installing user, Windows Media Load Simulator will not be able to stream using the MMS protocol.

With Windows Media Load Simulator, you can simulate the load of almost any number of clients. Not only can you set the number of clients, but you can also assign tasks to them. For example, you can have 30 clients playing files all the way through, 10 clients opening and closing connections, and 10 clients seeking through files. You can also monitor the effect of using the authentication and authorization plug-ins to authenticate clients before streaming to them. All of these tasks add to the load on the server and take up bandwidth on the network.

1. On the client computer, open Windows Media Load Simulator, and on the **Tools** menu, click **Configurations (Wizard)**.

2. Type the name of the server you want to target for the load test, such as Coho01.

3. Select the protocols to use for connecting to the server. See chapter 3 for a description of the different protocols that can be used with Windows Media 9 Series.

> **Note** If you select HTTP, ensure that HTTP streaming is enabled on your server. See the previous chapter for more information.

4. Add the names of the test files. The files and the protocols you selected are added to the list, as shown in figure 8.4.

144

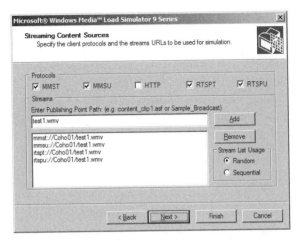

Figure 8.4 Specifying the files and protocols to use for load testing.

5.   Enter the number of clients you would like to simulate with each profile. For the first test, the Coho Winery Webmaster started with a conservative number and a straightforward profile, just to understand how the load simulation works. She used 10 clients in the **Long Play** profile, and 0 in all the others as shown in figure 8.5.

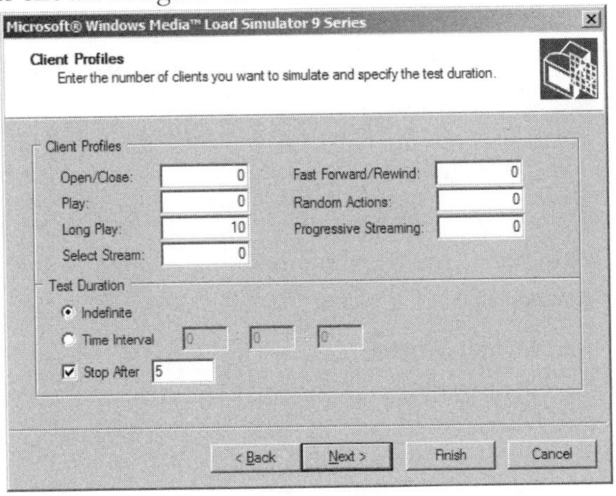

Figure 8.5 Selecting the load simulation profile.

Clients with the **Long Play** profile simply play the content. If the 10 clients are streaming a 100 Kbps file, you should see a total bandwidth of around 1,000 Kbps. The **Seek** profile simulates users seeking to different parts of files. You will notice during the simulation that bandwidth fluctuates with the content. As you add different profiles, the bandwidth increases as clients perform actions, like opening files, closing files, and seeking.

> **Note**   The Coho Winery Webmaster bypassed the next two pages of the wizard. She chose not to enable client-side logging because the results would be unreliable since no actual streams are being delivered, and she does not want to simulate user authentication because that would require her to use digest authentication, which is not a viable solution for the winery Web site.

6.   On the **Load Simulator Monitoring Options** page, click **Enable Load Simulator Logging**. This log shows the test results generated by Load Simulator. An entry is made for every instance in which a problem occurs with the client's streaming experience. After each test session, a set of summary statistics will also be recorded at the end of the log including information such as the total number of clients, total packets received, total number of streaming errors, and so on.

7.   Enable **Server Performance Logging**. This log collects server performance data. Data can only be collected when the load simulation computer uses an account that has administrative privileges on the server. You can also view the performance monitor on each computer or from the group in the Windows Media Services snap-in.

8.   On the client computer, open the following monitors, so you can view the health of the system during the test:

- **Task Manager** on the client computer to monitor **CPU Usage** on the **Performance** tab.

- **Load Simulation Status.** This tab on Windows Media Load Simulator shows when the test begins and ends, and streaming errors that occur.

9.   Start Windows Media Load Simulator and watch the server and client monitors.

10.   Reconfigure your test profile to change the number of clients connecting or the type of connections being made. On the second test, the Coho Winery Webmaster boosted the number of clients to 50 and added seeking, opening and closing, and additional tasks to the mix in order to stress the server even more. Figure 8.6. shows the updated test profile.

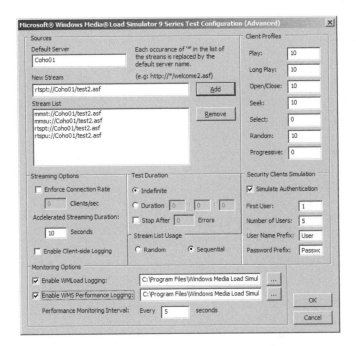

Figure 8.6 Updated profile for the second load test.

Interpreting Stream Errors

Streaming errors can occur when something has not been configured properly. For example, the simulator could attempt to do one of the following:

■ Stream using HTTP when the HTTP Server Control Protocol plug-in has been not been enabled.

■ Connect to a stream to which the user does not have access.

■ Stream a file that does not exist.

To track down errors, check all the monitors. For example, if you are receiving many client connection errors, but the CPU usage on the server and client computers are running low, the problem is probably caused by the configuration.

If the client CPU is running high, errors will show up that have nothing to do with server and network performance. Cut down on the number of clients and profiles and then check the client CPU again. You might notice that Windows Media Load Simulator requires more of the client computer's CPU and memory when it runs many tasks. You could try cutting down on the number of tasks if you want to increase the client count.

For example, the client computer can more easily handle 50 long play clients than the same number of clients opening files, closing files, and seeking.

Windows Media Performance Monitor gives you the most detailed picture of the server during a load test. With it you can view the amount of processor time used, number of Players connected for different protocols, and more. As the simulation runs, watch for problems such as an increase in late reads, memory, and processor time. If client errors occur in conjunction with an increase in these counters, either a slow CPU or slow hard drives could be to blame. If streaming errors are occurring, check bandwidth usage to see if it is running up against the limit of your network.

The **Monitor** tab also provides general information about your CPU usage, clients connected, and current allocated bandwidth. Select your server in the console tree, and then click the **Monitor** tab to view these statistics.

Studying the Test Results

When the load test is complete, review the test logs to identify problems or trends. The Coho Winery Webmaster cross-checked the server and load simulator logs as a means of pinpointing problems. Client logging was not enabled.

For example, the performance log noted a high processor time and late reads due to a large number of concurrent connections. Nothing unusual occurred on the server at that time, so she suspected the network or a configuration problem.

Next, she checked the Windows Media Load Simulator log for clients that reported a high number of failures. If a client reported failure to open, the server configuration was OK, and the server was not under stress, then she determined a slow network or a stressed client computer could be the problem.

Running Windows Media Load Simulator and reviewing test logs provides you with the information you need to correct configuration errors and set limits. You can set limits for the entire server or individual publishing points. To set limits, select the server or publishing point node from the console tree and click the **Properties** tab. Click **Limits**, and then set the limits appropriate for your situation.

Setting Limits

When deciding what limits to set, remember that it requires less bandwidth to stream a few high-bit-rate streams than it does to stream many low-bit-rate streams, even though the total bit rate is the same. This is because each connection requires a certain amount of bandwidth for protocol overhead. Many streams also require more processing power and reads from the hard drive. This is also true of short files and long files. As you saw with the simulation, short files require more opening and closing of sessions and seeking, which require more bandwidth and CPU time than long files.

If your computer and network are slow, try limiting the number of Player connections or the connection rate. Coho Winery, for example, limited concurrent connections to 40 as a result of testing. If you need to preserve network bandwidth, limit aggregate Player bandwidth. Coho Winery limited this to 70 percent of the total available bandwidth. Limiting connection acknowledgement can be useful if the server is overpowered by many authentication requests.

In this chapter the Coho Winery completed the testing of their streaming media site, adjusted the server configuration as necessary, and set limits to ensure optimal performance from their server. At this point, their system is ready to go live.

Monitoring server performance and making adjustments are an ongoing part of any streaming infrastructure as usage patterns change, content is updated or added, software is upgraded, and hardware and network configurations are changed.

In the next part we'll take the task of implementing a basic streaming media site and build upon it as we deploy Windows Media at an online movie company that provides live broadcasts of entertainment news while offering on-demand streams and downloadable content.

Part III

Internet Digital Media Business

In part II, we looked at a small company that adds streaming media to an existing site in order to enhance the value of the site. The scenario in this section focuses on a digital media-based business. Streaming issues such as quality, reliability, and cost have a direct effect on the bottom line in such businesses.

This part of the book describes setting up a production workstation for creating on-demand content, setting up an encoding workstation for encoding a live stream, writing server-side playlists, and using digital rights management (DRM) to protect content. A majority of businesses and organizations built around streaming media on the Internet focus on creating high-quality content, but rely on other companies to distribute the content. Therefore, we will focus on the content creation side of streaming, and explore the use of hosting services and content delivery networks (CDNs) for getting the content to an audience.

The section follows the process introduced in part II: envisioning, planning, developing, and implementing.

9

Envisioning and Planning

In this chapter, we introduce the scenario we will be exploring throughout part III by starting from the beginning of the process. We will explore the problem or opportunity that became the catalyst for the scenario. After describing the scenario, we will explore ways to plan the system that we will develop and implement.

Developing the Vision

The fictitious business Contoso Movies Online was started to take advantage of the opportunities that have emerged with the growth of the Internet and broadband communications. The founders of the company saw the potential of renting movies online. Users can come to the site, find the movies they want to view, pay a rental fee, and then download or stream movies to their computers. By being able to download or stream movies off the Internet, end users can enjoy instant access to their favorites. No longer do they have to drive to video stores and wait in long lines. In addition, the site can go beyond what a video store offers by acting as a movie resource for users, providing movie information and enabling users to preview clips and trailers before they rent. The site could even encourage the development of a community by offering chat rooms and other ways for users to exchange ideas and opinions.

After the founder put together her team of business partners and consultants, they met to decide on the vision for the enterprise. They needed a vision statement that would unite all activity around a central theme. This statement would then drive all internal activities from the purchase of stationery to site design to how they dealt with the film studios. They decided their vision would be *"To provide a one-stop Internet portal for the rental of movies online, distribution of fan-related movie information, and exchange of ideas."* The site must be engaging, useful, and provide a high-quality user experience. The goal of the site would be to become the primary location for everything related to movies.

Initially, the company founders focused on how to protect the movie properties they would rent. A studio would not be interested in allowing their movies to be rented online if they could easily be copied and pirated. The founders looked at a number of options, and then settled on a DRM solution using Windows Media Rights Manager. Movies could be encrypted with Windows Media Rights Manager, and then only users who pay the fee and receive the license could view the file.

After the mode of copyright protection was decided, Contoso's catalog of titles began to grow. The business team grew and development of the site began. E-commerce solutions and systems were added to the components behind the site, a hosting service was locked in, and the founders began to look for ways in which they could enhance the site.

In this part, we will not go into all the details of e-commerce and site design. Instead, we will focus on the following four primary areas of the site that involve the use of Windows Media:

- **Movie trailers.** Before end users commit to renting, they can view movie trailers for free.

- **Movie info channel.** There is one information channel for each of 10 film categories. End users can tune in to an info channel and view trailers and related movie information, such as interviews and special stories.

- **Live events channel.** About once a month, the site presents a live movie-related event. End users can tune in and view the entire event without commercial interruptions. Events include events such as movie premieres and Hollywood parties.

- **Movie rentals.** End users can view full-length features by streaming or downloading them.

Figure 9.1 provides a graphical view of how systems will be interconnected to provide the framework with which the content for the four areas can be created and distributed.

Videocassette recorders (VCRs) will be connected to a production workstation. Video, such as movies and publicity videos, will be captured on the workstation, and then sent over a broadband connection to the Internet hosting service. Web design elements, including the server-side playlists, will also be sent to the hosting service over the same connection. A remote encoding computer will be used to stream events for the live channel to the host via frame relay, a broadband Internet connection such DSL, or some other means. A laptop encoder can be used to save space and reduce setup time on location.

The hosting service will then distribute the content to its *edge* servers located around the world. Edge servers are a key component of the service's content delivery network (CDN). CDNs are advanced distribution systems that employ a decentralized network design, using edge servers to, in effect, move the content closer to the edge of the network where the end user is. CDN concepts will be described in chapter 12.

Contoso Movies Online will contract with an e-commerce service to handle customer transactions, and with a license provider to issue DRM licenses. After an end user successfully pays for a movie, the license provider generates and sends a license that is unique to the end user's computer. With a valid license installed on the client, the end user can view the movie.

In the remaining chapters of this part, we will design, deploy, and implement each of the four primary areas of the site. However, we will first expand our vision. Then we will analyze each of the areas in order to understand daily workflow.

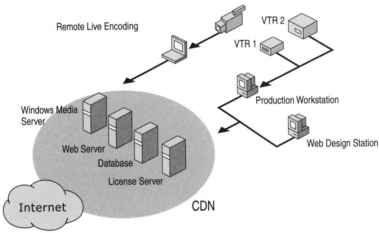

Figure 9.1 The Contoso Movies Online network topology.

Preparing Movie Trailers

Trailers are short films created by production companies to promote their films. The contract Contoso makes with a film company will include a description of the material to be supplied by them. As part of the agreement, they will make sure to receive a high-quality digital videotape of the entire film. They will also make sure to receive any appropriate publicity material, including stills, written information, and any promotional videos and trailers that can be used on the site. The contract will also include permissions to use the material.

When end users come to the site, they can browse the featured information on the home page, which includes special movie rental information and hot movie topics, or they can browse or search for a specific movie. After locating a movie, they link to the details page for the movie. On the details page, they can read reviews and movie information, view the movie, or they can view the trailer. When they click the link to view a trailer, Windows Media Player opens and the trailer streams to the user. Custom versions of the Player may be created for special content.

To implement movie trailers area on the site, we will need the following components:

- Trailers
- Production workstation
- Hosting service
- Presentation enhancements
- Web design

Trailers

Windows Media files will be encoded from videotape supplied by the film production companies or distributors. Contoso will request tapes in the Digital Betacam format, which is a standard used throughout the film and broadcast industries. This format will provide a high-quality transfer of a film. The trailers will be encoded at multiple bit rates. Typically, a streaming site provides two or three versions of a file or stream encoded for different bandwidths, such as 28.8 Kbps, 100 Kbps, and 300 Kbps. End users can then choose the version that is most appropriate for their Internet connection.

By using Windows Media, you can encode one file that contains multiple streams encoded at different bit rates. With Windows Media 9 Series, you can select different audio and video codec settings for each stream, as well as different frame sizes and other properties. The end user does not have to select a bandwidth; Windows Media Services selects the appropriate bit rate automatically based on current network conditions.

Production Workstation

To convert material on videotape to Windows Media files, Contoso Movies Online will need one or more production workstations. Each workstation must include VCRs to play back tapes from the studios, a computer to capture and encode the files, an audio mixer to adjust audio levels, a high-quality computer monitor, and audio speakers. The computer will use a video capture card that provides an SDI port to capture digital audio and video from the Digital Betacam.

Hosting Service

Contoso will use a third-party hosting service and CDN to host their Web and Windows Media-based content. With a CDN, end users connect to the edge servers that are closest to them, rather than one centralized server. The result is that end users receive a more reliable stream and therefore a better viewing experience. Contoso found that contracting with a hosting service and CDN is much less expensive and easier to manage than attempting to host the content themselves. Trailer files will be uploaded to the hosting service FTP site, and from there the host will propagate the files according to their content management system.

Presentation Enhancements

When end users choose to stream a trailer, it will open and play in Windows Media Player. A button will be displayed below the video frame that users can click to send them immediately to the rental page for the movie advertised in the trailer. In addition, Contoso will enhance the presentation of special trailers, features, and information in the Player with *borders* and *HTMLView*. These two Player features enable them to display collections of image files, digital media, text, and interactive elements in the **Now Playing** pane of the full mode Windows Media Player. The composition and functionality of the enhancements are implemented with script.

Web Design

ASP pages will be used to make the site easier to manage. For example, instead of creating individual details pages for every movie, Web designers can create an ASP page template and dynamically populate the page from information in a database when an end user accesses it. ASP pages will also be used to gather end user information.

The Movie Info Channel

With Windows Media 9 Series you can stream server-side playlists and control playback of the playlists with scripting. Server-side playlists can be accessed directly by users and played on demand, or they can be the source of a publishing point. If a playlist is the source of a broadcast publishing point, it plays just like any other broadcast. End users tune in to the broadcast in progress. For example, if you start a one-hour server-side playlist on a broadcast publishing point at 10:00 AM, an end user accessing the publishing point at 10:30 AM would begin viewing the playlist at the halfway point.

The online movie site will categorize their movies into 10 genres, and then create broadcast server-side playlists for each genre, which they will call "movie info channels." The playlists will consist of trailers in each genre and publicity material supplied by the studios, such as making-of shorts and interviews. The movie site will also produce interstitial videos to place in-between elements. Interstitial videos or clips are short transitional pieces that include branding information. They are also called bumpers. The following items could be part of the line-up for a playlist:

- Trailer 1   2:25
- Trailer 2   1:43
- Bumper 1   0:15
- Interview 1   3:04

- Bumper 2   0:20

- Trailer 3   2:14

- Trailer 4   0:45

- Bumper 3   0:13

- Making-of 1   5:31

A playlist will run for 15 to 20 minutes, and then repeat continuously in a *loop*. End users will then be able to access an info channel at any time from the home page or one of the genre pages. For example, an end user may tune in to an info channel at a point 10 minutes into a playlist and continue to watch for five minutes after it loops to the beginning.

Because the playlist is run from the server, there is minimal buffering and black between segments. Also, because they are accessed through publishing points, you can apply publishing point properties to a server-side playlist, such as limits and security. Wrapper playlists will be used with the channels to add a short intro video that every end user will see when they first connect to the publishing point, but before going to the playlist in progress. Chapter 11 describes how playlists and wrapper playlists are created and configured.

To implement movie info channels on the site, the Contoso staff will need the following components:

- Trailers and publicity material

- Production workstation

- Server-side playlists

- Hosting service

- Web design

Trailers and Publicity Material

Contoso will get this material from the studios. Trailers and the other material only have to be captured once. Then they can be linked to from the details page or other pages, or from a server-side playlist. For example, end users can view the trailer file for Movie 1 directly from the Movie 1 details page, or by viewing the movie info channel for the genre associated with Movie 1. If a movie fits in multiple genres, the same trailer file can be included on multiple playlists.

Production Workstation

A workstation will also be required to convert videotapes of other material. The server-side playlist can be created on any computer that has access to the host upload site.

Server-side Playlists

There will be one playlist for each of the 10 genres (for example, comedy, drama, action, children, and so forth). The playlist script is written using Synchronized Multimedia Integration Language (SMIL) in the Playlist Editor, which is installed with Windows Media Services. Scripts can also be written manually using a text editor program such as Microsoft Notepad.

After server-side playlists are written, they will be uploaded to the hosting service FTP site. Then Contoso personnel will use a server administration tool supplied by the host to configure the movie info channel publishing points and source the playlist files. To make changing the scripts easier, elements in a playlist can point to an ASP page instead of directly to a Windows Media file. This way new files can be added to the playlists dynamically by simply changing a database entry rather than by rewriting the playlist script.

Hosting Service

The hosting service will be used to deliver Web content as well as Windows Media files. In order to implement the info channels, Contoso will use a server administration tool supplied by the host, with which they can create publishing points. After the publishing points have been created, a playlist file can be changed by simply overwriting it, and then restarting the publishing point. ASP pages will be hosted with the other Web pages on a Web server.

Web Design

When an end user clicks the link for an info channel, the ASP page that the link points to will return the URL of the broadcast publishing point and open the stream in the Player.

The Live Events Channel

In addition to offering movies, trailers, and special shorts and features, Contoso Movies Online will present live events. This is another way the site owners plan to keep the site alive and fresh. Along with a live event, the site will run a chat which will be run by the event producer. The goal is to offer at least one live event per month. The owners realize that this is an ambitious goal, but they also see the competitive value of live events. Live events would draw many interested end users and help build the reputation of the site as a movie fan portal.

Unlike events on commercial television, the events on the live events channel can run as long as an event runs. The types of events will include movie premieres, special interview chats, and Hollywood parties. For example, to promote a movie, a production company could have one or more of the stars engage in a live chat from the set, which would include live audio and video.

Live television events can be expensive to produce. However, live events using streaming media can be done relatively inexpensively, because the technical requirements are often not as restrictive. And it would not be out of place to have part of the expense be absorbed by a production company. For example, a simple event could be done with one inexpensive digital camcorder, a fast laptop computer, and a broadband Internet connection. The only other expenses could be the production team, which may include a producer, camera operator, and someone to moderate the chat.

To view the event, end users will click the Live Events Channel link, which takes them to the Live Channel page. The page will include text and images to frame the page, and embedded chat and Windows Media Player ActiveX controls. The end user will be able to view the event, and perhaps log in to the chat room. In chapter 12 we will explore the Live Events Channel in greater detail.

To implement the Live Event Channel on the site, we will need the following components:

- Source
- Hosting service
- Web design
- Production equipment and staff
- Encoding computer
- Broadband connection to Internet

Content Source

The nature of the source will depend on the event. Not all events will be produced entirely by the Contoso team. Many can be produced by other companies and sent to Contoso as live audio and video. Then the Contoso team will encode the signal and send it to their hosting service. For example, a television station might produce a live premiere for Los Angeles viewers. Contoso could make a deal with the station to pick up the signal from a satellite and encode it with one of their production workstations. Another event might require a combination of teams and encoding on location. Each event will have to be planned individually.

Hosting Service

The service will receive the live stream from the encoder through a broadcast publishing point. The stream can be sent to the service using a dedicated frame relay connection, a broadband Internet connection, or even a dial-up Internet connection. To prevent Internet users from connecting directly to the encoder, Contoso will use encoder security to allow access only by the host server.

Web Design

A Live Event Channel page will be created that contains the embedded Player and chat controls. The Player will include playback controls, so the end user can start or stop the Player, or expand the image to full screen. Before or after the event, the Player will be black. At those times, the page can show event times and other information.

Any live event can be streamed simultaneously to the publishing point and to an archive file. After the event, the file can be made available to end users for viewing on-demand. The live event page will also include a link to view these archived events.

Production Equipment and Staff

If the production will be handled by the Contoso team, a producer or director will need to be assigned or hired, and plans made to gather the necessary equipment, supplies, crew, and connections. Then a production schedule will be created. The simple camcorder and laptop production can be expanded to include multiple cameras, a remote production truck, and a large crew, depending on the need and budget. For example, a studio may see the value in helping with the cost of a production as part of their marketing effort.

Encoding Computer

Regardless of the size of the production, one or more encoding computers will be required to convert audio and video to a digital media stream, and then send it over a network. Although one laptop can encode a live stream, if a large budget is on the line, it is always better to have redundant, reliable encoding computers. If you want to offer the stream at a number of different bit rates, you can encode an MBR stream. However, encoding MBR streams in real time requires a fast, reliable computer with abundant RAM. Rather than encoding with MBR, you can instead encode streams on multiple encoding computers.

Broadband Internet Connection

The most reliable and cost-effective means of getting the live stream from the encoder to the server is over a dedicated connection. Frame relay can provide adequate bandwidth and reliability. ISDN connections are also often used. If setup time and cost is a factor, you can use a broadband Internet connection, such as DSL or a cable modem. However, you should be prepared with a backup communications channel, such as a dial-up connection.

Movie Rentals

The primary business of the Contoso Movies Online site is renting movies. End users come to the site, select a movie they want to view, pay for the rental, and then either download or stream the movie with Windows Media Player.

The Contoso team decided early on that they would strive to provide the best user experience. To that end, they decided to use Windows Media 9 Series throughout their process. With Windows Media 9 Series Audio and Video codecs, the playback quality can exceed that of VHS, and can approach DVD quality, depending on the bit rate of the encoded movie. In addition to the codecs, Windows Media 9 Series features help ensure a high-quality stream, and Windows Media Rights Manager provides the necessary security. By encrypting the movie files, the online movies team can be confident that users will not be able to view them without paying.

After the end user enters valid payment information, a Windows Media Rights Manager license is downloaded. Then, when the Player accesses the movie file, either by streaming it from the server or playing it locally after it has been downloaded, the Player searches the computer for a valid license. If a valid license exists, the Player can begin rendering the movie.

In order for a license to be valid, a number of parameters in the license must match those in the encrypted file. Also, the license can only be used on the computer for which it was issued. If a user copies the Windows Media file to another computer, it will not play unless the user on that computer pays for another license. In addition, the times and dates must be valid.

The Contoso Movies Online site will place a time limit of 48 hours on the rentals. After that time, the license will expire. An end user can keep a downloaded movie without a license, or copy it and give it to friends. But if he or a friend attempts to play the file, Windows Media Player will automatically take him to the Contoso Movies Online site where he can pay the rental fee again and receive a new license.

To implement movie rentals on the site, we will need the following components:

- Encrypted movie files
- Windows Media hosting service
- E-commerce system
- License service provider

Encrypted Movie Files

As a movie is being encoded as a Windows Media file, it will also be encrypted. The encrypted file behaves just like any other file. For example, you can copy, move, rename, or download it. The only thing you cannot do is play it unless the computer you are playing it on has a valid license.

Windows Media Hosting Service

All movies on the site will be available for download or streaming. Files created for download will be hosted on a Web server, and streamed files will be hosted on a Windows Media server.

E-commerce System

After a user chooses to download or stream a movie, user information (such as a credit card number and e-mail address) will be gathered and processed through an e-commerce system. Such a system includes Web pages and software to communicate with the user and handle the purchase process, and a secure database that holds customer account information. The system will hook into third-party systems that authorize the purchase, adjust the user's account balance, and issue payments to Contoso. At the end of the e-commerce process, the system returns authorization information to the license provider or informs the user that payment has been denied.

Licensing Service Provider

During the encoding process, licensing information is entered into a license database owned or run by the license provider. Then, when an end user requests a license, the information is retrieved and used by a license server to generate a license. A business can maintain their own license server or contract with a third party. In our scenario, Contoso Movies Online will contract with a license service provider. To implement a license server, you need the Windows Media Rights Manager 9 Series Software Development Kit (SDK) and the Windows Media Encoder 9 Series SDK. You also need expertise in creating Web-based applications.

Running their own license server would give Contoso more direct control over the licensing process, but it would require extra staff to maintain the database and license properties for each movie title. At this early stage in the life of the company, it is more cost-effective to contract with a service to handle licensing. As the business grows, the licensing process can be brought internally by expanding the title acquisition team.

In this scenario, the license will be sent to an end user prior to downloading or streaming the content, so the end user is not even aware of the license process. If an end user attempts to play a downloaded file after the license has expired or on another computer, the Player opens the user's browser to a license acquisition URL, which is contained in the encrypted file. At that point, the user can choose whether to rent the movie again. In this scenario, the URL will point to a rental page on the Contoso Movies Online site. When the rental process starts, e-commerce and licensing processes will be initiated to fulfill the purchase.

Developing an Implementation Plan

With a solid vision in place, Contoso can begin planning how to deploy the systems that will implement the vision. From there they can study workflows and decide on staffing, facilities, and resource requirements. Contoso Movies Online will have business, creative, and process components.

The business component will consist of staff for managing the company and its finances, managing deals with production companies, acquiring products to rent, and acquiring publicity material. Acquisition managers will include Windows Media in their negotiations with production companies to demonstrate their commitment to quality. The managers will also demonstrate Windows Media Rights Manager and the e-commerce system to show how security and the payment process will work.

The creative component will consist of a small group of writers, artists, and producers who develop the content for the site. In addition to creating static text and graphics for the Web pages, the creative team will be responsible for creating the server-side playlists used for the movie info channels, and for producing events on the live channel.

The process component of the site will be engaged in creating content and getting it to the end user. Staff will include technical operators or editors for capturing and encoding the movies from videotape, and personnel for maintaining a database of movie titles and licensing information.

We will focus primarily on the areas of the process and creative components that relate to Windows Media.

Content Creation

The editors will capture and encode from videotape to Windows Media files. One person can handle the simultaneous capture of several movies and other material. For example, if Contoso has three workstations, an editor can start a movie capture on one workstation, and then set up captures on the other workstations while the first one is running. The editor will use the production workstations and other computers in the most efficient ways to create content quickly and with the highest quality.

The workflow for one capture is as follows:

1. **Receive videotape.** A work order will be generated by the acquisition team when a movie acquisition is made. The work order will be sent to the creative team, license coordinator, and editor containing information about the material that is to arrive from the production company, and what to do with the material. When an editor receives a videotape that matches the description on the work order, she will follow the instructions for encoding and encrypting the tape. Typically, a new movie will be encoded at multiple bit rates using a standard encoding template.

2. **Configure tape for playback.** Play the tape and set up the VCRs for proper playback of audio and video.

3. **Configure capture.** With the VCR configured, configure the capture program on the encoding computer. For highest quality, material will be captured to an uncompressed AVI file first.

4.   **Capture to AVI.** Capture videotape in real time to AVI. Monitor progress and watch for capture errors.

5.   **Check file quality.** Spot-check the captured AVI file.

6.   **Configure encoder.** Set up Windows Media Encoder to encode a Windows Media file from the AVI file. Because this process does not take place in real time, the speed of the processor does not have to be as high as that of the capturing computer. Therefore, multiple less-expensive computers can be used for this encoding process, freeing the main workstations for videotape capturing.

7.   **Encode and encrypt to a Windows Media file.** The time needed for this process can vary depending on computer CPU speed and memory.

8.   **Check file quality.** Spot-check the finished Windows Media file. In order to play the file, the editor must go through the process of obtaining a license, so this part of the process can be checked, too. The e-commerce service can create an internal account for testing licensing and playback.

9.   **Sign off work order.** The work order, which can be an e-mail document, is signed by the editor as being finished. Then it is sent to the acquisition manager, producer, Web designer, and license coordinator.

Licensing Configuration

The license coordinator works with the license service provider and manages the internal database of encrypted movies. The database maintained by the license provider for issuing licenses does not need to contain as much detail as the one that the license coordinator keeps. The internal database can be as complex as necessary, and can even include contract information from the production company. For license provider, the database needs to contain, at a minimum, the information included in the DRM profiles used by Windows Media Encoder for encrypting content.

Web Site Production

The producer's team develops the Web site, and maintains the information available to the end user. On a daily basis, the producer and team will be responsible for the following activities:

■   **Maintain movie info channels.** Design new line-ups, create the server-side playlists, send the playlist files to the hosting service, and configure the publishing points, if necessary. Then the producer will test playback, and create new material as needed, such as new interstitial segments and interview segments.

- **Coordinate receiving publicity material from studios.**

- **Create new movie details pages.** Initially, the Web designer will create Web page templates (ASP pages), so new pages can be quickly and easily added by creating and modifying records in the content database that the pages access. When the producer receives a work order from acquisition, she creates a new details page in the database.

- **Create static information.** The static information includes text and still images, which will be displayed on the home and movie details Web pages. The creative team writes copy, chooses images, and then keeps the pages fresh by adding viewer comments and other updates.

- **Produce monthly live events.** The producer will work with the acquisition team and the studios to organize and produce events on the Live Event Channel. The producer may contract with freelancers and attempt to leverage support from studios to create the events. She will also need to work with technical staff to coordinate the resources and production equipment to record, encode the video, and send it to the hosting service.

- **Design the site.** Initially, the Web designers will create the Web site. The site consists of those elements that the viewer uses to locate and play movies. In addition, the site includes all the code needed to interact with the e-commerce and licensing sites. The Web designer will also develop the custom Player enhancements for special presentations.

After the framework of the site has been built, the rest of the creative team will populate the site with content, including the encrypted movies, trailers, channels, and static information. On a daily basis, the Web designer will maintain and upgrade the site to make sure it runs correctly, and work with the creative team to make sure it is appealing and fresh.

Deploying Windows Media 9 Series

With a solid understanding of the workflow, the Contoso staff can build the facility. The biggest part of the Windows Media system will be the content creation facility, which will consist of two or more production workstations. Another component of the system will be a live encoding computer, which can be configured on a laptop. All other tasks can be performed on a computer with Web design and graphics programs, and office programs such as Microsoft Word and Excel. In the remaining chapters in this part, Contoso Movies Online builds the workstation and populates the Web site with fresh, engaging content.

10

Movie Trailers

In chapter 9, we saw how Contoso Movies Online developed their vision into an Internet business built around Windows Media 9 Series. They also began planning the four areas of the movies online site that relate to Windows Media: movie trailers, movie info channels, a live events channel, and movie rentals. In this chapter, Contoso completes the following tasks for creating and hosting movie trailers:

- Building a production workstation.

- Capturing and encoding content.

- Developing presentation enhancements for Windows Media Player.

Building the Production Workstation

To provide movies, trailers, and other video on their site, Contoso Movies Online must convert the video into Windows Media files. Then the files can be sent to the hosting service, and end users will be able to link to the files from the Contoso Web site and stream the digital media to their computers. To convert the video, the company will use two or more production workstations.

The basic components of a workstation are a playback VCR and a computer system. The VCR plays back the video, and the computer converts the video and stores it as a file. Contoso plans to use the workstations to convert all of their video. In the initial phase of the site, the company will need to convert many hours of video in order to have a broad enough catalog to open business. The company plans to have no less that 100 titles available before going online. That means that over 200 hours of video must be encoded. To help convert the initial volume of titles, Contoso may contract with outside encoding services.

In the early stages of business planning, the management team asked the questions: "Why not send out all conversion work? Why not keep the core business of the company focused on acquiring and renting movies?" The company decided to use a service to handle the hosting of the site and streaming content, an e-commerce provider to handle the purchase process, and a license service to handle issuing and maintaining DRM licensing. Why not farm out conversion as well?

The Contoso team is made up of people interested in the production of movies. As part of their charter, they decided that they want to have direct control over the quality of their content in order to provide the best user experience. By encoding their own material using the Windows Media codecs, tools, and services, they can work with the codec and encoder configurations to achieve the cleanest image and sound. And by contracting with a prominent CDN, they hope to provide their customers with the highest-quality stream. Other online sites may promote price or the size of their catalog. Contoso hopes to build their reputation on the quality of the end-user experience. The decisions were based on the vision and goals of this particular company. For your company, you may decide to use third-party encoding services exclusively, but handle your own e-commerce or focus on acquiring content only. The approach you take depends on your business model.

Today, video can be stored in a wide variety of formats. The company could receive material from a studio in several videotape formats, including Betacam SP, Digital Betacam, and S-VHS. Other popular formats include MiniDV, DV, DVCPro, DVCAM, Hi8, and Digital8. Video can also be stored on discs, such as DVDs, CD-ROMs, laser discs, and removable hard disc drives. Each format has its advantages and disadvantages, which help define how and when it is best used.

Contoso will standardize on the Digital Betacam format. This format is considered to be an industry standard for storing professional-quality video. However, the company will also purchase S-VHS and DVD decks to cover their bases. Again, quality is important to the company, so they will make the considerable investment in Digital Betacam decks.

Each workstation, therefore, will include a Digital Betacam deck and a computer system to store the converted video. The Betacam decks are fairly large, heavy, and expensive, so they will be permanently located at each workstation. The S-VHS and DVD decks are lighter and less expensive, so they will be made portable. For example, the DVD deck could be used for capturing on a workstation, and then moved to another area and used to view material.

Workstation Overview

Contoso will make the necessary investment in the workstations to ensure the highest-quality conversions. However, this does not mean they must purchase a lot of expensive production hardware and software. The company does not need to get in the business of editing and processing video and designing sound. They only need to convert video using methods and systems that provide the best possible quality. Therefore, they do not need dedicated video or sound editing tools. The Contoso staff will take the audio and video exactly as it comes from the studio and convert it to files, striving to make the finished files look and sound as close as possible to the original.

To that end, Contoso will require playback decks that reproduce good-quality images and sound; monitors, such as speakers and a video display, to check the quality of the playback; a capture card that accurately transfers or converts the source signals to the computer; a computer capable of reliably moving data from the card to a storage device; and a storage device that can quickly and reliably read, write, and store large amounts of data. If they do need editing or sound design services, Contoso can employ a third-party service.

Because Contoso Movies Online will most often work with digital video, they can expect a higher-quality capture of the video to their workstation computers. When transferring audio and video from analog sources (such as S-VHS tape) to digital format, quality is degraded in the conversion process. High-quality conversion of analog sources requires careful adjustment of audio and video parameters. For example, when converting an analog video to a file, you must adjust the color and brightness or video level of the picture, and the audio level. High-quality conversion also requires capture cards that are capable of accurately processing and sampling the analog signal.

With digital video, you do not have to convert an analog signal into digital samples; you merely play back the data on the VCR and copy it to the computer. It is very similar to copying a file, except that the source is a digital videotape. The only way the quality can be degraded is by capturing with a computer system that cannot handle the high volume of real-time digital media data. In Contoso's case, however, the workstations can handle the data transfer and storage at the speeds required. During the capture, the only conversions that take place are restructuring the data to a format such as AVI or Windows Media Format, and to a different pixel format. However, these modifications to the data do not require any adjustments by the Contoso staff; the format conversions are handled quickly and automatically. (For more information about pixel formats, see chapter 1.)

Thinking about the types of processing and configurations you will make is important in the early stages of planning a workstation, because you not only need to determine hardware and software requirements, you also need to know how much space the system will require and where you can locate it. For example, Contoso Movies Online will need to check the quality of the captured audio, so the space in which they locate the workstations should enable them to play the audio clearly and should block outside noises from sources such as air conditioners and elevators.

Workstation Placement

Contoso is located in a large loft environment with broad open spaces and cubicles. To avoid polluting the workspace with unwanted sound, the workstations will be located in an area with walls and a ceiling. Because the conversions will not require processing or editing, the sound level can be kept low; headphones can be used to spot-check the recording.

The small room must house at least two workstations, so the size of each system must be kept to a minimum. Therefore, the systems will use small audio speakers and small, accurate video displays. By accurate, we mean displays that correctly reproduce images. To help contain the sound, Contoso will also pad the walls.

Later in this book, we will describe how to build a compression suite in which a company can do some sound design and video editing. For more details, see chapter 15.

In addition to the two workstations, the room will house two or more encoding computers. These computers will do nothing more than encode Windows Media files from uncompressed AVI files. Because all of their work will be handled by software, these computers do not require audio and video capture cards or high-quality video displays. The computer CPUs, memory, bus speeds, and disk input/output speeds do not need to be as fast as those of the capturing computers because the process does not have to take place in real time.

When encoding from a file, you will get the same quality from a dual-processor, 1-GHz system as from a single 200-MHz CPU. The only difference is that a slower CPU will take much longer. However, once the encoding process has started, it does not require operator attention, so several computers can be configured to encode files while the operator monitors a capture on one of the workstations. On faster computers, the time it takes to encode a file can actually be less than real time. File-to-file encoding can be a good way to give old computers a second life.

Hardware Specifications

The following list describes the hardware that Contoso Movies Online will use in a production workstation:

- **Digital Betacam VCR.** They do not need a VCR that records and edits, so Contoso can save money by purchasing one that plays back videotape only. The deck needs to have a composite video output (so the encoding staff can view the tape with a video monitor) and an SDI video output. The SDI output provides standard, broadcast-quality digital video and connects directly to the video capture card. Figure 10.1 shows an illustration of a Digital Betacam deck.

- **Alternate video sources.** A number of other video playback devices can be purchased and shared between the workstations, such as S-VHS, DVD, laser disc, and MiniDV devices. Movies and other material will be requested from the studios in the Digital Betacam format. However, other video sources may need to be used.

Figure 10.1 A typical Digital Betacam deck.

■ **Waveform monitor and vectorscope.** These electronic instruments display a video signal in ways that enable you to check or adjust video levels and color according to television standards. A waveform monitor displays the video signal as a complex wave. A vectorscope displays the color components of the signal. Often, both instruments are combined in one device. Figure 10.2 shows a waveform monitor/vectorscope unit.

Figure 10.2 A typical waveform monitor/vectorscope.

Most tapes that Contoso Movies Online receives from studios will be digital, so they can bypass the setup process by using the SDI output. In those cases, they will not need a waveform monitor/vectorscope because the data is transferred directly without conversion or processing. However, Contoso will include a waveform/vectorscope in the workstation because it will enable them to properly configure the Digital Betacam when capturing from an analog tape.

The monitor/scope can be used to display the video signal from the alternate sources, such as the S-VHS and DVD decks. However, most consumer decks do not provide a way to adjust the video. The monitor/scope must have two inputs so Contoso can use it for both Digital Betacams. We will describe how to set up video later in this chapter.

■ **Video monitor.** You can view the video output of the VCRs on the computer video display. However, a small video monitor with two inputs is useful when the computer is busy with another task and you need to view a tape.

■ **Audio mixer and monitors.** To conserve space, Contoso will use a pair of small, professional-quality monitor speakers. Good-quality computer speakers are available from a variety of companies. For more critical listening, they can use a pair of good-quality headphones. Contoso will also use a small audio mixer to monitor multiple computers from one set of speakers.

■ **Video capture card.** There are several good-quality video capture cards that are recommended for use with Windows Media Encoder 9 Series. Contoso will use a capture card that provides an SDI input so that they can capture the digital video signal directly from the Digital Betacam VCRs.

■ **Workstation computer.** Contoso decided to use computers with dual 700 MHz processors or higher, 256 MB of RAM or more, and a fast PCI bus. Check the Microsoft Web site (http://www.microsoft.com/windowsmedia) for the latest requirements.

In the two-step process that Contoso will use, they will capture movies to an uncompressed AVI file first, and then encode a Windows Media file from the AVI file. The computer to be used for capturing will also be capable of encoding directly, using the one-step process. The PCI bus speed and the read/write speed of the hard drive are critical for capturing uncompressed audio and video. A fast CPU is required for capturing directly with the encoder because encoding includes compression, which uses a great deal of processor time.

■ **Raid array or fast hard drive.** When choosing a storage system, Contoso considered not only the amount of storage, but the read/write speed of the drives as well. An uncompressed movie requires a continuous read/write speed of at least 27 megabytes per second, and can require 80 to 120 GB of storage. After the movie has been encoded, the AVI file can be deleted.

■ **Network interface card (NIC).** The card must be capable of a speed of 100 mbps.

■ **Sound card for output.** Used to monitor the audio.

The following list describes the hardware that Contoso Movies Online will be using for their encode-only computers:

■ **Encode-only computer.** The minimum requirements for a computer to encode from file to file are a 500 MHz CPU and 32 MB of RAM. However, a 500-MHz CPU with 128 MB of RAM is recommended to run the encoder on Windows XP Professional. Again, the faster the CPU, the shorter the encode time. The computer will also require access to 80 to 120 GB of storage, which can be an internal hard drive or network share.

■ **NIC.** Same as the workstation computer.

Software Specifications

The following list describes the software required for a production workstation:

- **Capture utility.** The video capture card you choose often comes with a utility that enables you to do simple captures to AVI files, such as the Microsoft software Amcap, Windows Media 9 Capture, and Vidcap32. The Windows Media 9 Capture utility is pre-configured for capturing at standard video frame rates, which we will require for optimum quality.

- **Capture card driver.** Make sure the latest drivers and utilities have been installed for the video capture card.

- **Windows Media Encoder 9 Series and utilities.** When you install Windows Media Encoder, a set of utilities is also installed. These enable you to perform tasks such as simple editing of a Windows Media file and editing encoding profiles.

- **Windows Media Player 9 Series.** The Player can be installed from the Microsoft Windows Media Web site. You will need it to test playback of the files you create.

- **Windows XP Professional.** Windows XP Home Edition and Windows 2000 are also supported by Windows Media 9 Series. However, Contoso Movies Online will use Windows XP Professional because it supports computers with multiple processors. The hard disk must be formatted as an NTFS volume so files larger than 4 GB can be recorded.

Putting it Together

The equipment is laid out on a heavy duty computer lab bench and standard 19-inch equipment rack in the encoding room, as shown in figure 10.3. The computers are located on shelves above the bench; monitors and miscellaneous source devices are located on the bench; and the Digital Betacams, waveform monitor/vectorscope, and RAID arrays are mounted in the rack. With this approach, one operator can manage both workstations and one or more encode-only computers. A simple keyboard/video/mouse (KVM) switchbox is installed so the operator can control the three computers easily.

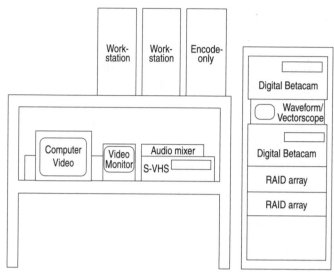

Figure 10.3 Layout of encoding equipment in the lab.

Of course there are many ways to enhance and customize the layout. For example, encode-only computers, arrays, source machines, and workstations can be added to increase productivity.

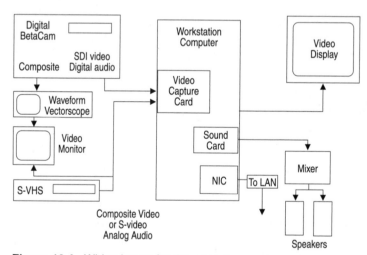

Figure 10.4 Wiring layout for the encoding equipment.

Figure 10.4 shows how a workstation is wired. In this layout, sources are hard-wired to workstations. As the facility expands, audio and video routing will be added so sources can be easily patched into different workstations. A workstation is built as follows:

1. Computer configuration. The video capture card, NIC, and audio monitoring sound card are installed according to the manufacturers' instructions.

2. Equipment mounted in racks. The Digital Betacams, waveform monitor/vectorscope, and RAID arrays are installed in the equipment rack. They place the waveform monitor/vectorscope between the Digital Betacams and at eye level to make it easier to see when configuring the VCRs.

3. Digital Betacam monitors. The Digital Betacams provide a number of output options. In the Contoso lab, they connect the composite video output to one input of the waveform monitor/vectorscope, and then connect the output of the waveform monitor/vectorscope to one input of the video monitor. Then they connect the other Digital Betacam to the second input of the waveform monitor/vectorscope. If the waveform monitor/vectorscope supports switching outputs, when the staff switches between the VCRs on the waveform monitor/vectorscope, the video will switch in the video monitor. If the monitor/scope does not support switching, you could connect the second input of the video monitor to the second Digital Betacam. For more information about the different audio and video formats Contoso will be working with, see the connector sidebar in chapter 2.

4. Digital Betacam main output. The SDI outputs of the Digital Betacam decks connect to the SDI inputs of the video capture cards (if supported). For audio, you can connect the AES/EBU digital audio outputs of the Digital Betacams to the video capture cards (again, if supported). In some cases, you can use the digital audio embedded in the SDI connection instead of making a separate audio connection. When playing back an analog tape, the Betacams convert the signals and output digital data through the SDI and AES/EBU ports.

5. S-VHS deck. The output of the S-VHS deck or other source is connected to the appropriate input of the video capture card. Many video capture cards support several input options. If your source device provides an S-video output, use that. Otherwise connect the video output to the composite input on the card. Also, connect the analog audio output of the device to the card. You can use a DV or IEEE 1394 (sometimes called FireWire) connection to record from a MiniDV camcorder or deck. If the source has a second composite video output, connect that to the video monitor.

    When setting up a capture session, you will use the capture dialog box to select which inputs to take audio and video from. For example, to capture from the Digital Betacam, you will choose SDI video and digital audio inputs.

6. KVM switch. The keyboard, video display, and mouse are connected through the KVM switch to the three computers.

7. Audio monitoring. The sound card line outputs of the three computers are connected to three input channels on the small audio mixer. Then the mixer output is connected to a pair of speakers. The operator can select which computer audio output to monitor by selecting the appropriate channel on the mixer.

8. Network. Finally the computers are connected to the LAN. Files can be copied over the network to other local computers or sent to the hosting service using FTP. An encode-only computer can also connect to source files located on an array over the network. Keep in mind, however, that the network does not provide enough bandwidth for real-time streaming of full-sized, uncompressed video.

With the workstations and production systems installed and running, the Contoso staff can now capture and encode content.

Capturing and Encoding Content

The two main programs Contoso Movies Online will use to create content are a simple AVI capture utility (such as Windows Media 9 Capture or Amcap) and Windows Media Encoder. First, they will capture the content from a videotape and save it as an AVI file on a workstation. Then they will encode the final Windows Media file from the AVI file. After they have successfully encoded the final file, they can delete the AVI file and capture another tape.

Configuring Encoder Options

The alternative to the two-step method is to capture and encode directly in one step with Windows Media Encoder. This method is certainly acceptable in many scenarios. It does not make sense to double the time it takes to capture and encode a movie for no good reason.

However, Contoso Movies Online wants to encode with the best possible quality, and that means offering content encoded for broadband connections. To do that they need to capture at full frame size (640 × 480) and full frame rate (29.97 fps). They also need to encode at a bit rate that gives acceptable image and sound quality. Contoso will target 700 Kbps. They also want to encode with multiple bit rates, so end users can view movies over slower broadband connections.

To capture and encode files the way Contoso wants them in one step would require a very fast computer system. Capturing and encoding in one step requires a fast CPU because of the high volume of data that must be compressed in real time. At the time of this writing, a computer with dual 2.5 GHz processors can capture and encode acceptable 700 Kbps files. However, if you want higher-bit-rate content or to encode files with MBR streams, you need a much faster computer.

Contoso will use the two-step method. However, when you decide what methods you are going to use, you should take a look at the features provided by the encoder and the utilities for optimizing quality, which include two-pass encoding, VBR, device control, and Windows Media Stream Editor.

Two-pass Encoding

The methods most often used to encode content employ one-pass encoding, in which compression is applied, the data is encoded, and a file or live stream is created in one step. As soon as you finish capturing a video, for example, you can view the finished file. With two-pass encoding, the content is analyzed during the first pass, and then encoded in the second pass based on the data gathered in the first pass.

Two-pass encoding can result in higher-quality content because more information about scene composition is available for optimizing bit rate, frame rate, buffer size, and image quality. The main drawback is that two-pass encoding can take twice as long. Also, you can only use the two-pass method for file-to-file encoding. It does not work for encoding a live stream, for example. You can, however, use two-pass encoding with device control to capture videotape to a file.

Variable Bit Rate Encoding

In most cases, you configure the encoder to create content that streams at a constant bit rate. For example, when you encode a file for 100 Kbps, no more than 100 Kbps of bandwidth is used when the file is streamed over a network. To achieve a constant bit rate, the encoder varies the quality of the content.

However, there may be situations where you want the quality to remain constant and the bit rate to vary. For example, if you plan to distribute a movie on a CD or offer it as a download only, you do not have to be as concerned with how much bandwidth is required to play back the content. In those cases, you can use VBR encoding. You can also combine VBR with two-pass encoding and get peak bit rate-based VBR, in which the bit rate varies, but does not rise above a bit rate limit that you specify.

Device Control

You can configure the encoder to automatically control playback of a device, such as a camcorder or VTR. For example, you can create an edit decision list of selected shots from a tape, and the encoder will automatically control the camcorder and encode the video. You can also use device control with two-pass encoding. For example, you can select a video segment from a tape, and the encoder will automatically capture the video and encode it using two-pass encoding. Device control only works with devices that connect through an IEEE 1394 port or that employ the Sony RS422 protocol, such as a Digital Betacam.

Windows Media Stream Editor

Rather than encode an MBR file directly, you can encode multiple single-bit-rate files and then combine them into one MBR file with Windows Media Stream Editor. This can be useful if you must capture and encode in one step on a computer that does not have a CPU that is fast enough to encode MBR at the same time. Windows Media Stream Editor, a utility that is installed with Windows Media Encoder 9 Series, also enables you to split one file into multiple files, and to support multiple languages by combining audio files.

Optimizing the System

As mentioned previously, Contoso Movies Online will encode in two steps. In the first step, audio and video are captured to an uncompressed AVI file. When capturing content, data must flow from the capture card, through the computer, and to the hard disk unimpeded in real time. If something slows or stops the constant flow, the whole process can fall apart. Without a system for controlling the flow on a slow computer, data would continue to pile up until memory ran out. To prevent a computer from crashing if it gets behind, a capture program deletes data and drops frames that the computer does not have time to process. You may not see an occasional dropped frame, but you would notice hundreds or thousands of them.

With a high-quality capture card, a fast computer, lots of memory, a fast bus speed, and a hard disk or disk array with a fast read/write speed, Contoso's workstations are capable of capturing high-quality video. However, they can take additional steps to help ensure the best capture quality.

You can minimize the amount of processing a computer is required to do by turning off any program or process that is not essential for the capture, such as anti-virus programs, screen savers, e-mail programs, and Web servers. Then create as little work as possible for the processor by capturing audio and video without compression. Not only does compression lower the quality of the content, it requires a great deal of processing speed and memory. A high-quality capture card can also help conserve CPU resources by performing pre-processing tasks such as deinterlacing and cropping. Also, formatting video data as an AVI file requires less processing than other formats, such as Windows Media Format.

As you capture, keep an eye on the capture program. A counter on the program interface shows the number of frames dropped. If a frame is dropped occasionally, you may be able to live with the results. However, if frames are dropped regularly, you should stop the capture and check CPU and memory usage. Many capture programs are designed to stop or slow the preview function if the processor cannot keep up with a capture, so do not be concerned if preview does not appear when you start capturing, or if the preview image is jerky. Use the number of dropped frames to determine the success of a capture.

When the capture is finished, you can start the second step of the process: using Windows Media Encoder to create a new Windows Media file from the AVI file. During this step, the encoder performs a number of processes that compress the original data to a smaller size and lower bit rate, and encodes the data to a Windows Media file. During this step, you should again turn off any unnecessary programs and services. However, because the process is not occurring in real time, the quality of the resulting file will not be affected and frames will not be dropped if the computer is not optimized for encoding. The processor works at its own speed when encoding from a file. Rather than dropping frames, the process simply takes longer.

As mentioned previously, digital videotapes are captured directly through the SDI port. However, when capturing an analog tape with the Digital Betacam, the waveform monitor/vectorscope will be used to properly adjust the video and color parameters. The videotape to be captured is inserted in the machine, and adjustments are made on the Digital Betacam while test signals recorded at the beginning of the tape are played back. After adjusting the machine with the test signals, the movie will play back with the proper video intensity and color. For more information about setting up the Digital Betacam for playing back analog tapes, see chapter 15.

Capturing Video to an AVI File

After inserting the videotape in the Digital Betacam and adjusting the video parameters if necessary, open the capture program, configure it, and then start the capture. Contoso will use Amcap or Windows Media 9 Capture because they capture AVI version 2.0 files, which permit file captures exceeding 2 GB. Keep this in mind if you choose another capture program. However, you will find the same types of settings on any capture card.

To capture video, the operator starts the capture program and follows these steps to configure a session:

1. On the **File** menu, click the **Set Capture File** command to specify the name and path of the capture AVI file to be created.

2. Select the audio and video capture device sources. The video capture card can be the source for both, or you could capture audio from a separate sound card.

3. Select **Preview** to display the source video in the capture program. You use preview to configure the video settings on the capture card. During capture, this displays the image that is being recorded. However, preview does not have to be enabled in order to capture.

4. On the **Options** menu, click **Video Format** to display the driver properties. These are the settings that affect the capture card directly. The settings are configured as described in the following steps.

5. On the **Source** tab, the following settings affect the incoming video:

    ■ For **Input**, select **SDI**. The capture card inputs video from the SDI connector, which is connected to the Digital Betacam. Because Contoso is sourcing a digital signal, the capture card does not have to do as much processing (such as color correction). Therefore, some settings are not available. The **SDI** input can also carry embedded audio. However, Contoso will use the digital audio input. To source from the S-VHS deck, select **Composite** or **S-video**.

    ■ For **Video Settings**, select **Bypass color correction**. Color correction processing on the capture card is bypassed because the video signal is digital. Even with bypass turned off, the settings you make to brightness, contrast, and saturation on the driver will not affect the captured video. If you are capturing from a composite or S-video source, you will need to configure these settings. For more information about configuring an analog source, see chapter 15.

    ■ For **Video Standard**, select **NTSC-M**. This is the video standard used in North America. You would select **PAL-BDGHI** if your source video is formatted using the PAL or SECAM standards.

6. On the **Format** tab, the following settings affect the video leaving the capture card:

    ■ For **Color Format**, select **YUV12 planar (I420)**. This is the standard color format used by Windows Media. The color format of digital video determines the arrangement of the digital information that describes the pixels that make up the images. The RGB32 format reproduces the most accurate image, but the size of a video file created with RGB32 is larger and the bit rate of the video stream is higher. Because Windows Media Encoder will convert the color format to YUV12 planar anyway, there is no point in capturing with a higher-resolution color format. For more information about color formats, see the pixel format sidebar in chapter 1.

    ■ For **Proportions**, select **CCIR601**, which reproduces the image with the same pixel proportions that are in the original Digital Betacam video, known as *nonsquare* pixels. Standard proportions create *square* pixels. If you use standard proportions with the Digital Betacam video, the image will appear squeezed horizontally. You should use standard proportions when capturing analog video.

    ■ For **Video Size**, select **Full**, which reproduces a full-size image with nonsquare pixels at 720 × 480 resolution. To cut file size in half, you can capture at 360 × 480 by entering the settings in the **Custom Size** boxes. This method produces an image that is squeezed to half its width. However, when you create the final Windows Media file, the encoder stretches the image back to normal width. The disadvantage is that image resolution is also cut in half, but often this method of reducing file size produces an image that is acceptable, and the height of 480 pixels enables you to enhance the quality using deinterlacing or inverse telecine, which are described in chapter 2. If file size and bit rate are still too high, you can capture at half size (360 × 240).

The other tabs of the driver dialog box provide additional settings. However, the Contoso staff will leave the default settings. For more information about these settings, see the documentation provided with the driver or video capture card.

After making the settings on the **Source** and **Format** tabs, close the dialog box.

7. On the **Options** menu, select **Audio Format**. The format is configured for **PCM audio, 48,000 kHz, 16-bit, Stereo**. Uncompressed audio will be captured, with the same sampling rate, bit depth, and number of channels as the digital tape. For analog tape, you can use any setting. However, for the best quality, you should not use a setting lower than 44,100 kHz, 16-bit.

8. Open the mixer by double-clicking the speaker icon in the taskbar or from the **Sounds and Audio Devices** dialog box. In the mixer properties, open the **Recording** mixer for the video capture card and make sure the **AES/EBU** digital audio input is selected. Notice that, when you select the digital input, the volume controls are disabled. As with the video, you cannot make audio level adjustments to an audio signal that is being captured digitally, because you are essentially copying the data from the tape to your hard drive. For analog tape, select analog **Line in**.

9. On the **Capture** menu, click **Set Frame Rate** and make sure the **Use Frame Rate** check box is not selected. Video will be captured at the same rate as the source video.

10. On the **Capture** menu, click **Start Capture**. The **Ready to Capture** dialog box opens. At this point the operator presses the **Play** button on the Digital Betacam deck. Two to four seconds prior to the start of video, she clicks **OK** to start the capture. It is easier to delete a second or two of black from the beginning of a capture than to have to recapture a movie because the first few frames were cut off.

11. To stop the capture, press the **ESC** key. The Contoso operator then renames or moves the capture file, if necessary. If you do not rename or move the

file, the capture program will record over it the next time you capture, unless you set a new default capture file name.

During the capture, keep an eye on the capture program status bar. It should display the number of frames captured, elapsed capture time, and the number of frames dropped. If frames are being dropped regularly, stop the capture and troubleshoot the computer. Remember, the capture program drops frames if any part of the data flow chain in the computer is not processing or transferring data fast enough. If computer specifications are adequate, you follow all the guidelines in this chapter, and the computer is operating correctly, the computer should not cause these problems.

You can check the performance of the computer during a capture by opening the Performance Monitor and watching for CPU and memory overload. Dropped frames in a digital capture can also occur if there is a problem with the videotape or VCR. If you suspect that, try capturing through the composite or S-video input.

Amcap and Windows Media 9 Capture were designed to capture uncompressed audio and video quickly and efficiently. If you want to add compression as you capture, you can use another capture program, such as Vidcap32. The Windows operating system comes with a number of codecs that you can apply to data during a capture. Keep in mind, however, that applying compression makes files smaller and bit rates lower, but will require more processing power and can result in more dropped frames.

Also, your capture utility must support capturing files larger than 2 GB, because even a compressed movie will require far more than 2 GB of storage. Vidcap32 does not support files larger than 2 GB.

If you use a capture card and utility that provides hardware compression, keep in mind that you will only be able to play back a hardware-compressed file on a computer on which that model of card is installed. Also, make sure the encoder supports that system of compression before investing in the card.

When the capture is complete, play the file in Windows Media Player and check for quality. Because Contoso is not using compression, the video images should appear with the same resolution and color as they did in the preview window. Also, they should not see any video or audio artifacts, such as blockiness and inconsistency in colors.

The main quality you should look for when checking an uncompressed capture is smoothness of motion. Any jerkiness or stuttering in the motion can be caused by dropped frames. If the number of dropped frames is high, you may want to capture the video again after checking to make sure unnecessary programs and services are closed and the computer is running smoothly. Keep in mind, however, that the video may not play back evenly because of the high bit rate of the uncompressed video.

After Contoso has captured the uncompressed AVI file successfully, they use Windows Media Encoder to compress and encode a new file.

Encoding to a Windows Media File

The uncompressed movie takes up 80 to 120 GB of storage space and streams at nearly 150 Mbps. However, after the movie has been compressed and encoded to a Windows Media file, size and bit rate will be substantially lower. The final Windows Media file will be several hundred megabytes and the bit rate that produces acceptable-quality broadband video can be as low as 300 Kbps.

To achieve this high level of compression, Windows Media 9 Series codecs and the encoder use a number of algorithms. A simple compression algorithm can achieve a 1:2 or 1:3 compression ratio. However, for streaming digital media over a network like the Internet, you need compression ratios in the neighborhood of 1:24.

In order for codecs to compress data that much and still produce acceptable audio and video, streaming media codecs must use more advanced compression techniques, such as psycho-acoustic and psycho-visual modeling. The codecs selectively eliminate and modify data so that the result appears and sounds acceptable, even though it is different from the original. For example, subtle variations in color can be reduced because that type of visual information is not that important to our perception. On the other hand, the codec must attempt to maintain the appearance of smooth motion because subtle details of motion are important to our perception.

Codec usage is somewhat subjective. One setting will not work for every type of audio and video. This is why Windows Media Encoder provides many different settings and predefined configuration profiles. You can use the pre-configured settings by selecting the destination for your digital media, the type of audio and video content, and the bit rate. Settings can be individually configured to optimize encoding to meet your particular needs.

The Contoso staff will use a pre-configured template and modify it to achieve the desired result. To encode the uncompressed AVI file, the operator opens Windows Media Encoder, and then follows these steps:

1. On the **Wizards** tab of the **New Session** dialog, select **Custom** session. The **Session Properties** dialog box of the new session opens.

2. On the **Sources** tab, specify to source from a file. Then enter the path and name of the uncompressed AVI file.

3. On the **Output** tab, select the **Archive to file** check box, and clear the **Push to server** and **Pull from encoder** check boxes. Then specify the file to encode.

4. On the **Compression** tab, specify the following settings:

   ■ For **Destination**, select **Windows Media server**.

   ■ For **Video**, select **Multiple bit rates (CBR)**.

- For **Audio**, select **Multiple bit rates (CBR)**.

- For **Bit rates**, select the **282 Kbps** and **764 Kbps** check boxes. For better quality, you can also select **Two-pass encoding** on this tab.

You could continue to the next tab from here and the Windows Media 9 Series audio and video codecs would be automatically configured with optimum settings. However, the Contoso staff will modify the following settings to achieve encoding results that are better optimized for their intended use:

1. Click **Edit**, and the **Custom Encoding Settings** dialog box appears. With the tabs in this dialog box, you can make fine adjustments to codec settings. The Contoso operator will modify several settings to enable nonsquare pixels so the output frame sizes are proportional to the dimensions of the source.

2. On the **General** tab, select the **Allow nonsquare pixel output** check box. On this tab, you can modify properties that affect the overall encoding process, such as selecting different audio and video codecs, and specifying the video format.

3. On the **764 Kbps** tab, enter a video size of **720 × 480**. End users connecting to the Contoso Windows Media server with a bandwidth supporting 764 Kbps will receive full-frame video. On the target bandwidth tabs, you can modify settings for each stream in an MBR stream, such as the frame size, frame rate, and video smoothness.

4. On the **282 Kbps** tab, enter a video size of **360 × 240**. End users connecting with a bandwidth supporting 282 Kbps will receive video at half the width and height.

5. Close the **Custom Encoding Settings** dialog box.

6. On the **Video Size** tab of **Session Properties**, select **Same as input** for **Pixel aspect ratio**.

7. On the **Processing** tab, select **Inverse telecine**. This process removes the redundant video fields that were added when the movie was transferred to videotape. For more information about inverse telecine, see chapter 1.

8. Click **Apply**, and then click **Start Encoding**.

The Contoso encoding operator will be able to view the encoding process in the **Video** and **Monitor** panels. The video display shows either the input video, output video, both, or a split screen.

When encoding is finished, the operator opens the file in Windows Media Player and checks the playback quality of the high-bit-rate stream. If you want to check the other MBR stream or streams, copy the file to a Windows Media server. Then play the file over a lower bandwidth connection or limit the bandwidth manually in the Player.

To limit Player bandwidth:

1.   Start Windows Media Player.

2.   On the **Tools** menu, click **Options**.

3.   On the **Performance** tab, select **Choose connection speed**, and then choose a speed that is between the stream you want to check and the stream above it. The server sends a stream that is no faster than the bandwidth selected.

The production workstation is now up and running, and the operator has created a high-bandwidth MBR file. After she is sure the Windows Media file plays as expected, she can delete the large AVI file and capture the next movie or trailer. She can also try other features of the encoder that enable her to improve quality and the end user experience, such as two-pass encoding, VBR encoding, and deinterlacing.

In the last part of this chapter, Contoso will create a border that adds functionality and branding to content in Windows Media Player.

Customizing Windows Media Player

Windows Media Player enables you to enhance the presentation of your digital media with a number of features and methods. In this topic, we will look at three of them: HTMLView, skins, and borders. Then we will see how the Contoso staff creates an HTMLView Web page and border that the Contoso Movies Online site will use to wrap around special trailers, features, and downloads.

The following list summarizes the features Contoso wants to include in its enhanced presentations:

■   Branding. The graphical treatment must include the company name, logo, colors, and other thematic elements. For end users, this will make a connection between the content and Contoso. Name recognition is very important for this young company.

■   Widescreen. To further promote the movie connection, the site will present all digital media in a widescreen aspect ratio. All digital media will be cropped or stretched (if necessary) to accommodate sizes of 320 × 176, 360 × 240, or 720 × 480.

■   **Rent now** and **Details** buttons. As end users view content, they can click buttons to display either information about the movie or the page that starts the rental process. Again, it is important that Contoso maintains the connection between the content in the Player and the Web site.

■ Extra movie info. Description text from each clip in a playlist will be displayed, providing the end user with additional information. The text will help build excitement for the movie and promote rental.

In the future, Contoso can expand on the information it provides to end users for each clip in a playlist. They can also add graphics, such as production stills, and can create custom borders for each exclusive program.

Customizing the Player with HTMLView

The simplest way to create a custom look in the Player is with the HTMLView parameter. All you have to do is add the HTMLView parameter to a Windows Media metafile with an .asx extension, and you can display a Web page in the **Now Playing** pane of the Player. If you want to display video, you add an embedded Player control to the page. You can also add elements like controls, links, frames, and tables. Figure 10.5 shows a sample Web page inserted using HTMLView.

When an end user clicks a link on the Contoso Web site for a special trailer or feature, a metafile is downloaded that contains a playlist of the digital media and an HTMLView element that embeds the Web page, such as the following:

```
<ASX version = "3.0" >
    <PARAM Name = "HTMLVIEW" Value = "HTMLView.htm"/>
    <Entry>
        <TITLE>Video #1</TITLE>
        <ABSTRACT>Text below video 1</ABSTRACT>
        <Ref HREF = "video1.wmv"/>
    </Entry>
    <Entry>
        <TITLE>Video #2</TITLE>
        <ABSTRACT>Text below video 2</ABSTRACT>
        <Ref HREF = "video2.wmv"/>
    </Entry>
</ASX>
```

The Player downloads HTMLView.htm and displays it in the **Now Playing** pane, and then begins playing the playlist. An example HTMLView.htm file is included on the companion CD. You can open the file in a text editor to see how it was constructed.

Basic HTML scripting is used to create and position the elements on the page. The title above the video frame comes from the **TITLE** element in the metafile, and is passed to the browser that is built in to the Player using the Player property **currentMedia.name**.

```
Title.innerHTML = Player.currentMedia.name;
```

The text below the video frame comes from the **ABSTRACT** element in the metafile, and is passed to the built-in browser using the **getItemInfo** Player method.

```
Description.innerHTML  =  Player.currentMedia.getItemInfo('Abstract');
```

Title.innerHTML and Description.innerHTML refer to the two DIV elements in the Web page that display the text. Finally, the video frame is embedded in the built-in browser using scripting for embedding the Player in a Web page.

```
<OBJECT id="Player" height = 176 width = 320
classid  =  "CLSID:6BF52A52-394A-11d3-B153-00C04F79FAA6">
    <PARAM name = "AutoStart"  value = "True">
    <PARAM name = "uiMode" value = "none">
    <PARAM name = "windowlessVideo" value = "true">
</OBJECT>
```

Note that the uiMode value is none. There is no need for the embedded Player to display playback controls because those controls are already available on the Player UI. There is no need to embed the control if you are not playing video content.

For more information about creating Web pages for HTMLView and how to use the application programming interface (API) for the Player, see the Windows Media Player 9 Series SDK. The SDK is also used for creating other presentation enhancements, such as skins and borders.

Figure 10.5   Using HTMLView to display custom Web content in the Player.

Customizing the Player with Skins

A skin is simply a user interface for Windows Media Player. For example, when you first open the Player, the interface you see is the full-mode skin. You can open the **Skin Chooser** feature and choose from a number of different skins that are installed with the Player. You can also download additional skins from the Internet. Figure 10.6 shows a skin that is included with Windows Media Player.

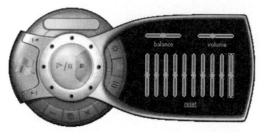

Figure 10.6   Skins can be used to personalize the Player interface.

The Player API enables users to create their own skins, and this makes skins particularly useful for online businesses. You can create your own user interface for the Player by creating image files and writing script that ties the art to the Player API. All the information for creating skins is located in the Windows Media Player SDK.

As you can see, you have complete artistic freedom to create any sort of look for the Player, and to lay out Player controls and interactive elements in any manner. The interface does not have to be rectangular or contain window elements, like a title bar. After creating a skin, you combine the artwork and script files into a compressed file. Then end users can download and install your skin from your Web site or some other method, such as a CD-ROM.

To understand how skins are created, we will see how Contoso created one that will be used as a border.

Customizing the Player with Borders

A border is a collection of image files, digital media, text, and interactive elements that displays in the **Now Playing** pane of the full mode Windows Media Player. To create a border, you create the graphics and then activate the elements with scripting in a skin definition file. Figure 10.7 shows a finished border in Windows Media Player.

Borders offer a user experience that can be similar to that of HTMLView. The difference is that HTMLView embeds a standard Web page, while borders embed Player skins. The main differences between a skin displayed as a user interface and a skin displayed as a border is that a border does not need to include controls that are already on the Player, such as a **Play** button, scroll bar, and **File** menu. In addition, a border can only display rectangular skins. Figure 10.8 shows an example of the Contoso Movies Online border with Player controls added to make it a skin.

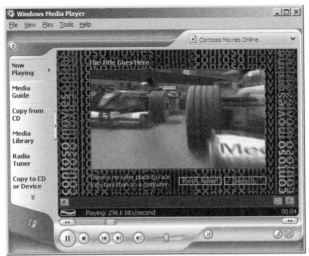

Figure 10.7   Borders are used to customize the Now Playing feature of the Player.

Figure 10.8   The Contoso Movies Online border as a skin.

Also a border file can include a playlist and digital media. For example, you can create a border file, also called a Windows Media Download Package, that contains the border skin, a playlist of music files, and the actual music files.

Contoso Movies Online will use borders to package exclusive behind-the-scenes programs. For example, a program can include a playlist of interviews, trailers, and behind-the-scenes clips of a movie that is about to be released. For the most part, the playlist will point to streaming media on the Windows Media server. However, a playlist in a download package can include a mix of downloaded digital media files and links to streaming media.

Building a Custom Border

All the information you need to create skins, borders, HTMLView, embedded Player controls, and programs using the Player API is contained in the Windows Media Player SDK. To try the samples in this topic, all you need are the Player and a text editor program, such as Microsoft Notepad.

To create the border, we will follow this process:

1. Create the artwork, design the border, and build the components.

2. Write the script. Using the script reference and samples in the SDK, write the skin definition file that associates the artwork to the Player API.

3. Package the border. Create the final file that the end user will download.

4. Deliver the border to the end user by adding a link to the Web page that downloads the border.

Creating the Border Artwork

The first step in creating the border is laying out, designing, and implementing the artwork that will become the border. To do that, you need to determine an optimum size for the border in the **Now Playing** pane, the size of the video frame, and the sizes and positions of the other elements in the border.

The border sample provided in the Windows Media Player 9 Series SDK describes a method for creating a border that is resizable, so the digital media and art elements will display correctly if the end user resizes the Player. Contoso, however, will use fixed-size elements because they want the video, text, buttons, and branding to display in a particular way.

The artwork consists of three files:

■   Background file

■   Mapping file

■   Hover image file

The background file, shown in figure 10.9, is a simple bitmap image file that contains the basic design and layout of the border. The colors used in the background are intentionally subdued, so the background does not compete visually with the video.

The skin definition file containing script, which will be created later, will add the video, text, functionality, and hover and mapping images to the background. To locate those components on the background, Contoso's artists will use a graphic design program to carefully measure the areas of the background where they will be positioned. For example, they know the area where the video will be displayed is 61 pixels in from the left edge, 35 pixels from top, 176 pixels high, and 320 pixels wide.

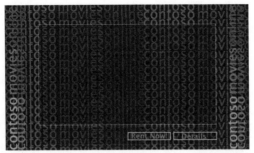

Figure 10.9 The background file used for the Contoso border.

The hover image file, shown in figure 10.10, is a simple bitmap image that shows the two buttons as they will appear when an end user moves the mouse pointer over them.

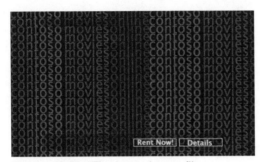

Figure 10.10 The hover image file.

The only areas of the image that will be seen are the tiny areas around each button. The content of the rest of the image does not matter. However, the size of the image and the position of the buttons must be exactly the same as those of the background. To accomplish that, the Contoso artists use a graphics program that enables them to create images in layers, such as Adobe Photoshop or Jasc Paint Shop Pro. Then they can build all the elements of the border or skin in one image file, and be assured that the elements are correctly aligned.

The mapping file, shown in figure 10.11, is a bitmap image that identifies areas of the image to which they want to add functionality.

None of this image will be visible to an end user. The two colored rectangles positioned over the buttons are used by the Player to map the areas on the interface to functions in the script. Mapping is implemented in script using the color value of a colored region in the image. The area on the left is green and has a color value of #00FF00. The red area on the right has a value of #FF0000. Those color values are used to create the script.

Figure 10.11   The mapping file used to identify interactive areas of the border.

Writing the Border Script

The script in the skin definition file is interpreted by Windows Media Player when it opens the border file. The script is written using the skin programming elements described in the Windows Media Player SDK to integrate the image files and add functionality to the border. We will not go into detail about how to script skins in this book. If you want to explore those topics and many more dealing with programming the Player, see the Windows Media Player 9 Series SDK.

The skin definition file created by Contoso contains the following script:

```
<THEME
    id = "ContosoMoviesOnline"
    author = "Contoso Movies Online"
    copyright = "(c) 2002 Contoso, Inc.">

    <VIEW
        id = "View1"
        backgroundColor = "#000000"
        backgroundImage = "MObg.bmp">

    <PLAYER
        openstatechange=
            "Info.value =
                player.currentMedia.getItemInfo('Description');" />

    <VIDEO
        id="CMO"
        left="61"
        top="35"
        height="176"
        width="320"
        stretchToFit="true">
    </VIDEO>
```

```
<BUTTONGROUP
    mappingImage = "MObg-MAP.bmp"
    hoverImage = "MObg-HOVER.bmp"
    horizontalAlignment = "left">

    <BUTTONELEMENT
        id = "RentNow"
        mappingColor = "#00FF00"
        upToolTip = "Rent Now!"
        onClick =
        "JScript: player.launchURL(
            'http://Contoso.com/RentPage.asp'); " />

    <BUTTONELEMENT
        id = "Details"
        mappingColor = "#FF0000"
        upToolTip = "Movie Details"
        onClick =
            "JScript: player.launchURL(
            'http://Contoso.com/MovieDetails.asp');" />

</BUTTONGROUP>

<TEXT
    ID="Title"
    left = "60"
    top = "15"
    foregroundcolor = "#C7BD03"
    fontSize = "8"
    fontStyle = "bold"
    value = "wmpprop:player.currentMedia.name" />

<TEXT
    ID="Info"
    left = "60"
    top = "217"
    width = "160"
    height = "26"
    foregroundcolor = "#E5AFD8"
    fontSize = "8"
    value =
        "JScript:player.currentMedia.getItemInfo(
        'Description');"
    wordWrap = "true" />

    </VIEW>
</THEME>
```

The skin definition file, Border.wms, is included on the companion CD along with the sample image files.

The instructions in the skin definition file are written in Extensible Markup Language (XML), which is similar to HTML. If you have used HTML to create Web pages, you will find that XML looks familiar. In general, XML scripting is used to set or retrieve the properties of elements. For example, the Contoso script describes the location and size of the video frame by setting left, top, width, and height properties. In scripting for skins, the API enables you to describe actions you want the Player to perform (methods), and to use actions generated by the Player (events).

To script a method or event, the examples shown here use Microsoft JScript. For example, in JScript you can assign the **launchURL** method to the **onClick** method of a skin button in the script:

```
onClick = "JScript: player.launchURL('http://WebSite');"
```

When a user clicks the button, the Player opens a browser to the Web site indicated in the URL. If you want to add more complex functionality to the script, you can assign a JScript file to the skin definition file that contains additional lines of code. For example, you could create a multi-line JScript function that is called from an **onClick** event handler.

The following descriptions provide an overview of the elements that are used in the sample script:

- **VIEW** elements contain the user interface details of a skin or border. Using **VIEW**, you can set the background image file or define a background color (black) for those areas not covered by the image file.

- **PLAYER** elements contain script that communicates directly with the Player. Most **PLAYER** elements are events, which are messages sent by the Player that can be used to trigger a method in a script. For example, in the Contoso script, the Player sends an **openStateChange** event, which triggers the method **getItemInfo** that gets the description text embedded in the current file or stream.

- **VIDEO** elements provide ways to manipulate a video window in a skin. For example, the Contoso script defines the location and size of the video window, and specifies that the Player should stretch the video (if necessary) to fit the defined size.

- **BUTTONGROUP** elements define a group of buttons. In the Contoso script, the hover image and mapping files are set with this element.

- **BUTTONELEMENT** elements define one or more buttons in a **BUTTON-GROUP**. Rather than define the button area using location and size values, skin definition files use color values in the **mappingImage** file. After setting the **mappingColor** value for a button, the button is then defined as the area or areas with that color value on the mapping image. When an end user moves the mouse pointer over a defined area, the same area on the hover image file shows through and a ToolTip appears. When an end user clicks the area, the **onClick** method of the button is called.

■   **TEXT** elements define how and where text appears on a skin or border. On the Contoso skin, one **TEXT** element places the name of each clip above the video window; another **TEXT** element places the description text embedded in a clip in an area below the video window. The other attributes in the **TEXT** elements define the size and location of the **TEXT** areas, and how you want the text to appear.

To create the skin file, create a folder on your computer that contains the following elements:

■   The skin definition file, Border.wms.

■   The background image file, MObg.bmp.

■   The hover image file, MObg-HOVER.bmp.

■   The mapping file, MObg-MAP.bmp.

These elements comprise the skin. If you double-click Border.wms, the Player will open and interpret the file, and the Player skin will change according to the definition in the script. In the Contoso case, however, the skin does not contain the usual skin functions, like play and stop, because Contoso will be using it as a border. In the next topic, we will follow the steps for creating a finished border, which is a Windows Media Download Package file.

Packaging the Border

To create border files, you follow a process of combining sets of files into single compressed files with a .zip file name extension. Then the end user only has to download one file that contains all the pieces. The end user does not need to do anything with the file, such as extract the individual files and install them. The Player downloads and reads the compressed file, and then handles the installation automatically.

The only additional file needed for the Contoso border is a Windows Media metafile that contains the playlist. To create the Windows Media Download Package that will implement the Contoso border, the designers do the following:

1.   Create a compressed file that includes the four files that comprise the skin. The compressed file will have a .zip extension.

2.   Change the .zip extension to .wmz (For example, Border.wmz). If you were to double-click the file, the Player would open and install Border.wmz as a skin.

3. Create a Windows Media metafile that embeds the skin as a border. The metafile contains links to the digital media that will play in the border, as well as a **SKIN** element that references Border.wmz. You can use a text editor to type the metafile script, and then save it with an .asx extension (for example Border.asx). The following script shows an example of a metafile with three playlist entries.

```
<ASX VERSION = "3.0">
    <SKIN HREF = "Border.wmz" />
    <TITLE>Contoso Movies Online</TITLE>
    <ENTRY>
        <REF HREF = "mms://WMServer/Trailer01.wmv"/>
        <PARAM NAME="Prebuffer" VALUE="true" />
    </ENTRY>
        <ENTRY>
        <REF HREF = "mms://WMServer/Trailer02.wmv"/>
        <PARAM NAME="Prebuffer" VALUE="true" />
    </ENTRY>
    <ENTRY>
        <REF HREF = "mms://WMServer/Trailer03.wmv"/>
    </ENTRY>
</ASX>
```

The **PreBuffer** parameter is used for seamless stream switching. If an **ENTRY** element contains this parameter and it is set to "true", the Player will begin to buffer the beginning of the following **ENTRY** before the current **ENTRY** ends, so the transition to the following file or stream will be as quick and will use as little buffering as possible.

4. Create another compressed file that includes the .wmz and .asx files. Change the .zip extension to .wmd, which makes this a Windows Media Download Package file. When an end user double-clicks this file, the Player starts, displays Border.wmz as a border, and plays the files in the .asx playlist. To make a complete download package, you can include the Windows Media files in Border.wmd, and then change the REF HREF values to reference the files locally, such as:

```
<REF HREF = "Trailer01.wmv"/>
```

Distributing the Border

To make the border available on the Contoso Web site, the site administrator copies Border.wmd to the Web server, and then adds links to it on the Web site. When a user clicks the link, the Player starts, downloads the Windows Media Download Package, installs the border, and plays the referenced Windows Media files. The border is saved on the user's computer as a playlist with the name that was entered as the title in the metafile. The user can view the border again by selecting the title in **Media Library**.

There are many creative ways to work with the Player and package digital media to customize the end-user experience. In the next chapter, we look at ways to package Windows Media files and streams, and create customized user experiences by working with server-side playlists.

11

Movie Info Channels

In the last chapter, the Contoso staff built a production workstation, and captured and encoded content from one of the video sources. Then they created a border in a Windows Media Download Package. In this chapter, they will develop the movie info channels by creating server-side playlists that include ASP pages that can deliver dynamic content. This chapter contains the following sections:

■ Info channel vision. An overview of the info channels.

■ Metafiles and packages. Describes options for presenting content with Windows Media.

■ Planning the info channels. Describes how the info channels will be constructed.

■ Implementing server-side playlists. Creating a mockup info channel.

Info Channel Vision

Movie info channels provide end users with a collection of trailers, publicity shorts, and other short video segments relating to 10 pre-defined movie genres. Interspersed in the mix are paid commercial messages and interstitial ads that brand the channel with the site. To reach the info channels, end users navigate to a genre page. Figure 11.1 shows a mockup of the Action/Adventure genre page.

End users can browse the page for the latest releases in that genre or they can click the Movie Info Channel link. The link opens Windows Media Player with the URL of a Windows Media metafile, which points to the Action/Adventure channel broadcast publishing point on the Windows Media server.

When the channel starts playing, the end user views a 10-second introductory image, such as the one in Figure 11.2.

Figure 11.1   A prototype genre Web page.

Figure 11.2   Branding art for the Action/Adventure channel.

Then the image switches to the channel in progress—the channel has already been running and the end user picks up the broadcast at whatever point is currently playing. From there, the user experience is similar to that of viewing a television broadcast. A channel line-up runs for approximately 20 minutes, then replays continuously. The following list shows a portion of a typical channel line-up:

Title	Source
Movie Trailer #1	\wmroot\Trailers\Trailer01.wmv
Movie Trailer #8	\wmroot\Trailers\Trailer08.wmv
Bumper #3	\wmroot\CMO\Bumper03.wmv
Exclusive Interview #7	Rtsp://RemoteServer/Int07.wmv
Behind-the-scenes #2	Httpd://StudioWebServer/BTS.asp
Commercial	Wrapper: httpd://AdServer/adRotator.asp
Movie Trailer #10	\wmroot\Trailers\Trailer10.wmv

Notice that, in this example, most of the content comes from the local Windows Media server. However, content can come from a number of sources. For example, Exclusive Interview #7 comes from a file on a remote Windows Media server, the URL of Behind-the-scenes #2 is generated by an ASP page on a Web server, and the commercial comes from a wrapper playlist, which points to an ASP page generating ads dynamically on an ad server. We'll look more closely at wrappers later in this chapter.

As far as the end user is concerned, the broadcast is continuous. He is not aware that the programming is dynamic and can even be personalized for him.

Understanding Metafiles and Packages

Windows Media provides many options for packaging and presenting content, and this enables you to create an engaging experience for end users. Most options deal with creative ways to use and program Player features, such as skins, borders, HTMLView, metadata, custom plug-ins that you can build to add functionality to the Player, and a versatile Player object model. The Windows Media Player SDK describes these options and how to implement them.

The SDK also describes how to package and present content using Windows Media metafiles. While the options just mentioned enable you to customize the look and functionality of the Player, metafiles enable you to customize the presentation of the content itself. The main function of a metafile is to create playlists, which are simply lists of digital media content.

Metafiles were originally created to provide a simple redirection function. When linking to a Windows Media stream on a Web page, rather than reference the stream directly, you reference a metafile that contains the URL of the stream. When an end user clicks the link, the metafile downloads and the browser opens Windows Media Player. The Player then interprets the contents of the metafile, locates the stream, and begins playback.

The reason for adding this redirection mechanism is that many browsers are not designed to handle streaming media protocols, like MMS and RTSP. For example, if you were to link directly to a file on a Windows Media server with a URL that began with "mms://", one browser might attempt to download the content and generate an error when it could not, while another browser might attempt to display the content as a Web page.

The basic metafile, then, acts as a simple redirector and contains a link to a file or live stream. Later versions of the metafile enable you to add multiple links to the metafile and create playlists of digital media content. You can also package the playlist with other content and create download packages.

Uses for Metafiles

The following sections summarize the different presentation solutions provided by Windows Media 9 Series metafiles.

Simple Redirector

The metafile contains the URL of one file or stream. The Player opens and interprets the contents of the metafile, and then plays the digital media. Metafiles are typically hosted on Web servers and linked to from Web pages with a URL such as http://WebServer/Content.asx. However, they can also be sent in e-mail messages or included in a download package.

Simple redirectors are a type of client-side metafile, meaning they are downloaded and interpreted by the Player software. Client-side metafiles use file name extensions such as .wvx, .wax, and .asx. You can use .wvx if the digital media contains video, .wax if it contains audio only, and .asx if it contains a mix of content types, such as a playlist that contains some audio and some video files.

Client-side Playlist

The same as a simple redirector, except that it contains multiple URLs of files and streams. The Player opens and interprets the metafile, and then plays each file or stream in order. The metafile can also contain descriptive information and URLs of image files, called banners, which are displayed on the Player. Links can be associated with titles and banners. When an end user clicks a linked banner, for example, the browser opens to the Web page in the link. As with a simple redirector, a client-side playlist uses .wvx, .wax, and .asx extensions.

Windows Media Download Package

A client-side playlist can be packaged with a skin, images, and possibly digital media content in a Windows Media Download Package file. Then the file can be downloaded by end users or delivered on other media, such as CDs. The Player opens the download package file, interprets the metafile and the skin definition file (if there is one), displays the skin as a border, and runs the playlist. Windows Media Download files use a .wmd file name extension.

Server-side Playlist

With a server-side playlist, the concept and end-user experience are similar to a client-side playlist, but the implementation is different. Instead of being downloaded from a Web server, a server-side playlist is hosted on a Windows Media server and is handled like a digital media file, using a protocol such as RTSP or MMS. You link to a server-side playlist file with a simple redirector file. The Player opens and interprets the redirector, locates the playlist, and then plays the server-side playlist as a stream, but without downloading it.

With a client-side playlist, the Player does the work of interpreting the playlist and locating the digital media. With a server-side playlist, the server does all that. A server-side playlist is written using Synchronized Multimedia Integration Language (SMIL), and has a .wsx extension. An example of a server-side playlist URL is rtsp://WMServer/Playlist.wsx.

Server-side Playlist on a Publishing Point

You can also make the playlist file the source of a publishing point. End users can then access the playlist by linking to the publishing point instead of the playlist file, using a URL such as rtsp://WMServer/PubPointPlaylist. One advantage of hosting a playlist from a publishing point is that you can customize the publishing point properties applied to the playlist, such as limits, security, and forward error correction. Another advantage is that you can broadcast the playlist. This is how Contoso Movies Online is going to implement the movie info channels. Each channel is a broadcast publishing point that sources from a server-side playlist.

Working with Metafiles

There are many ways to use these metafiles to create a custom presentation. We will use the following tools, which we will describe in more detail as we see how the Contoso staff creates a mockup of an info channel:

Wrappers

Think of a wrapper as a playlist that includes the source of a publishing point as one of its media elements. You can create a wrapper playlist for a publishing point that plays content when an end user first connects, when a publishing point source ends, and at points during a source playlist. For example, when an end user accesses a video file from a publishing point, a wrapper can be used to play an ad file before or after the video. Contoso will use wrappers in the info channel to display an image file before switching to the broadcast in progress, and to play an ad during the playlist.

ASP Pages

The entries in client-side or server-side playlists typically refer directly to a file or stream, such as mms://MovieServer/LivePublishingPoint. However, the entries can also point to content through an ASP page. For example, an entry in a playlist can point to an ASP page with a URL like httpd://AdServer01/AdRotator.asp.

The advantage of being able to access content through ASP pages is that you can create dynamic playlists. For example, you can serve ads in a playlist that are personalized to each end user, or you can add content on the fly to a playlist that is running. The Contoso info channel will use an ASP page to access a playlist that plays ads randomly.

Planning the Info Channel

Contoso planners want to build traffic to the site and keep people engaged once they arrive. They feel the info channel is one way to do that. The end user who wants a particular movie will locate the title and go right to the rental page. However, the planners feel that the info channels will appeal to users who want to browse. Each channel will repeat continuously, so a user can tune in at any point during the 20-minute broadcast.

In addition to trailers and insider movie fan information, the info channels will include MoreInfo banners and URLs. If an end user sees a movie she likes while viewing the channel, she can click the link and the details page for that movie will open. Figure 11.3 shows a banner as it appears in Windows Media Player.

Figure 11.3   An example of a MoreInfo banner on the Contoso Web site.

There will be 10 info channels, one for each movie genre. Each channel is a broadcast publishing point that sources from two server-side playlists: the main playlist and a wrapper. The playlists will source primarily from digital media content on the local Windows Media server. However, they can source from content on other servers.

The Contoso Movies Online staff will create a mockup of a movie info channel from the following components:

■ Broadcast publishing point. The address that Players use to access a movie channel. Publishing points are the basic components for configuring a Windows Media server. They connect the client to digital media content, such as a file, a directory of files, a live stream from an encoder, or a server-side playlist.

A publishing point is created from two basic pieces of information: a publishing point name and a source. A client accesses the name to receive the source content. For example, when a client accesses a movie info channel using the name of the channel (such as rtsp://WMServer/Channel01), the server streams the source content defined in the playlist. After you create either a broadcast or on-demand publishing point, you can configure properties and plug-ins that modify the operation of the publishing point.

- Main server-side playlist. The main source of the publishing point; the content that the end user has requested. The playlist is a metafile with a .wsx extension. It is located on a local hard drive or on a computer accessible over a network using a UNC path, such as \\RemoteComputer\Folder\File.wsx.

- Wrapper playlist. The playlist file that is added to the publishing point as a wrapper. End users play the wrapper playlist, if one is assigned, when they come to a publishing point. Therefore, in order for the main playlist to stream to end users, it must be an element of the wrapper. In the Contoso scenario, the wrapper playlist begins with an intro image file that plays for 10 seconds, and then cuts to the main broadcast playlist.

- ASP pages. Elements in the playlist that enable you to assign digital media sources dynamically. One ASP page simply returns the location of a playlist containing one digital media file; another returns a playlist with a random ad. In practice, ASP pages can be used to return URLs of dynamic playlists from an ad server, for example.

- Image files. These are used in the info channel publishing point in two ways. One is used as an introductory image in the wrapper playlist; the other is used as a MoreInfo banner.

- Digital media content. All movie channels will pull content from the same pool of Windows Media video files. Figure 11.4 shows how the digital media feeds into the info channel playlists.

In the WMRoot directory, for example, folders can be added to separate the types of digital media, such as movies, trailers, publicity material, bumpers, commercials, and playlists. When creating a playlist, the Contoso Movies Online producer views all the material available, and then lays the playlists out with content appropriate for each genre and for the best flow. The following table shows an example of part of the lineup of two channels.

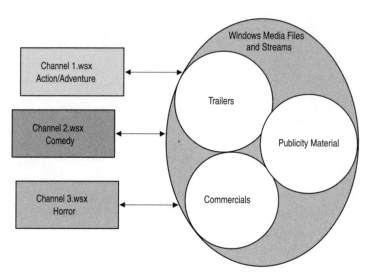

Figure 11.4   How files are added to the info channel playlists.

Channel 1.wsx	Channel 2.wsx
AdventureTrailer20.wmv	ComedyTrailer10.wmv
Interview05.wmv	Interview06.wmv
Bumper03.wmv	Bumper03.wmv
Ad01.asp (wrapper)	Ad01.asp (wrapper)
ComedyTrailer10.wmv	AdventureTrailer15.wmv
HorrorTrailer07.wmv	MakingOf03.wmv
Bumper04.wmv	Bumper04.wmv

Several of the media elements can be included in two or more channels. For example, the bumper files can be used on all channels, and there is a comedy trailer that fits in both the comedy and action/adventure genres. The Ad01.asp entry is accessed by switching to the wrapper playlist from the main playlist. Immediately after the ad returned by the ASP page ends, playback returns to the main playlist.

It may seem complicated and resource-intensive, but creating and implementing server-side playlists can be simplified by using ASP pages. For example, an entire playlist can be created dynamically and automatically by configuring an ASP page as the source of a broadcast publishing point. In the next part of this chapter, we will see how Contoso creates a mockup info channel that includes all of the components discussed here. We will see how they write the scripts, create the metafiles, configure the server, and then check playback of the publishing point.

Implementing Server-side Playlists

The Contoso producers will perform the following tasks to create a mockup of a movie info channel:

- Write the main server-side playlist file. We will see how to do this using the SMIL scripting language and a text editor, such as Notepad. We will also be introduced to the Playlist Editor.

- Write the wrapper playlist, adding the intro image file and dynamic ad.

- Write the ASP page that sends random ads to the wrapper playlist. Contoso will host the page from a Web server.

- Create a new broadcast publishing point and add the two playlists.

- Start the publishing point. Make sure the playlist is running correctly and check playback.

Writing the Main Server-side Playlist

To see how playlists work, we will run through a few examples of the playlists created for the info channels, reviewing the underlying concepts along the way. If you want details on the scripting language and the concepts, see the Playlist reference sections of the Windows Media Services online Help or the Windows Media Services SDK.

To make it easier to create playlists, you can use the Playlist Editor, which is included with the Windows Media Services installation. The editor displays a server-side playlist in a graphical interface that enables you to easily add and modify elements. In this section, we will see examples of creating the script in both a text editor and the Playlist Editor. Figure 11.5 shows the main server-side playlist for the mockup channel as it appears when opened in the Playlist Editor.

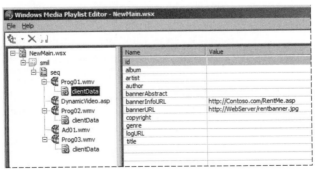

Figure 11.5   Editing a server-side playlist in Playlist Editor.

The area on the left provides a tree view. Each node in the tree is a playlist *element*, which is the basic component of a server-side playlist. You configure an element by setting its *attributes*. When you select an element in the tree view, the attributes are displayed on the right. You can add and remove elements, and change the position of elements in the list by dragging them. You can change the value of an attribute on the right by selecting the attribute and typing.

The tree view provides a visual representation of how a playlist is constructed. If two elements are at the same level in the tree, they are *peers*. For example, Prog1.wmv and Prog2.wmv are peers. Elements can also be *contained* inside other elements. We say the contained element is the *child* of the containing element. For example, a **clientData** element is a child of the Prog1.wmv element.

To understand how to create a playlist with elements and attributes, and what it means to contain elements inside other elements, you can see how this example was constructed. The example uses three types of elements:

- **smil**. This element defines the script as a server-side playlist. Every playlist has a **smil** element at its root. All elements contained in a **smil** element are part of the playlist. Also, elements contained in a **smil** element are played sequentially, starting with the first child element in the list. The **seq** element can be used within a playlist to play content sequentially.

- **media**. This element contains digital media. The first element in the playlist is a **media** element, Prog01.wmv. As you can see, there are a total of five **media** elements in the playlist. Because they are contained in a **smil** element, they play in order from top to bottom. Note that the second **media** element is an ASP page. When that element becomes active, the Windows Media server accesses the page to receive a server-side playlist, which contains digital media content. The source of a **media** element can be any supported source type, such as a file, a live stream, another publishing point, or another playlist.

- **clientData**. This element contains descriptive text and banner links that are used to display information and banners in Windows Media Player 9 Series. The example shown here includes banners for three **media** elements with **clientData** elements. The **clientData** elements contained in the **media** elements have two banner attributes set: **bannerURL** is the URL of the banner image (see figure 11.3), and **bannerInfoURL** is the link associated with the banner. Because the **clientData** elements are children of the **media** elements, the banners are only displayed when those **media** elements are active. If you were to add a **clientData** element containing title information to the **smil** element, for example, the title would display for the entire playlist.

The node at the top of the tree displays the file name and is not a playlist element. The playlist plays starting with the first **media** element and continues down the list.

After creating a playlist in the editor, you save it as a playlist file with a .wsx extension, and then you can add it as the source of a publishing point or a wrapper, depending on its intended use. A playlist is a plain text file. The following is the example playlist as it would appear in a text editor like Notepad.

```
<?wsx  version="1.0"?>
<smil  repeatCount="indefinite">
    <media src="Prog01.wmv">
        <clientData bannerInfoURL="http://WebServer/RentMe.asp"
        bannerURL="http://WebServer/rentbanner.jpg"/>
    </media>
     <media  src="httpd://WebServer/DynamicVideo.asp"/>
    <media syncEvent="Wrap" src="Prog02.wmv">
        <clientData bannerInfoURL="http://WebServer/RentMe.asp"
        bannerURL="http://WebServer/rentbanner.jpg"/>
    </media>
    <media dur="30s" src="Ad01.wmv"/>
    <media src="Prog03.wmv">
        <clientData bannerInfoURL="http://WebServer/RentMe.asp"
        bannerURL="http://WebServer/rentbanner.jpg"/>
    </media>
</smil>
```

This code shows a few more attributes not displayed in figure 11.5:

- **repeatCount**. With this attribute in the **smil** element set to indefinite, the entire playlist will loop continuously. If you were to set the **repeatCount** of another element, such as a **media** element, only that element and its child elements would repeat.

- **syncEvent**. This element is used primarily to activate an element in a wrapper playlist. In this case, when the **media** element with the **syncEvent** becomes active, playback switches to the element in the wrapper that has a begin attribute equal to the **syncEvent** value, Wrap. We will explain this further when Contoso creates the wrapper.

- **dur**. This element sets the length of time a **media** element plays. In this case, Ad01.wmv will play for 30 seconds, even if it is two minutes long.

Writing the Wrapper Playlist

The Contoso producers assigned a wrapper playlist to the info channel publishing point. When end users play the channel, they are actually playing the wrapper playlist, which contains the main playlist. Figure 11.6 shows the playlist in the Playlist Editor.

Figure 11.6   Editing a wrapper playlist in Playlist Editor.

Wrappers are typically smaller than source playlists because they are used to play ads only before, during, and after the main playlist. The wrapper example uses two new elements:

- **excl**. Unlike a **smil** or **seq** element that plays child elements sequentially, an **excl** element plays child elements based on the value of their **begin** attributes. An element with a **begin** value of 0s (zero seconds) plays first.

- **priorityClass**. This element can only be contained in an **excl** element. A **priorityClass** element enables you to control how one child element interrupts the playback of another.

To understand what happens when an end user begins streaming from the publishing point, let's look at the wrapper playlist script:

```
<?wsx  version="1.0"?>
<smil>
    <media  src="C:\WMPub\WMRoot\InfoChannelIntro.jpg"
    dur="10s"/>
    <excl>
        <priorityClass peers="pause">
            <media begin="0s" src="%requestedUrl%"/>
            <media src="httpd://WebServer/AdRotator.asp"
            begin="Wrap.end"/>
        </priorityClass>
    </excl>
</smil>
```

When an end user begins streaming, the elements contained in the **smil** element begin to play sequentially. The first element is the **media** element, InfoChannelIntro.jpg. This image file plays for a duration of 10 seconds (dur="10s"), then the next **media** element becomes active. The next **media** elements are contained in a **priorityClass** element, which is contained in an **excl** element. Because the **media** elements are child elements of an **excl** and **priorityClass**, the **begin** values determine which plays next.

The **begin** attribute of the first **media** element in the **priorityClass** is zero seconds, so it becomes the next active **media** element. The source (**src**) of the **media** element is %requestedURL%. When a **media** element with this source becomes active in a wrapper, playback switches to the stream that was requested by the end user: the source of the publishing point. For Contoso, the source is the main playlist. The source will continue to be active until it stops or ends, at which point control will return to the wrapper. If no other **media** elements are left to play in the wrapper, playback ends.

The other way to return control to a wrapper is to call **syncEvent** from the main playlist. In the main playlist, Prog02.wmv contains a **syncEvent** with a value of Wrap. When this element becomes active, control is returned to the wrapper, and the **media** element with a begin value equal to Wrap. In this example, the begin value is Wrap.end, which triggers the switch to the wrapper at the end of the element that is currently playing. Therefore playback will switch after Prog02.wmv.

The **media** element in the wrapper sources from an ASP page. AdRotator.asp returns a server-side playlist containing a local Windows Media file that is selected at random. In practice, an ASP page could be connected to an ad server. As the ad plays, the main playlist continues to play. End users who connect while the dynamic ad is active, and therefore miss the switch back to the wrapper, will receive Ad01.wmv from the main playlist. At the end of the dynamic ad, playback returns to the main playlist, picking up with the next element, Prog03.wmv.

Writing the ASP Pages

The last pieces of the mockup info channel are the ASP pages that return the dynamic video in the main playlist and the dynamic ad in the wrapper. DynamicVideo.asp contains the following script:

```
<% OPTION EXPLICIT %>
<HTML>
<smil>
<%
Response.Write("<media  src=""rtsp://WMS01/prog04.wmv""  />")
%>
</smil>
</HTML>
```

The script simply returns the URL of Prog04.wmv in a playlist. In practice, you could use a similar ASP page to simply slot in Windows Media files that you did not have final addresses for when you created the playlist. In this case, the producer did not have the address of Prog04.wmv, so she entered DynamicVideo.asp. Then, when she finally got the address, she created the ASP page. If a **media** element in a playlist is not a supported source, it is skipped, so DynamicVideo.asp will be skipped until it is available on the server.

The ad rotator is implemented with the following script:

```
<% OPTION EXPLICIT %>
<HTML>
<smil>

<%
Randomize
dim Index
Index=Int(3*Rnd+1)

select Case Index
case 1
    Response.Write("<media src=""c:\wmpub\wmroot\Ad02.wmv"" />")
case 2
    Response.Write("<media src=""c:\wmpub\wmroot\Ad03.wmv"" />")
case 3
    Response.Write("<media src=""c:\wmpub\wmroot\Ad04.wmv"" />")
end select
%>

</smil>
</HTML>
```

Each time the ASP page is opened, one of three ads is selected at random and returned to the playlist. You can use this form for creating far more complex and useful ad server engines. For example, you can use query strings in the playlist to send information to the ASP page, such as a user's name, IP address, and cookie information. For more information, see the Windows Media Services SDK.

Creating a New Broadcast Publishing Point

After finishing the files, the Contoso producers copy them to the servers: the ASP pages go to the Web server, and the server-side playlist files are copied to the Windows Media server. The ASP pages are online as soon as they are copied and have been given time to propagate to a CDN's remote or load-balancing servers, if necessary. The playlist files are also online and can be accessed directly. However, the playlists will broadcast from a publishing point.

The only way to create and configure a publishing point is with an administrator program that is connected to the servers, and server administration is usually reserved for server technicians who work for the CDN. Contoso has already worked out a process with the CDN for creating new publishing points. After copying the playlist files, the Contoso producer e-mails a request for a new broadcast publishing point to the CDN.

The request contains the name of the source and wrapper playlists, and a proposed name for the publishing point.

The server technician creates the publishing point, adds the two playlist files, and sends a metafile back that the producer can use as a redirector for the publishing point. The name of the Contoso publishing point is InfoChannel, and the following is an example of a redirector metafile script for InfoChannel.asx:

```
<asx version = "3.0">
    <title>Info Channel</title>
    <entry>
        <ref href = "mms://WMServer01/InfoChannel"/>
    </entry>
</asx>
```

The producer can copy the metafile to the Web server, and then add a link to it from a movie genre Web page. She could also rewrite the metafile, for example, to change the title and add more descriptive text. Notice that the metafile is a client-side script, so it is written using the Windows Media metafile programming reference instead of SMIL. However, even though the two use a different language and syntax, many of the display properties and attributes are the same. For example, title and author do the same things in both playlists.

Anything added to the metafile will override the same attributes in the server-side playlist. For example, you could intentionally override title text. You could even add more entry elements and create a client-side playlist. Then you would have a client-side playlist that has the info channel publishing point as one of its elements.

Starting the Publishing Point

The broadcast publishing point can be configured to remain stopped until the first client accesses it. Contoso, however, asks the CDN to start the publishing point as soon as it is configured.

When an end user clicks the link on the movie genre page, InfoChannel.asx downloads to Windows Media Player. The Player opens the metafile and connects to the publishing point. The intro image plays for 10 seconds, and then playback switches to the playlist in progress.

We have seen how Contoso Movies Online made detailed plans for building the movie info channels, and then created a mockup channel with server-side playlists that contain dynamic content. In the next chapter, we see how they produce an event for the Live Event Channel.

12

Live Events Channel

In the last chapter, the Contoso producers laid the groundwork for the movie info channels. In addition to providing broadcast channels with features and fan info, the Contoso Movies Online site will bring exclusive live events to the Web. For example, the site could run live coverage of a big movie premiere or exclusive, unedited interviews.

The live event channel is a broadcast publishing point. When broadcasting an event, a live encoding computer on location streams over a data connection, such as a T1 line, DSL connection, or even a phone line, to the publishing point on the host Windows Media server. End users then come to the live channel Web page and link to the publishing point through the CDN to view the event. The same process is used for any live broadcast on the Internet, such as a radio station.

We will take a look at the process Contoso goes through when producing a live event and streaming it on the Internet. There are as many ways to produce a live event as there are live event opportunities. However, our main focus will not be on describing all the possible ways to produce live events, but on how to use Windows Media in a live event context. To do that, we will describe how a live event might be produced by Contoso.

We will also explore what happens to streaming media content after it has been encoded. Like most content providers on the Internet, the Contoso Movies Online site will take advantage of a hosting service. We will look at the role of a hosting service and how content is distributed using a CDN.

This section includes the following topics:

- Producing live Web events. An overview of producing live events destined for distribution as streaming media.

- *Ivanhoe* wrap party. A description of the event and how the Contoso Movies Online producers approach production.

- Pre-production. A description of the phase of a production when the vision becomes a plan.

- Production. A description of the events that take place when the plan is implemented and production proceeds.

- Content delivery. A description of how on-demand content, live streams, playlists, and metafiles gets to the end user by using a CDN.

Producing Live Web Events

What does the implementation or production of a live Web event look like? If we place live production on a cost scale, we see a wide range of possibilities: everything from inexpensive Webcams to full-scale broadcast-quality productions. The live event Contoso will produce falls somewhere in the middle of this cost range. Contoso's production planning will strive to keep costs as low as possible. However, they will pattern the approach to production of a live event after what on-air broadcasters have been doing for many years.

Contoso Movies Online will use a broadcast production model because end users have preconceived ideas of what the quality of a video production should be like from having watched television for over 50 years. Contoso wants to provide an appropriate level of technical and production quality, because end users will judge their site based on the experience they have with the live video. If the experience is good, there is a greater likelihood that the end user will perceive the Contoso site as being a useful and engaging portal for movies and information. The Contoso producers will also be using the same type of equipment, like video cameras and audio mixers, and they will want the event to look and feel like a broadcast.

The video and audio signals that will be encoded are standard signals used throughout the world. For example, Contoso can rebroadcast (with permission, of course) the signal from a television station, or obtain rights to stream a signal from a satellite or microwave link. If they decide to produce their own event, Contoso can do the same things a broadcaster would do—for example, rent broadcast equipment, satellite time, and hire freelance technicians and artists. The entire production infrastructure can be identical to that of doing a broadcast up to the point of encoding the signal to a Windows Media stream.

There are many similarities between broadcast and live streaming media production. However, there are also a number of differences that can help keep costs down and add value to the event, for example:

- No time constraints. Broadcast programming is traditionally limited by time constraints. This limit comes from other factors limiting the size and scope of the broadcast medium, such as the cost of running a station or network, and government regulations. Time is translated directly to money, making broadcast time expensive. Most programming is, therefore, limited to a tight and inflexible time block, with breaks for commercials and other format restrictions.

Webcasting, on the other hand, has no such time restrictions. For example, you do not have to try to squeeze a three-hour event that starts at 6:42 pm into a one-hour block that starts at exactly 7:00 pm. The Internet and streaming media as media do not create time barriers.

■ Cost barriers. Not only do cost barriers restrict broadcast time, they restrict many other facets of broadcasting, such as who can be a broadcaster and what one can broadcast. FCC licenses are very difficult to come by, and once you have one you need an expensive transmitter and all of the technical infrastructure. On the other hand, one can become a Webcaster with an inexpensive computer, a video camera, and a connection to the Internet. There are Internet Service Providers (ISPs) that provide live streaming services for a monthly fee. Without the technical and cost barriers, the Contoso Movies Online site can produce quality live events that are easily within their budget.

■ No content barriers. Again without regulations from entities such as the FCC and organizations, and without the cost barriers, an Internet broadcaster has more freedom to create many different types of content for many different types of audiences. For years, Web site owners have taken advantage of this freedom in the text and images they create. You can extend the advantage to streaming media and take viewers to places they have never imagined and are not possible with traditional broadcasting.

■ No presentation barriers. Broadcast television imposes many restrictions on the presentation of content that do not apply to streaming media. Broadcast television is carried with an analog signal that reproduces an image of a set size and quality. Streaming media, on the other hand, is a digital stream that has the potential of carrying, reproducing, creating, or doing anything that a computer is capable of.

Currently, a stream of data formatted into Windows Media packets carries audio and video. The audio and video can be streamed at a number of different bit rates with different codecs, frame sizes, frame aspect ratios, and audio quality levels. You can then embed one or more video frames in a Web page and script the page so the stream displays static images.

When planning how to use Windows Media, you can take advantage of the systems and lessons learned in broadcasting, while leveraging the features and freedoms available only to the Internet broadcaster.

Ivanhoe Wrap Party

To describe the production of a Web broadcast, we will follow along as the Contoso team creates an event for the Live Event Channel. The event is an end-of-production party for the cast and crew of a fictitious movie, *Ivanhoe*, based on the book by Sir Walter Scott. The "wrap party," will be held on the production's soundstage in Los Angeles. Contoso Movies Online has negotiated the exclusive rights to be there with their cameras and to stream the event on their site.

End users can come to the live channel page and join the party. Coverage of the party will include interviews with the stars. There will also be speeches by the director and studio executives, as well as some live musical entertainment. The evening will be loosely structured and filled with surprises. The coverage will begin at approximately 8:00 PM, and will run until approximately 10:00 PM, but there is no time limit. Two of the movie's actors have agreed to host the Web event, and end users can interact with them and the stars by joining the online chat.

The first step in putting together the production after the agreements have been formalized is planning: deciding how to accomplish the production and making all the necessary arrangements. This stage is called pre-production.

Pre-production

The site producers must create a Web event that is engaging and captures the excitement of the party, while maintaining control of the budget. They want to keep the spontaneous quality of the event, because that will be a draw for end users. However, to make it all work, they must carefully plan the production so the producers and crew are prepared for the spontaneity.

To that end, the producer works closely with the people who are putting together the party, such as the event planners, caterers, and facilities team. She meets with all of the people involved and scouts the location, taking careful notes and making sure everyone who should know is aware of the Web production. For example, the producer makes sure that her crew can set up their equipment on the soundstage, they have access to electricity, and security will allow them to enter the studio lot. She must also inform the cast and crew of the production details, and obtain their permission to photograph them and capture their voice. Her job is to head off every possible problem so the production runs smoothly and efficiently.

We will not go into all of the details that a producer must consider. Instead, we will leap ahead to the point where all the plans have been put in place.

Production Plan

Everything about the production plan takes the need for spontaneity into account. Without the luxury of a final script or rundown, the producer prepares for a variety of possibilities. She has scouted the area where the party will take place, and she has determined that the lighting will be dim, the area will be noisy, electricity will only be available in certain areas, and the events will be unpredictable.

She works with her technician, and they decide to create a main staging area near the soundstage entrance. At this location, they will set up the main production equipment, such as the video switcher, audio mixer, encoding computer, and chat computer. One camera will be located near this station with one of the hosts.

Party guests will use this entrance primarily, and will then move out to the main party area. To capture party guests in this area, the producer will use a wireless camera and microphone. The second host will stay with the wireless setup, and will roam from group to group, interviewing guests and narrating the events for the viewers. They also plan to bring backup equipment and a supply of expendables, such as batteries.

The producer and technician are the only members of the crew who actually work for Contoso Movies Online. All other cast and crew members are freelance artists and technicians hired for the event. The small production team consists of the following people:

- Producer. During the event, she will oversee the production and retrieve questions from the chat room.

- Technician. Oversees the technical aspects of the pre-production and production. During the event, the technician will help set up and configure the encoding computer, and then monitor the stream.

- Hosts. The on-camera hosts of the Web broadcast are two actors from the movie. The producer feels that because they were part of the cast, the party guests will be more open to participating in the Web event.

- Director. In addition to being in charge of the flow of the Web event, he will operate the video switcher and audio mixer.

- Camerapersons. One for each camera. The cameraperson operates the camera and communicates with the hosts to set up segments that will be interesting to broadcast.

In addition to using freelance cast and crew, the producer will rent most of the equipment and obtain expendable items, such as tape, from the rental companies. The exception is the encoding computer, which has been preconfigured with the encoder settings they will use. In this plan, equipment will be set up in an area near the stage door. Another option would be to hire a complete mobile video production setup that includes the crew, equipment, and a production van. However, the producer decided she could cut costs by having the equipment set up on tables and portable equipment racks. Figure 12.1 shows the configuration of the equipment.

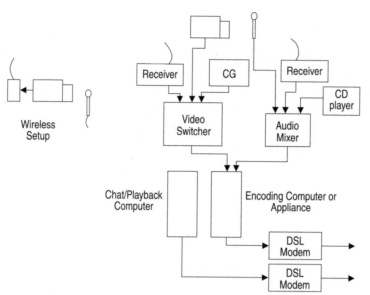

Figure 12.1   Configuration of equipment for broadcasting a live event.

The following are descriptions of the equipment and how it is set up:

- Character generator (CG). A device for generating titles that can be super-imposed over video. Titles will be added to the video to show who is being interviewed. Before and after the event, and during intermissions, it will also be used to tell viewers what is happening, such as, "Stay tuned. The event will begin momentarily." A computer with an appropriate titling program may take the place of a character generator device.

- Cameras. A local camera will be connected directly to the video switcher; the other will be connected to a small transmitter. The cameras will be small and portable. Semi-professional or high-end consumer camcorders can be used. If camcorders are used, they can also record their signals to videotape as a backup.

- Wireless video system. The system will consist of a small transmitter attached to the remote camera and a receiving station near the video switcher. Wireless systems by companies such as Coherent and Dynapix can be purchased or rented. The output of the receiver will be fed into the switcher. Figure 12.2 shows a Coherent transmitter the size of a matchbox. Portable wireless systems provide a great deal of mobility for events like the Ivanhoe party. They can also be used for many other applications, such as Web cams and surveillance.

├─1.5in / 3.9cm─┤

Figure 12.2   An example of a small video transmitter.

- Wireless audio system. Similar in concept to the wireless video system. The audio transmitter is contained in the handheld microphone, and the receiver is located near the audio mixer.

- Wireless intercom system. The director will communicate with the camera operators and the hosts by using a wireless system, such as those from Comtek, Lectrosonics, and Clearcom. An Interrupted Foldback (IFB) system can be used, so the crew will be able to hear instructions from the director mixed with the audio being encoded.

- Audio mixer. Mixes the audio from various sources into one signal that feeds the sound card on the encoding computer. Sources include the local microphone, the receiver for the wireless microphone, and a CD player that will be used to provide background music when the microphones are not live.

- Video switcher. Switches between video sources and can be used to superimpose titles on the video. Sources include the local camera, the receiver for the wireless camera, and the character generator.

- Video monitors. Not shown in the diagram are five small video monitors, which will enable the director to view video from the sources, and to view the preview and program video from the video switcher.

- Computers. One will be configured as the encoding computer; the other will be used to administer the chat and view playback from the Internet. To encode, the Contoso team will use a dual-processor computer with 256 MB of RAM and a 20 GB hard drive, running Microsoft Windows XP Professional. The chat/playback computer will run Windows XP Professional with more modest hardware requirements, a sound card, and speakers.

  During the event, Windows Media Player will be connected to the live stream over the Internet, so the producer, technician, and director can check the stream as it is being received by clients. A second encoding computer could be used as a backup; however, the computer the crew will use has proven to be reliable. Another encoding option is an encoding appliance, such as those from Winnov, Pinnacle, and Vcast. An appliance is a dedicated encoder device that can offer additional reliability and signal processing features.

- DSL modems. Two DSL connections will be used: one to send the encoded data, the other to administer the chat and check Internet playback. A number of other connection types can be used, such as partial T1 or frame relay. However, DSL provides a cost-effective solution for this event.

- Audio monitor. The technician will operate the audio mixer and monitor the audio closely using professional-quality headphones. Due to the amount of noise in the environment, speakers cannot be used.

- CD player. An inexpensive CD player will be used to provide background music during those times when the microphones are not live, such as before and after the event.

It is important to note that there are many ways to set up a live production, and every event will require a different configuration. The goal of a production is to create an engaging experience for the end user, but that does not mean you have to spend a lot of money, use a lot of equipment, or hire a large crew. It does mean that you should be aware of how to create a live show, and all the opportunities and pitfalls that come with creating an event.

Broadcast Infrastructure Planning

When Contoso Movies Online first set up their contract with the CDN service that would also host their Web and Windows Media-based content, a process was established for how to set up broadcasts for the live channel. Each CDN or ISP will have a different process. However, there is some basic information that is common to all broadcast configurations that must be communicated. To understand what information is needed, let's look at what happens to the live stream during a broadcast.

First, Windows Media Encoder compresses and encodes the audio and video into a stream that consists of a series of packets containing data. Then the stream is sent over a network as a live or broadcast stream. The stream can also be sent to a storage device where it is written to a file, or both written to a file and broadcast. Once on the network, the live stream from the encoder is most often received by a Windows Media server that then delivers the stream to multiple players.

You connect a server to the live stream from an encoder by using the URL of the encoder, which consists of the HTTP protocol, the IP address of the computer, and the port number assigned to the encoder session, such as http://EncodingComputer:8181. Multiple instances of the encoder can stream data from a single computer. For example, you could use three video capture cards to feed into three encoders. To differentiate the encoder instances, you assign different port numbers to each one. For example, the encoders could be assigned port numbers 8181, 8182, and 8183. You could also split the video stream from one capture card to two or more encoder instances, and configure each to encode at a different bit rate. For example, the Osprey video capture card can use SimulStream software to split the video. You could also encode an MBR stream with one encoder instance.

You can connect the Player directly to the encoder and receive the live data packets. In practice, however, you do not typically connect the Player directly to an encoder except for monitoring. Maintaining connections requires processing time, and you should reserve as much processor resources as possible for encoding. Besides, Windows Media Encoder is limited to five client connections. To distribute a live stream, you use a Windows Media server, which can handle hundreds (or even thousands) of connections.

Distributing a Live Stream

To distribute a live stream from a Windows Media server, you create a broadcast publishing point that sources from the encoder, using the encoder's URL. Then users can connect to the server by entering the URL of the publishing point, such as rtsp://WMServer/LiveStream. Note that you connect to an encoder using the HTTP protocol, and to a server using the MMS or RTSP protocols. You can stream from a server using HTTP if the server is configured to do so.

To deliver a live stream to a hosting service or CDN, a connection is established, typically over the Internet. To do that, the encoding computer can be assigned a static IP address and configured with a high-speed connection to the Internet. The hosting service can then connect using the IP address. If the computer cannot be assigned a static address (for example, if the computer might be connecting through different ISPs), you can use a dynamic DNS service. The DNS service enables you to change the IP address associated with a fixed domain name. The Windows Media server publishing point can then refer to the fixed domain name, such as http://ContosoDynamicName01:8181. When the IP address of the encoding computer changes, you can use a utility provided by the DNS service to update the address associated with the fixed domain name. This is the system Contoso will use for the *Ivanhoe* event, because the DSL provider for the event is different from the provider used at the Contoso office.

To set up the connection for the event, therefore, the producer will supply the hosting service with the fixed domain name of the encoding computer, ContosoDynamicName. If they were to use a backup encoder, they would also need to supply a domain name for it. The Contoso producer would also inform the hosting service if she will be encoding multiple streams on an encoding computer.

To create a publishing point, a server administrator needs two basic pieces of information: a name for the publishing point (such as LiveEvent01) and a source (http://ContosoDynamicName01:8181). According to Contoso's arrangement with the hosting service, the producer will supply the publishing point name and encoder domain name, and the hosting service will then configure the publishing point and send back the port number that a technician will add to the encoder configuration. If multiple publishing points are required for additional streams, the hosting service will provide port numbers for each one.

Setting up Encoder Rollover

Typically, a broadcast publishing point is configured to source directly from an encoder. However, it can instead point to a server-side playlist that contains a media element that sources from the encoder. The advantage of using a playlist is that a failover or rollover mechanism can be built into the publishing point. With rollover, you can configure two or more redundant encoding computers to automatically switch to a working encoder if the encoder that is live fails. The following playlist shows an example of a simple rollover.

```
<?wsx  version="1.0"  encoding="utf-8"?>
<smil  repeatCount="indefinite">
    <media  src="http://Encoder01:8181"/>
    <media  src="http://Encoder02:8182"/>
    <media  src="C:\WMPub\WMRoot\Standby.jpg"  dur="10s"/>
</smil>
```

As mentioned in the previous chapter, elements contained in a smil element play sequentially from top to bottom. In this example, the playlist starts with Encoder01. As long as a stream is received from Encoder01, the playlist does not change to the next media element. If, on the other hand, a problem occurs and the stream stops, the server switches to the next media element, Encoder02. If neither encoder sends a stream, the playlist switches to an image that displays standby text, such as the image in figure 12.3.

Figure 12.3 Image displayed if previous elements in the playlist are not available.

The image plays for 10 seconds, and then the playlist loops to the top of the list. If one of the encoders starts streaming again, the server will resume streaming from that point in the playlist. If not, the playlist will repeat every 10 seconds until an encoder is started.

Live Event Production

The day of the event, the cast and crew arrive as early as possible to set up. All equipment is laid out and wired. Then the equipment is turned on and tested.

The technicians connect audio from the mixer output and video from the switcher to the capture cards on the encoding computer. Then they connect the NIC to one of the DSL modems. The chat/playback computer is connected to the other DSL modem. The DSL modems are then connected to the phone lines carrying the two DSL lines.

The technicians then turn on the encoding computer and load the session file that was created ahead of time for the live stream. The session file is configured with the following properties:

- On the **Source** tab, click **Source from Devices**, and select the video and audio capture cards.

- On the **Output** tab, click **Pull from encoder**, and type the port number supplied by the hosting service.

- On the **Compression** tab:

  - The **Destination** is specified as **Windows Media server**.

  - **Video** and **Audio** has **Multiple bit rates (CBR)** selected.

  - For **Bit rates**, only **148 Kbps** is selected.

- On the **Video Size** tab:

  - The **Crop Method** is **Widescreen 1.78:1**.

  - The **Resize Method** is set to **No resizing**.

The Contoso Movies Online site sizes all video to this aspect ratio so it has a more cinematic look. With these settings, the top and bottom 30 pixels of the image are cropped.

In addition to the property settings, the technicians will configure the encoder to reject all connection requests for the stream except from the Windows Media server at the hosting service. As mentioned earlier, Windows Media Encoder will only support up to five connections. If the address of the encoding computer were to become known on the Internet, it would be open to a denial-of-service attack if only five clients connected to it directly. To restrict access to the encoder, open the **Broadcast Security** dialog from the **Tools** menu, and enter the IP address of the host server in the **Allow** area. In Contoso's case, they get the address from the hosting service. The address is also displayed as a **Client** on the **Connections** tab of the **Monitor** panel once they start encoding.

After everything has been set up, the Contoso technicians send a test stream to the host. They can, for example, use the character generator to create an appropriate title, play some test music on the CD player, and start encoding. The producer contacts the host to start the publishing point. If they are using a rollover playlist, the IT person at the host service will see that the media element associated with the live encoder is the active media element in the playlist.

The technician then opens the Player on the chat/playback computer and connects to the publishing point to check that the data is getting through, and that streaming quality is acceptable. If a connection is not made, they can turn off broadcast security to allow all connections, and then see if they can connect directly to the encoder with the Player on the playback computer. If you have difficulty making a connection, double-check settings and make sure the domain name, if you use one, resolves properly to the encoding computer.

A half-hour before the show, the director can play some music with a title announcing the start time. The producer can set up and check the chat system, and the technician and camera operators can check all audio and video signals one last time.

Using Content Delivery Networks

Most businesses that create content for the Internet use a third-party hosting service to handle distribution to end users. This includes both businesses that use their Internet presence as an extension of their primary business and e-businesses that rely entirely on the Internet. In the early days of the Internet, site owners often built and maintained their own servers. Today, however, the Internet is very different: there are many more sites, bandwidth requirements are higher, the technology required to construct a site is more complex, businesses demand reliability and more security, there are many more end users, and they demand low latency and rich content. It is still possible to do it yourself, but it often makes more sense to delegate that task to a service that specializes in the delivery of content.

The business of delivering content has grown and become specialized. Most commercial sites are no longer hosted on a single server, but employ a hosting service that uses many servers interconnected to provide reliability and speed. They also use other devices, like firewalls, to improve security. There are specialized servers that handle only certain types of applications, such as e-commerce, licensing, and streaming media. There are specialized storage devices that hold large amounts of data, and backbones that transfer billions of bits per second. In order to compete as a hosting service today, a business must make huge investments in hardware and infrastructure and needs a team of professionals with the expertise to plan and build reliable solutions. For a business focused on creating content, it is more cost-effective and productive to contract with a service that has the hardware and infrastructure, and that understands the complex business of hosting large volumes of data on the Internet. These services are often called content delivery networks (CDNs).

CDN Concepts

Possibly the greatest recent advance in distribution technology has been in the development of systems that decentralize the hosting of content. The concept of decentralization is easy to grasp. The closer a client is to a server, the faster and more reliably the client will be able to access and receive content, and the less it will impact network resources. Decreasing the distance between client and server is good for the network and the end user. Decentralized distribution is often called "edge serving" because the servers are located closer to the edge of the network—closer to the users.

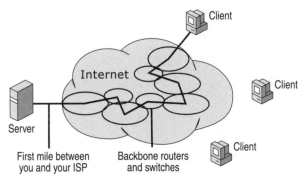

Figure 12.4   A traditional, centralized network.

The traditional approach to hosting content is the centralized configuration shown in figure 12.4. The route that data must take to get from server to client can be very long and can pass through many routing devices on the way. Every device that data must be routed through, and every mile of cable that data must travel, adds to the potential latency a client experiences. Also, it is more likely that data will be received with missing or corrupt packets. These problems can be very annoying for end users, especially when attempting to stream a video, for example.

Figure 12.5 shows how decentralizing distribution solves these problems. In a decentralized solution, multiple servers are located at the edges of the network. By delivering data from an edge server, problems that occur in the first mile, with backbone devices and ISP peering, are greatly reduced. Multiple servers also help balance server load. End users are more likely to receive a high-quality stream if it is coming from a computer that is servicing fewer clients.

Edge serving has been combined with other technologies and given the umbrella name "content delivery network." A true CDN is a business that provides a large-scale deployment of edge servers, such as nationally or globally, and provides technology, often referred to as intelligence, that redirects clients based on a number of criteria, in order to optimize server and network load.

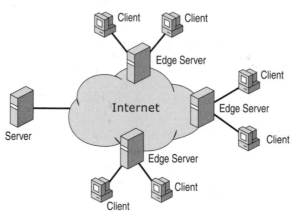

Figure 12.5   A decentralized content delivery network.

Streaming with CDNs

CDNs are particularly advantageous for the delivery of streaming media content. When streaming, a server must maintain a continuous connection with a client, not only sending each client a steady stream of packets, but resending packets that are not received properly and handling client requests, such as changing streams, pausing, and seeking.

By using the decentralized design and intelligent redirection of a CDN, network congestion and server load can be managed. Also, problems that occur in one area do not affect other areas. The job of the main (or *origin*) server is no longer to host content for all clients. The origin server is used primarily to distribute content to the edge servers, and to host light content, such as small files. The heavy content, such as large, high-bit-rate streaming media files and images, are delivered from the edge. Network resource usage is minimized and the end user experience is improved. By locating numerous edge servers in areas that handle a heavy volume of Internet traffic, the amount of traffic can be reduced and end users receive content faster and more reliably.

A number of processes are used for redirecting client requests to edge servers. A common way to do this is to use the client IP address to find the closest edge server. CDNs also use a number of techniques, many of them proprietary, for locating the closest server and redirecting clients to the server with the least load and best network conditions.

If you are a content provider, you can think of the CDN that is hosting your content as a black box. All you need to care about is that the content you create gets to the client, and the end user experience is the best it can be. However, there are three concepts that will help you understand how a CDN does its job, so you will understand how to better work with your CDN.

■   Cache/proxy servers intercept client requests and stream content locally.

- Prestuffing enables you to copy content to edge servers in anticipation of playback requests.

- Stream splitting enables you to deliver broadcast content.

Cache/Proxy Servers

Edge servers are a type of cache/proxy server: they cache content and proxy requests. By "proxy" we mean the server intercepts requests from clients and attempts to handle them locally. By "cache" we mean the cache/proxy server saves content locally.

A typical cache/proxy server scenario works like this:

1. An end user requests content from the origin server.

2. The cache/proxy server intercepts the request and attempts to deliver the content from its cache.

3. If the content is not cached, the cache/proxy server directs the request to the origin server.

4. As the origin server streams the content to the end user, the cache/proxy server adds a copy to its own cache.

5. A second end user requests the same content from the origin server.

6. The cache/proxy server intercepts the request and streams the content from its local cache.

Prestuffing

If it is known that a file will receive a high number of plays, it can be preloaded (or *prestuffed*) on the edge servers before a client requests it. By prestuffing content, the CDN can head-off client requests and minimize streaming from the origin servers. It is even possible to have a very simple origin server configuration on a relatively slow connection, and plan on prestuffing all content automatically. Using this system, the origin server is accessed from the Internet only one time, to copy the files on it to the edge servers.

Stream Splitting

The caching system only works if the digital media or other content is a file. To handle live streaming, another approach is needed because it would not make sense for edge servers to cache a broadcast. For example, caching the stream from a movie info channel or a 24-hour news service would not be the right solution for hosting a live stream from an edge server. This is not to say there is no value in a content provider archiving a broadcast so that it can be streamed on-demand as a file afterwards. However, in that case, the archived file would be handled like any other file.

To handle a broadcast stream, edge servers use a system called *stream splitting*. The system is patterned after the cache/proxy system described earlier, except the stream is not cached; it is split so that one stream from the origin server feeds multiple clients.

A typical stream-splitting scenario works like this:

1. An end user requests a broadcast from the origin server.

2. The cache/proxy server intercepts the request.

3. If this is the first request for the broadcast, the cache/proxy server sends the request to the origin server and then redistributes the stream to the client.

4. A second end user requests the same broadcast from the origin server.

5. The cache/proxy server intercepts the request and splits the stream, thereby serving both clients.

Deploying a Delivery System

Figure 12.6 shows how all the components connect for delivering content from Contoso Movies Online to the end user through a CDN.

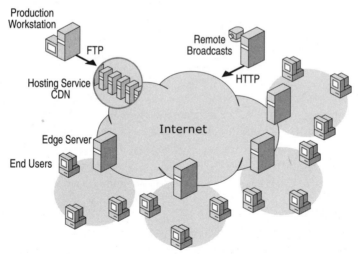

Figure 12.6   The Contoso Movies Online distribution topology, using a CDN.

The production workstations located at Contoso headquarters connect to the corporate LAN, which connects to the Internet through an ISP. The ISP in this case is the hosting service, which is also the CDN. (However, the ISP, hosting service, and CDN could be separate businesses.) Many different scenarios are possible when the Internet is used as the common means of data distribution. The FTP protocol is used to copy (or *publish*) files to the hosting service, from which point the CDN distributes (or propagates) the content to edge servers throughout the network.

The HTTP protocol is used by the encoder to send a live stream over the Internet to the hosting service. In the *Ivanhoe* scenario, the encoding computer connects to the Internet over DSL, which could be provided by the same service that provides the ISP, hosting, and CDN services. In other scenarios, the encoded stream could be sent to the Internet over a dial-up connection in, say, Toronto, or over a partial T1 connection in New York. The video signal could also be picked up via satellite at Contoso headquarters, encoded, and delivered live to the host. The Internet provides the common data delivery system for getting content to the host, as well as getting it to the end user.

Working with a CDN

The CDN that Contoso Movies Online contracted with prestuffs all digital media content to the edge servers. It also prestuffs most of the Web content, such as Web pages and images. There are certain light files that are not cached at the edge, such as small text files that contain movie news and regularly updated information. These files are not cached because it can take time for content to propagate, especially if a CDN has thousands of edge servers. Therefore, if certain content must be changed frequently, it is hosted on the origin server. Late-breaking movie news and information can easily be hosted on an origin server if the data load is very light. CDNs provide systems, such as custom tags, for creating dynamic Web pages that enable you to choose the source of the content.

Many CDNs, such as Akamai, Speedera, and Conxion, provide interfaces that enable their customers to publish content to the servers and work with their publishing points. Customers can use an interface to copy content via FTP to the host server, and can create broadcast publishing points that source remote encoders. Customers can also create publishing points that source from playlists. For example, a customer can copy a server-side playlist to a folder on the host Windows Media server, and create a publishing point that sources from the playlist. Then the customer can modify publishing point properties if necessary, such as add authentication and authorization. Most CDNs also enable customers to monitor their content, and provide customers with logs that show details such as client usage and errors.

In this chapter, we saw how Contoso Movies Online produced a live event, and looked at how Contoso makes use of hosting services and CDNs. In the next chapter, Contoso adds the final touch to the movies online site: enabling the site to generate revenue with movie rentals. They do that by first encrypting the movies with Windows Media Rights Manager, and then sending licenses to those end users who pay the fee.

13

Movie Rentals

In part III, you've seen how Contoso Movies Online built a production workstation for encoding content and produced a live event. We also saw how they created three types of content: on-demand content, server-side playlists for the movie info channels, and broadcast content for the live event channel.

In this chapter, we will walk through the process by which the Contoso staff will create a fourth type of content for the site: Windows Media files that have been encrypted using Windows Media Rights Manager. With their inventory of movies secure, the Contoso Movies Online team can move ahead with the rest of their plans to create an e-commerce system and implement their model for generating revenue with movie rentals.

Windows Media Rights Manager is the Microsoft DRM solution for protecting Windows Media-based content. The encryption process is half of the system. In order to fully understand how Windows Media Rights Manager works, we will also describe the process of generating and sending licenses to clients so the content can be played. In this chapter we will explore Windows Media Rights Manager, how it ties into the e-commerce solution, and how to create a sample Windows Media Rights Manager solution.

Protecting Your Content

Most security measures protect content by controlling access to it, such as through an access control list (ACL) on a network share. Windows Media Rights Manager, on the other hand, protects a Windows Media file or stream by securing the data itself through encryption. In order to play an encrypted stream, an end user obtains a license that contains the key for decrypting the data. By tying issuance of a license to receiving a fee or some other criteria, you can maintain tight control over who has access to your content and how it is used. In that sense, Windows Media Rights Manager can become an important part of a business model.

There are other ways to secure data. Some methods, such as hiding the URL, are not secure enough for a business model. Methods like these can only work if the content that is being hidden has no value for anyone except those who already have the URL. If your content has market value and you need to restrict access to it, then you need to implement a truly secure system.

A more secure method would be to use the Windows Media server to apply authentication and authorization to a publishing point, or to an individual file or stream. Then give end users who pay a fee permission to access the content. This type of system has been used for pay-per-view scenarios. The system works fine, but it can be cumbersome to maintain. For one thing, you need access to the server in order to update the permissions list. For many content providers, such as Contoso Movies Online, obtaining permission from a hosting service to access security on a Windows Media server might not be possible.

More importantly, authentication and authorization only secure the path to the content. If the content is moved or copied to a location that is not secure, the content is vulnerable. There are also applications available that capture streams to local files. If an end user had one of these programs, all she would have to do is pay to access the stream, and then record it to her hard drive. Then she could freely make copies and distribute the file. And of course, authentication and authorization does nothing to protect files that are downloaded or distributed on CDs, for example.

Windows Media Rights Manager protects the content itself. No matter where you locate the file or what you do with it, the file remains protected. You can, for example, distribute protected files on a CD for free or encourage end users to share files. End users can have the protected content, but they will not be able to play the files until they receive a license, and for that you can charge a fee.

Of course, a revenue model is only one use for Windows Media Rights Manager. A corporation could use rights management to restrict who can view sensitive company information. For example, rights management could be used for business-to-business communication to restrict viewing of a live conference over the Internet. And again, simply having knowledge of the URL or of a valid user name and password will not enable a user to view a Windows Media Rights Manager-protected stream, because the content itself is encrypted.

How Windows Media Rights Manager Works

In order to maximize the security of the Windows Media Rights Manager system, a number of interlocking features and algorithms are used. The goal of Windows Media Rights Manager is to make compromising the system and playing content without authorization as difficult as possible. To that end, Windows Media Rights Manager designers have created a complex system that takes many potential security breaches into account. The system can be a challenge to understand, and requires software development expertise to implement. For that reason, many businesses, including Contoso Movies Online, choose to contract with third-party DRM license service providers. The provider handles the complexities of the system, maintains license records, and issues licenses to clients.

With a licensing service to handle content security and an e-commerce service to handle transactions and accounting, Contoso can concentrate on the content: acquiring the titles and encoding the movies with encryption. Windows Media Encoder makes working with Windows Media Rights Manager easy. Through the encoder, you can access a license provider service that will create a DRM profile on your computer. You can then use the DRM profile to encode and encrypt files or live streams in one step.

All of the code and components to create custom solutions for licensing Windows Media Rights Manager content can be found in the Windows Media Rights Manager 9 Series SDK. The Windows Media Encoder 9 Series SDK is also required to generate DRM profiles for the encoder. The SDKs also provide information on how Windows Media Rights Manager systems work. A licensing system can be created using a number of scripting and programming languages. For example, a complete licensing system can be written with ASP pages and VBScript, and hosted on a Web server.

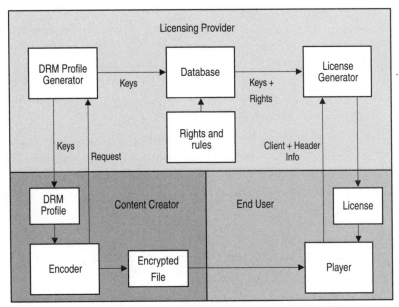

Figure 13.1 Using Windows Media Rights Manager in a DRM system.

Figure 13.1 provides an overview of the Windows Media Rights Manager system. To understand the overall functioning of a Windows Media Rights Manager system, we have combined a lot of the details. The diagram shows a typical Windows Media Rights

Manager scenario. Keep in mind, however, that because you create systems with SDKs, there are many possible solutions.

Three entities are involved in a Windows Media Rights Manager system: the license provider, content creator, and end user. Security is provided by encrypting content; however, at least half of the system is involved with the other part of the process, which is selectively enabling end users to decrypt the files so they can be played.

The following process describes the content creation part of the Windows Media Rights Manager scenario in the diagram:

1. The content creator opens Windows Media Encoder and sends a request for a DRM profile to the license provider. The DRM profile contains all the data needed for configuring the encoder to encrypt a file or live stream.

2. The profile creation process opens in the encoder. Typically, the process consists of one or more forms created by the license provider, such as the one in figure 13.2. The content creator fills in details, such as the movie title, and selects the rights that apply. For example, you could apply a special offer to a movie that allows a customer to play it once at no cost. All of the basic rights and rules have already been established with the provider.

3. The license provider generates a DRM profile on the encoding computer from the information just provided and from existing account information. The DRM profile contains a license key seed, which is one of two components needed to generate a key. The key is used to encrypt the file or stream. The DRM profile also contains information that is added to the content header of the file or stream, including a license acquisition URL.

4. The content creator adds the DRM profile to the encoding session and a key ID is created, which is the other component needed to generate a key. Figure 13.3 shows a DRM profile in **Session Properties** after it has been added to a session and the key ID has been generated.

5. Information used to create the DRM profile is also saved in a license provider database.

6. The content creator encodes the movie with the DRM profile and key ID, and then copies it to the Windows Media server.

When the file is made available for streaming, end users can come to the site and pay to rent the movie. The site could also enable end users to purchase movies. The only difference between configuring Windows Media Rights Manager for purchasing and for renting is the way in which rights are applied in the license. For rentals, you would configure the rights with an expiration time of, say, 48 hours, or a limited number of plays. For movie purchases, you would simply give the file unlimited plays and no expiration.

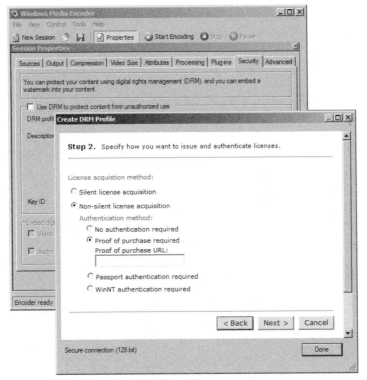

Figure 13.2   Creating a DRM profile.

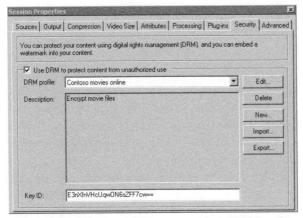

Figure 13.3   The properties created for a DRM profile.

After an end user's payment has been approved by the e-commerce service, the license provider receives approval and the licensing process begins.

1. E-commerce and content identification information are received by the license provider. Content information comes from the Web page through which the end user ordered the movie. E-commerce information is sent by the e-commerce provider. Typically, the only e-commerce information needed by a license provider is whether license issuance has been approved.

2. Content information is used to locate the DRM profile record in the license provider database. The content information on the Web page could be a simple ID number, which is used by the database engine to locate corresponding information that should not be exposed to the public, such as the license key seed.

3. Rights associated with the content are also retrieved from a database. Rights determine how the content can be used. For example, you can set the number of plays for a file or stream and an expiration date.

4. Content information, the key used to protect the content, and rights are used to generate a unique license, which is then issued to the client. When the license is issued, it is installed on the end user's computer.

5. The end user can then download or begin streaming the movie.

6. Windows Media Player searches the computer for a valid license. If the license exists, the movie plays.

This method for obtaining a license is called *silent predelivery*. With this method, the end user may not even be aware a license process is occurring. With predelivery, a license is generated before an end user begins playing encrypted content. After receiving the go-ahead from the e-commerce service, the download or streaming process begins. During the first few moments of the process, the license is generated and installed on the client without any need for further intervention by the end user.

Predelivery can be made moments before streaming begins or at any other time prior to playing the content. You could create a subscription service by predelivering a license that covers a number of files or streams. An end user could then purchase a license that covers content that will be delivered over several months or a year, for example.

An end user can also obtain a license through the standard delivery method, which involves the use of the license acquisition URL that was added to the content header when the stream was encoded. This is the method shown in figure 13.1. With standard delivery, the license acquisition process begins after an end user attempts to play encrypted content. Whenever an end user starts to play an encrypted file or stream, Windows Media Player checks the computer for a valid license. If there is none, the Player extracts the URL from the content header and opens the Web page. The page used by the Contoso Movies Online site will guide the end user through the process of paying for a movie rental, and then issue a license.

With this method, an end user does not even have to receive the encrypted stream from the content owner's site. For example, an end user could copy the file from a friend's computer, from a CD, or from another site. It does not matter where the file comes from because the only way to play the file is by obtaining a license from the Web page identified in the license acquisition URL.

Creating a Rights Management System

In this part of the chapter, we will create a Windows Media Rights Manager system using sample files from the companion CD. The samples are included with the whitepaper, "Developing a License Provider Service for Windows Media Encoder." The whitepaper provides details on how to set up a license provider service that supports DRM profiles in the encoder. We will run the samples and describe the process, but we will not go into the details of using the programming objects and methods. We will also use a VBScript-based program instead of the Visual Basic-based program described in the whitepaper.

To run the sample Windows Media Rights Manager process, you need a computer running Windows 2000 Server, Windows XP Professional, or Windows Server 2003. You will use the computer to both encode and encrypt a Windows Media file from a video file, and issue licenses to play the file. In order to issue licenses, you will set up the computer as a license server.

To run the sample, you need to install the following software and services:

- Microsoft Internet Information Services (IIS). Install IIS using the **Windows Components Wizard** in the **Add or Remove Programs** utility in Windows **Control Panel**.

- Windows Media Encoder 9 Series SDK (available on the companion CD).

- Windows Media Encoder 9 Series (available on the companion CD).

- Windows Media Rights Manager 9 Series SDK. For information about how to get the SDK, go to the MSDN Web site (http://msdn.microsoft.com/library) and see the article, "Getting Started with Windows Media Rights Manager SDK," located in the Digital Rights Management area.

You will also need a sample video file. For the exercise, choose a short video to minimize the wait for the encoding process.

Creating a License Server

After the required software has been installed, set up the computer to issue licenses for the sample process:

1. Create the following folder in the IIS default Web site: %systemdrive%\inetpub\wwwroot\wm.

2. Copy the sample files IssueLicense.asp and IssueLicense_ns.asp from the CD to the new folder.

3. From the Windows Media Rights Manager SDK sample folder, copy Global.asa to the new folder. The SDK sample folder is installed in %systemdrive%\WMSDK\Windows Media Rights Manager.

4. Open the IIS snap-in. In **Properties** for the \wm folder, create a new application. Then in **Execute Permissions**, select **Scripts and Executables**. In creating a new application, you are designating the wm folder as the starting point (application root) for the application, which in our case generates licenses. For more information, see IIS Help or Quick Start in the Windows Media Rights Manager SDK.

5. Stop and then restart the World Wide Web Service so the new settings take effect.

In the following steps, you will get a *certificate* and *revocation list* for your license server from the Microsoft Web site. The certificate enables the computer to issue licenses. The revocation list contains all the application certificates of Player software known to be damaged or corrupted and prevents the server from issuing licenses to those copies of the Player. The entire process can take less than a minute to complete.

1. In a browser, go to http://licenseserver.windowsmedia.com. Click **Enroll to get a new certificate**, and then follow the instructions. After the form has been submitted, an e-mail message will be sent to you containing a token that you will use in the next step.

2. Return to http://licenseserver.windowsmedia.com, and click **Complete the enrollment with your e-mail confirmation**. In this form, enter the token number, and complete enrollment.

3. Return to http://licenseserver.windowsmedia.com, and click **Download the latest License Service Information** to install the latest revocation list.

Your computer is now ready to issue licenses.

Encoding and Encrypting a File

In the following steps, you will use a program written with VBScript to encode and encrypt a video file. The program runs using Windows Script Host, which is included with the installation of your Windows operating system. You can use any video file with an .avi, .mpg, or .wmv file name extension as the source.

Keep in mind that, as you follow the process, you will be performing the tasks of both a license service and a content creator on the same computer. In practice, the content creator requests a DRM profile from a license service, which is most often a third-party provider.

Also, think about how the sample process relates to the overview diagram in figure 13.1. Most of the work of encrypting streams and issuing licenses is done automatically with the DRM components on the license server, Windows Media Encoder, and Windows Media Player. The task of developing a Windows Media Rights Manager process is mainly about making sure the different components have the correct information to do their jobs, such as the key ID, license key seed, and content ID. As you follow the process, notice how the information is exchanged between components. In running the samples, we are not concerned with who has access to the information. In practice, however, information like certificate, seed, and key values should only be shared with trusted employees and vendors.

1. From the CD sample folder, copy DRMEncoderScript.vbs to an empty folder, such as c:\DRMsample, and then double-click the file.

    The program starts running. The user interface for the simple VBScript-based program consists of a series of message and input boxes. Each box stops execution of the program and either informs you of what the program is doing or asks for input.

2. Click **OK** to close each message and advance to the next part of the program.

    As you do, the program generates and exchanges information between DRM components. The components use the information to create a key and content header. The first five messages display values for **MS LS Root Certificate**, **Licensor Certificate**, **private key**, **public key**, and **signed public key**. The two certificate values were generated on your computer when you enrolled at the Microsoft certification site. The three keys are generated by the program and are used to sign the content header. By signing the header, you increase security and prevent tampering with the encrypted file.

    In practice, the certification values would be associated with the license provider server, and the keys would be generated by the license provider server prior to creating a DRM profile.

3. In the input box, type the URL of the license provider site, and then click **OK**. In the sample, the site is the wm folder, http://MyComputer/wm.

    The program creates the DRM profile and installs it automatically on the encoding computer. In practice, the license provider server would create the DRM profile on the encoding computer. The programming method that generates the DRM profile sends certain information back to the provider. The provider then saves this in a database and uses it later to generate a license. In our case, the information that would be returned to the license provider is saved in two text files.

4. Click **OK** to close the next four messages that show new information generated about the version 7 public key, DRM profile ID, license key seed, and the key ID.

   The DRM profile and a pre-defined encoding profile are used to create an encoding session. The session contains the settings that will be used to encode and encrypt the video file. When the DRM profile is added to the session, a key ID is generated. A key is generated from the key ID and the license key seed. This new key will be used to encrypt the content. The key ID will also be added to the content header. You can use the same key ID if you want multiple files or streams to share the same license. You can use this method for a subscription model for example.

   The version 7 public key is used during license acquisition to verify the version 7 portion of the content header.

5. In the next two input boxes, enter the paths and file names of the input (source) and output video files. The sample program encodes and encrypts a file using a fixed encoding profile. In practice, you would configure your own encoding properties in Windows Media Encoder.

6. Click **OK** to encode and encrypt the file. For a large file, the process can take several minutes.

To summarize, the DRM profile creation process and the process of adding the DRM profile to the encoder session uses or generates the following information:

- License acquisition URL. When a Player attempts to play the encrypted file without a valid license, it will open the Web page associated with this URL so the end user can obtain a license. The URL is contained in the DRM profile and added to the content header when the file is encoded.

- Private key. This key is added to the DRM profile and will be used to sign the content header.

- Signed public key. Used in signing the header.

- Licensor certificate. Generated when the license server is certified.

- DRM license server root certificate. Generated when the license server is certified.

- Version 7 public key. Generated during the DRM profile creation process. The value is used to verify the version 7 portion of the content header. The value is added to the DRM profile and the license provider database.

- DRM profile ID. Generated during the DRM profile creation process. The value identifies the DRM profile. The value is added to the DRM profile and the license provider database.

■ License key seed. Generated during the DRM profile creation process. The value is used with the key ID to create the key that is used to encrypt the file. This value is added to the DRM profile and the license provider database.

■ Key ID. A new key ID is generated each time a DRM profile is added to an encoding session. The DRM profile itself does not contain a key ID.

Notice that there does not have to be any content-specific information included in a DRM profile. In the sample, the key ID is the only content-specific information, and it is not part of the DRM profile. Therefore, the same DRM profile can be used to encrypt multiple files and streams.

At this point, the DRM profile is on the computer. After closing the VBScript-based program, you can open Windows Media Encoder and the DRM profile will appear in the list on the **Security** tab in **Session Properties**. Later, you can use the DRM profile to try encoding other content, such as a live stream. However, we will continue with the sample process.

The first part of the Windows Media Rights Manager process is finished and an encrypted file has been created.

Transferring Information to the License Server

The license server requires two pieces of information in the DRM profile in order to issue licenses: the version 7 public key and the license key seed. Typically, this information would be kept in a secure database. In our sample, we will copy the information from two text files to a Global.asa in the wm folder of the IIS default site. The sample ASP pages will then retrieve the key and seed values to generate the license.

1. Open LKSEED.txt and PUBKEYV7.txt in Notepad. The files were created by DRMEncoderScript in the same folder as the script file.

2. Open the Global.asa file in Notepad.

3. Copy the LKSEED text to the Application("seed") value in the Global.asa. Paste over the placeholder value, xxx, and delete any trailing spaces. For example, the line in the Global.asa might look like this:

   ```
   Application("seed")  =  "QE9foBvvww99901Mma"
   ```

4. Copy the PUBKEYV7 text to the Application("contentserverpubkey") value in the Global.asa.

5. Save and close the Global.asa. All other information to license the content will come from the content header and client information when a request is received from the Player.

Generating a License to Play the File

In the following steps, your computer will act as license server and client. In this sample, we will use the standard method of delivering a license. Again, refer to the diagram in figure 13.1 as you run through the steps.

1. Locate the output file and double-click it. Windows Media Player opens the file and launches the license acquisition URL, which is IssueLicense.asp on your computer's Web site.

   To obtain a license, the Player provides the license server with client information and the content header. Client information includes the type and version of Player and DRM component, and a unique client DRM identification. The content header consists of the following information:

   - Key ID. The value that is used to encrypt and decrypt the file.

   - Content ID. An optional value that uniquely identifies the Windows Media file.

   - License Acquisition URL. Carried over from the DRM profile.

   - Individualization version. An optional value that specifies the minimum version of individualization that an end user's Player must have to play the file.

   - Attributes. Optional values that a content creator can add.

   The ASP page runs the following processes automatically, resulting in the issuance of a license.

2. Check the individualization version. The version number in the header is used to determine whether the Windows Media Player DRM component is up to date. If not, the message in figure 13.4 is displayed, and the end user can choose to update the component. If they do not update, they will not be able to play the content.

3. Retrieve public key and license key seed from Global.asa.

4. Retrieve content header and client information.

5. Generate a key by using the key ID from the content header and the license key seed.

6. Set the rights, which determine how the end user can use the content. In the sample, the rights contained in the ASP page enable the client to play the file twice. After the second play, the client is prompted to obtain a new license. In practice, rights would be stored in a license provider database, and would be retrieved based on information contained in the content header.

7. Generate the license by using the information that has been gathered. Notice that security is maximized by integrating information from three sources: the content, the license provider database, and the client.

8. Send the license and store the unique license on the client computer. The license cannot be moved or copied, and is associated with the computer on which it is issued.

9. A **Play** button appears on the Web page displayed by the Player, enabling you to play the file.

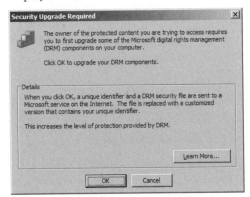

Figure 13.4 The error generated by a Player that is not individualized.

In practice, e-commerce processes can be inserted after the content header and client information have been retrieved. For example, a short series of e-commerce pages can gather payment information and then return an authorization code, which either allows the license process to continue or stops it.

Note that a license can be sent using silent or non-silent delivery. If the Player is set for silent delivery, licenses are sent automatically. If the Player is not set to acquire licenses automatically, the IssueLicense_ns.asp page is called. The only difference between the two methods is that a confirmation message is displayed when non-silent delivery is selected.

This sample demonstrates license delivery using the license acquisition URL. To use predelivery, you would typically initiate the license process from a Web page. After authorization was received, the page would pass content information to the license service provider. The license would then be generated and sent to the client, prior to the content being played.

Developing the Contoso Movies Online Solution

The Contoso Movies Online site will encode and encrypt movie files using DRM profiles. One DRM profile can be used for multiple movies, with the same license key seed used to encrypt the content and generate licenses. The part of the encryption process that differentiates the content is the key ID, which is generated each time session properties are saved prior to encoding. To increase security, however, a new DRM profile that contains a new seed is generated periodically.

To set up Windows Media Encoder in order to create a new DRM profile and encrypt content, the Contoso staff do the following:

1. In **Session Properties** of the encoder, configure settings to encode content, such as adding a source, setting the output, and setting the compression.

2. On the **Security** tab, click **New**.

3. Select a license provider or add a new one, and then click **Generate**. The provider's DRM profile configuration Web page opens.

4. Enter the appropriate information, and then start the process on the page. A DRM profile is installed on your computer.

5. Select the **Use DRM to protect content from unauthorized use** check box, click the new DRM profile, and then click **Apply**.

When the operator starts the encoder, the stream will be encrypted. The key ID can be saved in a database if it will be needed in the future to encode content that uses the same license. If the operator enters a key ID value in **Session Properties**, the encoder will use that value rather than generate a new one.

DRM profiles will be used primarily to secure movie content. However, they can also be used to encrypt a live stream. For example, the site could have an exclusive deal to cover an important event that they would want to charge a rental fee for or offer only to special customers. In that case, a new DRM profile, a different set of rights, and a new sign-up page may be required. The process is basically the same as for renting movies, except a live stream would be received by a client instead of an on-demand stream.

The Contoso Movies Online site is ready to create Windows Media files and live streams, and the CDN is prepared to deliver the content to end users over the Internet. With the new production workstation, site personnel can capture and encode video received from production companies, and they can encrypt movies and other rental content with Windows Media Rights Manager. In addition, the producer can use the Playlist Editor to create server-side playlists for the info channels, and she has a system for producing live events.

In part III, we focused on creating content and relying on outside services for distributing the streams. In part IV, we see how a larger company plans and deploys a complete Windows Media system on an enterprise network. The company will deploy systems for creating content, and will also deploy servers and configure the network infrastructure to distribute live and on-demand content to every desktop in the enterprise.

Part IV

Enterprise Intranet Streaming Media

This part describes how to assemble and integrate a streaming media system in an existing large-enterprise network: setting up Windows Media servers, cache/proxy servers, and encoding workstations. This part also describes the development of a Web portal that can be used as a one-stop site for users to locate on-demand and live streaming content on an intranet.

This information is primarily intended for IT professionals, working in an enterprise setting, who are looking toward a large-scale Windows Media deployment. In the first chapter of this part, we will look at the process that goes into envisioning and planning a large-scale deployment.

14

Adding Streaming Media to Enterprise Networks

This part is about deploying and using Windows Media on a large-scale enterprise intranet. Rather than describe every possible way to configure a streaming media system, we will focus on one scenario that covers a number of deployment issues. The scenario is built around a fictitious, medium-to-large company with branch offices worldwide. The company creates about 70 percent of its streaming media content internally, typically in the form of live, one-to-many broadcasts and on-demand presentations, many of which incorporate Microsoft PowerPoint slides. The rest of the content is redistributed by permission from external sources, such as corporate education programs, financial and news programs, and videos from vendors received through satellite or cable.

To deliver the content, the company uses a streaming media network topology that decentralizes distribution. Steaming media content is first hosted on three origin servers that reside in the company's main data center. The three Windows Media servers are configured in a cluster, so the load is balanced across them. From this media server "farm," the content is distributed to users through a network of cache/proxy servers. By employing a number of servers throughout a large enterprise, a company can effectively spread out bandwidth usage.

How Are Enterprise Deployments Different?

Enterprise systems are different from commercial systems on the Internet because of the network environment and the role digital media plays. In an enterprise, the network is controlled by the company; network usage is more predictable because the company decides how it is used. This is not the case on the Internet. Also, in an enterprise, digital media is used for a different reason. On the Internet, it is a commodity; in an enterprise it is a tool used to communicate and educate.

For these reasons it would appear to be easier to deploy and use streaming media in an enterprise than on the Internet. However, enterprises have their own set of challenges. Even though the network environment is more controlled, it is not always robust and flexible enough to handle many different types of traffic, such as streaming media. Also, most enterprises are not in the business of producing content. Where many Internet sites, such as radio stations, are built around the production of creative content, to an enterprise such as an insurance company, content creation is a small part of its corporate vision. For many large corporations, it is difficult to justify spending a lot of time and resources on digital media without a very clear return on investment.

In the scenario presented, we will see how a company solves these problems by approaching deployment of a streaming media system as an extension of the existing infrastructure. In other words, they are adding value to what is already there. Through business planning and justification, solid project management, and integration, the streaming media system can and should be regarded as an extension of the business model.

When deploying a Windows Media streaming system in an enterprise, you should consider the following business tasks:

■ Identify stakeholders. These are the people who have a stake in the streaming media business. Make sure you know who they are, and that they are aligned with the business vision.

■ Build a business plan. Just like every other part of the enterprise, the streaming media business should have a structure and defined boundaries.

■ Manage risk. As you detail the plans of a system, you should indicate where problems could occur and make sure you have the time and resources available to handle them. This book provides you with information so you can identify and understand potential problems.

■ Adapt and integrate Windows Media into other enterprise systems. Windows Media is an extension of the existing infrastructure, so you need to know how all the parts fit together.

■ Manage the system effectively. After deployment, an effective business plan must include an effective operating plan.

As we have seen in previous sections, it doesn't take a lot to begin streaming over a network. The size and complexity of a streaming media system depends on the scale of your streaming media requirements. Much of planning a system is understanding what scale means in terms of deploying a Windows Media system, and how you can take advantage of scale to optimize resources and the end-user experience.

Scaling a Deployment to Fit

The smallest-scale deployment of Windows Media Technologies is copying one low-bit-rate file to a Web server. The largest-scale deployment can include multiple servers deployed throughout a network, and content management and delivery systems that distribute streams to thousands of end users. With Windows Media components, you can build the system to fit your needs. If you have planned your deployment properly, you can scale up at any time by simply adding to what you already have.

Windows Media Technologies enables you to scale horizontally and vertically. For example, you can add more distributed servers as your enterprise expands, and upgrade the processors on servers to handle greater loads. Security, manageability, and upgrade-ability are also scalable. These are properties that give you the flexibility to manage the growth of the streaming infrastructure as demand increases.

In creating a business plan, you can include a calculation for cost per stream to better understand your return on investment. For example, if you invested $20,000 in a system that serves 1,000 streams per day, the cost per stream in one year would be $0.07. You can compare the figure to the cost per employee associated with other distribution methods, such as videotape or live classroom instruction. You could also use the figure to help determine the scale of your system by comparing deployment and operation costs to cost benefit for employees. As you study the figures, look at the return over time, and factor in the quality of the user experience. For example, ask yourself, are end users more or less likely to retain information when streamed to their desktop rather than sitting in a large meeting?

Scale is not just about the size of your audience and the quality of your content. The scale of your vision may also increase once you start to see the possibilities. One video may spawn a series of videos once users see how effective it is. Other people and groups may have ideas for content. Soon one video turns into one hundred. People on your intranet discover the effectiveness of communicating with streaming media and start demanding more. You may discover that the true value of a streaming media system can be determined by its positive effect on productivity or morale.

You can scale the size of a streaming media deployment, and you can also scale features within that system. A company may have originally deployed Windows Media simply to replace videotape distribution, for example. However, once a Windows Media system is in place, users can take advantage of many other features. With live streaming, the CEO can reach everyone instantly with video that can incorporate PowerPoint slides and animations. As more users become familiar with Windows Media 9 Series, they may discover server-side playlists, new ways to distribute content, and other features. You can then implement load-balanced servers and cache/proxy servers to handle the additional load. If hard disk speed and capacity become an issue, drive arrays and Network-Attached Storage (NAS) systems can be added to handle a large number of concurrent high-bandwidth streams. With Windows Media, you can start at whatever level is appropriate and then scale up, scale down, or expand the system in whichever direction gets the job done. Windows Media products are building blocks that fit together in a nearly unlimited number of ways.

In the first part of this chapter, we will describe the process that a Windows Media deployment person or consultant might undertake when sizing up a potential installation. You can use this process when determining the scope of your deployment. You do not get a better streaming media system by simply purchasing more equipment. The key to using the scalability of Windows Media to design the right system is knowing your requirements and the full scope of Windows Media capabilities. Deploy the solution that is appropriate now, and that will scale for tomorrow.

The Enterprise Deployment Scenario

A final, working streaming media system is the realization of a vision. As in previous sections of the book, we will start by describing the complete scenario. Then we will spend the rest of the section exploring how a company builds the scenario from the ground up. Again, we will not attempt to describe every possible solution.

This scenario is based on a fictitious company, Fabrikam Transportation, that manufactures mass transportation vehicles such as buses and tram cars. The company is headquartered in Toronto, with important subsidiary facilities in the United States, Mexico, and several countries in Europe.

Keeping the lines of communications open and flowing is vital to the success of the company. Assembly and manufacturing operations in Toronto, Detroit, Stuttgart, and Düsseldorf can move smoothly only if the information is current, complete, and correct—if parts are held up in Detroit, Toronto needs to know that now. The sales and marketing division in New York cannot be held up because of slow network connections to Toronto. E-mail and the telephone provide instant one-to-one communication, and today streaming media provides instant one-to-many communication.

Figure 14.1 shows a simplified topology of the Fabrikam streaming media system. Fabrikam has 15,000 employees and contractors internationally. Streaming media reaches 9,400 desktops. The main data center in Toronto, which is the company's manufacturing center, serves the bulk of the workforce. Multiple remote data centers throughout North America and Europe connect to Toronto through a wide area network (WAN) that uses Asynchronous Transfer Mode (ATM) technology. The remote data centers then serve nearly 100 remote work sites.

Sites that are local to a remote data center enjoy a high-bandwidth connection. Bandwidth available to remote sites varies depending on the type of connection. Medium-bandwidth sites typically connect with DSL; low-bandwidth sites and employees connecting to the corporate network through remote access typically use dial-up or 56 Kbps frame relay connections. Other users connect wirelessly with laptop computers and Pocket PCs.

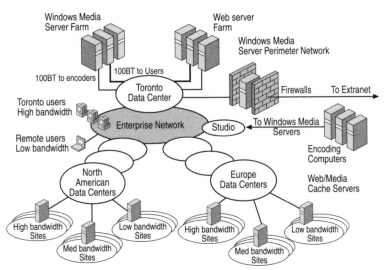

Figure 14.1   The network topology used for streaming media at Fabrikam.

Fabrikam Network Resources

There are three Windows Media servers and three Web servers in the Toronto data center. The two sets of servers are configured with the Network Load Balancing (NLB) service. These server clusters are referred to as the Windows Media and Web server farms. Each server has a 1000 Base-T connection to the data center backbone for providing streaming content to users. Each also has a separate 100 Base-T connection to internal management systems, and the Windows Media servers have 100 Base-T connections for receiving content from live and on-demand encoding computers and production workstations.

A Windows Media server located in the data center perimeter network (also known as the "DMZ") provides streaming content to special users, such as partners and customers, on the Internet. This is referred to as the company's "extranet."

Most end-users view streaming presentations on their desktop computers. Employees without desktop computers connected to the corporate LAN (such as those in the plants, remote sales staff working on laptops, and home users) can view streaming media content on computers, on Windows Media-enabled set-top boxes in resource centers located near manufacturing areas, and in meeting rooms with video projection systems.

The Origin Servers

Designing a streaming media system is an additive process, starting with a core system and building outward as needed. The core of a Windows Media distribution system is a server. The server sits in the center. Content is sent from one or more encoding computers to the server, and content is streamed from the server to one or more client computers.

At Fabrikam, the intranet origin servers are actually server farms that appear to the client as a single Web or Windows Media server. Single servers could be used, but connecting multiple servers together in a cluster using NLB enhances the availability and scalability of the servers.

- Availability means that there are enough servers to handle the load if one should fail. By using NLB, a server can be removed from the farm for maintenance with no system downtime. The only service disruption is to the users who were streaming from the server at the time it was taken offline.

- Scalability means that a server can grow to meet increasing performance demands. Multiple servers that have been configured as a cluster to act as a single server provide a high level of scalability. To further enhance scalability, you can easily add more servers, storage, and processors to the cluster as the need arises. For example, a storage area network (SAN) could be added to increase storage capacity and reduce the load on the servers.

The Web server farm delivers Web content to users' browsers and to other programs, such as Windows Media Player. Web servers are included in a discussion of Windows Media Services because there are many instances in which Web servers are used in conjunction with streaming Windows Media-based content. On-demand PowerPoint presentations and the Media Guide are two examples that will be described later.

A user requests Windows Media-based content using the URL of the cluster, such as rtsp://WMServer/content.wmv. The NLB cluster receives the request and the NLB service uses a statistical mapping algorithm, which is distributed on each server, to determine which server will handle the request. The determination is based on the current load across all servers in the cluster.

By using computers with multiple NICs, the gigabit Ethernet network can be dedicated to servicing client requests. Server management functions are moved from the main network to separate network systems, so that more network resources are dedicated to handling user traffic. A Virtual LAN (VLAN) can be created to logically isolate management functions.

The Windows Media server farm hosts on-demand and broadcast unicast content and multicast streams. To receive unicast content, Toronto-based clients connect directly to the origin servers; clients outside Toronto connect to cache/proxy servers. For more details on how the origin servers are configured, see chapter 17.

The Corporate Network

Clients connected to the main LAN in Toronto enjoy a 100 Mbps Fast Ethernet network. Clients there can stream VHS-quality video directly from the origin servers. Care is taken, however, to make sure the total aggregate bit rate from the origin servers does not overwhelm the network. Most of the time, the total bit rate is moderate. Windows Media server client logs give the company a picture of bandwidth usage. Fabrikam logs show that during business hours, the average streaming media bandwidth usage on the Toronto LAN is less than 15 megabits—roughly 50 clients connected concurrently viewing a 300 Kbps unicast stream. Of course, over a period of a day that can amount to thousands of viewers.

There are situations when unicast connections could exceed the capabilities of the network. For example, an archive of a live broadcast of the CEO announcing the year's profits is timely enough that many users will want to play the stream at the same time. To handle the load, the company sets limits on the server. When the bandwidth limit is reached, the server starts denying client connections.

This method effectively limits load on the network and servers. But it does not limit the frustration of users who cannot receive a stream. Therefore, broadcast content and on-demand content that is expected to receive a high number of concurrent connections will be delivered using multicast streaming to help eliminate network traffic problems. To help manage unicast traffic, the company will employ remote servers.

Remote Networks

Desktop computers at each branch location are also connected to 100 Mbps LANs, which provide more than enough bandwidth to support e-mail and intranet needs within the LANs. Bottlenecks, however, can occur over many of the WAN circuits. Users in New York access a North American data center in Detroit through an ATM network, which provides a high-bandwidth, 25-Mbps connection. European data centers, on the other hand, use a frame relay connection, which provides only 128 Kbps of bandwidth for local users in Stuttgart and London. As you can see, many unicast connections could quickly consume much of the bandwidth in the segments serving the data centers. A frame relay connection could barely handle one stream.

To protect the bandwidth in the WANs, usage must be reserved for critical data exchange, such as sales and production documents. Streaming media is therefore handled by using remote servers with cache/proxy plug-ins and by content management.

Cache/Proxy Servers

Cache and proxy service functions are most often hosted on a single server, called a cache/proxy server. These are computers or devices that intercept and handle client requests made to origin servers. For example, a system can be set up so that, when a client makes a request to stream a file or open a Web page from an origin server, a cache/proxy server that is closer to the client intercepts the request and delivers the content from its cache. By using cache/proxy servers, you can ease the demand on the origin server and the network segments that converge around it. The result is a more efficient use of network resources and bandwidth, and a better user experience because there is likely to be less buffering.

Fabrikam uses cache/proxy servers to help move content closer to users so that the load is taken off of the WAN, the network segments leading up to the origin servers, and the origin severs themselves. End users and clients are often referred to as being at the "edge" of a network because that is where the requests originate; likewise, when cache/proxy servers are used to move content closer to the edge, they are sometimes called "edge servers."

Edge devices and servers are the key components of a decentralized network topology, the type of network topology that is being used for the Fabrikam scenario. A centralized topology with one origin server handling all requests works on small or medium-sized networks. However, on medium or large, complex networks that are made up of network segments of different types and bandwidths, it makes more sense to distribute content through edge servers that cache and proxy content. The alternative would be to upgrade the entire network infrastructure to handle the increased bandwidth demand, which would not be an economical option for Fabrikam at this time.

This decentralized network is called a content delivery network (CDN). Within an enterprise, this type of network is sometimes called an eCDN. Several methods are used to move the content from the origin server to an edge server, and then from the edge server to a client. If the content is a file, it can be cached automatically, or copied in advance of demand. Copying content in anticipation of an end-user request is sometimes called *prestuffing* or *preloading*. If the content is a live stream, it can be split by an edge server. All of these methods are detailed in chapter 20.

Content Management

Managing Windows Media-based content is simple if you have only a handful of files to stream. However, a company that understands the value of communicating with audio and video will, over time, accumulate many hundreds of files that need to be made available online. In addition to streaming audio and video, the company must be able to handle all the different types of content that go into a rich-media production, such as images, text, Web pages, script, and metafiles. And if a decentralized topology is used, the files must be made available on multiple remote edge servers as well as on the origin server.

The CDN system used by Fabrikam does more than decentralize the topology; it includes systems for helping the company manage its on-demand content on the network. There are basically three ways to move content from the origin server to the remote servers:

- Manual distribution. An administrator manually copies the files to remote caches. Obviously, with 100 or more edge devices, this may not be the most effective solution. However, it can be used to quickly copy files to a new server.

- Scheduled distribution. A third-party or custom program is used to automatically copy files according to a schedule. Using scheduled distribution, you can work around time zone differences and prestuff files after business hours when there is low traffic on the WAN.

- Automatic caching. Most cache/proxy solutions use this method. With automatic caching, content is not added to the remote cache until a user requests it. The first time a file is requested, it is played from the origin server and concurrently sent to the cache. Subsequent requests play the file from the cache.

Most CDN systems enable an administrator to use a combination of automatic, manual, and scheduled distribution. For example, you might decide to prestuff a file that you know will receive many plays, such as a quarterly financial report.

Perimeter Network Servers

At Fabrikam, like many enterprises, the data center has a perimeter network that contains Web and Windows Media servers that are accessible to users on the Internet. The perimeter network sits between the corporate network and the Internet. Firewalls surround the perimeter network servers and filter network traffic based on protocols and ports to keep Internet users from gaining unauthorized access to internal intranet computers.

Figure 14.2 shows how the firewalls are used. Internal users can copy files and distribute live streams through the first firewall to the perimeter network Windows Media server. External users can request and play content from the perimeter network server, but are prevented by the second firewall from gaining access to other applications on the server, and by the first firewall from gaining access to the corporate network.

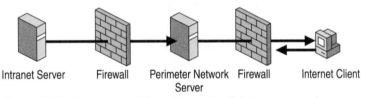

Intranet Server   Firewall   Perimeter Network Firewall   Internet Client
                                   Server

Figure 14.2 Locations of firewalls on the Fabrikam network.

Many firewalls are configured by default to block streaming media packets sent using the UDP protocol. In order for Internet users to stream content, the ports needed for UDP traffic can be opened on the firewall. However, if the ports cannot be opened, Windows Media Player is configured by default to *roll over*, or switch to receiving a stream using the TCP protocol automatically. The TCP protocol and port 80 are used for most Internet traffic.

At Fabrikam, the Windows Media server on the perimeter network enables Internet users to play files, such as maintenance training videos, public financial reports, and marketing information. Authentication and authorization plug-ins are enabled on the server to restrict access to a select group of users who are part of the company's extranet, including partners, dealers, and repair facilities.

Production Workstations

One set of encoding stations is indicated in the topology. In practice, however, live and on-demand content can be delivered to the servers from multiple encoding computers over the corporate network. For example, a remote encoding station can be set up in Stuttgart to encode on-demand content. The content can then be hosted on the Toronto origin servers. Most often, videos are produced in the production facilities of the Media department in Toronto. The department creates most of the live and on-demand content using its studio and editing facilities.

Also, PowerPoint slides can be synchronized to recorded video of a presenter by using Microsoft Producer. The resulting presentation can be packaged into a final on-demand video. These Producer presentations can be recorded and edited by the Media department or in a special mini-studio like the one described in chapter 18. The studio provides users who have little knowledge of video production with the tools to produce their own videos. The finished presentations can then be uploaded to the Web server and Windows Media server for international distribution.

Media Guide Portal

The Media Guide portal is an intranet Web site on which end users can link to live streams, and search for and link to on-demand content. The portal is built on Microsoft SharePoint Portal Server, so it is modular and extensible. In addition to providing a one-stop location for accessing streaming content, the Media Guide portal provides a simple way for users to upload material destined for the Windows Media server. Users can also request production resources and help, and schedule live broadcast time. SharePoint and the Media Guide are described in chapter 16.

Multicast Broadcasting

Multiple users can connect to a single broadcast delivered using multicast streaming, and bandwidth usage is no more than that of one user. Because bandwidth usage is low, producers can offer users a choice of bit rates with little additional impact on network bandwidth. For example, two encoders can be used to record single streams that support different bit rates, such as 100 Kbps and 300 Kbps.

After a live event, producers can use multicast to broadcast an archived file of the event from server-side playlists. The playlists can be set to loop repeatedly so users can tune in and view the event at any time. Again, thousands of users can connect without adversely affecting the available bandwidth on the network. Playlists are described in chapter 11.

Before a company can broadcast using multicast, the entire network must be multicast-enabled. In an enterprise the size of Fabrikam, routers are used to connect large network segments, and on many of the routers multicasting may be disabled by default. Also, many hubs and switches may not be designed to segment multicast traffic and might need to be replaced. Token ring configurations also present barriers to multicast. to address thse issues, Fabrikam studied the network infrastructure to identify and reconfigure devices to handle multicast traffic. On those segments of the network that could not be enabled, unicast delivery was used. Chapter 22 describes how Fabrikam enabled multicast streaming.

Developing the Vision

During this part of the deployment process, needs are identified, ideas are brainstormed, and individuals or groups are tasked with developing a deployment plan.

Defining the Need: Distributing Video

Most company-wide communication was handled in e-mail and through the intranet before there was streaming media at Fabrikam. These systems are both fast and easy to use. The Web sites of individual departments provide anyone in the company quick access to static information in the form of text and graphics. For example, the site belonging to a machine shop in Detroit can be viewed by a sales representative in New York. The representative can locate details of part designs instantly and relay the information to customers.

The other main method of one-to-many communication was videotape. Television was used for training, corporate communications, inter-departmental information sharing, and in many other applications. Text and static graphics have their place, but there are many instances where video can be added to create a more engaging and effective presentation. For example, one can certainly explain how to install a bus engine transmission with text and graphics, but a carefully constructed video—or a video with supporting graphics—can be far more effective.

Videotape, however, has many drawbacks. Duplicating and distributing tapes is slow and expensive, especially compared to sending an e-mail. Managers at Fabrikam saw the intranet as a way to solve the problem. Rather than deal with tapes, why not distribute videos over the network?

A few departments experimented with downloading video files. End users could click a link on a Web page, download files to their computers, and then play them with Windows Media Player. The system worked when audiences were small, but a large number of users attempting to download files could overwhelm the network. The problem with video is its size. A broadcast e-mail message is a tiny percentage of the size of a video file. If the intranet were to be a viable mechanism for distributing video over the network, it was clear that a more robust system was needed.

Fabrikam also had a system in place for delivering live video. Many thousands of dollars were spent wiring the Toronto facility for closed-circuit television and satellite delivery. The system was expensive to maintain, and live television broadcasts required a lot of time and resources to set up. It was difficult to justify a specialized system that was used to deliver live television sporadically to select groups. Every time there was an expansion or change, there was no budget left for rewiring the closed-circuit TV and purchasing more monitors. And without upgrading and maintaining the system, it slowly lost its capability to reach a large number of employees, and was used less and less. If live video were to ever be viable, it would need to reach a large number of employees inexpensively.

Brainstorming

Windows Media provides a robust solution for distributing pre-recorded and live video to Fabrikam employees over the company's existing intranet. The entire Windows Media system is designed around using network resources efficiently and to deliver high-quality video to end users. With streaming media, the infrastructure and equipment are already in place; Windows Media adds value to what is already there. Windows Media would enable the company to distribute video inexpensively, efficiently, and quickly.

Fabrikam planners brainstormed other potential uses for Windows Media. The company makes heavy use of PowerPoint slides to deliver one-to-many messages in groups with live presenters. Fabrikam management was intrigued with Microsoft Producer as a means of making the presentations more widely available. Users could create their presentations, and then use Producer to record them. Then they could publish the presentations to intranet Web sites and a Windows Media server, and anyone in the company with access to a desktop computer could view the presentations on demand.

The security department saw a potential use for streaming media in facilities maintenance and security. The signals from hundreds of security cameras could be encoded and hosted on a secure site. The areas could then be monitored from any number of remote locations. The streams could also be archived, which could eventually eliminate the need for videotape.

The marketing and customer training departments saw the potential for reaching customers over the Internet, via the company's extranet. Material could be produced internally and hosted on a Windows Media server outside the internal network. Marketing material could be aimed at attracting new customers, and training material could provide current customers with the latest safety and maintenance information.

The employee professional development department saw an easy way to train and educate employees at their desktops. Desktop instruction could eliminate much of the need for classroom-based training that required a live instructor, expensive office space, and travel time for employees. Producer could be used to capture lessons, which could then be made available to employees worldwide. Even manufacturing saw the opportunity for using video and Windows Media to study their processes.

Assigning Action Items

In the next phase of the problem-solving process, a system needed to be designed around Windows Media, and an implementation plan formulated. Action items were assigned to two internal groups. The IT department was asked to draw up a network topology that included Windows Media, and to decide how it was to be implemented. The Media department was to make recommendations on how to produce the content.

Once the system was in place, IT would maintain the servers and infrastructure. They would use the Enterprise Deployment Pack for Windows Media Player to package the Player and settings into a simple one-click setup program. Then they would add a section to their Web site from which users could download the Player and obtain setup help.

The groups decided to deploy Windows Media in three stages. At the end of each stage, a fully operational system would be in place. Subsequent stages would add on to what was already there without disrupting the operation of the preceding stage.

The company had several reasons for deploying in stages. First, there was no critical reason for pulling out all the stops and doing a large-scale deployment that would require lots of resources. The current systems were working. There was no reason to stop using them right away or to disrupt their use. Also, the new system was not merely a hardware upgrade. Deployment would affect workflow patterns, schedules, and corporate culture. The Windows Media-based system could be blended in with the current system over a reasonable amount of time.

Second, managers wanted immediate results. They didn't want to wait until the system was completely finished before using Windows Media. This makes sense; completing every area of Windows Media deployment takes time and resources. If deployment begins with the origin servers, there is no need to wait until all of the cache/proxy servers are configured before the company can start streaming in Toronto. Also, there were certain points during deployment when slowdowns could occur, such as when configuring routers and switches to pass multicast packets. The process of configuring the infrastructure could take place during and after the time when on-demand streaming was being implemented.

Third, IT knew from experience that unexpected things could happen. A phased approach would make it easier for IT to locate trouble spots. Rather than build the entire system and then test it, it made more sense for them to build, test, and release continuously as they proceeded—making sure a setup was successful before adding on to it.

Developing the Implementation Plan

In this part of the deployment process, the IT and Media departments divide the deployment into tasks and define the phases. Even if your deployment is comparatively simple, you should go through a similar process to make sure you have considered every angle.

The original objective of the Windows Media deployment was to replace tape distribution and enable one-to-many broadcasting. The system that the IT and Media departments designed achieved those objectives. It also anticipated future objectives that did not incur additional cost in material and time. For example, a Windows Media server is required to do broadcasting. For no extra cost, the server also supports server-side playlists, streaming over a wireless network, and authorization and authentication.

Phases of Development

Fabrikam managers decided to divide deployment into three phases. At the end of each of the following phases a complete, working system will be in place:

- Phase I: Base system. Users in Toronto will be able to create and stream on-demand content, and they can locate content with the Media Guide portal site.

- Phase II: Extended system. Users worldwide will be able to stream on-demand content. Live unicast broadcasting will be available on a limited, local basis.

- Phase III: Enhanced system. Users worldwide will be able to stream broadcast content; a kick-off series of training programs will be available on-demand; and usage reports and a user feedback system will be in place.

At the end of the last phase, the system will be fully operational according to the original plan. In addition, hundreds of popular videotapes will be available online, as well as the kick-off training series.

In your plan, you may want to start with a pilot phase in which you build and test representative samples of the full deployment. For example, you could build one production workstation and provide streaming media to a subset of the entire network. In this way, you could gather baseline information and receive useful feedback from end users. The pilot program would enable technical support personnel to learn about the system before they attempt to answer user questions, and would enable IT personnel to test configurations before opening up the system companywide. A pilot program can help you manage risks and ultimately help ensure success with less cost. In this scenario, however, Fabrikam jumps ahead to full deployment.

Establishing a Timeline

Figure 14.3 shows the proposed timeline for completion of Fabrikam's streaming media deployment.

Because our focus is on Windows Media deployment, we will not go into system planning in depth. A complete deployment plan would require more detail in the schedule, and of course an understanding of the availability of personnel, resources, and budget. A deployment such as the one we are describing could run anywhere from three months to two years, depending on available resources. You would also have to include requirements, content identification and prioritization, and other business-specific needs, and it would follow the basic deployment process: gathering requirements, designing, testing, building a pilot, deploying, operating the system, and gathering usage data for evaluation.

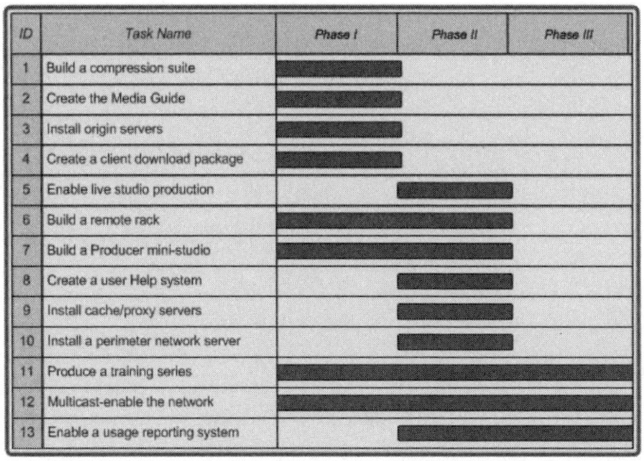

ID	Task Name	Phase I	Phase II	Phase III
1	Build a compression suite	████		
2	Create the Media Guide	████		
3	Install origin servers	████		
4	Create a client download package	████		
5	Enable live studio production		████	
6	Build a remote rack	████████		
7	Build a Producer mini-studio	████████		
8	Create a user Help system		████	
9	Install cache/proxy servers		████	
10	Install a perimeter network server		████	
11	Produce a training series	████████████		
12	Multicast-enable the network	████████████		
13	Enable a usage reporting system		████████	

Figure 14.3   A timeline helps schedule deployment tasks.

The Fabrikam timeline consists of the following tasks:

- Build a compression suite. A production facility for creating and converting audio and video content to Windows Media files. The suite integrates with the existing facility that handles production and post-production of videos.

- Create the Media Guide. A Web site for users to locate and access Windows Media-based content.

- Install origin servers. The Windows Media server farm that originates the distribution of content.

- Create a client download package. Users can download the package and install Windows Media Player.

- Enable live studio production. Upgrading an existing facility for live broadcasting over the intranet.

- Build a remote rack. A portable equipment rack used for encoding on location.

- Build a Producer mini-studio. A small production facility intended for use by any employee to record and edit presentations for on-demand delivery.

- Create a user Help system. A system to explain how to use the Producer mini-studio.

- Install cache/proxy servers. The system of servers used to decentralize the distribution of Web and Windows Media-based content.

- Install a perimeter network server. The Windows Media server from which users on the company's extranet can stream content.

- Produce a training series. A series of training videos intended to kick-off the new streaming media system.

- Enable multicasting on the network. The ability to deliver multicast streams where possible throughout the corporate network.

- Enable a usage reporting system. A system that combines logging data from all servers and creates reports showing client usage.

As you can see in the timeline, several of the tasks overlap. At the same time that the Media Guide, compression suite, and origin server are to be deployed, work is to begin on the Producer mini-studio, the training series, and making sure all routers in the company are multicast-enabled. Also, development of a usage tracking system would be started during the second phase.

The tasks identified on the chart were divided between the Media and IT departments, both of which developed plans for completion of their portions. Representatives of both departments planned to meet regularly to make sure the deployments were coordinated.

The Media Department Plan

The Media department will provide support for content creation and the Media Guide, and producers in the department intend to work with the training department to create the training series.

Planning for Content Creation

The Media department will provide content creation support for the streaming media system. Their primary tasks were to design a system for transitioning away from videotape and to provide support for live production. The initial design addressed those basic requirements. It consists of a workstation for encoding on-demand content, and four computers dedicated for live encoding, which will be located in the Media department's small studio.

The design team knows that the basic systems will not be enough. They know how important PowerPoint presentations are for communication, and they know that users can make their presentations available to a wider audience with Microsoft Producer. They also know employees want to originate live broadcasts from more locations than the Media department's studio. So with all this in mind, the Media department designers came up with five solutions:

Compression Suite

In phase I of the deployment plan, a compression suite will be built. The suite will be located in the Media department and operated by an employee of the department who has expertise in audio and video production, computer-based editing, and sound design. The suite will be integrated with the department's professional production environment. The equipment and wiring used in the suite will be broadcast quality. Broadcast-quality equipment and infrastructure not only result in higher-quality sounds and pictures, but are designed for durability.

Live Studio Production

In phase II of the deployment plan, two encoding computers will be added to the equipment rack in the Media department's studio control room. The encoders can be configured to provide a number of concurrent live streams. The streams can provide multiple bit rates, fault tolerance, or a combination of both. For example, a typical configuration will provide two bit rates, such as 56 Kbps and 300 Kbps, and a backup for each. Users will be able to connect to either stream through the Windows Media server. If an encoder stops working, the publishing point on the server will automatically roll over to the backup stream and the Player will continue with only a momentary pause for buffering.

Remote Rack

In phase II of the deployment plan, a portable system will be built that includes all the equipment needed to encode live presentations and events. The system consists of various hardware devices mounted and wired in a short equipment rack contained in a large shipping case. The rack contains all of the equipment necessary to capture audio and video and encode it to a live stream. The case can be shipped to remote sites pre-wired. All the production team will have to do is plug in one or more cameras and microphones, and then connect the rack to AC power and the corporate network.

Producer Mini-studio

In phase II of the deployment plan, a mini-studio will be completed that employees can use to record Producer presentations. Rather than take the time to give the presentations multiple times to multiple groups, employees can create presentations and record them in the self-service studio. Then individuals or groups can stream the recorded presentation. The Media department decided a small investment in a Producer production studio up front would enable employees to make better use of their time, therefore saving the company money in the long run.

User Information

In phase II of the deployment plan, documentation will be created that gives users information about how to use the Producer mini-studio. The information will be posted in the studio. The same information will be available online on the Media Guide site.

Planning for the Media Guide Site

The Media Guide Web site will be the main portal that Fabrikam employees use to access the rich store of on-demand and live content available to them. The Media department was tasked with developing and maintaining the site. Initially, the site will be developed by the department's Web design team with input from content producers. Once online, the site will be updated and maintained by members of the production scheduling team. Because the site will be run by people who are not trained Web designers, it needs to be easy to update and require low maintenance.

The Media Guide will include the following minimum functionality:

- On-demand content list, search, and link. Several ways for users to locate on-demand content.

- Live content calendar, search, and link. Several ways for users to locate broadcasts.

- Announcements. Timely information regarding important video programs.

- Information and help. How to use the site and locate content.

- Production requests. A system for requesting production resources.

- Content upload. A system for adding content to the site.

- Windows Media Player download package. A way for users to download and install the correct version of Windows Media Player.

The Web designers decided a database-driven site would be the best way to go. They chose Microsoft SharePoint Portal Server to provide the structure for the site. A SharePoint Portal site is easy to develop and change, and will provide all the functionality they anticipate needing. As the database grows and the team discovers new needs, the Web team can either create a custom site or purchase a third-party solution.

Planning for the Training Series

Fabrikam offers its employees free training courses. The training department decided to work with the Media department to record many of the courses and offer them online. Then employees could take online courses at any time, and the training department could reserve instructors and classroom space for those situations that required live instruction, such as CPR training.

As a pilot project, the training department identified a course on shop floor safety, which it will turn into a series of four lessons, each lasting about 25 minutes. Employees can sign up for the course online and immediately begin with lesson one. At the completion of the course, employees will take a quiz and fill out a short survey to prove that they went through all the material. If they complete the course successfully, the result would be added to their employee records.

The training and Media departments will work together to shoot and edit a videotape, and then convert the tape into synchronized presentations with Producer. The two departments will take what they learned from the process and develop a streamlined system for converting more courses to Producer presentations.

In addition to creating the pilot series, the training department will work with the Web designers to create an online training sub-portal site of the Media Guide site. Employees will be able to sign up for a course and then view it using the sub-portal site.

The IT Department Plan

The IT department will integrate Windows Media Services into the current intranet infrastructure, and then maintain the system. Their tasks consist of deploying the origin servers, deploying cache/proxy servers, enabling routers and switches for multicast, developing a client download package, and developing a system for usage reporting. These tasks are very broad. Within each task is potentially one or more layers of subtasks, which will be assigned to various managers in the department. For example, the task of deploying cache/proxy servers includes subtasks such as selecting and ordering the hardware and coordinating with remote IT personnel.

Origin Servers

In phase I of the deployment plan, the IT department will configure and install the Windows Media server farm in the Toronto data center. The IT department will purchase the computers and any supporting hardware, and then configure them with Windows Media Services and the NLB service. They will do all configuration on their test bench before installing the computers in a rack in the data center.

Installing Windows Server 2003, Enterprise Edition, and Windows Media Services is fairly straightforward. That part should take a technician only a few hours. However, keeping the computers on the bench will give them a chance to try out features and test scenarios before putting the server farm online. For example, they can run Windows Media Load Simulator to emulate the effect of multiple clients connecting to a server.

Once in place, the server farm will be administered remotely from the data center control room using Microsoft Management Console (MMC). They also plan to install Windows Media Services Administrator for the Web and give certain people in the Media department permission to administer the server and add files. For example, the production assistants who work with the Media Guide will be able to create and configure publishing points for broadcasts and copy Windows Media files to the server.

Client Download Packages

In phase I of the deployment, the IT department will create a custom download package for Windows Media Player. Every employee in the company will then be required to install the package before they can play company content. The package will ensure that everyone in the company has the same version of the Player, and that it is configured properly. For example, Stuttgart users will install a special download package that properly configures Windows Media Player to access content from the Stuttgart servers. Managers may decide to turn off features that corporate users won't need. The primary location from which users can download the package will be the Media Guide site.

Cache/proxy Servers

In phase II of the deployment plan, the IT department will work with their subsidiaries to install cache/proxy servers in nearly 100 remote sites in North America and Europe. Lessons learned during the installation of the Toronto servers will be applied to the installation.

An administration and content management system will also be installed. The system will enable IT personnel in Toronto to administer the remote servers, manage the content on them, and eventually gather usage data. The content management part of the system will enable personnel to view the content that is on the servers, and then add to or remove content. For example, they will be able to prestuff files and remove dated material.

The IT department will also create and distribute configuration files (commonly referred to as Pac files) to all end users. The files automatically configure proxy settings in Internet Explorer, so the browsers send URL requests through the appropriate proxy servers.

After the cache/proxy servers are in place, on-demand content will be available to every desktop in the company. Live broadcasting will also be available on a small scale.

Perimeter Network Server

Also during phase II, a Windows Media server will be installed on the company's perimeter network located in the data center. The server will be configured similarly to the origin servers, except it will not use the NLB service. Because the server will be exposed to the Internet, it will host its own content and operate in isolation from the intranet servers.

Multicast-enabled Network

At the end of phase III of the deployment, the routers, switches, and other devices on the worldwide corporate network will be enabled to pass multicast packets. Three months have been allocated for this task in order to provide small teams of technicians in each subsidiary enough time to check each network segment. In a system as large as Fabrikam's, it is not unusual to find hundreds of routers and switches located in all points of an enterprise. Hubs and switches cannot segment multicast traffic. Many of these devices may need to be replaced. Routers simply need to be checked to make sure multicasting functionality is enabled.

After all devices have been enabled to pass multicast traffic, multicast broadcasting will reach most points of the company. For areas of the network that cannot be multicast enabled, end users can receive a unicast stream from the cache/proxy server. The cache/proxy server used by Fabrikam will include the ability to split live streams. This means that the server can receive one unicast stream from the origin server, and then split it among multiple local clients.

Usage Reporting

During phase III of the deployment, a system will be developed that collects usage information and creates reports. This information can be used by various groups to plan future use of the streaming media system. For example, the training department might receive reports showing the number of users who actually streamed course content, which courses they were selecting, and for how long they played the presentation. This information could give them a better idea of how to design courses. IT planners could study usage reports to gauge network bandwidth usage. Media guide production assistants could use the reports to better schedule live broadcasts and to inform producers and potential clients.

During the final month of the deployment, IT developers will look at a number of solutions, including specialized, third-party solutions that automatically retrieve logging data from any number of servers, compile the information, and then create a variety of reports.

Implementation Plan Summary

In this chapter, we provided a context for the high-level implementation tasks so that you would see how a company might organize their needs and ideas. A Windows Media deployment follows the same process as any other deployment or project. Every deployment starts with a need; the need drives a vision; the vision becomes the solution; the solution drives the plan; and the plan drives the deployment process.

In the rest of this section, we will follow the company plan to deploy, test, and use the Windows Media streaming media system.

Phase I. Base system

Task	Subtask	Groups
Content creation	Build compression suite.	Media
	Begin encoding selected, archived videotape programs.	Media
Portal development	Develop and test Media Guide using SharePoint Portal Server.	Media
	Test and release.	Media
	Create client download package.	IT
Server deployment	Configure and test the Windows Media server farm on test bench.	IT
	Locate and install servers in data center.	IT
	Configure servers remotely.	IT
	Test and release.	IT

Phase II. Extended system

Task	Subtask	Groups
Live studio production	Configure existing studio for live production.	Media
	Install two live encoding computers and a remote control computer in studio control room.	Media
	Test and deploy.	Media
Remote encoding rack	Build, test, and deploy.	Media
Producer mini-studio	Locate and configure office space for mini-studio.	Media
	Install equipment.	Media
	Test and deploy.	Media
	Create user Help information.	Media
Cache/proxy servers	Install and configure cache/proxy servers.	IT
	Initiate content management system.	IT
	Install and configure a Windows Media server in the perimeter network.	IT
	Test and release.	IT

Phase III. Enhanced system

Task	Subtask	Groups
Interactive online training series	Produce a kick-off series, created using Producer.	Media, Professional development group
	Create a sub-portal site for the training programs.	Media, Professional development group
	Test and deploy.	Media, Professional development group
Multicast-enabled network	Upgrade and configure routers, switches, and hubs.	IT
	Test multicast reception in all segments of the network.	IT
	Plan and deploy large-scale test broadcast.	IT, Media
Usage reporting and feedback	Portal team works with IT to monitor usage and identify problems.	IT, Media
	Portal team and IT work on a report template for logs.	IT, Media
	Portal site adds feedback feature.	IT, Media
	Feedback information and identified problems are sent to IT user help group.	IT, Media

In the next chapter, the compression suite is designed, built, and tested. Then production begins.

15

Phase I: Content Creation

In this chapter, we see how Fabrikam builds a compression suite. This will be the primary workstation used in the company for capturing and encoding audio and video content to Windows Media files. At the center of the suite are two encoding computers. The computers can be used for live encoding. However, the suite is primarily designed for creating and working with on-demand content: capturing audio and video from a source, such as tape, and encoding it to Windows Media files.

The only difference between live and on-demand encoding is the destination of the stream. With live encoding, the stream is sent over a network; with on-demand the stream goes to a storage device. However, the production process behind the two streams is different. With live production, processes are geared toward immediacy, efficiency, and reliability: redundant encoding machines are used to provide fault tolerance, and there is more pressure to make everything happen correctly once in real time. With on-demand content, processes can be geared for production and technical quality. Without a real-time source, producers can spend time editing and processing the video. The compression suite enables the producer or technician to focus on creating a quality on-demand product.

Designing the Compression Suite

The room that houses the compression suite will be treated with sound absorption material to eliminate some of the sound problems introduced by hard walls. The room will also be quieter than a typical office or control room. Equipment will be enclosed in sound-treated equipment racks and noise from air vents will be reduced. Professional audio speakers and computer monitors will be used so that the producer or technician can judge the true sound of an audio track and the true color of a video. In short, the compression suite is designed so a professional production person can optimize capture and compression settings for a high-quality encoded product.

Figure 15.1 shows the components of the compression suite, which will be described in detail later in the chapter.

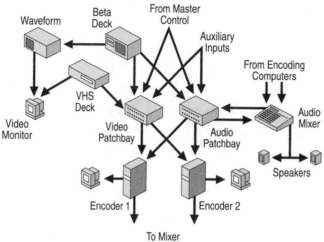

Figure 15.1   The Fabrikam compression suite.

Audio and video patch bays will allow the editor or sound designer to route signals from a number of sources into either or both encoding computers. The sources include professional Digital Betacam and S-VHS video cassette recorders (VCRs) located in the suite, a line from the Media department's Master Control, and local auxiliary inputs into which any source can be connected. The audio from the computers is routed into the monitor section of the mixer, which feeds two small professional speakers.

Encoding Considerations

There are advantages to encoding from a file to a file over encoding from a live source to a file, and the compression suite is designed with those advantages in mind. When you encode from a live source, your computer must convert the audio and video signals, compress the streams, and encode them to Windows Media Format in real time. If you are encoding to a file, the computer must also handle writing to disk in real time. Live encoding, therefore, requires fast CPUs, 256 MB of RAM or more, a fast internal bus that can transfer large amounts of data quickly, and a storage system capable of fast write speeds for long durations.

When encoding from file to file, however, Windows Media Encoder 9 Series takes as long as necessary given the available system resources. In other words, processing time is not related to the playback time of a digital media file when you encode from a file. For example, a source file that plays in five minutes can take ten minutes to encode on a very slow computer, or only one minute on a very fast computer.

With live encoding, a five-minute videotape or live presentation takes exactly five minutes to encode. As you can imagine, real-time encoding runs into problems when more processing power is needed than a computer is capable of providing. If the processing power of the computer cannot keep up with the demands of encoding a live source, Windows Media Encoder automatically reduces the encoding quality. If reducing the quality isn't enough, the encoder drops frames, skipping over material it does not have the processing power to handle.

This also applies to encoding a live stream from a file. Whenever real-time processing is required, the encoder will reduce quality if the processor cannot keep up. Therefore, you will generally get higher quality when you encode from a file to another file. When you encode from a file, you can also take advantage of two-pass encoding, in which a file is processed twice in order to optimize the quality.

With quality and computer power in mind, there are two ways to approach encoding on-demand content: direct real-time encoding and two-step encoding. Each method is described below.

Direct Real-time Encoding

You can encode from a real-time source, such as a live event or videotape. Though real-time encoding can result in lower quality, there are situations when this is the most efficient and appropriate way to encode.

While encoding in real time, you should monitor the status of the encoding computer by watching the CPU and memory usage percentage in the Performance Monitor. If you notice high CPU or memory usage and a degradation of quality while encoding from a tape, you can rewind the tape and encode the video again with lower compression settings, such as a smaller frame size or lower frame rate.

You can also configure the encoder to temporarily store content as it is being captured, and then automatically compress and encode the content when the capture is finished. Using this method, the quality of the encoded file is less likely to be adversely affected by an overburdened computer, because the CPU-intensive processes of capturing and encoding are performed at different times.

Another problem with direct encoding is that not all editing programs can work with Windows Media files. (Microsoft Producer, Sonic Foundry Vegas Video, and Adobe Premiere are three examples of programs that can work directly with Windows Media files.) Simple editing is often necessary when encoding from a real-time source in order to remove unwanted material from the beginning and end of a file.

Two-step Encoding

The encoding process can also be broken into two steps. First, the video is captured as an uncompressed AVI file. Then the uncompressed file is encoded with the final settings. After the final file is encoded and checked for quality, the original can be deleted.

The reason for encoding in two steps is to optimize quality by not requiring the processor to compress the digital media in real time. The compression process requires the most computation. By doing each process separately, computer resources are used more efficiently, resulting in a higher-quality final product. The two-step method should be used if content contains high motion or detail, is being encoded at a high bit rate, the CPU or memory utilization is peaked, or you simply want the best quality.

If you need to edit or process the video by using a program that does not import Windows Media files, capture the content in real time as an uncompressed AVI file, which most programs do support. Then encode a Windows Media file from the edited AVI file.

Finding a Room for the Compression Suite

The first step in building a compression suite is to locate an appropriate space to house the equipment and operator. The room must first provide a good environment for sound. If you encode only video, you could locate encoding computers in a busy cubicle. A separate room allows you to isolate the sound so extraneous background noise from air conditioners, group chatter, and traffic don't interfere with the sound from the video. Conversely, the suite should provide some isolation of the video sound from people working in offices and meeting rooms.

In addition to isolating sound, the room should be sonically "dead," which means there are no excessive standing waves. Basically, standing waves occur in a room when sounds at certain frequencies get trapped between hard walls and start resonating, creating a very fast echo or delay. You can eliminate most standing waves in the upper frequency range with soft and irregular surfaces, such as carpeting and acoustic tile.

To soften the hard walls, you can apply sound absorption panels, such as those from Markertek and the Sonex panels from Illbruck. Figure 15.2 shows an example. Sound absorption panels consist of a flexible foam material that is fairly inexpensive and easy to apply. You can use an adhesive or simply nail it up.

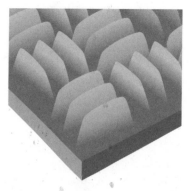

Figure 15.2 Sound absorption panels are used in the compression suite.

Fabrikam decided to locate the suite in one of the rooms previously used for off-line video editing. The room has all the features they are looking for, with enough space for one operator and the equipment, which takes up about as much space as the VCRs and edit controller did previously. Figure 15.3 shows the layout of the room and the location of the furniture and equipment.

The room is the size of a small office, 8 ½ by 12 feet. They apply sound panels to the walls behind the technician and adjacent to the door. They also apply small sections of paneling above the desk.

The compression suite uses standard, adjustable-height office tables. A 44-inch high equipment rack sits on the floor to the right of the technician, and the encoding computers are housed in a wheeled enclosure located under the desk on the left.

The video equipment fits into a standard equipment rack that accepts 19-inch rack-mountable components. To reduce equipment noise, detachable doors are added to the front and back of the unit, and the inside of the rack is lined with sound panels. Fabrikam also creates an enclosure for the computers to reduce the noise from the fans and drives. The enclosure has front and back doors and sound treatment on the inside walls.

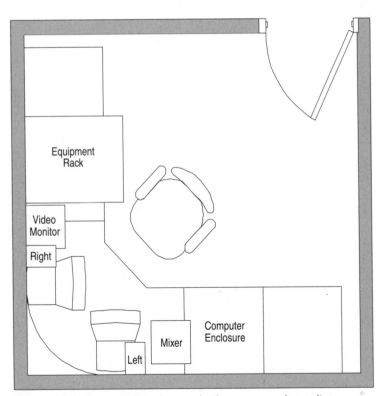

Figure 15.3 Layout of equipment in the compression suite.

Installing the Hardware

The Media department chooses hardware that complements the quality standard of the facility. Years ago, the department made the decision to go with professional, broadcast-standard equipment and infrastructure throughout. It was an expensive decision, but the company has been happy with the choice.

If you or your company have considered building a video production department, you have probably gone through the process of deciding what is too much, and what is not enough. Many companies begin by purchasing low-quality consumer equipment, and then later regret it. They saved money initially, but down the road they realized that they really did get what they paid for.

Consumer-grade equipment has a limited number of features because it is simplified for users with little knowledge of and experience with video production. Broadcast-grade equipment, on the other hand, is designed to provide experienced users with a rich set of features and controls. For example, a broadcast camcorder enables the user to manually control most video functions in order to fine-tune a high-quality image. Consumer-grade equipment is also not usually as rugged and durable as broadcast-grade equipment.

Fabrikam, like many other companies, invested in inexpensive S-VHS consumer equipment initially. Then, after realizing the value of video in corporate communications, they decided the investment in a higher-quality system was worth the price. They wanted the same level of production and technical quality they had in their other communications media, like print and signage. The compression suite will be integrated with the department's professional production environment.

Setting up the Equipment Rack

The rack chosen by Fabrikam is roughly half the height of a standard equipment rack. The outside dimensions are 43.5 inches by 23 inches, and it is 30.5 inches deep. The front door has smoked plexiglas, so the technician can watch the machines with the door closed.

They will install the following equipment in the rack:

Digital Betacam VCR

A professional-grade VCR that is used in the broadcast and video production industry, and is the standard video recorder used in the Media department. All video produced before the mid-nineties was recorded using the older Betacam format. When Digital Betacam became widely available, the department upgraded all machines, and now most production is shot and edited using this format. Note that the older non-digital tapes will play in the digital VCRs.

You may have standardized on a different tape format, such as MiniDV or an S-VHS format. Whatever the case, the machines you install in the suite should accommodate the formats you are using.

S-VHS VCR

The S-VHS format is most often used for consumer recording. However, the company uses the format as a distribution medium. Video is edited and archived at the highest quality, Digital Betacam, and then copied to S-VHS tapes. When a taped program is encoded, the Digital Betacam master tape is used first if available. The S-VHS VCR is most often used to encode a video shot by an employee outside the Media department.

Waveform Monitor

The waveform monitor enables an operator to adjust the video output of the Digital Betacam to video standards when playing back an analog tape, or when capturing from the composite video outputs. There is no point in connecting the waveform monitor to the S-VHS VCR because it has no output adjustments.

The monitor provides two views of a video signal that a technician can display separately on the monitor screen: the waveform view and vectorscope view. The waveform view shows the video frame as a graph, with the bright areas appearing near the top and darker areas near the bottom. The technician adjusts the video level and setup controls to optimize the light and dark areas of the picture using the waveform as the reference. The vectorscope display shows the relationships of the colors in the video frame. The technician adjusts the phase or hue controls and the color level or intensity using the vectorscope as the reference.

Video Patch Bay

Enables the technician to route video signals from various sources to the encoding computers. A patch bay consists of two rows of connectors: the top row is normally outputs; the bottom row provides inputs. A short video cable, called a patch cord, connects an output to an input.

In the compression suite, the outputs consist of the two VCRs, two trunk lines to the patch bay in the studio control room, and an auxiliary output. The trunk lines are used to feed signals from VCRs or the video switcher in the studio. For example, an interview can be recorded live in the studio control room and patched through to an encoding computer in the compression suite, where it can be encoded to a file. The auxiliary output is an open connector in the suite that can be used to connect extra equipment. For example, a camcorder can be connected to the encoding computers through the auxiliary output.

Audio Patch Bay

Like the video patch bay, it enables the technician to route audio sources to the encoding computers. The audio patch bay provides identical connections to the video patch bay. The only additional connections are inputs to and outputs from the audio mixer.

Blank Panels

The bottom of the rack includes an empty space that can be used for expansion. The space could contain more sources such as a MiniDV deck, or processing gear such as an audio limiter/compressor to keep audio levels constant. The space is filled with blank panels to help reduce equipment noise.

Setting up the Computer Enclosure

The enclosure will be a simple plywood box with wheels. The Media department leverages the Fabrikam facilities woodworking shop to build the box. The alternative to a plywood box would be another equipment rack that contained rack-mounted computers. In this scenario, however, Fabrikam will use standard computers that are not designed for rack mounting.

The enclosure contains two identical encoding computers with the following specifications:

- Computers. Dual processors rated at 2-GHz or better, 256 MB of RAM, and 80 GB or larger hard drive. The hard drive must be capable of a sustained data writing speed that is at least equal to that of the highest bit rate at which video will be captured. The internal bus speed must also be fast enough to handle the throughput. For uncompressed video, the rate is about 27 Mbps.

- Video capture card. A video capture card, such as one from the Viewcast Osprey 500 series or a Winnov Videum card, will be used to capture audio and video. The card must provide a variety of input and output options, such as professional SDI digital video, composite video, and balanced audio connections.

- IEEE 1394 card. With this card, digital media and control data can be transferred to and from devices, such as digital camcorders, that support the IEEE 1394 standard. Sometimes called FireWire, this external bus standard supports a data transfer rate of up to 400 Mbps. An alternative to using IEEE 1394 cards is using a device that employs USB 2.0 technology for captures.

- Network Interface Card (NIC). Connects the computers to the corporate network. Full duplex, 100 BT NICs will be used to provide a data rate high enough to support transfers of large amounts of data, such as uncompressed AVI files.

■   CD/DVD burner. CDs and DVDs can be created for archiving projects and large files. These media provide an inexpensive, robust, and easy way to archive large digital media files. Also, their small size makes them easy to store. The company also plans to look into large-scale permanent Digital Asset Management systems, such as the solution from Bulldog Group. But for the moment, CDs and DVDs offer a good short-term solution.

Setting up the Desktop

The desktop is raised slightly to accommodate the computer enclosure. Besides a keyboard, mouse, and computer switcher to switch keyboard and mouse between the two computers, the following equipment sits on or above the desktop area:

■   Mixer. The compression suite uses a small 8-input, stereo mixer to monitor encoding computers. A source can also be patched into the mixer if additional audio level control is needed. For example, the audio on a poorly recorded tape might need to be boosted or equalized. Companies that make small mixers include Mackie, Tascam, and Behringer. Figure 15.4 shows a typical small mixer.

Figure 15.4   A small audio mixer is used in the compression suite.

■   Speakers. Two small speakers will be mounted on the wall on either side of the technician. Fabrikam will use small, professional-quality speakers, such as those from KRK, JBL, and Tannoy. They will also choose speakers that are powered, meaning the final amplifier that powers each speaker is built into the speaker enclosure. With powered speakers, the line-level monitor output from the mixer can feed the speakers directly. If unpowered speakers were used, they would need an additional power amplifier between the mixer and the speakers.

- Speaker-mounting hardware. Mounts the speakers directly to the wall and provides a way to aim the speakers. The hardware is available from a number of manufacturers.

- 20" computer monitos. A high-resolution monitor with reliable color reproduction. As with the audio monitor, the video monitor serves as the reference.

- Video monitor. A small, 9-inch monitor with a switchable input. The output of the Digital Betacam or S-VHS VCR can be viewed directly on the monitor.

Installing Software for the Compression Suite

Both computers will run Microsoft Windows XP Professional, with as many of the background processes and graphics-intensive options as possible turned off—in other words, a plain, blue background with classic Windows display settings and only those processes left running that are required for encoding, as shown in figure 15.5. Programs such as screen savers, Web services, antivirus programs, computer management systems, and instant messengers require processing cycles that can be used for encoding. Also, turn off file sharing while capturing to conserve disk bandwidth.

You should not turn off programs that are needed for security or required by company policy, but the objective is to have as much processing power and memory as possible dedicated to capturing and encoding. The display color quality should be set to 24 or 32 bits so the highest-quality image is reproduced on the screen.

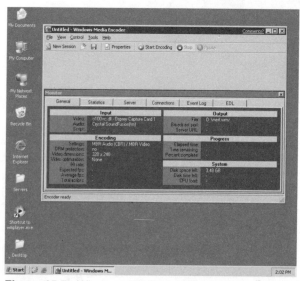

Figure 15.5 Windows XP Professional with nonessential features turned off.

The Fabrikam staff will install the following programs on the computers:

- Windows Media Encoder 9 Series. This is the encoding software used to create Windows Media files from a live source or another file. The encoder installation also includes a number of useful tools and utilities.

- Video editor. A program that supports direct editing and rendering of Windows Media files. An editing program will enable a technician or producer to edit files or captured digital media into a final form. Several programs include a variety of features and enhancements, such as titling and transition effects. With Producer, Vegas Video, and Premiere, for example, Windows Media files can be added to an editing project and mixed with other supported formats, and effects and transitions can be applied. Then the project can be rendered as a final Windows Media file.

- Digital audio workstation. A program such as Sonic Foundry Sound Forge or Syntrillium Software Cool Edit. With a digital audio workstation, a technician can perform detailed audio editing and processing. The program should support Windows Media files.

- Microsoft Producer. A program that enables PowerPoint presentations to be synchronized with video and audio. A final presentation can then be published to a Web server or Windows Media server. The Producer mini-studio that will be built in the second phase is where users can record themselves giving the presentation. The compression suite can be used to edit, synchronize PowerPoint slides, and create the final presentation.

- Video capture program. Typically this is included with the installation of the video capture card software. The Microsoft programs Windows Media 9 Capture and Amcap may be included with a capture card driver. The programs can be used to capture uncompressed audio and video to an AVI file.

Building and Wiring the Compression Suite

After the hardware is installed, we can wire the components. We will look at the professional connectors and cable used to connect inputs and outputs, and provide an overview of the wiring tasks.

Audio Cables and Connectors

The standards used for analog audio inputs and outputs are different for professional and consumer equipment. Professional audio equipment often uses *balanced* connections;

consumer equipment uses *unbalanced* connections. Standard signal levels and other audio characteristics also vary for each type.

We won't go into all the details of audio circuits here. Suffice it to say, when connecting devices, a balanced circuit has three connections (high, low, and ground), and an unbalanced circuit has two connections (high and ground.) If a connection is made between a balanced input and a balanced output, or unbalanced input and output, the signal levels and audio characteristics will usually match, and the audio signal will be optimized. If a connection must be made between an unbalanced and balanced input or output, a device that matches the level and audio characteristics, such as a matching transformer, can be inserted.

In the case of the compression suite Fabrikam is building, all the equipment in the chain provides professional balanced connections, except for the consumer S-VHS VCR. To solve that problem, they will route the audio through the mixer, which accepts both types of inputs.

Balanced audio is routed by using an audio cable with two wires surrounded by a wire sleeve called a shield. The high and low signals are connected to the wires, and the ground is connected to the shield. Balanced connections typically use an XLR connector. The XLR connector and other connectors are pictured in the port and connector sidebar in chapter 2.

Unbalanced audio is routed using an audio cable with one wire and a shield, and typically use RCA, quarter-inch, or eighth-inch connectors. There are quarter-inch and eighth-inch connectors that can support three internal connections, called tip-ring-sleeve (TRS) connectors, that can support three internal connections. One connection is made to the tip of the connector, another to a ring just below the tip, and a third to the sleeve below the ring. TRS connectors can be used for a balanced line, but in computers they are more often used to carry a stereo signal, where the tip is the left signal, the ring is the right, and the sleeve is common.

The shield on an audio cable is connected to ground in an audio device, which is usually the metal chassis or shield surrounding the electronic components. The chassis is then connected to the ground connector on the AC line, which ultimately connects to a metal pipe or long metal stake driven into the ground. Grounding is very important in audio circuits for preventing external electrical fields from interfering with the low-voltage audio signal.

Video Cables and Connectors

Shielding is even more necessary with video signals. Video signals are routed through a coaxial cable that can contain several layers of shielding. The video coaxial cable for carrying standard composite video has one wire surrounded by shielding. Cables used for carrying other types of video signals, such as S-video and IEEE 1394 data, can contain multiple wires with shielding. Video production facilities typically standardize on a particular type of video signal to make video routing easier.

The Media department has chosen the NTSC standard for composite video. Composite video consists of one analog signal that is a composite of the red, green, and blue components of a video image, and the synchronization pulses that a video monitor or television uses to display the image. NTSC is the standard system used in North America and some other countries. Other standards used in the world are PAL and SECAM. (For more information about video standards, see chapter 2.)

Even though the department has standardized on composite video for its routing system, connections can still be made directly using other types of video. The video capture card the Media department uses will be able to input various types of video. For example, a technician can connect a digital camcorder directly to the card using the IEEE 1394 digital connector.

The BNC connector is the professional connector for composite analog. It is also used for SDI video, which is the standard in broadcast digital video. A Digital Betacam deck can be connected directly to the capture card with the SDI connector, providing the most direct—and therefore the highest-quality—transfer of video. RCA connectors are often used instead of BNC connectors for composite video on consumer-grade equipment. However, many analog devices, including the S-VHS VCR, have S-video ports that provide a higher-quality analog video signal than composite video. You can, for example, connect the S-VHS VCR directly to the capture card with an S-video cable.

Video Wiring

As you can see in figure 15.6, one end of most of the video lines connects to the video patch bay; the other end connects to an input or an output of a device. The exceptions are the two connections between the VCRs and the waveform and video monitors. Both VCRs provide two composite video outputs, so one video output can be routed to the monitors and the other to the patch bay.

The waveform monitor, like most professional devices, has two BNC input connectors for each input, even though only one source at a time can be connected to an input. The reason for the extra connector is so signals can be looped through to other devices. One cable runs from the Digital Betacam to one BNC connector. Then another cable is run from the loop-through connector to the video monitor. The signal from the Betacam is displayed on the waveform and the video monitor. Keep in mind, if a device has a termination switch next to the loop-through connectors, termination must be turned off if loop-through is used; otherwise termination must be on.

For higher-quality captures, the SDI outputs of the Digital Betacams are connected directly to the capture cards. When capturing digitally, the waveform monitor is not used because the video parameters do not need to be adjusted. For more information about capturing digitally, see chapter 10.

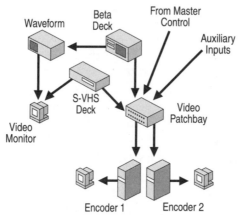

Figure 15.6   Wiring for video equipment in the compression suite.

Audio Wiring

The concept behind the audio wiring is the same as for video. One end of every line connects to a patch bay input or output, and the other end to a device (see figure 15.7). Because all of the devices are stereo, two lines must be run for every connection.

The main output and the inputs of two channels of the mixer are routed to the patch bay. This provides the technician with a way to mix two signals, adjust levels, or add mixer equalization to a source before it is fed to the encoding computers. For example, suppose audio levels fluctuate significantly on an S-VHS tape. The S-VHS VCR can be patched into the mixer, and the mixer output can be patched into the encoding computer. Then the levels can be adjusted during capture.

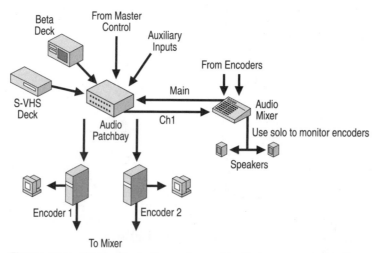

Figure 15.7   Wiring for audio equipment in the compression suite.

The outputs from the two encoding computers are fed into two channels of the mixer, and the powered monitor speakers are fed from the mixer's monitor outputs. "Solo" buttons on the mixer channels are used to monitor either or both encoding computer outputs. The channel faders are normally turned all the way down. This is to avoid a feedback loop when the mixer output is connected to an encoding computer input. A feedback loop is created when the output of a device is fed back into its input. Feedback can caused damage to electronics and speakers, not to mention your ears.

As with digital video, the AES/EBU connections on the Digital Betacams and capture cards are used to capture audio digitally. (Again, see chapter 10 for more information on digital capture.)

Creating Windows Media Files

After the wiring is complete, the technicians can test the suite by capturing and creating a Windows Media file. They will use the two-step capturing method because it will work with high-bit-rate content, which pushes the capabilities of the system. First, the technicians will capture an uncompressed AVI file, and then they will compress and encode the file to a Windows Media file that plays back at 100 Kbps.

Configuring Playback on the Digital Betacam

The basic operation of a Digital Betacam deck is not much different from that of a consumer S-VHS machine. The main difference is that a Betacam deck enables you to adjust many playback and recording parameters.

When a professional videotape recording is made, color bars and a test audio tone are recorded at the beginning of the tape. These are audio and video reference signals that you can use to adjust the VCR during playback so the sound and picture are the same as those recorded. Figure 15.8 shows the configuration of color bars displayed on a video monitor. The top section of bars are, left to right, 80 percent grey, yellow, cyan, green, magenta, red, and blue.

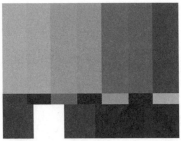

Figure 15.8 The color bars used to calibrate video playback.

Figure 15.9 shows properly-adjusted color bars as they would be displayed on a waveform monitor. The waveform monitor displays two seemingly identical side-by-side images. Each represents one field of a video frame. The video and color intensity of each bar is displayed on the graph, as well as other video components used for synchronizing the signal.

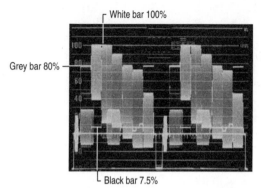

Figure 15.9   Calibrated color bars as displayed on the waveform monitor.

Color is adjusted by using a vectorscope. To explain how this instrument works, you need to know a bit about the NTSC standard. Color intensity is differentiated the same way as video intensity, by changes in voltage. The hue of the color (green, purple, yellow, and so forth), on the other hand, is differentiated by phase relationships in the color or chrominance signal. These phase relationships can be seen by displaying the chrominance of a video signal on a vectorscope, which displays phase relationships as degrees in a circle. For an overview of phase relationships, see the "Creating Color with Phase" sidebar. Figure 15.10 shows color bars displayed correctly on a vectorscope.

If you are using the SDI connectors to capture a digital tape, the data is transferred directly to the computer, bypassing conversion and processor circuits. Without these circuits in the video signal chain, the video quality is better. However, direct transfer means you cannot adjust video parameters. If you connect to a composite output while playing back either a digital or analog tape, you access the video after the digital stream is converted to an analog signal and a processor has been applied. The quality is not as good, but you can adjust the video. In the following discussion, we will assume that the composite output is being used.

The Digital Betacam provides many controls, but the four you will use the most are Video, Set up, Chroma, and Chroma Phase:

- ■   Video. This control adjusts the overall intensity or brightness of the video. While playing the color bars, adjust the Video control so the grey bar on the left is at 80 percent on the waveform scale. The white bar should be no higher than 100 percent.

- Set up. This control adjusts the black level. While playing the color bars, adjust the Set up control so the black bar on the right is at 7.5 percent on the scale. The 7.5 percent area is marked by a double line.

- Chroma. This control adjusts the intensity of color. As you adjust Chroma, the shape on the vectorscope changes in overall size. With chroma all the way off, the shape is a point in the middle, which represents zero chrominance, or black and white.

- Chroma phase. This control adjusts the hue of all colors. As you adjust the phase with the vectorscope, the shape rotates. For example, if you rotate the phase 40 degrees clockwise, the red bar would appear magenta and the cyan bar would appear green.

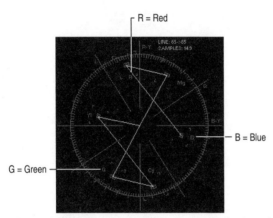

Figure 15.10   Calibrated color bars as displayed on the vectorscope.

Six small boxes located just inside the outer circle represent the colors in the color bars: R is red, B is blue, G is green, and so forth. You adjust the color so the vertices of the six angles of the shape created by the color bars align with the six boxes in the scale.

Like color bars, the tone recorded on the audio tracks is the reference with which you can adjust the audio output level on the Betacam, and the input level on the encoding computer. Typically, the tone is recorded at 0 decibels (dB). Decibels is the standard measurement of relative signal level. If you adjust the level control so the meter registers at zero on the scale, the audio will play back at the same level it was recorded. Figure 15.11 shows a VU (volume units) meter displaying a tone set to 0 db.

VU meters are used to ensure that audio levels are maximized and consistent without exceeding the upper limit of an audio circuit and recording medium. As you raise the level above 0 db, the signal will at some point become distorted. It will become increasingly distorted as you continue to raise the level. When you are adjusting audio from a source other than a test tone, you should typically keep the level as close to 0 as possible without going over too often. For most audio amplifiers and tape recorders, this method will provide the optimum sound level without objectionable distortion.

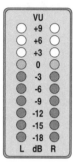

Figure 15.11   A VU meter is used to measure audio levels.

Figure 15.12   This audio signal measures -18 dB on a digital audio meter.

With analog devices, there are different levels of distortion. If the audio peaks over 0 db occasionally, you may not even notice any difference in the sound. With digital recording, on the other hand, no distortion is added to the sound until the clipping point is reached, and no sound can be recorded above that point. In other words, there is either no distortion or total distortion. Therefore, clipping must be avoided. On digital recorders, you see meters that have no indication above 0 db (or clipping). To allow some headroom, often sound engineers will set an upper limit at -18 db, and keep audio fluctuations at or below that point to avoid clipping. Figure 15.12 shows a digital audio meter with the test tone set at -18 dB.

As with video, if you capture audio digitally, conversion and processing circuits are bypassed, so you cannot adjust audio levels.

Creating Color with Phase

The NTSC television standard was adopted in North America for television standards in the early 1940s, during the days of black-and-white television.

Until recently, television signals were analog signals, a system established in the 1930s that had color grafted onto it in the early 1950s. In this system, the signal was broadcast by breaking up and transmitting (or recording) images as a series of lines, one after the other. The signal itself is based on a varying voltage.

The television signal bandwidth is 6 MHz. When color was added, the original monochrome signal, called luminance (Y), was given the largest portion (0-4 MHz) of the channel, or bandwidth. This contains the brightness information and the detail.

In addition to the Y signal, color television includes two additional chrominance (C) signals, which contain color information for the orange-cyan signal (1.5 MHz) and the green-purple signal (0.5 MHz). These signals are added together to form the C signal.

A color television signal starts off looking just like a black-and-white signal. An extra chrominance signal is added by superimposing a 3.579545 MHz sine wave onto the standard black-and-white signal. Right after the horizontal sync pulse, eight cycles of a 3.579545 MHz sine wave are added as a color burst, as shown in figure 15.13.

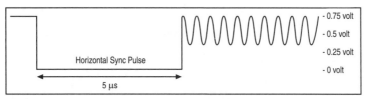

Figure 15.13 Elements of a color video signal.

Following these eight cycles, a phase shift in the chrominance signal indicates the color to display on the receiving television. The amplitude (or maximum absolute value) of the signal determines the color saturation. The following table displays the relationship between color and phase:

(continued)

Creating Color with Phase   *(continued)*

Color	Phase
Burst	0 degrees
Yellow	15 degrees
Red	75 degrees
Magenta	135 degrees
Blue	195 degrees
Cyan	255 degrees
Green	315 degrees

A black-and-white television filters out and ignores the chrominance signal. A color television picks it out of the signal and decodes it, along with the normal intensity signal, to determine how to modulate the red, green, and blue components.

Patching the Signals

After configuring playback on the source, the technicians patch it to the encoding computer. They plug one end of a video patch cord into the Digital Betacam output, and the other end into an encoding computer input. Then they patch audio channels 1 and 2 of the Digital Betacam into the left and right channels of the encoding computer.

Preparing the Encoder for Capturing

To prepare the encoder to capture uncompressed audio and video, the Fabrikam technicians first make sure audio and video are present at the inputs of the capture card. Then they can adjust audio and video so the levels match those coming from the Digital Betacam. If the video capture card does not provide audio output, they can use a second sound card or built-in sound system to monitor sound. If you are capturing digitally with the SDI, AES/EBU, or IEEE 1394 ports, you cannot adjust video and audio parameters.

To properly adjust the input audio level on the computer, you need a volume control and an audio meter. You can use an audio program that provides an audio meter, such as Sound Forge or Cool Edit. Follow these steps:

1. Open the audio program's recorder dialog box, and then make sure monitoring is active.

2. Open the volume controls by double-clicking the speaker icon in the taskbar. If the speaker icon is not displayed in your taskbar, click **Start**, click **Control Panel**, then double-click **Sound, Speech and Audio Devices**. Make sure the correct recording device is selected.

3. In the **Properties** dialog box for the **Volume Control**, select **Adjust volume for Recording**. The recording controls adjust the signal entering the video card. The playback or master volume controls adjust the audio output.

4. As you play back the bars and tone, adjust the **Line In** control to match the meters on the Betacam, such as -18 db.

5. Open the **Master** or **Playback Volume** controls, and adjust the **Line In** control to adjust the monitor volume.

6. On the mixer, press the Solo button on the encoding computer channel and adjust the monitor level to hear the sound through the computer.

7. After the input and output levels are adjusted, close the volume controls and audio program. Once set, the volume controls should not need to be readjusted as long as the audio entering the computer has been adjusted properly.

Setting up the Video

Video levels are adjusted in the video capture program—in this case Windows Media 9 Capture. The technicians select the video capture card as the source and enable the preview function, so they can view live video as it is coming into the card. Configuration options are in the video source configuration dialog box. You will typically find the following four video setting controls, which correspond roughly to the four controls on the Digital Betacam:

- Brightness. Controls the intensity of the picture (same as the Video control).

- Contrast. Controls the range between the brightest and darkest parts of the picture (similar to the Set up control, except Set up only adjusts the darkest parts).

- Saturation. Controls the color intensity (same as the Chroma control).

- Hue. Controls the hue of all colors (same as the Chroma phase control).

  The Fabrikam technicians follow this procedure to set up the video levels.

1. Turn Saturation to 0, and adjust Brightness about half-way on the slider control.

2. While viewing playback of color bars, adjust Contrast and Brightness until whites are as white as possible, blacks are black as possible, and all the gray bars are differentiated.

3. Turn up Saturation until color intensity seems correct. Avoid turning it up too high.

4. Adjust Hue for the correct colors.

Video configuration is not as objective as that of audio without meters or scopes to work with. Software waveform monitors and vectorscopes are available from companies such as Digital Media Works and VideoForge, and they will give you more control over video setup. If you do not use a software monitor, make sure your video monitor is correctly adjusted before you make adjustments to the video capture card.

After the input levels have been set, the technicians configure the capture program with the following settings:

■ Enter a name for the output file. Make sure the location to which you will save the file has ample storage space. One minute of uncompressed video with a frame size of 320 × 240 requires approximately 200 MB.

■ Select **Full Frames (uncompressed)** as the video compression type, and select **None (PCM)** for audio compression.

■ Enter **YUV12** as the color format. This is the color format Windows Media Encoder uses when encoding the final file.

■ Enter a video size, such as **320 × 240**, and a frame rate, such as **30**.

Capturing Video from Tape

Now the technicians can cue the videotape to a point about five seconds before the start of the program. They start the tape, then start the capture. It is important to make sure the program is capturing before the video starts. Keep in mind there is a small delay between the time at which you click the button to start the capture and when the program actually begins capturing frames.

As the capture proceeds, the technicians monitor the quality of the video and check the CPU load and remaining disk space counters with **Performance Monitor**. If the CPU exceeds 75 percent, and certainly if it hits 100 percent occasionally, the quality of the final encoded video might be adversely affected. A computer with the same specifications as those used in the compression suite are capable of capturing uncompressed video with full-frame size and frame rate without overloading the CPU.

When the source ends, the technician stops the capture. They allow a few seconds of black or extra space after the program before stopping the capture to make sure the source is not cut off. Then they open the file in Windows Media Player and play it back to check the capture quality. When you do a capture, remember to check the beginning and end to make sure program material was not cut off. If everything looks and sounds good, you can encode the final compressed file. For more information about using the encoder, see chapter 7.

Editing the Captured Video

If there is excess black or other non-program material at the beginning or end of the uncompressed file, or if there are parts you want to remove or move to a different location, you can make those changes using a video editing program. Some programs do not support editing Windows Media files, which is one reason for initially capturing the video to an AVI file.

Figure 15.14   The captured video file being edited in Vegas Video.

Figures 15.14 and 15.15 show AVI files open on the timeline tracks of Vegas Video 3.0 and Adobe Premiere 6.5. In both programs, fade transitions have been added, which are represented graphically as volume or video intensity graphs overlaying the beginning and end of the audio and video tracks. In Premiere, video transitions are represented by blocks in a transition track.

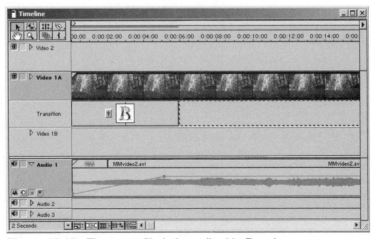

Figure 15.15   The same file being edited in Premiere.

As you edit, preview the video periodically to make sure it plays back as expected. Most computer-based editing programs perform "nondestructive" editing and processing, which means you can make as many edits and add as many effects as you want, and the source video file is unaffected. As you edit your clip, you should regularly save your work. When you save, you are really only saving the editing decisions and settings, not the actual video content. The decisions and settings are saved as projects. When you have finished a project, you will use a render function. When rendering, the programs create a new file using the content and your editing decisions and settings. With Producer, Vegas Video 3.0, and Premiere 6.5, you can render the final video as a Windows Media file directly.

In this chapter, Fabrikam built and tested the compression suite to be used by the Media department. In the next chapter, they design and implement a simple Media Guide portal.

16

Phase I: Media Guide Portal

In the last chapter, Fabrikam built the compression suite that the Media department will use to capture and encode Windows Media-based content. In this chapter, we will look at the other task the department took on in phase I of the company's streaming media deployment: organizing the corporation's sizable store of video content and making it available online.

Right away, Media department planners knew that simply making videos available online wasn't enough; they would also need to find a way for users to locate the content. The first solution was to keep the system the way it was. The company could announce and distribute Windows Media files the same way it does videotapes. For example, a manager or producer could send out an e-mail message announcing or promoting a video. The URL could be sent in the e-mail message so all recipients could simply click the link and the video would stream to their Player.

Of course, e-mail is a good tool if active promotion of a video is desired. However, e-mail promotion is a passive experience for the user. Users shouldn't have to sit and wait for an e-mail message to come along in order to watch an important video or presentation. The company needs a system, like a video store or library, for the user who wants to search for a particular video. The solution is to develop a Web site on the corporate intranet that can provide access to a library of video content. The Web site will be a one-stop location for all the end user's video needs.

With a Web site, access to a video is not restricted to only those employees receiving an e-mail message. Anybody with access to a computer is a potential viewer. By adding security measures, such as digital rights management (DRM) or authentication and authorization, even confidential content could be distributed through this site.

The Media department decides the best way to announce and distribute streaming media content is to build a robust Web site that aggregates all the video content produced in the company, provides security for sensitive material, and provides a quick and easy system for users to locate content. Live content can be represented, as well as the large store of on-demand content. The site will serve as a virtual library, providing a way for users to actively participate in locating material. It will also serve as a portal for announcing and promoting new content and events. Fabrikam calls the site the "Media Guide."

Creating a Specification for the Media Guide

The Media Guide Web site will be the main portal that Fabrikam employees can use to access the rich store of on-demand and live content available to them. The Media department will develop the site, and will be responsible for design changes and updates. Production assistants working with the production scheduling team will maintain the content and manage daily operation of the site. Because the site will be run by production people who are not Web designers, it needs to be easy to update and require low maintenance.

The Media Guide will include the following minimum functionality:

- On-demand content list, search, and links. Users will be able to locate on-demand content by browsing for Windows Media files and Producer presentations in a hierarchical list view or by performing a keyword search. When users locate the content they want to view, they can click the link on the page to start playing the content.

- Live content calendar, search, and links. Users will be able to locate a broadcast by browsing through a calendar or by performing a keyword search. Users can click the link to view the event (or a lobby page if the event hasn't begun).

- Announcements. Production assistants will be able to add or edit announcements, which will appear on the Media Guide home page. For example, the announcement feature can be used to promote a special live event or on-demand file, such as a speech by the CEO, or give users special instructions or information.

- Information. The guide will provide users with additional information. One immediate use for the information feature is a help system, which will describe how to use the site. The Producer mini-studio documentation will also be included, as well as instructions on how to schedule live events and production resources. They may also produce a video guide using Producer.

- Production requests. Employees can use the site to request production resources. Online forms will be used to collect information. The information can then be used to book time in the studio or remote production assistance. Users can also request live event coverage and to have their on-demand content made available on the site.

- Content upload. Site administrators will have access to the Media Guide administration site. From this location, they can configure the site and upload files.

- Windows Media Player downloads. The Media Guide will also serve as the primary location from which users can download and install Windows Media Player. The company can use the Enterprise Deployment Pack to create a custom Player download package. This allows Fabrikam to configure the Player to take advantage of features such as progressive download of content and faster seeking within videos. They can also use this functionality to pre-install codecs. The IT department will create the package and host it on the Media Guide site. The package will ensure that everyone in the company has the same version of the Player, and that it is configured properly.

Creating the Media Guide Portal

The Web designers needed a solution that would scale, provide a number of fairly complex functions, and contain complete administrative functionality. They decided a database-driven site was the way to go. Rather than take many months to build and test a solution, they decided to use an existing portal software solution.

Microsoft SharePoint Portal Server, which was designed for use in enterprises to help people share information, will provide the structure for the site. A SharePoint Portal site can be customized to suit the Media department's needs, and will provide all the functionality they needed for now. As the database grows and the team discovers new needs, the Web team can create a custom site or, if necessary, purchase another solution. Regardless of whether you decide to go with a simple Web site, an off-the-shelf portal solution, or a custom site, the basic concepts for building a Media Guide portal apply.

SharePoint Portal Server uses workspace folders to hold the information or links to information, and it uses a dashboard site to search for and manipulate information. SharePoint refers to content files as documents, but any type of information can be contained in a workspace, including text files, audio and video content, Windows Media metafiles, installation files, and Web pages.

Security on the site is configured by defining user roles. A user can be a reader, an author, or a coordinator.

- A reader can search for and read documents, but cannot add them to the workspace.

- An author can add new documents to a folder, edit all documents in the folder, delete any document from the folder, and read all documents in the folder.

- A coordinator for the workspace manages content in the top-level folder and can perform workspace administration tasks.

Most of the people who use the Media Guide site at Fabrikam will be readers. The production assistants will have coordinator status. The site can also make use of Sharepoint NTLM authentication, which works with the company's Active Directory-based security.

SharePoint provides a number of features for managing production process workflow and documents, including version control and document publishing by multiple users. SharePoint is designed to work as a many-to-many solution; where many users can share information with many others. However, the Media Guide will use the server more as a one-to-many portal. Although many people can submit information and digital media content for the site, only a few users (the production assistants) will have permission to actually add files to and edit files directly on the site.

Microsoft Producer enables users to publish on-demand PowerPoint presentations directly to the SharePoint portal. When they do, metadata, such as title and description, is also published and included automatically in the site's indexing system. After a presentation is published to the site, end users can immediately use the SharePoint search engine to locate it. To make it easier for users to record and publish their presentations, users can request permission to publish directly, and appropriate user permissions can be configured in SharePoint.

Understanding SharePoint Portal Server

SharePoint holds the Media Guide site in a storage area called a workspace. The only way to view and manage the workspace is with Web folders. To use Web folders, you must enable this feature on your SharePoint Web server. Then you or another coordinator can open the workspace in a Windows Explorer window on a remote computer and manipulate the documents, folders, categories, and site settings roughly the same as you would view documents and folders locally. You can also use Web folders in Office applications like Excel and Word. The main difference between Web folders and regular file folders is that you work with the items on a Web server through a URL.

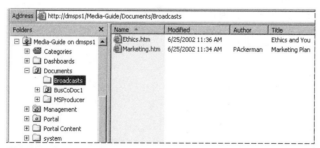

Figure 16.1   Viewing the Media Guide workspace in SharePoint.

Figure 16.1 shows the Media Guide workspace opened in a Windows Explorer window. As you can see, the Media Guide workspace contains folders and other components. Fabrikam Web producers have already added the folders and files that you see in the Documents folder. All of the other folders were created automatically when they added the workspace. The System and Portal folders contain site resources like images, ASP pages, and script files. Normally, these files are only accessed by Web designers to perform modification of the site. Most often work is done in the Categories, Documents, Management, and Portal Content folders.

- Categories. This folder contains special folders called Category folders, which store and organize documents into a hierarchy of topics and subtopics.

- Documents. This folder is where documents such as Web pages, Windows Media files, and Word documents are added, stored, or removed. You can create a hierarchy of subfolders to organize the files. In this case, the producers have added folders to hold broadcast information, documents, and Producer presentations.

  When a document is added, SharePoint attaches a document profile. You use profiles to give documents a presence in SharePoint. For example, you can add a document description in a profile, which can be displayed by SharePoint on a Web page. If you assign one or more categories to a document, the document also shows up automatically in the Categories folder.

- Management. This folder contains tools and folders that configure and manage the workspace, document profiles, and content sources.

- Portal Content. This folder contains default folders used to configure and manage the information displayed on the Web site.

You configure the site and document profiles by right-clicking a folder or an item in a folder and changing its properties. The information you add and configurations you make to the workspace are then displayed on Web pages called dashboards. End users access the Media Guide through the home dashboard, as shown in figure 16.2.

A dashboard is composed of a number of Web "parts," which can provide different views of the information in the workspace. For example, the Video Categories Web part displays workspace document categories and provides links to expanded views. Web parts can also contain other content and provide all sorts of different functions. For example, the MSNBC Weather Web part displays local weather when it is expanded. You can use the default Web parts that come with SharePoint, select from a Web part gallery, and create your own Web parts using the SharePoint Portal Server Resource Kit.

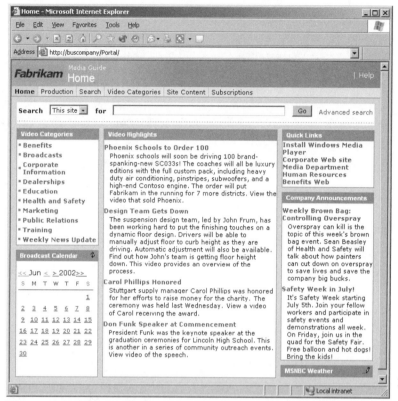

Figure 16.2   The dashboard page created for Fabrikam's Media Guide.

Installing SharePoint Portal Server

SharePoint Portal Server installation requires four steps:

1. Run the SharePoint Portal Server setup wizard to install the server.

2. Run the New Workspace Wizard to create a workspace on the server. The wizard requires a workspace name, and other information that is optional. You can also designate the workspace as an index workspace. SharePoint contains an index engine that decreases the time it takes users to search through a large number of documents.

3. Run the Client Components for SharePoint Portal Server setup wizard to install the components that will allow you to administer the server. You can also run this wizard on the other computers from which you will be administering the workspace. The components enable you to publish files directly from other

Microsoft Office programs. For example, you could write an announcement for a broadcast in Microsoft Word and then save it directly to the workspace.

4. Add a Web folder that points to the workspace. To do that in Windows 2000 or Windows XP, add a new Network Place in **My Network Places**. The Fabrikam workspace is named Media Guide and is located on the server Dmsps1, so the address of the workspace and Web site is http://dmsps1/ Media-Guide. When you double-click the new Network Place, the workspace opens in a Web folder. When you access the URL in a browser, the home dashboard opens.

Web Distributed Authoring and Versioning (WebDAV) is used to access site management features and perform file management. Once WebDAV is installed in Internet Information Services (IIS) on the Web server, computers with the WebDAV client can access the site with Web folders and in Office applications.

After installation, security is configured for the site. For Fabrikam, the Web design team and production assistants who will be performing daily work on the site are assigned the coordinator role. Everyone else is assigned the reader role, except for those who will use Microsoft Producer to publish presentations to the Media Guide; these users are assigned the author role. After roles are established, site design can begin and content can be added.

Designing the Media Guide Site

Design work for the Media Guide site is focused on providing functionality for the two primary user types: production assistants who will maintain the content, and end users who will access videos from the site. The work is divided into the main user task areas. Web parts and dashboards must be built and configured to enable users to do the following tasks:

■ Find and play on-demand content.

■ Find and play broadcast content.

■ Submit production requests.

■ Upload content.

■ Publish Microsoft Producer projects.

■ Maintain the site.

■ Publish and read information, promotions, and announcements.

■ Install Windows Media Player.

Building a Web part requires knowledge of scripting with a language such as Visual Basic Scripting Edition (VBScript) or JScript. Basic dashboard design can be handled by users with knowledge of Web page design.

In addition to enabling these user tasks, the Fabrikam Web producers decide to make changes to the appearance of the site. For each of the dashboards that can be selected on the taskbar, they change the style sheet to the Tropical style included with SharePoint and add the Fabrikam logo to the header. Advanced designers can create custom style sheets that change the entire look of the site.

In the following topics, we will describe the intended end user and production assistant experiences. Then we will see how Fabrikam configured SharePoint to implement their design.

Finding and Playing On-demand Content

End users will come to the site primarily to look for and play on-demand or broadcast content. They can come to the site to find content they already know about, such as videos advertised through e-mail messages, or to browse for content in a certain category.

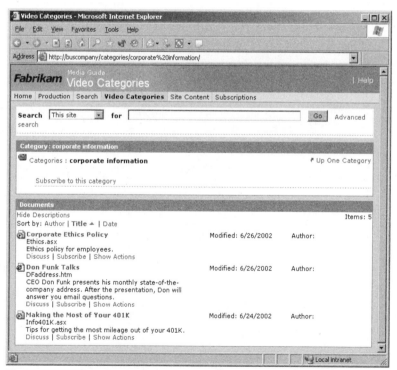

Figure 16.3 Viewing the Corporate Information category on the Media Guide site.

When an end user enters the URL of the Media Guide site (http://dmsps1/Media-Guide), the home dashboard opens as shown in figure 16.2. Users can browse or search for a particular item. To browse, they access Video Categories either on the page or from the dashboard on the taskbar. The experience is similar to browsing through folders. Users can click a particular title and the video will play in Windows Media Player.

Figure 16.3 shows the Video Categories dashboard with the Corporate Information category displayed. The first item in the list is an on-demand Windows Media file, Ethics.asx. The item "Don Funk Talks" points to a Web page for viewing a broadcast. Before the broadcast, the user accesses the Lobby page that contains information about the broadcast and downloads related PowerPoint slides to the user's Internet cache.

The production assistant can add or remove content by dragging files and dropping them into subfolders of the Documents folder, or by saving or publishing content to the folders. After adding content, the production assistant opens the properties for the content and enters profile information. After properties have been added, SharePoint automatically adds the document to the appropriate categories and enters the information into its database, which can then be retrieved by the Web parts to display that information.

Publishing a File

There are basically two types of on-demand content: video files and Microsoft Producer projects, and each is handled differently. The Producer process will be described later in this chapter. This is the process an assistant would use to publish a Windows Media file:

1. Copy the Windows Media Video file to a location on the Windows Media server. Let's say Driver01.wmv is copied to a publishing point called Safety on the server WMS01.

2. Create a Windows Media metafile with an .asx extension. A simple text editor program such as Microsoft Notepad can be used. The contents of the file looks like this:

```
<ASX version ="3.0">
     <Title>Driver Safety</Title>
<Entry>
     <Title>Driver Safety Part 1</Title>
     <Author>Max Bennett</Author>
     <Copyright>2002</Copyright>
     <Ref href="mms://WMS01/Safety/Driver01.wmv" />
</Entry>
</ASX>
```

A metafile can be created automatically with the **Announcement Wizard** in Windows Media Services.

3.   Save the metafile to the local hard drive. Give it a descriptive name, such as DriverSafety.asx, keeping in mind that the name will be displayed on the site.

4.   Drag the file to the site folder.

If you create the metafile in an Office application or another program that supports Web folders, and you have installed the SharePoint client, you can click **Save as** to save directly to the Web site location and add profile information in one step.

5.   In the Media Guide workspace, open the properties dialog box for Driver-Safety.asx, and then open the **Document profile** dialog box from the **Profile** tab. Type some descriptive information, assign one or more categories and keywords, and attach the appropriate document profile template, ASX. Figure 16.4 shows the **Document profile** dialog box.

Figure 16.4   Configuring profile information for an .asx file.

The ASX profile template was created by the Web designers when the site was originally configured. You can create a new profile in the **Document Profiles** folder of the **Management** folder.

6.   Close the dialog boxes. Figure 16.5 shows the file as it appears to a user who is viewing the Training category.

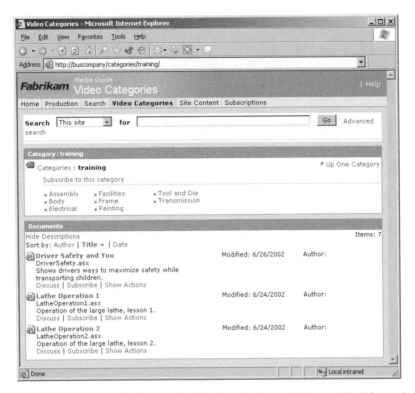

Figure 16.5   DriverSafety.asx is displayed, along with its profile information.

Implementing the Site Design

Very little work is needed to accommodate on-demand content. Video Categories and Video Highlights on the home page are default Web parts that were simply renamed from Categories and News. The Video Categories and Site Content dashboards are also simply renamed.

Before any content is added, a base set of categories and subcategories is created in the Categories folder, as shown in figure 16.6. A beginning set of document folders is also added.

A custom document profile template, ASX, is also created. The default Base profile template, which is assigned by default to files added to the Documents folder, does not include a Category property. Because the Media Guide designers want all metafiles to show up in categories, they create an ASX profile that includes the Category property. The ASX profile template is assigned to the Documents folder so it can be available to all content added to that folder. The ASX profile template enables a production assistant to assign a title, categories, a description, and keyword properties to a Windows Media file or Web page.

Figure 16.6   Folders for various content categories in SharePoint.

SharePoint has two features that can be useful for sites with large amounts of content: category assistant and indexing. Category assistant is an automated categorization tool. You "train" the assistant with a sample set of documents, and then you can enable the assistant to place new documents in the correct categories automatically.

Indexing is a feature for handling searches of very large numbers of documents. Windows Media metafiles are fairly small documents compared to Word documents, but if a site has thousands of files, the workspace index can dramatically reduce search time. The index is updated automatically whenever content is added or removed.

SharePoint also enables you to add content sources that are outside the workspace. You can enable indexing of these external sources, and SharePoint will automatically update the index to include these files.

Finding and Playing Broadcast Content

An end user can locate a broadcast in several ways: with the Broadcast Calendar, by browsing the Broadcast category, from Video Highlights, or with Search. We have already seen the process for locating content through a category or by searching. The Broadcast Calendar, however, is used specifically for locating broadcasts. Figure 16.7 shows the calendar on the home page.

Though the other methods can be used, the calendar is probably the most obvious and intuitive to an end user. The calendar is displayed on the home page, so it is the first broadcast-related item the end user sees when entering the site. The end user clicks a date and the Search dashboard opens with the broadcasts scheduled to air on that date. The user can then click the title and link to the broadcast, or add it to her calendar in Microsoft Outlook.

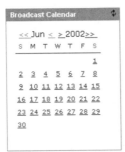

Figure 16.7 The Broadcast Calendar helps users find broadcast content.

To SharePoint, a broadcast is just another document, like those used for on-demand content. The difference is the contents of the file. A Windows Media metafile for a broadcast points to a broadcast publishing point, which points to a live encoder or playlist. A broadcast Web page contains the elements used in the broadcast. To an end user, however, a broadcast is very different from an on-demand viewing experience, which is why the calendar Web part was created.

For the calendar to work, a new document profile was created that includes the property AirDate (see figure 16.8).

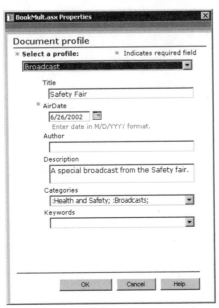

Figure 16.8 A new document profile form for broadcast presentations.

A Broadcasts folder (with the Broadcast profile assigned to it) was also added to Documents. A production assistant uses the same process to add a new metafile or Web page for a broadcast, except he places it in a subfolder of the Broadcasts folder, and then selects the Broadcast profile. He enters all the usual information, and then enters the date the broadcast will occur in AirDate. After information has been added to a property, it can be used by the SharePoint search engine.

Implementing the Broadcast Search Feature

To support broadcast search, two new items must be created: the calendar Web part and the Broadcast document profile template.

The calendar is a new Web part that contains script to display a calendar and invoke a search using the AirDate property. A Web part can be created using HTML, VBScript, JScript, or XML. The script for creating a dynamic calendar and performing the search is embedded directly in the Web part. The SharePoint Portal Server Resource Kit contains information about creating custom Web parts and using the document properties to invoke a search.

The Broadcast profile template contains a set of default properties, as well as the new AirDate property for specifying the event date. New properties can be created when you run the **Add Document Profile** wizard. When adding a property, you give it a name, assign a type, and choose whether information for the property is required.

The Media department is planning to create only a handful of broadcasts per month at first. That is why the search method was chosen. In the future, it is possible that the number of broadcasts will increase to a point where they overlap. When that happens, a log-style Web part can be created to list events chronologically, with time and date headings. For now the calendar, search, and browse methods, combined with the Video Highlights Web part, provide adequate functionality.

It is possible some broadcasts will be designed for presentation directly in Windows Media Player instead of through a Web page. Not all broadcasts require a lobby page, and there may be continuous broadcasts (such as rebroadcasts of radio stations). In these cases, users will link directly to a metafile, which will open the Player and stream the broadcast.

The .asx file and the multicast information file (with an .nsc extension) will be located in a folder on the workspace. (Because the two files are located in the same directory, a relative URL can be used in the .asx file to point to the .nsc file.) The profile for the .asx file will include the broadcast category and other useful information. However, the .nsc profile will not include a category or information in order to partly hide it from end users. If a user should attempt to open the file, the browser will display it as a Web page rather than in Windows Media Player, because MIME types on most browsers are not set up for .nsc files.

With additional scripting using Collaboration Data Objects (CDO), calendar functionality can be handled using Microsoft Outlook and Exchange servers. The calendar displayed on the home dashboard can link to the Exchange database. By integrating messaging, live event scheduling, coordination, and other messaging features can be used in the Media Guide system.

Submitting Production Requests

Most end-users will use the site to play content. However, the site can be used to submit a request for production resources through the Media department. The initial Media Guide will include a request form for production services, such as shooting, editing, and duplication. Other forms will be added later for users who want to submit finished Producer presentations and other content. The Production dashboard could eventually become a sub-portal for the Media department, and could include information about the facilities and instructions about creating videos.

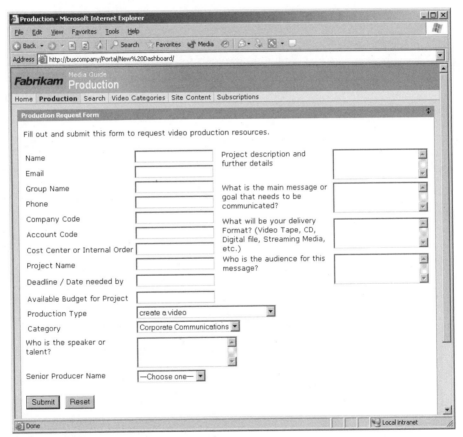

Figure 16.9   The production request form.

The request form opens when an end user clicks Production in the taskbar. The home page does not lead end users to the form, although some may discover it when they browse the site. Most likely, users will come to the form after reading the online help page for the site or after contacting the Media department. Figure 16.9 shows the production request form.

When an end user clicks Submit, the completed form is sent in an e-mail message to the Production Request alias. A production assistant opens the e-mail message, reviews the form, and contacts the end user directly to work out details.

The form is a Web page that was created with a Web design tool, like Microsoft FrontPage. After the form was created, it was added to a new Web part. Submit sends the contents of the form; Reset reloads the page, erasing whatever the user has entered.

Uploading Content

Initially, the production assistants in the Media department will be the only ones with permission to publish content to the site. Author-level roles may be given to certain individuals or groups, which will allow them to copy files to a limited set of folders. Security can be set on individual files or on folders to grant or deny access to individuals or groups.

Production assistants copy or publish Windows Media Video files to the Windows Media servers, and Windows Media metafiles to the Media Guide workspace, following the steps outlined previously.

Producer projects will be handled differently.

Publishing Microsoft Producer Projects

Users can create Microsoft Producer presentations, and then submit them for inclusion on the Media Guide site. First an end user creates and saves a presentation in Producer. Then he contacts the Media department or fills out a production request form on the Media Guide site. A production assistant will provide publishing locations on the Media Guide workspace and the Windows Media server. The user can then run the **Publish Presentation** wizard in Producer to encode the files and folders for the presentation. He can then copy these file and folders to the appropriate Media Guide workspace.

If the user needs production assistance from the Media department, he can use the **Pack and Go** wizard in Producer, which creates a compressed file of the project. He can then copy this file to a public location on a Media department file server, and a production assistant will create a finished presentation.

When a request is received, a production assistant creates a new folder for the content in the MSProducer folder on the Media Guide workspace. She will also create a new folder for the Windows Media files on the Windows Media server. Then she gives the end user author permission to access the Media Guide and the Windows Media server folder. After the user publishes the presentation, he can notify the production assistant. She will add categories to the presentation page and test playback of the files.

In chapter 19, we will go into more detail about using Producer to capture, edit, and publish content.

Maintaining the Site

The Media department decides to create a short document of maintenance procedures for the production assistants. The document includes information about the following topics:

- Keeping the home dasboard fresh. This will be the page that is visited the most by users. Information and links in the Video Highlights and Company Announcements Web parts must be current, and Quick Links must be current.

- Maintaining the on-demand folders. Make sure the content is current and working: Make sure Windows Media metafile and Web page links continue to be valid. When a file is removed from the Windows Media server, the metafile or Web page associated with it should also be removed.

- Maintain the Broadcasts folder. Make sure metafiles and Web pages are current and coincide with the broadcasts scheduled through production requests. For example, if a broadcast is canceled, the metafile and Web page should be deleted.

- Content sources. If additional content sources are used, make sure the content is maintained and indexed.

- Storage maintenance. Make sure the workspace has adequate hard drive space, that old files and folders are archived or removed, and that basic disk maintenance is performed. If the workspace becomes too crowded, add external content sources.

Publishing Information, Promotions, and Announcements

On the home dashboard of the Media Guide site, an end user can browse the Video Highlights and Company Announcements Web parts, which provide information about special broadcasts, presentations, and company events. The user can click the title of a video to play it, or click an announcement to receive more information. The end user can also click Help in the banner area to get information about accessing information on the site.

Up to this point, the production assistant has added metafiles and Web pages to the Documents folder. She also assigned ASX or Broadcast profiles to the documents, which enable indexing and categorization. However, the Video Highlights and Company Announcements Web parts are handled a different way. Content that appears in these Web parts is added to the News and the Announcements folders, respectively, which are located in the Portal Content folder. The Portal Content folder is located at the root of the workspace. The Web parts automatically reflect whatever content is in these folders. In other words, if you want to add an item to Video Highlights, all you have to do is add a document to the News folder.

Creating Company Announcements

Company Announcements are used to highlight special events. Documents in the Announcements folder are for the most part Web pages. Documents added to the News folder have a News Item profile attached to them by default. Documents added to Announcements have an Announcement profile. Both profiles include only Title and Description properties. Therefore, a document added here cannot be included in a category; it will only appear on the home dashboard Web part or as a search result. When an end user clicks the title in the Web part, the document opens. For example, an end user can read the description of a special video and click the title to open the metafile and play the video.

However, it is often more efficient if an announcement or video highlight points to a Web site outside the Media Guide site, such as the corporate Web, or to a metafile located in the Documents folder. A Video Highlight file could be a Web page that contains descriptive text and a link. But a production assistant may want to link the end user directly to a video that is located with the other videos in the Documents folder.

To accomplish that, Fabrikam adds the Web Link profile to the Announcements and News folders. The production assistants can choose whether the link associated with the title opens the document or points to another source. For example, to create a Video Highlight entry that contains a title, descriptive text, and a link that points to a metafile in the Documents folder, the production assistant follows these steps:

1. Create a file and add it to the News folder. This can simply be a text file that contains one character. Only the profile properties that are associated with the file are used; the contents of the file are ignored.

2. In the News folder, open the **Document profile** dialog box for the file.

3. Choose the Web Link profile.

4. Type the **Title**, **Description**, and the **Link** to the metafile in the Documents folder (for example, http://dmsps1/Media-Guide/Documents/On-Demand/DriverSafety.asx). Do not enter a category, because the metafile is already categorized.

When the end user clicks the title in Video Highlights, the metafile will open and play the file. The same steps can be used to add a link to an external Web site in the Announcements folder.

Adding Custom Help Content

A Help link is included in the right side of the banner area. The link opens a document that describes to users how to navigate a SharePoint site. While this can be useful, the Media department decides to add their own information to the pages. For example, the original help pages described dashboards in general. The Media department replaces these with pages that describe specific features of the Media Guide site.

The pages are located in the **Resources** folder of the root **Portal** folder. They are mixed with other site resources, so a little bit of detective work is needed to locate all the help resources. You can open the Help pages in a browser and look at page properties to find the file name of the page. For example, the first main content page is ptl_home.htm. After locating the pages, you can copy them to another computer and open them in a Web editor, such as FrontPage. Copy the customized pages back to the **Resources** folder. You might want to save the original pages in case you need to restore them, and use the same file names so links continue to work.

Installing Windows Media Player

Before end users can play content from the Media Guide site, they must install Windows Media Player from the Media Guide site. The link is located in the Quick Links Web part on the home dashboard. This link points to an installation file that was customized by the company's IT department. They used Enterprise Deployment Pack for Windows Media Player to create the custom installer. All the end user has to do is click the link and a preconfigured Player is installed with custom company settings.

The Enterprise Deployment Pack is expected to be available from the Windows Media Web site. After installing the Enterprise Deployment Pack, an IT technician runs a wizard that guides them through the creation of the custom download file. Custom Player installation files can be created with preconfigured proxy server, protocol, and port settings. An installation file can be created for clients with slow connections, so that the automatic upgrade and codec download features are disabled. If the company creates a custom skin, the skin files can also be automatically applied to the Player. Additional installation files can be created for configuration changes and upgrades, as needed.

After running the wizard, the installation file is copied to the Quick Links folder. The Base document profile is used, and "Install Windows Media Player" is entered as the title. If the company creates multiple installation files, the Quick Link document can be changed to one that links the end user to a Web page from which a selection can be made.

At this point two of the three tasks in phase I of the streaming media deployment have been completed: on-demand content can be created with the compression suite and end users can locate streaming media content in the Media Guide. In the next chapter, we follow the configuration and deployment of the Windows Media server farm at the Toronto headquarters. After the servers have been deployed, on-demand content and limited broadcast streaming will be available in Toronto.

17

Phase I: Server Deployment

Phase I of the plan to deploy Windows Media at Fabrikam involves building a system that enables the company's content producers and IT professionals to create on-demand content and stream it throughout their Toronto headquarters. They also plan to have limited broadcast capability.

In chapter 15, we saw how they built the compression suite for creating the on-demand content. In chapter 16, we saw how they designed the Media Guide portal Web site where end users can find content to stream or download. In this chapter, Fabrikam puts together the last piece of phase I: installing the Windows Media server farm in the data center. After the Windows Media server farm is installed, the basic deployment is complete: users can record and encode content in the compression suite, they can publish content to or find content on the Media Guide site, and they can stream content to their desktops from the Windows Media server farm.

Updating the Fabrikam Data Center

The data center at Fabrikam is typical of those in medium-to-large enterprises: multiple racks of servers and network infrastructure components that support business applications used throughout the company. The data center also provides access to the Internet. The corporate Web server farm is dedicated to internal communications, but another Web server is located in the data center perimeter network and can be accessed by the company's partners and customers over the Internet.

The data center will house the Windows Media server farm, which will include the primary servers for streaming digital media to desktops and conference rooms throughout the company. A Windows Media server will also be installed in the perimeter network so selected content can be streamed over the Internet.

Users in the Toronto headquarters will connect directly to the server farm to stream on-demand and broadcast content. After phase II of the implementation is complete, end users outside Toronto will receive on-demand content that originated on the server farm, but that is actually streamed from a cache/proxy server. After phase III is complete, most end users will be able to receive multicast broadcasts originating from the data center server farm.

Windows Media Server Specifications

The Windows Media server farm will be added to a rack in the area with the other intranet Web servers and devices. A cluster of three servers will handle all streaming media. The IT department decides to purchase computers that will be able to handle the projected load over the next two years. Utilization of these computers should not exceed 50 percent of CPUs, hard drives, and network resources.

Fabrikam purchases computers with dual processors running at 2 GHz. The computers will originally have 512 MB of RAM, upgradeable to 1 GB, and bus speeds of 400 MHz. When hosting streaming media content, RAM, hard drive capacity and speed, and internal bus speed are very important.

The servers contain five hot-swap hard drive bays. The IT department will use two 18 GB drives for storing the operating system, back-up files, and applications. The remaining slots will contain 36 GB drives and be used for storing Windows Media files and other content. In the future they will switch over to a RAID disk array system to provide fault tolerance. The Network Load Balancing (NLB) service provides one level of failure protection. However, hard drives have the highest failure rate in a streaming media server system, and a RAID 5 array would reduce the cost of drive replacement. In this case, however, Fabrikam decides to use the drives built into the server.

If possible, digital media content should be kept on a separate drive from the one used for the operating system. Hosting streaming media content is very different from a server perspective than hosting Web pages, images, and other static data. When a Web page is sent, for example, the hard drive is accessed for a second or two while the data is read into a memory buffer and sent to the client. One hard drive can serve many Web pages and images concurrently because data access times are comparatively short.

When streaming digital media content, on the other hand, data must be sent continuously. A storage system must be able to handle multiple concurrent streams for much longer periods of time, and this places a heavy demand on hard drives. By using separate drives for the operating system and applications, the content drives do not have the additional burden of storing and retrieving system data. Newer systems with bus speeds of 400 MHz or higher can help move the data quickly from the drives into memory. To decrease the load on the hard drives and the system bus, large amounts of RAM are helpful for storing and sending data.

Besides the removable hard drives, the only other hardware needed is three NICs: one 1000BT NIC for streaming content to users, one 100BT NIC for administrative use, and one 100BT NIC for content management.

In this configuration, the Fabrikam staff have plenty of room to expand as demand increases. 100 GB of content storage should be sufficient for now, considering it could hold over 2,400 hours of content streaming at 100 Kbps. Larger drives (or an external disk array) can be added to the computers, if needed. It is far more likely that network bandwidth will be saturated before the load on the servers becomes a problem.

RAM can be added if memory utilization is high. The CPU speed should not be an issue. If demand increases to a point where the CPU usage is above 50 percent and additional RAM does not help, more servers can be added to the media server farm. A Windows Media deployment can scale both vertically (by increasing host resources, such as CPU speed and RAM), and horizontally (by increasing the number of servers). If Windows Media server resources are increased, network bandwidth should also be increased to handle more concurrent streams. If network bandwidth becomes an issue, the IT department can also investigate adding cache/proxy servers throughout the main office to spread out the load on the Toronto network.

Configuring the Windows Media Servers

The server farm will initially be built on the bench in an isolated test environment. After it has been configured and tested, it will be installed in a rack in the data center and moved into production. The IT department builds servers offline because it is easier to add and configure software in a controlled environment. Working with the server offline also enables IT people to tweak the configuration, see how the system will handle various loads using Windows Media Load Simulator, and try out Windows Media Services 9 Series features, such as server-side playlists.

The hardware is assembled first. The NICs are installed in the servers, and memory is added, if it is not preconfigured by the manufacturer. Then the five hard drives are inserted in the servers.

The computers are started and the hard drives are configured. The first disk, an 18 GB hard drive, is split into two equal partitions. The primary partition contains the operating system, and the extended partition is left open for applications, such as a content management system. The second disk, an 18 GB hard drive, is also split into two partitions: one is used for backing up files; the other is used by the content management system for content storage. The remaining three disks, 36 GB each, are formatted with single partitions. All disks are formatted as NTFS volumes because NTFS provides better performance, security, reliability, and configuration features than the FAT32 file system.

Windows Server 2003, Enterprise Edition, is installed on each of the servers. During installation of the network components, the installer lets you choose whether to join a workgroup or a domain. Since the Fabrikam team will initially test the server farm in a closed LAN on the bench, they configure these machines to join a workgroup called LAN. Each computer is then given a name such as LAN01, LAN02, and LAN03. Each machine is also given an appropriate administrator password. (See the Windows Server 2003 Help for more information about strong passwords.)

After Windows Server 2003 is installed on each computer, a technician logs on as the administrator and installs Windows Media Services from the Windows Server 2003 CD.

The first thing you will notice after logging on is the **Manage Your Server** wizard. You can use this wizard to add the streaming media server role to the server, and the wizard will install Windows Media Services. The **Manage Your Server** wizard can also be used after Windows Media Services has been installed to open the Windows Media Services Administrator snap-in. In this case, the technician bypasses the **Manage Your Server** wizard in order to install and configure Windows Media Services manually.

Installing Windows Media Services

To install Windows Media Services, the technician does the following:

1. Open **Control Panel**, double-click **Add or Remove Programs**, and then start the **Add/Remove Windows Components** wizard.

2. Open details for Windows Media Services. All of the listed components will be used in this installation, including:

   - Multicast and Advertisement Logging Agent. This installs the components used to generate client usage logs for multicast broadcasts, and to collect client data by using the LogURL attribute in a playlist. Fabrikam will not use the advertisement agent, but they will log client usage for multicasts. Unicast logging is handled by the Logging plug-in. With multicast, on the other hand, there is no connection between the server and client. To log multicast usage, the client sends usage data back to the server, and Internet Information Server (IIS) handles logging the data using the multicast agent.

   - Windows Media Services. This installs the primary Windows Media Services functionality, and is a required component of a Windows Media server.

   - Windows Media Services snap-in. This is the primary interface used to administer the server. The interface is run in the Microsoft Management Console (MMC).

   - Windows Media Services Administrator for the Web. This installs the Web pages and components for administering a Windows Media server over the Web. Most technicians will connect to the server by using t he Windows Media Services snap-in for the Microsoft Management Console (MMC). However, the Web interface will enable users with administrative permission to connect to and configure the server through a browser.

After the components have been installed on all servers, Windows Media Services is ready to run. Microsoft Internet Information Services (IIS) is also installed and configured automatically because it is used for multicast logging and to host the Web administrator. To use these features, the installation software configures IIS to allow ISAPI applications, server-side includes, and ASP pages.

Setting up the Test LAN

After the servers have been configured, a technician could simply install them in the data center rack and they would be ready to host content. However, it is generally better to run the server offline for a period of time just to make sure there are no problems. Only after the servers have been configured and tested properly should they be placed on the production network.

At this point the technicians will set up each server in a closed LAN that is isolated from the production network. Later they will run some tests to make sure everything has been configured correctly, and to make any needed configuration changes offline. They can also try different configurations to optimize performance or reliability. For example, they might want to see what happens when using different client usage limits or when applying different authentication and authorization settings to a publishing point.

With Windows Media Load Simulator, the Fabrikam staff can see how the server and network handle a number of different client streaming scenarios. If necessary, they can use data from the load simulation tests to set limits or reconfigure the server.

Testing Considerations

To fully test the server farm offline, the closed testing network will consist of the three servers, an encoding computer, and a client computer. Figure 17.1 shows the layout of the test LAN and the temporary IP addresses that are assigned to the computers.

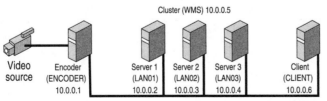

Figure 17.1   Configuration of the network for testing Windows Media servers.

The encoder should be capable of encoding a 100 Kbps stream. Even though the content will only be used for testing, the quality of the content should be high enough to accurately determine the quality of the stream coming from the server.

In addition, the encoding computer must run Windows Server 2003 because it will be used to manage the server cluster with the Network Load Balancing Manager program and Windows Media Services snap-in for MMC. Keep in mind that, in a production environment, Windows Media Encoder 9 Series would typically run on Windows XP, and the encoding computer would almost never be used to manage a server. In the lab, however, the encoding computer can play a dual role because you can control the network environment. If you want a more realistic configuration, add a separate computer for managing the servers.

The video can come from any number of sources. A video tuner connected to cable TV or a VCR playing a movie are good choices because they provide a steady stream of high-motion video, which will produce realistic, high-bit-rate content. If you do not have a video capture card, an inexpensive USB camera can be used as a video source.

The client computer has a CPU and RAM similar to the servers, and it runs Windows XP Professional. A slower CPU can be used if you plan to test server output with only one instance of Windows Media Player. However, Windows Media Load Simulator needs a client computer that can handle requesting and playing multiple concurrent streams. If you configure Windows Media Load Simulator to simulate the affect of 100 or more clients connecting to and streaming from a server, the computer must be able to handle all of these clients requesting and streaming content. Windows Media Load Simulator does not require nearly as much CPU and memory as 100 actual clients, because it does not attempt to decompress and process the streams. Nevertheless, Windows Media Load Simulator does require enough processing power to provide valid test results.

Setting up the Test Environment

The Fabrikam technicians install Windows Media Encoder 9 Series on the encoding computer, and then install Windows Media Load Simulator on the client computer. They also make sure Windows Media Player 9 Series is installed on the client. The computers need NICs. A 100-Mbps switch or hub connects the computers. After configuring the client and encoding computers, the technicians connect them and the server computers to the network switch, using the 1000Base-T NICs for the servers. For this testing session, the technicians will not use the administration and content management NICs.

The technicians set the computer names, make each a member of the same workgroup (LAN in this case), and give them static IP addresses as noted in the following table. The cluster address will be set when they configure the NLB service.

Computer	Name	IP Address
Encoder	ENCODER	10.0.0.1
Server 1	LAN01	10.0.0.2
Server 2	LAN02	10.0.0.3
Server 3	LAN03	10.0.0.4
Server cluster	WMCluster	10.0.0.5
Client	CLIENT	10.0.0.6

Finally, they create a user that is common to all computers, such as LAN, and give the user administrative permission on all computers. (They will need to remove this user from the server when putting the servers into production.)

If you plan to use WMS Negotiate Authentication or WMS Digest Authentication to secure publishing points in production, you can add a domain controller to the lab configuration. After adding the controller, the test computers must be configured to join the domain.

After the computers have been connected, the technicians check for basic network connectivity. They log on to each using the common user account. Then they use the **Run** dialog box on each computer to type the names of the other computers and view shared folders. For example, on the client computer, the technician types "\\Encoder" in the **Run** dialog box and clicks **OK**. He should be able to view shared folders on the other computers without entering a user name and password for those computers.

With all computers on and network connectivity confirmed, IT can configure the servers with the NLB service.

Configuring Network Load Balancing

In the test scenario, NLB Manager will run on the encoding computer to manage the server cluster. You could also manage from the client computer, but that computer will be very busy during the tests. You would not be able to manage the cluster from one of the server computers because this test will use load balancing in unicast mode. In this mode, you cannot access cluster hosts from one of the servers in the cluster because the media access control (MAC) address for each host is the same. In production, the administration NIC will be used to manage the cluster, and this will enable technicians to supply separate MAC addresses to the servers for administrative access. For more information on NLB, see the sidebar.

Network Load Balancing

NLB is one of the two clustering services offered by Windows Server 2003. Available in all editions of the Windows Server 2003 family of operating systems, this service routes incoming Internet Protocol (IP) traffic across clusters of servers. NLB enhances both the availability and scalability of Internet server-based programs such as Web servers, streaming media servers, and Terminal Services. By acting as the load-balancing infrastructure and providing control information to management applications built on top of Windows Management Instrumentation (WMI), NLB can seamlessly integrate into existing Web server farm infrastructures.
NLB features include the following:

- NLB Manager. Can be used as a single point of configuration and management for NLB clusters.

- Virtual clusters. Can be used to configure hosts in a cluster with different cluster IP addresses.

- Support for multiple NICs. Can be used to bind NLB to multiple network cards.

- Bi-directional affinity. Commonly used to cluster Internet Security and Acceleration (ISA) servers for proxy and firewall load balancing.

- Internet Group Management Protocol (IGMP) support. Can be used to limit switch flooding when NLB is configured in multicast mode.

For more information about the Network Load Balancing feature in Microsoft Windows Server 2003, see the product documentation.

Creating the Cluster

NLB is automatically installed and running on the servers. The Fabrikam technicians simply configure IP addresses on the 1000Base-T network adapter and the servers will start using load balancing. NLB Manager lets the technicians create, configure, and monitor the load balancing clusters remotely from the encoding computer.

The technicians follow these steps to configure and start the server cluster.

1. To start NLB Manager, on the encoding computer, open **Administrative Tools**, and then click **Network Load Balancing Manager**.

2. In the console tree, right-click **Network Load Balancing Clusters**, and then click **New Cluster**. The **Cluster Parameters** wizard starts.

For complete details about configuring clusters, see the NLB Manager Help. The following steps will describe the testing parameters set up by the Fabrikam technicians.

3. In the wizard, enter the following information:

    ■   For **Cluster IP configuration**, type the static IP address for the cluster (10.0.0.5), a subnet mask (255.255.0.0), and full Internet name (WM-Cluster). These are placeholder values for the test LAN. When they take the servers online, the technicians will need to change this information to work with the Fabrikam network.

    ■   For **Cluster operation mode**, select **Unicast**. Multicast with IGMP multicast support is not required for load balancing the media servers. This selection does not affect unicast and multicast as it relates to streaming Windows Media.

    ■   Connect to one host that is to be part of the new cluster, and select the interface. In this scenario, the technicians type 10.0.0.2, click **Connect**, and then select the 1000Base-T interface.

    A new cluster is added to NLB Manager. Next, the technicians will add the remaining two servers.

4. Select the cluster in the console tree, and start the wizard to add a new host. In **Connect to one host that is to be part of the new cluster and select the interface**, type the IP address of the next server, click **Connect**, and then select the 1000Base-T interface.

5. Repeat step 3 for the remaining server.

After you make a configuration change in the manager, the NLB service must make the changes on the servers and confirm that there are no errors. This process can take several seconds. Also, the service must perform a *convergence* operation whenever the state of the cluster changes, such as when a host is added, removed, or reconfigured. During convergence, the hosts exchange messages to determine a new, consistent state.

When intranet clients connect to the cluster address (WMCluster), NLB redirects them to one of the three servers in order to balance the load on the servers. Clients can also connect to an individual server by accessing its dedicated IP address, such as 10.0.0.2 (LAN01). When clients connect in this way, load balancing is bypassed.

To receive a multicast stream, clients do not connect directly to a server, so it would not make sense to use all three computers in the cluster for this purpose. In fact, there is no advantage to using multiple servers for multicasting, and it would only add unnecessary complexity to the system. When hosting a multicast broadcast, one server will be used to handle the multicast stream, such as LAN01. Users will connect to WMCluster for unicast streams, and the multicast group streaming from LAN01 for multicast.

Network Load Balancing Considerations

The NLB service can help balance server load and can provide fault tolerance when a server goes off line, but keep the following points in mind when using NLB with Windows Media Services.

Fast Reconnect

This is a new feature of Windows Media Services 9 Series that enables clients to reconnect to a server after a temporary network outage and resume streaming from the point at which the outage occurred. Fast Reconnect works by using state information held in temporary storage on the server. Therefore, in order for the client to resume a stream, it must reconnect to the server that holds the state information for the interrupted connection. In an NLB setup, however, the client could be sent to a different server when it attempts to reconnect.

This problem is handled by changing the client affinity setting in the port rules for a host. Open the properties dialog box for each host in the NLB cluster, locate the port rules for the host, and then change the **Affinity** option to **Single**. All traffic from a particular client will then be routed to the same cluster host.

For testing, however, leave **Affinity** set to **None**. Otherwise Windows Media Load Simulator, which is running on a single client, will connect to only one of the NLB servers. If that happens, you won't be able to test the entire cluster.

Server Applications

NLB effectively redirects client requests when a server is no longer available. However, the NLB service is not aware of other server applications or the content on a server. Even though Windows Media Services may be stopped, for example, NLB will continue to redirect clients to the server. Therefore, NLB does not replace using server rollover in Windows Media metafiles.

Also, content must be mirrored properly across the cluster. All servers must contain the same digital media files, file structure, and publishing points. If the cluster is used for a broadcast using unicast streaming, the broadcast publishing points on all servers must be running and configured identically. You can automate the mirroring of content with Distribute File System (DFS), which is included with Windows Server 2003.

The Fabrikam scenario uses the NLB service, which is software load-balancing functionality included with Windows Server 2003. Several hardware-based products are also available from companies such as Cisco and Foundry.

Network Testing Procedures

With the NLB service successfully installed, the Fabrikam team can begin streaming content over the LAN. The following checklist summarizes the setup of the server and closed LAN.

- Install server hardware. Install the NICs, add memory if necessary, and install the hard drives.

- Configure the hard drives.

- Install server software. Install Windows Server 2003, Enterprise Edition, and then install Windows Media Services. The Windows Media Services snap-in is installed on the encoding computer.

- Configure encoding and client computers. Install Windows Media Encoder 9 Series, a video capture card, and a NIC on the encoding computer. Attach an audio and video source, such as a camcorder, VCR, or TV tuner. Install Windows Media Load Simulator, Windows Media Player 9 Series, and a NIC on the client computer.

- Configure networking on all computers. Add static IP addresses and make all computers members of the same workgroup (LAN). Create a common user with administrative permissions on all computers. The technicians will create an additional user when they test security.

- Configure NLB on the servers. Open NLB Manager on the encoding computer, and then create a new cluster, adding the three servers as hosts.

- Connect the computers and check connectivity.

In the next part of the bench configuration, the technicians will run the following tests:

Test Number	Test Name	Description
Test #1	On-demand Load	Stream multiple Windows Media files.
Test #2	Broadcast Unicast Load	Stream a broadcast to multiple clients using unicast connections. Then stream a mix of on-demand and broadcast streams.
Test #3	Multicast	Stream a broadcast to a client using multicast. Then stream a mix of on-demand and multicast content.
Test #4	Security	Restrict access to a publishing point using authentication and authorization. If necessary, add a domain controller to test NTLM or Kerberos authentication. Test #4 will use a security method that does not require a domain controller.

(continued)

(continued)

Test Number	Test Name	Description
Test #5	Unicast broadcast playlist with wrapper	Stream a broadcast playlist with a wrapper to multiple clients.
Test #6	Windows Media Services Administrator for the Web	Open and examine the Web administrator interface.

Note that it is not essential that you run all or any of these tests. The purpose of the tests is to check the basic configuration, to establish a performance baseline, to confirm performance expectations, and to try different settings offline.

During testing, the Fabrikam technicians will accomplish the following tasks:

■ Confirm that everything works.

■ Configure the Windows Media server to deliver on-demand and broadcast streams to clients.

■ Analyze test results and make configuration changes if necessary.

■ Configure IIS, if necessary. If you added the Multicast and advertisement logging agent and Windows Media Services for the Web during Windows Media Services installation, IIS is also installed and configured automatically for handling these features. If changes were made to IIS after the installation, however, the features may have to be configured manually.

■ Configure the server for logging unicast and multicast connections.

■ Configure security for Windows Media Services Administrator for the Web.

■ Test streaming a broadcast playlist with a wrapper.

Test #1: On-demand Load

This is the most basic test and will tell you more about the system than any of the others. The Fabrikam technicians will create five or so test files with the encoder, and then stream them to the client.

Encoding Test Files

The first step is to create the test files. The technicians follow these steps to encode content for the tests:

1. Connect a video source to the video capture card and audio card.

Use a capture utility, such as Microsoft VidCap32 or Windows Media 9 Capture, to confirm that the capture card driver is working properly by setting the program to preview the incoming video feed.

Open the volume control and confirm that the audio driver works, and the audio is set properly. You can use an audio program that has an accurate audio meter to set up the sound level.

After you have confirmed the driver works, close the capture program.

2. Open Windows Media Encoder 9 Series.

There are many ways to configure the encoder. However, for these tests, the technicians will use the **New Session** wizard and preconfigured compression settings. In the **New Session** dialog box, they click the **Capture audio or video** wizard, and then make the following selections:

- Select the video and audio capture devices.

- Enter a file name and path to be used for the first output file, such as c:\media\test1.wmv.

- In **Content Destination**, select **Windows Media server**.

- In **Encoding options**, select **Multiple bit rates (CBR)** for video and audio. In **Bit rate**, select only the **125** Kbps check box for the first file. For the other four or five files, use different bit rates, and try a file that contains two or three bit rates. For example, encode a file at 160 Kbps and another at 332 Kbps.

- Enter metadata such as title and author.

3. Encode 30 to 60 seconds of the video source. As the encoder runs, the technician keeps an eye on **CPU load** in the **Monitor** panel. If the load is consistently over 60 to 70 percent, the quality of the encoded video may be compromised. You can lower CPU usage by closing programs like screen savers and instant messengers. You can also try closing the **Video preview** panel.

You can also configure the encoder to store content temporarily as it is being captured, and then compress and encode the content automatically when the capture is finished. When doing so, the CPU-intensive processes of capturing and encoding are performed at different times, so the quality of the encoded file is less likely to be adversely affected by an overburdened computer. If CPU load is still high, you will have to lower the encoding bit rate.

4. Open the file in Windows Media Player and check playback. Then repeat steps 2 and 3 to create the remaining test files.

5.   After encoding five or six files, copy them to the default publishing point on each Windows Media server. When Windows Media Services is installed, a set of folders is created. The folder %systemdrive%\WMPub\WMRoot is set as the default publishing point and contains some more sample files that can be used for testing. Move the default publishing point and the content, if necessary, to the new data volume designated for digital media content.

Checking Server Configuration

With the files available to the Windows Media server, the technicians will open the Windows Media Services snap-in and configure the cluster.

1.   On the encoding computer click **Start**, click **Administrative Tools**, and then click **Windows Media Services**. The Windows Media Services snap-in opens.

2.   In the console tree on the left, add a group, and name it Cluster.

3.   Add each Windows Media server to the Cluster group.

4.   Right-click **Windows Media Services**, click **Export console configuration**, and then enter a location and name. The next time a technician opens the Windows Media Services snap-in, he can reopen the group by importing the configuration file.

5.   In the console tree on the left, expand each server, and then expand **Publishing Points**. On each, click the default publishing point, and then click the **Source** tab in the details pane. The new files should appear in the **Source** list. If you add files after opening the **Source** tab, click the **Refresh** button to update the list. If you copy files to a new data volume, make it the source of the default publishing point.

6.   By default, the root publishing point is set to deny new connections as a security measure. Before content can be streamed from the publishing points, a technician must click the **Allow new unicast connections** button on the row below the list on each server.

7.   On each server, on the **Properties** tab, click the **Logging** plug-in and enable client logging. The client log provides a detailed record of client activity, such as listing all clients, the streams they played or attempted to play, times, and errors. The Fabrikam test will not necessarily use this log. However, logging adds to the load on the servers and will therefore give a more complete picture of the server as it would function in production.

Streaming Files

With the server cluster configured, the technicians can start streaming content to Windows Media Player. These are the procedures used for the test:

1. On the client computer, open Windows Media Player 9 Series.

2. Open and stream one of the test files. In the **Open URL** dialog box, type the URL of the file (rtsp://WMCluster/test1.wmv). If the file streams correctly, the technicians can go on to the next test and use Windows Media Load Simulator. If there is a problem, they will retrace their steps and locate the source of the problem. The following are potential problem areas:

   - Wrong URL. The Player displays the error message "File or path not found." Make sure that the file is in the default root folder, and that the file name and path are correct in the URL.

   - Network connectivity. The Player displays the error message "Server not found." The Player might not find a server because of a mistyped URL or a problem with the network cable or switch.

   - NLB service. The Player displays a "Server not found" error if the load balancing service is not working. Try streaming the file directly from a server, using a URL such as rtsp://LAN01/test1.wmv.

   - Security. Windows Media Player displays the error message "Access is denied." Authorization and authentication have been added to the server or publishing point, and the user who is logged on to the client computer does not have access.

   - Codec. The Player error indicates that you are attempting to stream a file for which there is no codec installed. The Player attempted to download the codec, unless the download codec feature was disabled, but could not locate the codec site to install it.

If your client computer is running an earlier version of Windows, such as Windows 2000, you can use Windows Media Player versions 6.4 or 7, but you will not be able to use the new features that are available only with Windows Media Player 9 Series. Also, earlier versions of the Player do not include the new Windows Media 9 Series codecs.

If your streaming media system must support earlier versions of Windows Media Player, copy one of the files you just encoded to the client, then reconfigure the client computer and connect to the Internet. When you attempt to play the file, Windows Media Player will automatically download the new codecs. Once the codecs are installed, reconnect the client computer to the closed LAN.

Alternatively, you can encode the files with a custom compression setting using an earlier codec.

Configuring Windows Media Load Simulator

Windows Media Load Simulator approximates the processing and network usage of one or more clients streaming content from a server. Windows Media Load Simulator does not use the streams, so it does not need to use the client computer's CPU and RAM to decompress and render the streams. Without having to decompress the streams, one computer can simulate the load of a hundred or more clients. Even though the data is not used, the streams are very real from the point of view of the server and the network. The server and network behave during a simulation the same as they would under a real load.

Windows Media Load Simulator should not be used to test server load over the production network because it can affect the operation of the entire network. However, Windows Media Load Simulator is sometimes used to establish a performance baseline, which is difficult to do in a lab environment. If you choose to use Windows Media Load Simulator in production, be aware of the security, operational, and network risks involved in doing so.

As you run Windows Media Load Simulator, check the performance of the Windows Media server computers and the streams that they are delivering by using the Windows Media Performance Monitor. The Performance Monitor gives you the picture from the server side. At the same time, Windows Media Load Simulator displays streaming errors that are generated as it attempts to connect, stream, and seek within streams. After you run a simulation, you can check the performance and error logs created by Windows Media Load Simulator. All of this information will give you an understanding of how the servers will function under various load conditions.

As the Fabrikam technicians set up Windows Media Load Simulator, you will see that many different usage scenarios that can be created. You can simulate the load of almost any number of clients. You can set the number of clients and assign various tasks to them. For example, you can have 30 clients playing files all the way through, 10 clients just opening and closing connections, and 10 more seeking in files. You can also monitor the effect of using authentication and authorization. Handling security and client control add to the load on the server and bandwidth usage on the network.

Before opening Windows Media Load Simulator, make sure you log on to the same user account that was used to install the program (usually the administrator account). This is important because Windows Media Load Simulator installation makes changes to the Windows Media Player configuration file that is individualized for each user. If you do not log on as the user who installed Windows Media Load Simulator, you will not be able to stream using the MMS protocol.

The following procedures are used to configure Windows Media Load Simulator for testing:

1.   Open Windows Media Load Simulator.

2.   On the **Tools** menu, click **Configurations (Wizard)**.

3.   In the wizard, enter the following information:

   ■   Enter the name of the target server for the load test. In this case, the
       Fabrikam technicians enter the cluster address (WMCluster).

   ■   Select the protocols to use. Select both MMS protocols (**MMST** and
       MMSU) and both RTSP protocols (**RTSPT** and **RTSPU**), but not **HTTP**.
       The MMST and RTSPT options use the TCP/IP transport protocol;
       the MMSU and RTSPU options use the UDP transport protocol.

   ■   Add the names of the test files. The files and the protocols selected are
       added to the list, as shown in the figure 17.2.

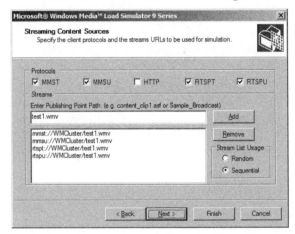

Figure 17.2   Files have been selected for the streaming test.

   ■   Enter client profiles. A profile is a client behavior. Enter the number of
       clients you would like to stream content for one or more behaviors. Figure
       17.3 shows a sample profile configuration.

   ■   Test duration. The Fabrikam technicians will stop the simulator manu-
       ally, but you can specify a test duration.

   ■   Enable **Client-side Logging**. Select this check box to send client
       activity information to the Windows Media server logging system on
       each server. You may want to use the logs to study the simulation re-
       sults, such as to see how NLB redirects client requests. However, be-
       cause the simulator does not actually use the streams, the information
       may not tell you very much.

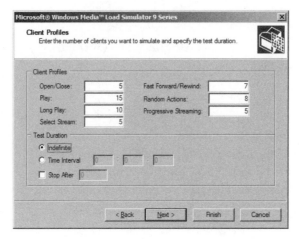

Figure 17.3 A client profile configuration.

■ Enable **Load Simulator Logging**. Select this check box and enter a
location for saving the log file. This log shows the test results generated
by Windows Media Load Simulator. An entry is made for each client
describing the client's streaming experience. Figure 17.4 shows a sample
client entry taken from a log opened in Microsoft Excel.

Figure 17.4 Load Simulator log information can be viewed in Excel.

■ Turn off **Server Performance Logging**. This log records the server
performance monitor. However, because clients will be connecting to
the cluster, no performance information can be obtained to create the
log. You can view Windows Media Performance Monitor on each computer or from the group in the Windows Media Services MMC snap-in.

HTTP is not enabled when you install Windows Media Services because it uses port 80 by default, which is the same port used by IIS. If you want to try HTTP streaming, enable the protocol in the Windows Media Services snap-in and change the HTTP port number. Then add the port number to the URL in Load Simulator (for example, http://WMCluster:8090/test1.wmv).

For the client profiles, you may want to start with a conservative number and a straightforward profile, just to see how the program works. For example, you might enter 10 clients in the **Long Play** profile, and 0 in all the others. Clients with the **Long Play** profile simply play the content. If the 10 clients are streaming a 100 Kbps file, you should see a total bandwidth of around 1000 Kbps. Clients with the **Seek** profile simulate users seeking to different parts of files. As you run the simulation, you will notice that bandwidth fluctuates with the content. With different profiles, the bandwidth increases as clients perform actions, like opening and closing files and seeking. For more information about the meaning of the different profiles, see Windows Media Load Simulator Help.

After you are comfortable with the results, you may want to see what happens when 30 clients connect and play content all the way through, five receive content through progressive streaming, and 10 seek or change playback position within files. Simply streaming a file adds one kind of load to the server. Opening, closing, seeking, and other client actions add another kind of load. As you add different profiles, you can see how different aspects of the server are affected by watching the performance monitors.

Before you can run a simulation, you must place a Windows Media file with the name WMLoad.asf in the root folder of each server (\WMPub\WMRoot). Any Windows Media file can be used. Pick one that is small, copy it to the WMRoot folder, and rename it.

This file serves as a simple security measure to prevent unauthorized simulations against a server. The file can be any Windows Media file. The important thing is the name. Without this file present in the default root folder, Windows Media Load Simulator will not stream from the server. Windows Media Load Simulator is designed to test loading in a protected environment. In production, the program could be used to launch a denial of service attack. To prevent unauthorized users from running simulations, remove the file when the servers are in production.

To view the performance of the system during the test runs, the Fabrikam technicians open the following system monitors:

- Client Task Manager. On the client computer, run **Task Manager** and keep an eye on **CPU Usage** on the **Performance** tab.

- Group details. In the Windows Media Services MMC snap-in on the encoding computer, watch the group of servers in the details pane, which will show connections and bandwidth usage.

■   Server Performance Monitor. Expand each server in the group, and then click the **View Performance Monitor** button on the bottom row of the **Monitor** tab for each server. You can add or remove performance counters to get different views of the servers, and you can view the performance of the whole server or individual publishing points. You can also monitor load-balancing operations by creating a Windows Media Performance Monitor configuration with all the servers listed in a common view. For more information about the counters, see Windows Media Services Help.

Running the Simulation

At this point, the Fabrikam technicians start Windows Media Load Simulator and watch the monitors. The following sections describe what they watch and how the information can be interpreted:

Load Simulation Status

This tab on Windows Media Load Simulator shows when the test begins and ends, and lists streaming errors that occur during the simulation when a setting has been configured improperly. For example, an error is raised when Windows Media Load Simulator attempts to stream using HTTP when the HTTP Server Control Protocol plug-in on the server has been disabled, attempts to connect to a stream to which the user does not have access, or attempts to stream a file that does not exist.

Barring configuration errors, streaming errors can occur if the server, network, or client computer cannot process a request or handle a stream. To track down errors, check the other monitors. For example, if you are receiving many client connection errors, but the CPU usage on the server and client computers are running low, there is a good chance the problem is caused by a configuration error and not server load.

Client Performance

If the client CPU usage is running in the high percentages, errors will show up that have nothing to do with server and network performance. Cut down on the number of simulator clients and profiles. You might notice that Load Simulator requires more of the client computer's CPU and memory when it runs many tasks. You could try cutting down on the number of tasks if you want to increase the client count. For example, the client computer can more easily handle 50 long-play clients than the same number of clients opening, closing, and seeking.

Server Performance Monitors

These indicators provide the most detailed picture of a server during a test run. You can view **% Processor Time**, number of players connected for different protocols, and many more counters. As the simulation runs, watch for problems such as an increase in **Late Reads**, **Memory**, and **% Processor Time**.

If client errors occur in conjunction with an increase in these counters, either a slow CPU or slow hard drives might be a problem. If streaming errors are occurring, you can also check the bandwidth usage to see if it is running up against the limits of the network.

Group Details or Monitor Tab

For a high-level picture of the simulation, check the indicators in **Group details** or the **Monitor** tab for each server. These screens will show you general information, such as CPU usage, total number of clients connected, and the current allocated bandwidth.

With a server farm like the one Fabrikam is using, CPU usage will be very low, late reads probably nonexistent, and errors very rare when running simulation tests. It is more likely that problems will originate on the network or the client computer. If the servers are functioning and configured properly, the server farm should be able to handle thousands of client connections, depending on the bit rates being streamed and number of different streams. As the Fabrikam technicians increase the number of clients, they will probably begin to see network errors, such as errors reading from the network and failed network connections. The 1000-Mbps network can handle far less traffic than the server, and the one client computer can handle even less.

If you need to stress test a server, you can add more client computers and a faster network. However, doing so would not give a realistic picture of the servers in production. You can try several different client scenarios, and then run a simulation overnight. In the morning, you can check memory usage and glance through the logs to note any unusual errors. Typically, the limiting factor for streaming on-demand content is hard drive input and output. The limiting factor for streaming live content is the CPU.

Analyzing the Test Results

The logs show a lot of detail that can be used to create accurate reports. Client usage logs generated on the servers (like the one shown in figure 17.5) can be compiled and used to create detailed client demographic reports, for example. Commercial Web sites can base customer billing on the length of time clients stay tuned to a stream or the number of hits a file gets.

At Fabrikam, client logs can be used by the IT department to locate streaming errors. If the cause of an error isn't obvious, they can use the times on the client log to reference a performance log.

Each record in the client log corresponds to an event from the client. The log in figure 17.5 shows a few seconds of a Windows Media Load Simulator run. Client logs from simulations will not always give you useful information because the simulator does not always provide the server with the same information an actual Player would provide. But you can glance through it for large blocks of streaming errors, for example.

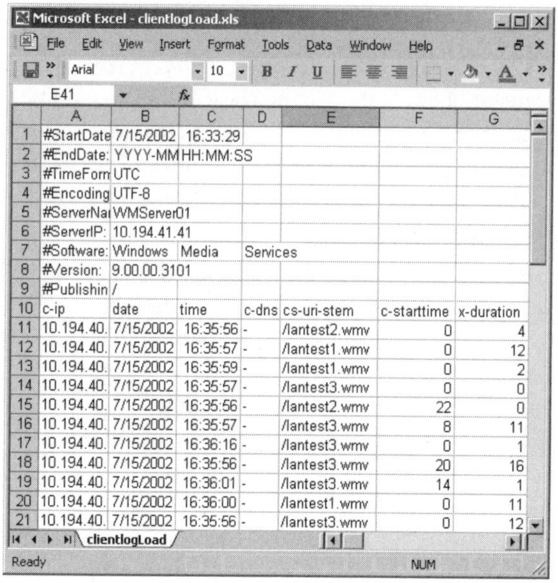

Figure 17.5 Client usage logs provide details about streaming activity on the server.

If you note a problem at a given time, such as a large number of playback errors, you could cross-check logs created by the performance monitors for each server. If you looked at the performance log for that time, you might note a high processor time and late reads value due to a high number of concurrent streaming players. If there was nothing unusual on the server side at that time other than an unusually high number of clients, you might suspect the network or a configuration problem.

You could then check the Windows Media Load Simulator WMLog and look for clients that reported a high number of failures. Figure 17.4 shows the data for one client in the log. The first part of the log records the error activity that printed out in real time during the simulation run on the **Load Simulation Status** tab on Windows Media Load Simulator. If a client reported failure to open, configuration was correct, and you knew the server was not under stress, then you might suspect a slow network or a stressed client computer.

The Windows Media Load Simulator tests have several purposes. First, they enable you to pick up any gross configuration errors in the server, try different server settings, and learn how the server operates. Simulations can also be used to configure limits on the server. Figure 17.6 shows the **Limits** list on the **Properties** tab of a server. You can set limits for the entire server or individual publishing points. If your computer and network are slow, try limiting the number of player connections or connection rate. If you need to preserve network bandwidth, limit aggregate player bandwidth.

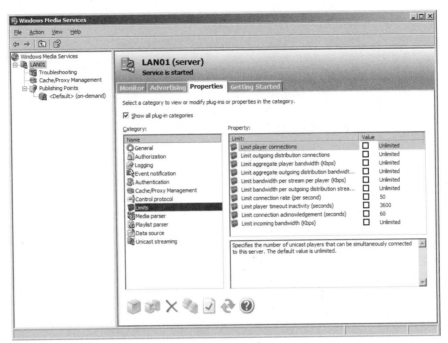

Figure 17.6   Configuring usage limits for a server.

The Fabrikam server farm itself can most likely handle more processing and streaming than the network. However, if you are running Windows Media Services on a slow computer or if network bandwidth is an issue, you can place limits on bandwidth and the number of client connections. When deciding what numbers to use, keep in mind that it requires less bandwidth to stream a few high-bit-rate streams than it does to stream many low-bit-rate streams, even though the total bit rate is the same. This is because each connection requires a certain amount of bandwidth overhead.

Delivering a large number of streams also requires more processing power and reads from the hard drive. This is also true of short files and long files. As you can see with the simulation, playing many short files requires more opening and closing of sessions and seeking, which requires more bandwidth and CPU time than would long files. Try simulations against many short files, and then try the simulation again with a few long files. Also try adding clients that just seek, open, and close files.

Try to estimate what the typical and peak mix of content and playback behavior will be in your enterprise. It will only be an estimate, but this will provide testing results that are more applicable to your particular scenario than simply entering random client profile numbers. The lab test is the first of enterprise performance baselines. In a production environment, more tests should be done during deployment to make sure the lab results are accurate.

Test #2: Broadcast Unicast Load

A stream is the same whether it comes from a file or a broadcast source, so you can gather most server performance data by using on-demand content. However, there are some differences in how the streams are delivered and used that you should be aware of. For example, streaming a live broadcast is easier on the server computer because the hard drive is not used. Even if you are broadcasting a file or a playlist of files, disk access is low compared to streaming on-demand content. Therefore, you will probably not see late reads with a broadcast. The client cannot seek and broadcasts often have a longer duration, so there is usually less client interaction. On the other hand, a unicast broadcast can have more concurrent connections, because all users must tune in at the same time. Therefore, you are more likely to see an increase in bandwidth usage and CPU time.

With multicast, of course, an increase in the number of clients does not increase the connections or the load on the computer. As far as bench testing, it is a good idea to set up and run a unicast broadcast, so you can see how the system works and so you know what to expect when the server is online, even if, as in the Fabrikam scenario, most of your clients will receive broadcasts using multicast streaming.

The main point of this test is educational. You will see the process of creating a broadcast to better learn how broadcast publishing points and live encoding work. We will see how the Fabrikam technicians run Windows Media Load Simulator on the broadcast publishing point to measure the difference in load between on-demand and live streaming. We can also see what happens when they run a simulation that includes a mix of live and on-demand streaming, different bit rates, and an MBR stream.

Encoding a Live Stream

The Fabrikam technicians start by configuring the encoder to capture and encode a live stream, and then they start the stream. The technicians follow these steps to complete the process:

1. Connect a live video source to the video capture card. Then check for connectivity and make sure the audio level is adjusted correctly.

2. Open Windows Media Encoder 9 Series.

3. Run the **New Session** wizard as in test #1. This time, however, select the **Broadcast a live event** wizard. Enter the following information:

   ■ Select the video and audio capture devices.

   ■ Select the **Pull from encoder** option. With this option, the publishing point will initiate the connection to the encoder.

   ■ Type a port number, such as 9090, or click **Find Free Port** to have the encoder choose one.

- In **Encoding options**, select **Multiple bit rates (CBR)** for video and audio.

- In **Bit rate**, select the **125 Kbps** check box for the live stream. Make sure the other bit rates are not selected.

- Enter information to be displayed in Windows Media Player. Note that, if you later choose to add metadata to the announcement file, the information in the announcement file will supercede the information added here.

4. Start encoding.

Configuring the Server

Now the Fabrikam technicians test the live stream from the encoder, and configure a broadcast publishing point on the server.

A technician starts by checking the stream from the encoder. He does this by opening Windows Media Player on the client computer and entering the encoder URL, which consists of the HTTP protocol, the name of the encoding computer, and the port number (such as http://encoder:9090).

By default, up to five clients can connect directly to the encoder. You can change the default value to accommodate up to 50 clients by editing a key in the system registry. However, maintaining connections adds to the load on the encoding computer. Typically, you will direct clients to connect to a Windows Media server which can handle many more connections.

After confirming that the encoder is streaming, the technician creates a publishing point on the server to host the stream.

1. On the encoding computer, open the Windows Media Services MMC snap-in and import the configuration file that includes the cluster group.

2. In the console tree on the left, expand each server and its publishing points.

3. On the first server, right-click **Publishing Points**, and click **Add Publishing Point Wizard**. In test #1, the Fabrikam technicians used a predefined on-demand publishing point. In this test, they will create a new broadcast publishing point. For more information about publishing points, see chapter 3.

4. Enter the following information in the wizard:

   - For **Publishing Point Name**, enter LiveTest.

   - For **Content Type**, select the source of the publishing point. In this case, the source is an encoder.

   - For **Publishing Point Type**, select **Broadcast publishing point**.

- For **Delivery Options**, select **Unicast streaming**.

- For **Encoder URL**, enter the location and port number of the source (for example, http://encoder:9090).

- Select the check box for unicast logging. Client usage logs will be created for the publishing point.

- To complete the wizard, select **Create an announcement file (.asx) or Web page (.htm)**, and do not choose to start the publishing point when the wizard finishes. The **Unicast Announcement Wizard** starts.

5. The **Unicast Announcement Wizard** helps quickly create an announcement file for the publishing point. For more information about announcement files, see chapter 3. Enter the following information in the wizard:

   - For **URL to content**, enter the URL that will be contained in the announcement file. Windows Media Player will use this information to locate the content. The URL uses the MMS protocol, and contains the name of the server followed by the publishing point. Change the URL to point to the cluster, such as mms://WMCluster/LiveTest.

   - Enter a path and name for the announcement file, which has an .asx file extension. Save the file in a folder in the IIS root of the first server, such as \\LAN01\Inetpub\wwwroot\ASX. In the test, the Player will access the file from IIS on one of the servers. When the server goes online, announcement files will be hosted on the Fabrikam intranet Web server farm.

   - Enter a title, such as **LiveTest**.

   - Do not choose to test the file when the wizard finishes.

   The publishing point is set up and the announcement file that points to it is created. And the encoder has been started.

6. Repeat steps 3, 4, and 5 for the remaining servers. You can skip step 5 if you want, and merely copy the announcement file to the same location on the other servers.

7. Click the **Start publishing point** button on each of the servers. The broadcast publishing points start after successfully connecting to the encoder. However, the encoder does not need to be encoding for the publishing point to start; it just needs to be open and configured. If a client connects to a running publishing point that hosts an encoder that is not encoding, the client will go into "waiting" mode until the stream from the encoder begins.

The announcement file is a plain text file that contains information used by Windows Media Player to locate the content. It also contains metadata information that defines text and graphics that display on the Player, as well as multicast logging information. As you become more familiar with using Windows Media Services 9 Series, you may find that it is easier to simply write your own announcement files in a program such as Microsoft Notepad. The following is an example of an announcement file:

```
<asx version = "3.0">
    <entry>
        <ref href = "mms://WMCluster/LiveTest"/>
    <Title>LiveTest</Title>
    <Author></Author>
    <Copyright></Copyright>
    <Banner></Banner>
    </entry>
    <Title>LiveTest</Title>
    <Author></Author>
    <Copyright></Copyright>
    <Banner></Banner>
    <LogURL href = ""/>
</asx>
```

Notice that the only metadata used here is for the title. Other metadata, such as author and copyright, are empty. An announcement file can also be a client-side playlist file simply by adding more <entry> elements containing content.

Playing the Live Stream

At this point, the Fabrikam technician opens Windows Media Player on the client computer and enters the URL of the announcement file (for example, http://WMCluster/ASX/LiveTest.asx). The Player opens the .asx file, interprets the script, and then opens the stream using the URL contained in the file (mms://WMCluster/LiveTest). The Player also displays any metadata contained in the file or stream.

You can access Windows Media-based content in the Player directly with the MMS or RTSP protocols, or you can access it through an announcement file. Announcement files are primarily used to provide a redirection function because content URLs are most often passed to the client on a Web page, and many browser MIME types are not set up to handle audio and video content. For more information about announcement files and client-side playlist files, see chapter 3.

Running Load Simulator and Analyzing Results

The same process is used for setting up Windows Media Load Simulator as for testing on-demand streaming, except the technicians point Windows Media Load Simulator to the broadcast publishing point. For example, the **Streaming Content Sources** page might look like figure 17.7.

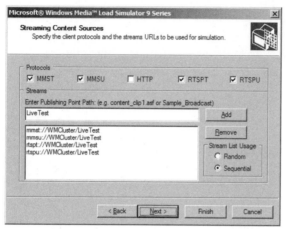

Figure 17.7   Using Windows Media Load Simulator on a broadcast publishing point.

You can use the same types of client profiles as were used for testing on-demand streaming. Keep in mind that clients cannot seek within content during a broadcast, and long-play clients will stay connected as long as the stream runs. As you run a simulation, notice the difference in activity between the on-demand and broadcast tests. In general, content usage is also very different. With on-demand content, there is often more client activity because users have more control over playback. With a broadcast, clients may stay connected longer, so the load on the server is lighter, even though more clients may be connected.

Try different profiles and compare the two types of streaming. Add on-demand files to the mix of content sources and see how the server performs. Try adding another bit rate to the encoder, so it streams multiple bit rates (for example 100 and 45 Kbps). The added processing load should be very noticeable on the encoder, but should have little effect on server processing.

In summary, the server typically has to work less to deliver 100 broadcast streams than it does for the same number of on-demand streams. The server does not have to access a hard drive, so processing time and hard drive usage are not issues. The processor also works less because there is less client interaction. However, all of this is offset by the fact that there are often more concurrent connections, which add to server load and require more RAM. The added connections also require more network bandwidth.

Test #3: Multicasting

The whole point of setting up a multicast broadcast was merely educational. There is no real need to run a load simulation because multicast client connections do not place a load on the server. For example, no clients, one client, or 4,000 clients all have the same impact on server load and bandwidth usage. For this reason, Windows Media Load Simulator is not designed to stream a multicast broadcast.

To test multicasting, the Fabrikam technicians will receive the broadcast with a Player on the client computer, and another Player on the encoding computer. After they see how multicast streaming works, they can run Windows Media Load Simulator to see how the server handles a mix of multicast and unicast on-demand streaming, which will provide a more realistic picture of the servers in production.

When a client connects to a unicast stream, the server sends header information before it starts sending the content. The header is a small package of information that tells Windows Media Player about the stream, such as what codecs will be needed to decompress the stream, how large the video frame will be, how data packets are laid out, and so forth. The Player uses this information to prepare for the data that follows. For example, the Player downloads and installs codecs if necessary, and then loads them into memory. Without header information, a stream cannot be played because the data cannot be interpreted.

With a multicast stream, the Player does not connect to the server to receive the stream, so it must get header information from another source. That source is the multicast information file. To connect to a multicast stream, the Player first opens the announcement file, which is typically hosted on a Web server with a URL such as http://WebServer/Multicast.asx. Then, rather than connect to a file or publishing point, the Player connects to the multicast information file by using the address contained in the announcement file. For example, the following announcement file points to the information file Multicast.nsc.

```
<asx version = "3.0">
    <entry>
        <ref href = "http://WebServer/Multicast.nsc"/>
    </entry>
</asx>
```

The Player then opens the multicast information file to retrieve the header information and the IP address and port of the multicast. The Player makes a request for the stream over the network, which is received by routers and other network devices. If the stream is available, the multicast traffic is routed to the Player. Unlike an announcement file, the multicast information file contains binary information that can be read by the Player, but cannot be read or edited using a text editor. The only way to make a multicast information file is by using the wizard on the server.

For Fabrikam's test, they will host the announcement and multicast information files on the LAN01 Web server.

Enabling Multicast Logging

Only one server, LAN01, will be set up for delivering the multicast stream. All three servers in the Fabrikam cluster will continue to host unicast streams. Before setting up our test scenario, the Fabrikam technicians will set up LAN01 for logging multicast clients. They will enable multicast logging on the publishing point and check the log after completing the test, but they won't necessarily use the test log results for anything.

Client logging for unicast streaming is fairly straightforward because the server maintains a connection with every client. Detailed information about clients, such as how long a client plays a stream and the name of the content, is readily available. Logging multicast clients, on the other hand, requires a more complex system because the server makes no connections with clients. In order to log client activity for a multicast, the client sends usage data to a multicast logging URL. The URL points to a logging file on a Web server. Fabrikam will use the logging file wmsiislog.dll, which they installed with Windows Media Services. The Windows Media Services SDK can be used by developers to create custom logging files that may handle the logging data differently.

Here is how the logging system works for multicast: The Player opens a multicast information file (.nsc), which contains configuration information, including the logging URL. When the Player stops receiving the multicast stream, such as when the end user clicks **Stop**, the Player sends a string of client data to the logging file specified in the URL. The data contains usage data for the entire session, such as the player IP address, the start time, and playback duration. This information is then added to a multicast log on the server. To minimize data on the network, the Player only sends logging data when it stops receiving the multicast.

To set up the server to receive multicast usage information from clients, make sure IIS is running and then do the following:

1. Locate the folder containing the logging file, wmsiislog.dll, which is installed by default in the %systemdrive%\Wmpub\Wmsiislog folder.

2. Right-click the folder, and then click **Sharing and Security**.

3. On the **Web Sharing** tab, share the folder on the default Web site, and enter an alias, such as "WmLog." Then assign executable permissions to the directory.

This creates a virtual directory. The URL of the directory is now the logging URL, which can be used by any broadcast publishing point that uses multicast streaming and requires client logging.

Other necessary settings were added to IIS and the system registry when the Multicast and Logging Agent was installed. If you find that logging is not working when you run a multicasting test, try reinstalling the agent.

After the server goes into production on the corporate network, the logging file can be moved from the Windows Media server to a Web server. Logging does require some

CPU time and memory to perform, and this is one task that can be offloaded to another computer.

Encoding a Live Stream

This test uses the same setup as described in test #2. Make sure the capture devices are configured and video is being received. You can use the same encoder configuration, but select only one bit rate to encode. A stream that contains multiple bit rates cannot be delivered using multicast because MBR streams require a direct connection between the client and the server.

In practice, when a multicast broadcast is produced by the Fabrikam Media department, they will use two or three encoding computers, or two or three instances of the encoder on one computer, each set up for a different bit rate. The encoders will then feed two or three multicast publishing points, and end users can choose the bit rate that is appropriate.

After the encoder is configured, start encoding.

Configuring the Server

The Fabrikam technicians test the encoded stream, and then configure a broadcast publishing point for multicast delivery.

1. On the server (LAN01), open the Player and connect directly to the encoder to make sure the server is receiving the stream. You can skip this step if nothing has changed from the previous test.

2. On the encoding computer, open the Windows Media Services MMC snap-in with the cluster group, and start the **Add Publishing Point Wizard** on LAN01. Then enter the following information:

    ■   For **Publishing Point Name**, enter LiveMulticast.

    ■   For **Content Type**, select **Encoder (a live stream)**.

    ■   For **Publishing Point Type**, select **Broadcast publishing point**.

    ■   For **Delivery Options**, select **Multicast**.

    ■   For **Encoder URL**, enter the same URL that was used in test #2 (for example, http://encoder:9090).

    ■   After the wizard finishes, choose to create an .nsc file. The **Multicast Announcement Wizard** starts.

3. In the **Multicast Announcement Wizard**, enter the following information:

- For **Files to create**, select **Multicast information file (.nsc) and announcement file (.asx)**.

- For **Retrieve stream format information**, choose for the server to automatically retrieve stream formats from the encoder.

4. On the next wizard screen, the wizard will attempt to connect to the encoder and download the header information from the live stream. Make sure the encoder is configured and streaming before going to the next page of the wizard.

5. Enable client logging for the publishing point, and then enter the URL of the logging file (such as http://LAN01/WmLog/wmsiislog.dll).

6. Save the multicast information file and the announcement file on the default Web site. For example, you could create ASX and NSC folders within the Home folder. In production, the metafiles will be hosted on the intranet Web servers.

7. Specify the URL of the multicast information file. If the Fabrikam technicians placed the multicast information file in a folder called NSC, the URL would be http://LAN01/NSC/LiveMulticast.nsc.

8. Enter any necessary metadata, then finish the wizard.

The wizard creates the files, retrieves stream format information from the encoder, and automatically configures and enables the multicast plug-in with default values. Before testing the stream, let's look at how the plug-in was configured.

To see the configuration information, click the **Properties** tab for the new publishing point, then click the **Multicast streaming** category. The wizard has already enabled the WMS Multicast Data Writer plug-in. Now, open the properties page for the plug-in.

An IP address and port number have been assigned to the publishing point automatically. You can use these settings. After setting up a broadcast system, you may want to explicitly assign a multicast IP address. The standard class D IP addresses range from 224.0.0.0 to 239.255.255.255. Addresses 239.0.0.0 to 239.255.255.255 are defined as administrative addresses and are used for private networks.

If you select the **Enable unicast rollover** check box, a client can connect to the publishing point by using unicast streaming if it cannot locate the multicast stream. This is useful if a stream must be available to all clients on a network, but devices like routers and firewalls are configured to stop multicast packets. If you do not select the **Enable unicast rollover** check box, it will force clients to connect to the multicast stream only.

The properties dialog for the plug-in also enables you to enter a **Time-to-live (TTL)** value. This setting affects how routers handle multicast traffic. For more information, see the Understanding Time-to-live sidebar.

If you change any settings in the multicast plug-in, you must create a new multicast information file.

Now start the publishing point. If all information was entered correctly and the publishing point is receiving the stream specified as the source on the **Source** tab and in the multicast information file, the publishing point will start streaming.

Playing the Live Stream

To test the live stream, a Fabrikam technician opens the Player on a client computer, and then opens the URL of the announcement file (http://LAN01/ASX/LiveMulticast.asx). The Player will follow the path in the announcement file to the multicast information file, which it will use to locate and play the multicast stream.

On the server **Monitor** tab, the technicians will see that there are no connected unicast clients. You can connect as many clients to the stream as you like and no load will be added to the server. Except for the multicast client usage log, there is no way of knowing how many clients are connected to a multicast.

Now the technician opens the Player on the encoding computer and connects to the multicast, if the CPU can handle the extra load. At this point they have two Players connected to the stream, and no additional load on the server.

Next, the technician clicks the **Monitor** tab, and then clicks the **Allow new unicast connections** button. Then he stops the Player on the client computer and re-connects to the publishing point using unicast streaming, with a URL such as mms://LAN01/LiveMulticast. Even if a publishing point is configured for multicast, you can still connect using unicast streaming.

Understanding Time-to-live

Routers on a network play an important role in delivering multicast streams. When a unicast stream is requested by a client, one connection is established between the server and a client. With multicast, on the other hand, there is no connection between client and server. When a multicast publishing point is started, the network routers and switches handle client requests and direct the multicast packets. The server merely sends the stream. Without routers to control the stream, multicast packets would flood every part of the network.

(continued)

Understanding Time-to-live   *(continued)*

You can control where the stream goes by configuring the devices and the multicast stream. Using TTL, you can restrict the scope of a multicast. For example, you can restrict the scope to a building or a plant, or, as in the case of Fabrikam, to headquarters. The TTL value determines how many router hops a multicast packet can pass through. Every time a packet passes through a router, the TTL value is decremented by one. When a packet has a TTL of 0, the router stops forwarding the packet. For example, with a value of 32, the packets will pass through 32 routers. When it hits the router 33, the packets go no further.

The routers themselves can also be configured or enabled to control the traffic. One way to control traffic is to configure the router to pass only multicast packets with certain IP addresses. This allows you to restrict multicasts to given network segments. We will cover configuring routers and switches for multicasting in chapter 22.

In the Fabrikam scenario, however, the IT department may want to allow multicasting only. If that is the case, they can click the **Deny new unicast connections** button on the **Monitor** tab. With multicasting enabled and new unicast connections denied, clients will only be able to connect through multicast. With new unicast connections denied, the technician can try connecting using the unicast URL, and then try connecting to the multicast.

You can check which protocol and method Windows Media Player is connected with by opening the **Statistics** dialog box in the Player, and then clicking the **Advanced** tab. If the Player is using multicast streaming, the **Protocol** box will show **MMS (Multicast)**. It will display a protocol, such as **RTSP (UDP)**, if it is streaming unicast. This **Statistics** dialog box is very useful for seeing how the Player is receiving a stream. If **Protocol** shows **CACHE**, for example, you know the Player has downloaded a file and is playing it from the local cache.

If you plan to offer both unicast and multicast, you can set up the multicast plug-in so that a client will automatically roll over to unicast stream if it is unable to connect to the multicast stream. Rollover is currently turned off in the Fabrikam scenario.

To disable multicast in the Player, a Fabrikam technician does the following:

1. On the publishing point, click the **Allow new unicast** connections button.

2. In the **Option** dialog box in the Player, click the **Network** tab, and clear the **Multicast** check box.

3. Open the announcement file in the Player (for example, http://WMServer01/ ASX/LiveMulticast.asx). The Player will not be able to connect to the stream from the publishing point. This is similar to the experience of an end user who is behind a firewall or network device that does not pass multicast traffic.

Now the Fabrikam technician can enable unicast rollover:

1. Go back to the server and open up the properties for the Multicast Data Writer plug-in.

2. Enable unicast rollover and make sure **Use this publishing point** is selected.

3. Close the properties dialog box, stop the publishing point, create and save new announcement and multicast information files, and then restart the publishing point.

4. Attempt to connect with the Player. The Player will open the announcement file, then the multicast information file. Because it cannot stream multicast, the Player will roll over to a unicast stream.

5. Check the **Statistics** dialog box in the Player. It should indicate **RTSP (UDP)**. The **Monitor** tab on the server will also indicate one unicast client connection.

The following table summarizes the basic procedures needed to configure unicast and multicast broadcasts, or both with rollover enabled or disabled.

Broadcast Type	Procedure
Unicast only	Make sure the **Allow new unicast connections** button is selected, and disable the **Multicast Data Writer plug-in**. Connect using a unicast URL, such as MMS://Server/PubPoint.
Multicast only	Make sure the **Deny new unicast connections** button is selected. Enable and configure the **Multicast Data Writer plug-in**. Create an announcement file and a multicast information file.
Both, without rollover	Make sure the **Allow new unicast connections** button is selected. Enable and configure the **Multicast Data Writer plug-in**. Create an announcement file and a multicast information file.
Both, with rollover	Make sure the **Allow new unicast connections** button is selected. Enable and configure the **Multicast Data Writer plug-in**. Enable unicast rollover. Create an announcement file and a multicast information file.

351

If you want, run Windows Media Load Simulator with a modest number of clients. Connect to a publishing point using unicast streaming with the RTSPU, RTSPT, MMSU, and MMST protocols. Then connect to the multicast stream with Windows Media Player. Windows Media Load Simulator is not designed to connect using multicast streaming, but you can test the effect on the server of providing unicast and multicast streams at the same time. You can also create broadcast unicast publishing points on the other servers in the cluster, and source each from the encoder. Then run Windows Media Load Simulator against the cluster.

You will see that adding a multicast broadcast has almost no negative effect. The multicast requires so few system resources it is hardly noticed. The multicast stream is more likely to be affected by a congested network before there is a problem from an overloaded server.

With unicast streaming, a client is guaranteed to receive all or most of the data packets intact. This is because there is a connection between the client and server, so the client can request that packets be resent by the server if they do not arrive or they arrive with data errors. With multicast, on the other hand, there is no client/server connection. If packets do not arrive intact, there will be a hole in the stream because the Player cannot request new packets. For this reason, multicast streaming always works best on reliable, uncongested networks.

Stop the multicast stream on Windows Media Player and locate the multicast client log on the server. After the Player stops, it sends usage information to the multicast logging file indicated by the logging URL it received from the multicast information file. If you have followed the steps in this section, there should be a multicast log file on the server, which will contain the usage information sent from the clients.

By default, the multicast logging files are created in the %systemroot%\system32 \LogFiles\WMS_ISAPI folder. A new file is generated every day and whenever a multicast publishing point is created or changed. If the log is empty, wait a few minutes and try again. There is a delay between the time when a client stops and the time when information gets logged. For more information about how to read the log, see Windows Media Services Help.

Test #4: Security

Before any server is deployed on their corporate network, Fabrikam technicians make sure security features have been properly configured to protect the server and the content contained on it. The security features provided by Windows Server 2003 and Windows Media Services cover the following areas:

■   Computer security. If the computer is not secure, Windows Media Services will not be secure. Read the Windows Server 2003 Help, and then use the documented security features and methods to make sure that the data and software on the computer are as safe as possible.

- Content security. Authentication and authorization plug-ins can be enabled on Windows Media servers to restrict viewing of sensitive content. You can customize restrictions for individual files, groups of files in publishing points, live streams, and playlists. For example, Fabrikam could host sensitive marketing material on a publishing point that was restricted to certain individuals or groups, and host unrestricted, public material on a general publishing point. Another publishing point could carry a restricted live unicast stream of a crucial meeting with a new client. Another way to secure content is to use Windows Media Rights Manager. This method adds encryption to the digital media itself. For more information, see chapter 13.

- Windows Media Services Administrator for the Web security. This tool provides an easy and versatile way to administer Windows Media servers in situations where the MMC snap-in cannot be used. You can administer one or more Windows Media servers by using a browser to connect over an intranet to this administration Web site. To ensure that the server is administered only by those who have permission, set up security for the administration Web site on your computer.

In this test, Fabrikam technicians secure content on the default publishing point by adding and configuring authentication and authorization, and then attempting to access the content as an authenticated user and as an unauthenticated user.

Publishing point security checks users two ways before they are given access to secure content. The first check is authentication, which compares the user name against a password. The second check is authorization, which compares the authenticated user name against a list of users who have permission to access the content. Windows Media Services plug-ins provide the following methods of authenticating and authorizing users:

- WMS Anonymous User Authentication. Enables unauthenticated users to access content without being prompted for a user name or password.

- WMS Negotiate Authentication. Uses the Negotiate protocol to determine whether Kerberos or NTLM authentication is used. Both types of authentication use a challenge/response encrypted authentication mechanism.

- WMS Digest Authentication. Uses a challenge/response HTTP authentication protocol that does not require a password to be sent over a network. Instead, the plug-in uses a hashed version of a password to authenticate the user.

- WMS NTFS ACL Authorization. Enforces permissions that were set on files and directories in an NTFS file system when streaming from an on-demand publishing point.

- WMS IP Address Authorization. Enables you to allow or deny access to content for specific IP addresses.

- WMS Publishing Points ACL Authorization. Enables you to allow or deny specific users, servers, or groups to access content for all publishing points on a server or for a specific publishing point.

For testing purposes, Fabrikam use simple security methods that work on a closed LAN that does not have access to a domain server. The Negotiate plug-in relies upon established user logon credentials that are authenticated using NTLM or Kerberos authentication. In the closed LAN system, the user is known to all three computers, so the user can access secure content on the server by successfully logging on to the client.

A technician needs to configure the following security options on each server.

1. On the first server, select the default on-demand publishing point. Check the **Source** tab to make sure the test files created in test #1 are still there.

2. On the **Properties** tab, click **Authentication**, and then enable the WMS Negotiate Authentication plug-in.

3. Click **Authorization**, and enable the WMS Publishing Point ACL Authorization plug-in.

4. Open **Properties** for the publishing point to see the list. By default the Everyone group has read permission, and any administrator on the computer has full permission.

5. Remove the Everyone group. BUILTIN\Administrators should be the only group with access to the files on the publishing point.

The technician opens Windows Media Player on the client computer and attempts to access a file in the default publishing point. Because the technician is logged on as user Lan and is an administrator, the file plays with no challenge.

Now he creates a new user named NoConnect on the client computer, and then logs on as that user. When he attempts to play the file from this account, the technician will be required to enter a valid user name and password. After he has received authorization to play a file, he can play the file repeatedly without having to enter user name and password again—as long as he does not close the Player.

If the Fast Cache feature is enabled on the publishing point, clients can cache content as it is being streamed. You may notice that once you access and play a file, you do not have to enter login credentials again, even if you restart the Player. This is because the Player is streaming the content from its cache and not from the server. You can see whether the Player is streaming from the cache by checking the **Advanced** tab in the **Statistics** dialog box. The **Protocol** box will display **CACHE**. To prevent Players from caching, you can disable **Fast Cache** on the server. This option is in the **General** category on the **Properties** tab.

Performing security functions does add to the load on the server. If you anticipate many concurrent connections using authentication and authorization, you can create a test of this functionality by using Load Simulator. However, you will need to add a domain server that is set up to authenticate users on the closed LAN, because Load Simulator uses Digest authentication.

Before leaving the security test, the Fabrikam technician returns the default publishing point to its original configuration by adding the Everyone group with read-only access. In the next test, we will see how Fabrikam sets up and runs the sample broadcast playlist that is installed with Windows Media Services.

Test #5: Unicast Broadcast Playlist with a Wrapper

A playlist is a file that contains a list of digital media items. When you open the file in Windows Media Player, the digital media items play one after the other until the Player reaches the end of the list. The file itself does not contain the audio and video files or streams. Rather, it contains only the links to or URLs of the content. The digital media items referenced in a playlist can be any file or stream that Windows Media Player can play, including still images. For more information about playlists, see chapter 11.

There are two types of playlist files: client-side playlists and server-side playlists. A client-side playlist is downloaded by the client, typically from a Web server. The client then locates and plays the digital media items in the list. The end user can stream the playlist from beginning to end, and can control playback with the pause and seek controls.

The only difference between a client-side playlist and an announcement file is the number of digital media elements. An announcement is created by the server and points to one file or publishing point. You could edit an announcement file and add more elements, and you would have a playlist. Client-side playlists have .asx, .wvx, or .wax file name extensions.

A server-side playlist does about the same thing as a client-side playlist, except that it is hosted on a Windows Media server. With a server-side playlist, the server locates and streams the content to the client. Server-side playlist files can be created by using the Playlist Editor, which can be accessed from the **Source** tab in the Windows Media Services MMC snap-in. Server-side playlists have .wsx file name extensions and are based on the Synchronized Multimedia Integration Language (SMIL) 2.0 language specification. (See appendix A for details about SMIL elements and playlists.)

You can make server-side playlists available to users in three ways: directly, through an on-demand publishing point, or through a broadcast publishing point. To access a server-side playlist file directly, a client connects to the playlist file with a URL such as mms://WMServer01/serverside_playlist.wsx. Using this method, the end user experience is similar to downloading a client-side playlist.

A more interesting use of a server-side playlist is to make it the source of a publishing point. You can create an on-demand publishing point named Plist, for example, that sources serverside_playlist.wsx. Then a client can stream the playlist by connecting to the publishing point with a URL such as mms://WMServer01/Plist. Hosting a playlist from a publishing point enables you to apply publishing point properties and plug-ins to the playlist. You can also view and edit the playlist on the **Source** tab or in the Playlist Editor.

An even more interesting use of a server-side playlist is to make it the source of a broadcast publishing point. When you broadcast a playlist, users can tune in and play the content in progress. For example, a CEO speech can be rebroadcast by looping a server-side playlist that references the archived file of the live speech. This is preferable to offering the archive as an on-demand file because you can use multicast streaming, which saves bandwidth on the network.

You can also add *wrappers* to publishing points. A wrapper is a type of playlist that defines content that all clients receive before, during, or after playback of the requested publishing point content. For example, say a publishing point hosts a radio station. You can add a wrapper to the publishing point that contains a 30-second introductory file, which every client receives when they first connect.

In this test, the Fabrikam staff will use the sample playlist file, serverside_playlist.wsx, that was pre-configured as the source of a broadcast publishing point during installation of the server. Figure 17.8 shows the **Source** tab of the sample publishing point.

When a playlist is the source of a publishing point, it displays in a small editing pane on the **Source** tab. The tree view on the left side of the pane displays the elements of the playlist arranged hierarchically. When you click an element, you can view its attributes in the pane on the right. In the editor pane, you can drag elements to new positions, add or remove elements, and change their attributes. If you want to do more extensive editing, you can open the file in the Playlist Editor.

The sample playlist consists of five elements: a **smil** element, and four **media** elements. A **media** element is the basic component of a server-side playlist. The other element types are used to control the behavior of elements contained within **media** elements. In the sample, playback of the **media** elements is controlled by the **smil** element, which causes the **media** elements to play sequentially.

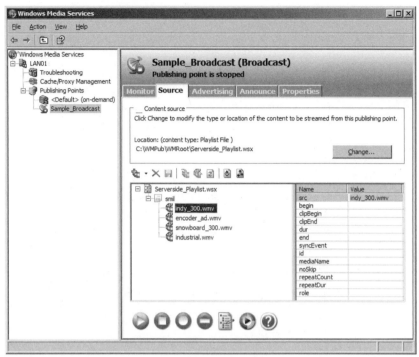

Figure 17.8   The sample broadcast publishing point.

The Fabrikam technicians won't make any changes to the playlist. They will just configure the publishing point to loop the playlist so it will start over after it reaches the end. The following steps describe how a technician will turn on the sample broadcast publishing point:

1. On the first server, click the Sample_Broadcast publishing point, and then click the **Source** tab.

2. To loop the playlist, click the **Loop** button in the Playlist Editor controls, shown in figure 17.9.

3. Click the **Allow unicast connections** button on the **Monitor** tab, and then start the publishing point.

4. Repeat steps 1 through 3 for the remaining servers.

Figure 17.9   The **Loop** button in the Playlist Editor controls.

If you make changes to the playlist, click the **Save** button in the Playlist Editor controls. Even though the playlist editing pane displays your changes, they will not take effect until they are saved in the playlist file.

On the client computer, the Fabrikam technician opens Windows Media Player and connects to the publishing point with a URL like mms://WMCluster/Sample_Broadcast. The Player starts streaming the broadcast that is already in progress. As the playlist runs, a green arrow points to the element that is currently playing. There is the usual buffer delay between what is currently streaming and what the Player is rendering. At the end of the last item, the playlist starts over.

Next, the technician will add a wrapper to the playlist. The sample wrapper playlist included with the Windows Media server plays advertisements at the beginning and the end of the broadcast.

1. On each server, on the **Advertising** tab, check whether Wrapper_playlist.wsx and the correct path are displayed in **Wrapper location**. If not, browse to the file and select it.

2. Select the **Use a wrapper with this publishing point** check box.

3. On the **Source** tab, turn off looping so the playlist plays through once and stops. If the playlist does not end, the closing ad will never be displayed.

4. Repeat steps 1 through 3 for the remaining servers.

The technician can now start the publishing point and connect to it with the Player. The introductory ad (a still image) plays first, and then the broadcast is displayed. After the end of the playlist, the closing ad plays.

To see how the wrapper works, you can open it in the Playlist Editor or the Wrapper Editor. On the **Advertising** tab of any server, click the **Wrapper Editor** button. Select **Edit existing playlist file**, and open Wrapper_playlist.wsx. The playlist opens in the Playlist Editor shown in figure 17.10.

The wrapper playlist consists of three **media** elements contained in a **smil** element. The proseware_leadin. jpg file is an image. Notice in the details pane that the image has a **dur** value (duration) of 10s, or 10 seconds. The second **media** element, %requested-Url%, plays the source that the end user requested. The third **media** element is a closing ad. When a user connects to the publishing point, the image is displayed for 10 seconds, then the wrapper switches playback to the requested URL (the playlist defined as the source of the publishing point). When the playlist ends, playback returns to the wrapper and the file poweredby_wms.wmv plays.

You can set the publishing point to loop, and then run Load Simulator. Try a mix of clients playing the publishing point and on-demand content. You can also set up the server to multicast the playlist, and test a combination of unicast and multicast client connections.

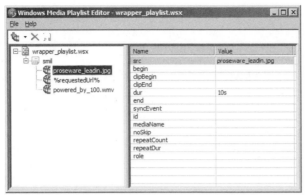

Figure 17.10   The wrapper playlist as it appears in the Playlist Editor.

Test #6: Windows Media Services Administrator for the Web

The Fabrikam installation of Windows Media Services included Windows Media Services Administrator for the Web. In this test, a technician will open the Web administrator to test its functionality.

The company would like to allow certain users who cannot connect to it through the MMC snap-in to administer the server. This includes some production assistants in the Media department who need to be able to create and manage publishing points. With Windows Media Services Administrator for the Web, these users can manage Windows Media servers from computers that are running an operating system other than Windows Server 2003, that are separated from the server by firewalls, or that are using a low-bandwidth Internet connection.

During installation of Windows Media Services, the Web site files were copied to the server, and IIS was configured. The technician can open the administrator site and view or modify server settings.

1.   On the client computer, open Internet Explorer to the administration site on the first server with the URL http://LAN01:8080/default.asp. The Security Settings page opens.

When you view and make changes to a Windows Media server with the Web administrator, the data is sent over the network as IP packets. To protect the configuration data and your credentials from being intercepted and used to gain access to the server, you need to use a secure form of data transfer. The first page you see provides information about how to do that.

Secure Sockets Layer (SSL) provides a high level of security by encrypting data before it is sent over the network, and authenticating users with digital certificates. As it stands, the Web site can only be accessed by users with

Administrator group permissions on the Windows Media server. However, this does not prevent someone from intercepting the IP packets sent between the client and server. By using SSL, you increase the security of the system.

2. Click **Administer the local Windows Media Server**. The Web administrator opens with an interface similar to that of the snap-in. You can do things like add publishing points, change sources, enable plug-ins, and change properties.

   You can also manage multiple servers from one Web administrator site. For example, you could open the other servers in the cluster from the same interface. Doing so, however, requires using a fairly complex security system because a remote user's credentials must be passed through to the other servers. See Windows Media Services Help for details on how to set up such a system. Alternatively, you can simply open a separate browser for each server.

3. Repeat steps 1 and 2 to connect to the remaining servers in the cluster.

After the server farm is installed in the data center, Administrator permissions can be set for the computer. Also, SSL can be added to the Web administrator. SSL requires a connection to a certificate authority (CA) that provides authentication and certification services.

Final System Checks

Windows Media Services provides many more features that you can explore before moving the servers into production. You can also gain experience with publishing points, server-side playlists, and all the related properties and plug-ins. When you are not using the server farm, you can connect Windows Media Player or Load Simulator and run overnight streaming tests to make sure everything has been configured correctly for your environment. This will also tell you more about the server's potential strengths and limitations. If you run into problems at any point, retrace your steps, and check Windows Media Services Help for troubleshooting tips.

After the Fabrikam technicians have thoroughly tested the servers on the bench, it is time to install them in the data center and connect them to the network.

Releasing Servers into Production

Before the servers leave the test bench, the Fabrikam technicians remove any settings and files they placed on the server for testing, including the following:

■ Remove WMLoad.asf from the Windows Media server root directories. If this file is not removed, users can run Windows Media Load Simulator against the server. Prevent unauthorized users from adding a WMLoad.asf file.

■ Remove static IP addresses used for testing, and replace with final static IP addresses and domain names provided by the IT department for the hosts and the cluster.

■ Remove the test users Lan and NoConnect. Make sure the Everyone group has read-only access, and that the BUILT-IN\Administrators account has full access to the default publishing point.

■ Remove test Windows Media files and publishing points. You may want to leave some content temporarily to test the server after it is online.

■ Change any test properties and plug-ins. For example, you may have experimented with adding client connection limits or authentication and authorization.

■ Change the **Affinity** setting in NLB to **Single**. The Fast Reconnect feature of Windows Media Services 9 Series can only work if Windows Media Player reconnects to the same server.

After installing the server and connecting it to the network, do the following:

■ Install Windows Media Services snap-in on the computers that will be used to monitor the Windows Media servers. After installation, create a group in the Windows Media Services MMC snap-in and add the cluster servers, and then connect to the cluster with NLB Manager.

If you add more servers, you can add them to this group. You could also create more groups to monitor additional servers and clusters. This can be useful after adding cache/proxy servers.

■ Add the users who will need to use the MMC snap-in to the server's Administrators group. Only those users who are in the Administrators group on the server can open the server in a remote management interface.

■ Configure security for Windows Media Services Administrator for the Web. To provide the highest level of security, use SSL.

■ Run through some tests with one or two clients.

❑ Stream on-demand content from the root directory.

❑ Stream the sample broadcast playlist.

❑ Check operation of Windows Media Services Administrator for the Web.

With the server and Media Guide online, and the Media department prepared to create content, phase I of the Fabrikam deployment is finished. In the first part of phase II, we will see how Fabrikam configures the existing studio in the Media department for live production, and then installs encoding computers for live production.

18

Phase II: Live Production

In phase I of the Fabrikam company plan to deploy Windows Media, a system was built that enabled the Media department to create on-demand content, the IT department to host the content, and end users with desktop computers to locate the content in an online Media Guide and stream it to any computer connected to the corporate network.

In phase II of the plan, the system will be extended: the Media department adds live encoding capabilities and a Producer mini-studio, and the IT department adds remote servers. At the completion of phase II, users worldwide will be able to stream on-demand content, and there will be limited live streaming at the company's headquarters in Toronto.

In this chapter, we will see how the company adds encoding computers to the existing Media department studio. With this functionality, the studio can be used to originate live broadcasts. The Fabrikam staff will also create a Windows Media "road kit" that can be transported to any location for remote live or on-demand encoding.

Upgrading the Production Studio

Fabrikam has a small studio that can be used for recording video of individuals or small groups. The studio was originally constructed to record a weekly company news program that was distributed on tape. The studio has also been used to record talks by managers that include PowerPoint slides, interviews that are edited into other programs, and voiceovers. (A voiceover is an audio-only recording of an announcer or narrator that is later edited into a finished production.)

The complete studio consists of the studio space, control room, and equipment room. The studio space is where cameras record people and objects; the control room is where the audio and video are mixed before going to tape; and the equipment room is where the VCRs and other equipment that do not require constant attention are housed.

To add the capability to produce live programming from the studio, the Media department will simply add encoding computers and some additional equipment. Most of the infrastructure is already in place.

Production Styles and Considerations

The studio is already equipped to record "live to tape," meaning complete programs can be produced and recorded to tape in real time. With only minimal changes, the Media department can encode programs live to the company intranet. For example, once the live encoding computers are installed, the Media department can broadcast a live news program. Studio personnel can also reconfigure the studio to broadcast a speaker giving a PowerPoint presentation, or any number of other similar live-to-tape productions.

The other styles of production commonly used are *continuity* and *documentary*. With these production styles, a program is shot in individual elements, such as interviews, shots of buses on the assembly line, and computer graphics. Then the program is assembled in an editing suite. The program elements are shot "out of continuity," meaning the elements are not necessarily recorded in the order in which they will appear in the final production. For this reason, these styles cannot be used for live production.

In general, it is easier and less expensive to create an edited production from elements shot out of continuity than to attempt a live production, especially if your facility is not capable of live-to-tape recording. Even if you have live-to-tape capabilities, a live production requires more planning and an experienced production team. However, live production has the advantages of timeliness and immediacy, and it can also save production time once a process has been developed for doing live production.

Planning for live-to-tape production includes writing a script or outline, making sure everyone involved knows their roles and the flow of the production, and rehearsing, if possible. For a weekly news show, the producer only needs to write the script and edit the news clips in advance. For a one-time event, a week of pre-production may be required to make sure all the pieces fall into place.

Elements of a Live Production

A typical live production requires attention to the following elements:

Sets

The set is the area created for the camera to photograph (or *shoot*). Often, corporate videos call for nothing more than a simple, featureless, blue background. If you add anything to a set, the end user will assume it has something to do with the content of the video. Everything in the video frame should focus the end user's attention on the content.

Lighting

Lighting serves two basic purposes. First, television cameras require more light than the human eye, so additional lighting will often be needed to bring the light level up to a point where the camera can capture a high-quality image. Second, lighting serves an artistic purpose, enabling you to model the image and create an effective look. In general, you will want to create a pleasant effect that doesn't distract the viewer's attention from the content.

Scripts or Rundowns

A script typically contains the words a speaker will read. An outline or *rundown* provides a structure for a live program. In either case, a script or rundown is not just for the speaker—it is the blueprint for a production, the instrument that holds a live production together. The director, producer, audio engineer, and camera operators cannot do an effective job without a complete script or rundown.

Talent

This is a broadcast term used to refer to the people who are seen or heard in a video (for example actors, presenters, narrators, and interviewees). Talent do not have to be professionally trained. However, the talent chosen to deliver the message in a video should have the skills to communicate effectively.

Cameras

Video cameras capture light and convert it to an electrical signal (see figure 18.1). Many modern cameras then convert the signal into a digital stream. The camera is the beginning of the signal chain that will end up as an image on the end user's monitor. It is important to start off with the best quality possible, because there is no way to improve quality once a signal is recorded; you can only change the appearance of the video recording, but you cannot increase the quality of the recorded information. There is a variety of inexpensive, high-quality video cameras on the market today.

Audio

An audio system consists of the components to capture or create sound (such as microphones and CD players), components to process and mix the sounds (such as a mixer), and components to record sound (such as a tape recorder, VCR, or encoder). An audio system is typically less expensive and complicated than the associated video system, but that does not mean audio is less important. Most of the message of a video is carried through the audio.

Figure 18.1   An example of a modern, professional video camera setup.

Directing and Switching

A director is in charge of the production of a film or video. In a live video production, the director follows the rundown or script, and gives timing instructions to the camera operators and audio engineers. In short, the director controls what goes on the tape or into the broadcast.

In a smaller production, a director may also operate the video switcher that changes camera angles and adds visual effects, such as titles. Everyone on a live crew wears intercom headphones, through which they receive instructions from the director, and can provide feedback.

Assistants

Though many small productions are done with one director and two camera operators, one or more assistants are often needed on larger-scale productions to handle miscellaneous tasks, such as moving set pieces and equipment, and rolling tape. One very necessary assistant task is running the teleprompter, if one is used.

Producer

Every situation is different, but the producer is most often the person who organizes the production. The producer is also often the writer and liaison between the crew and the customer or client.

During a live production, the talent reads the script or follows the rundown and performs; the camera people shoot angles of the action; the audio person mixes the sound and manages the sound quality; the director manages the flow of the program, selects appropriate camera angles, and rolls in video clips when called for; the assistants help run

VCRs, check encoding quality, operate the teleprompter, and other miscellaneous tasks; and the producer makes sure the director has what is needed to manage the production.

The audio and video is captured in the studio, mixed in the control room, and then sent as audio and video signals (called the program signals or *feed*) to the encoding computers. There the signals are split, encoded into four streams, and sent over the network to publishing points on the Windows Media server. Clients then use Windows Media Player to connect to the server and stream the program.

The Studio Space

The Fabrikam Media department studio is 30 by 40 feet—large enough to hold a small set and two cameras on wheeled pedestals. The studio has a tall ceiling with an overhead grid on which the studio crew can hang lights. With the lights off the floor, there is more space for sets, cameras, and other equipment. Sound absorption baffles, such as the panels used in the compression suite in chapter 15, are hung above the grid and attached to the walls.

Sets are modular, and can easily be taken apart and arranged for different situations. A typical set consists of a thin carpet and desk placed on two risers pushed together near a corner. The risers are each four feet wide, eight feet long, and one foot high. The carpet keeps foot noise down and helps deaden reverberation in the room. The desk is raised so it is easier for the cameras to shoot the talent at eye level. If the studio needs to shoot an interview, the desk can be removed and two or three chairs arranged on the risers.

The background is a large seamless piece of blue cloth called a *backdrop*. The backdrop can be changed to a different color or texture. The talent is placed far enough away to prevent shadows from falling on the backdrop.

Additional equipment, such as computers and a video monitor on a rolling stand, can be brought in when needed. When not needed they are stored in a small room next to the studio. Each camera and pedestal includes a teleprompter, so the talent can read scripts or notes while looking into the lens. Nothing in the studio is permanent: lights can be moved, sets can be changed, and cameras can be removed from the pedestals and used for shooting on location. The studio can even hold a small audience.

The Control Room

Adjacent to the studio is the control room. This is where the components of a live program are assembled in real time. The control room also contains editing equipment, so the room can be used to edit a continuity style production. The small room has an area for mixing the audio, an area for switching between video sources, and an area in which the producer and customer can sit and observe or take notes.

The audio area contains an audio mixer for blending multiple audio sources, such as two on-camera presenters and sound on videotape. The area also features two high-quality audio monitor speakers and various audio processors, such as an audio limiter that keeps the audio level below a set threshold to prevent distortion.

The video area is centered on a video switcher, as shown in figure 18.2. A director uses the switcher to change from one video source to another, such as from a studio camera to a prerecorded videotape introduction. Switchers also do effects such as layering video sources and adding transitions. The person controlling the switcher, the director or technical director, controls the flow of the program. He calls shots and communicates other timing information by using a headphone intercom.

Figure 18.2   A compact, portable video switcher.

A bank of monitors above the switcher enables the director to view all the sources. Remote control units enable him to start and stop VCRs, which are located in the machine room next to the control room. A character generator next to the switcher enables him to add titles with a variety of font styles. A computer editing system sits on the opposite side of the switcher. After the Fabrikam technicians install the live encoding computers, an additional computer monitor, keyboard, mouse, and a KVM switch will sit next to the editing system.

The studio and control room are designed to facilitate live-to-tape production, so adding live Windows Media-based production functionalty is easy. The output audio and video signals are simply rerouted from a VCR to the encoding computers. Distribution Amplifiers (DAs) are used to split the signals to multiple destinations. This will enable the director to, for example, encode on two computers and record a backup tape simultaneously. Once the encoders are in place, the studio can begin sending a live stream to tape, to a disk, to the intranet, or to the extranet.

The Machine Room

A small machine room is located next to the control room. It is used to house equipment that does not require constant attention, and that would add to the noise level and require space in the crowded control room. This is where the VCRs and the editing system computer are located, and where the two encoding computers and the remote control computer will be installed.

Figure 18.3 shows multiple encoding computers installed in a large machine-room rack at Microsoft. The patch bay to the right enables operators to quickly change the routing of source signals to encoders.

Figure 18.3 Encoding computers installed in a typical machine room.

Fabrikam will install two encoding computers that can provide multiple streams encoded at different bit rates, and these will be able to feed multiple broadcast publishing points on the sever. Redundant streams can also be encoded as a backup. The third computer will run the Windows Media Services Administrator for the Web and Windows Media Player. The director will be able to view and operate the computers in the control room from a single monitor, mouse, and keyboard by using a KVM switchbox. The entire live production, from switching video sources to controlling the server, can be run by the director from one location.

An alternative to the KVM switchbox would be to connect to the encoding computers by using Remote Desktop Connection in Windows XP. You could use this method if the computers were located too far from the control room to use the KVM switchbox. Keep in mind, however, that you cannot open and control the encoder unless the remote computer sound setting is configured as **Leave at Remote computer**. Also, Remote Desktop Connection draws on system resources that could be used by the encoder. Make sure the encoding computer has adequate processing power and memory before using this method.

Figure 18.4   A typical control room layout.

Figure 18.4 shows the encoder control room at the Microsoft in-house video production facility. Microsoft makes extensive use of live and on-demand streaming media. In this control room, source signals, streams, and encoding computers can be monitored, and encoders can be controlled remotely. If you have programming skills, you can create a program for controlling Windows Media Encoder remotely by using the Windows Media Encoder SDK.

Configuring Live Encoders

The Fabrikam staff first mount the three computers in a rack in the machine room, and then wire them to the KVM switchbox in the control room. The diagram in figure 18.5 shows a simplified view of the signal flow.

From the main outputs of the audio mixer and video switcher, the signals are split by DAs, and then sent to the patch bays. From there the signals can be routed or patched to a number of destinations, including the two encoding computers. The encoded Windows Media streams are then sent to the servers.

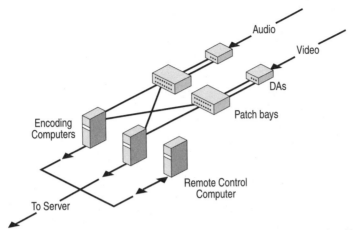

Figure 18.5   Configuration of computers and equipment in the Fabrikam studio.

The remote control computer is also connected to the servers over the network. The audio output of the computer is fed into the control room mixer so that the broadcast audio can be monitored. The audio output will not be monitored continuously because of the delay added by Windows Media Player and the encoders.

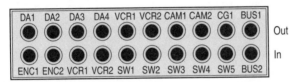

Figure 18.6   Typical layout of a video patch bay.

Most of the inputs and outputs in the facility are wired into the patch bay to simplify signal routing. Figure 18.6 shows a section of the video patch bay. Outputs are typically on the top row; inputs are on the bottom row. The DA outputs show up at the patch points labeled DA1 through DA4.

The patch bay is laid out so each output can be "normalled" to the input below it, meaning the output is connected internally to the input unless a signal is rerouted with a patch cord. In this patch panel, the four DA outputs are normalled to the encoding computer inputs and VCR inputs. The outputs of the two VCRs, two cameras, and the character generator are normalled to switcher inputs SW1 through SW5. BUS1 and BUS2 are the two video lines to the compression suite, and they are not normalled. You can, for example, patch the output of a VCR or DA to BUS2, and then patch that signal into one of the encoding computers in the compression suite. The audio patch bay is similar.

Computer Specifications

To encode live streams, the Fabrikam studio will use two dual-processor computers with 256 MB of RAM and 20 GB hard drives. Both computers will run Microsoft Windows XP Professional. Windows Media Encoder 9 Series will be used to encode.

In addition to encoding live streams, the computers can be used to save archive files, so they will need large hard drives. However, Fabrikam will not use the hard drives for long-term storage.

The only additional hardware each computer will need is a video capture card. The 100-Mbps network interface card (NIC) is typically included on the computers. To save money, Fabrikam will use desktop-style computers placed on shelves mounted in the rack.

For the remote control computer, Fabrikam can use a less-powerful, single-processor computer running Windows XP Professional. This computer will be used to control the broadcast publishing point with the Windows Media Services Administrator for the Web, and to check playback of the encoded stream. They can install the three computers in the rack first, and then install and configure the software. They will name the computers LiveEncoder01, LiveEncoder02, and RemControl.

Encoding Appliances

Several manufacturers, such as Winnov and Pinnacle, offer dedicated encoding appliances. An encoding appliance simplifies setup and operation because all it does is encode multiple streams. Most appliances are designed to be rack-mounted and offer additional production features, such as Web-based remote management and monitoring. You simply plug in the audio, video, and network, configure the encoders, and then start the encoders running.

The main downside of an encoding appliance is that it might not meet corporate platform and security standards, or enable you to easily upgrade the encoder and codecs.

Configuring Encoders and Servers

Fabrikam will run multiple instances of the encoder on each computer. Because only one program can capture from an audio or video capture device at a time, they could install multiple capture cards and then configure each instance of the encoder to source from a different set of capture cards. Instead, they will use a program or plug-in that splits the audio and video streams from a single capture card. An example of stream-splitting software is Osprey SimulStream, which can be used with Osprey video capture cards. By splitting the streams from a single card, Fabrikam can save the cost of additional capture devices and make configuration easier.

Configuration of the multicast system begins with the encoders. As you will remember from testing the server farm, encoder configuration information is required in order to create a multicast information file. This information is added to the multicast file and passed on to Windows Media Player as header information. Without encoder configuration information, the Player cannot receive the stream. If you use unicast streaming, header information will be sent automatically when a client connects to the server, so a custom encoder configuration could be entered moments before the encoder is started. With multicast, on the other hand, the server needs that information up front.

Creating Standard Encoder Configurations

You could grab encoder configuration information automatically from the encoder when you create the multicast information files. If you use the push method of live encoding, you can create and send the multicast information files with the encoder.

However, to make setting up a broadcast easier, the Media department works with the IT department to create a standard set of broadcast encoding templates. By standardizing, new multicast information files do not have to be created for every live event. Standardization also enables the IT department to maintain control of bandwidth usage on the network. For more information about the push and pull methods of encoding, see the Connecting the Encoder and Server sidebar later in this chapter.

To create standardized encoder configurations, the Fabrikam technicians do the following:

1. Decide on two or three standard bit rates. For example, 56 Kbps and 300 Kbps would be good bit rates for Fabrikam. Remote locations using frame relay can connect to the 56 Kbps stream, and the 300 Kbps stream can be used by local clients with high-speed connections and fast computers. A 300 Kbps stream can be displayed at full-screen in conference rooms and media centers in the factory.

2. Configure the encoder. You can use the preconfigured templates or create your own custom configurations for each bit rate. After you enter a configuration, start encoding. Check the quality and bit rate. If you plan to do a lot of low-motion video, such as talking head videos, you can increase the quality setting to get sharper images or lower the frame rate to 15 fps because you are less likely to notice a reduced frame rate with low motion. For information about how to configure the encoder, see the test topics in chapter 17 or Windows Media Encoder Help.

3. Save the configuration. After finding the right balance of quality, frame size, and frame rate for each bit rate, save the configurations as encoder session files with .wme extensions and as encoder stream format files with .asf extensions. For example, if you choose to standardize on 56 Kbps and 300 Kbps, you will create four files: Enc56K.asf, Enc56K.wme, Enc300K.asf, and Enc300K.wme.

4. Copy the session files to the other encoding computers, and copy the stream format files to a location on the server that will originate the broadcast. After creating the standard configuration files, do not change encoder settings that affect how the audio and video are encoded, or you will not be able to start the publishing point. For information about generating these files, see Windows Media Encoder Help.

   Because each encoder has an identical configuration, the session files created on one encoding computer will work on the other one. The only settings that are different are the computer names and IP addresses. However, these settings can vary because they do not affect the audio and video.

5. On the server, establish standard publishing points for live multicasts. For example, the Fabrikam staff will create the following multicast publishing points:

Publishing Point	Source
Channel 1	Rollover56.wsx
Channel 2	Rollover300.wsx

Fabrikam will run two instances of the encoder on both computers: one instance will use the Enc56K.wme session file, and the other will use the Enc300K.wme session file. If an encoder or computer fails, the server-side playlist files Rollover56.wsx and Rollover300.wsx will switch to the encoder on the other computer. To add fault tolerance in case of server failure, they can also stream from identical publishing points on one of the other Windows Media servers in the server farm, and then implement server rollover in a client-side playlist.

Setting up a Publishing Point

The Fabrikam technicians follow this procedure to set up a publishing point on one of the Windows Media servers:

1. Open the Windows Media Services MMC snap-in, and then add the Windows Media server that you want to use for multicast broadcasting.

2. Open the **Add Publishing Point Wizard**. You can create publishing points manually using the **Advanced** method, but the wizard helps configure the multicast automatically.

3. In the **Add Publishing Point Wizard**, do the following:

   - Enter Channel 1 as the publishing point name.

   - Select **Playlist** as the content type.

- ■ Select **Broadcast publishing point**.

- ■ Select **Multicast**.

- ■ Choose to create a new playlist and add two media elements: the 56K encoders on both computers, for example, http://LiveEncoder01:9090 and http://LiveEncoder02:9090.

- ■ Save the playlist for future reference.

- ■ Select the **Loop** check box. Each playlist has two entries. With **Loop** checked, if the stream stops in the current entry, the server will play the other.

- ■ Launch the wizard to create an .nsc file.

4. In the **Multicast Announcement Wizard**, enter the following information:

- ■ Make a multicast information file (.nsc) and announcement file (.asx).

- ■ Add the Enc56.asf and Enc300.asf stream format files.

- ■ Enable logging, and enter the URL of the logging file.

- ■ Enter locations for the multicast information and announcement files.

- ■ Check the URL of the multicast information file.

- ■ Enable archiving, and enter a location and name for the file.

5. Repeat steps 1 through 4 for the other publishing point. Name the publishing point Channel 2 and add to the playlist the 300K encoders on both computers, http://LiveEncoder01:9091 and http://LiveEncoder02:9091.

Figure 18.7 shows the playlist on the Channel 1 publishing point.

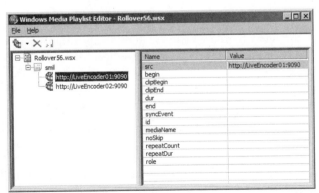

Figure 18.7   Configuring the playlist for publishing point "Channel 1."

Windows Media Services Administrator for the Web will be used to control the broadcast publishing point from the remote-control computer, but it cannot be used to create multicast information (.nsc) files. Therefore, you must use the Windows Media Services MMC snap-in on a computer running Windows Server 2003 to initially configure the multicast publishing point. Once the publishing point has been configured, Windows Media Services Administrator for the Web can be used to start, stop, monitor, and configure other properties of the publishing point. If you want to create multicast publishing points with a remote control computer, it must be running Windows Server 2003.

Preparing the Encoders

The last configuration step for the Fabrikam technicians to do is to prepare the encoders on each computer. These steps are followed to complete the process:

1. On LiveEncoder01, start Windows Media Encoder, and open the session file Enc56K.wme.

2. In **Session Properties**, on the **Source** tab, change the audio and video sources to the first capture card output.

3. On the **Output** tab, select the **Pull from encoder** check box, and enter the port number 9090. (This port number should match the one entered in the Channel 1 server-side playlist.)

4. Click **Apply**.

5. With the 56K encoder still open, open a second encoder.

6. Configure the second encoder by first opening Enc300.wme, and then selecting the second capture card output for the audio and video sources, and port 9091 on the **Output** tab. (This port should match the one used in the Channel 2 server-side playlist.)

7. Repeat steps 1 through 6 for the second encoding computer, LiveEncoder02. The encoders on both computers should be configured identically.

8. Start the encoders and the publishing point.

End users will access Channel 1.asx to receive the 56 Kbps stream, or Channel 2.asx to receive the 300 Kbps stream. Because the two stream formats are built into the multicast information files for each publishing point, you can use either session file with either encoder. The playlist for each channel will indicate that the first encoder is playing. End users can connect to the Channel 1 publishing point and stream the content from LiveEncoder01:9090, or they can connect to Channel 2 and stream from LiveEncoder01:9091.

Encoder Rollover

To see how encoder rollover works, you could stop the 56K encoder on LiveEncoder01. **Media** elements with a **smil** parent element will play in sequence from first to last. When the encoder stops, the server begins streaming the next element in the list, LiveEncoder02:9090. When it does, Windows Media Player buffers and begins playing the new stream. If you restart the encoder on LiveEncoder01 and stop the encoder on LiveEncoder02, the playlist goes back to the first element in the list. This happens because you have enabled looping.

Keep in mind that, while having the ability to do rollovers can be very useful, if the encoding computers are properly configured and running with adequate CPU and RAM in a controlled environment, there is no more risk of an encoder failing than most other components in the signal path. Also, the computers are capable of encoding more than two streams. You could, for example, create a third stream format and session file for 100 Kbps, and then encode three streams from LiveEncoder01 to a third channel on the server. You could also use LiveEncoder02 to encode an entirely different live program and send it to additional publishing points.

If you do not use encoder rollover, you can source the publishing point directly from the encoding computer. You can ease the setup of encoders and multicast broadcasts by creating standardized session and stream format files and applying the formats to all standardized publishing points.

You can add fault tolerance to the multicast server by mirroring the broadcast publishing points on another Windows Media server in the server farm, and by implementing rollover with a client-side playlist. To create a client-side playlist, you can modify the announcement files and the file names of the multicast information files to add the fail-over server.

The following script shows an example of the Channel 1 announcement file with a rollover added:

```
<asx version = "3.0">
    <entry>
            <ref href = "http://WebServer/WMS01Channel 1.nsc"/>
            <ref href = "http://WebServer/WMS02Channel 1.nsc"/>
    <Title>Channel 1</Title>
    <Author></Author>
    <Copyright></Copyright>
    <Banner></Banner>
    </entry>
    <Title>Channel 1</Title>
    <Author></Author>
    <Copyright></Copyright>
    <Banner></Banner>
    <LogURL href = ""/>
</asx>
```

The multicast information and announcement files for both servers are hosted on the Fabrikam Web servers. They will need one announcement file for each channel. The technicians rename each multicast information file, adding the name of the server it points to. Then they change the href parameter of the first ref element to point to the primary server information file, and they edit the second ref element to point to the rollover server file. If WMS01 fails during the multicast event, Windows Media Player will attempt to connect to the second server, which is called out in WMS02Channel 1.nsc.

One last option you should consider is broadcast security, which enables you to deny or allow access to the live stream from an Encoder. For more information, see chapter 12.

Configuring Servers for Live Production

When setting up for a live production, the Fabrikam technicians follow these steps:

1. Decide the layout of the encoders and publishing points, as shown in the following table.

Publishing Point	Source:	Encoder Session
Channel 1	Rollover56.wsx, Enc56.asf	Enc56.wme
Channel 2	Rollover300.wsx, Enc300.asf	Enc300.wme

2. Configure the publishing point sources to point to the associated rollover playlists.

3. One hour or so before the event, open the encoders with the appropriate session files. Then start encoding test streams, such as color bars and a test tone.

4. Start the publishing points. Test connectivity to each publishing point by connecting to it with Windows Media Player on another computer, such as the remote control computer. The technicians could also select end users in edge locations throughout the company to check playback.

5. Near the start of the program, show a title slide announcing the start time. The title slide can contain additional configuration information if appropriate. You could also add a countdown clock and include some pre-show music.

6. Moments before the program starts, click the **Start archiving** button on the **Source** tab of each publishing point.

After the live production, technicians stop the publishing points and the encoders. Then they check the archive files. If necessary, they can edit content from the beginning or end of the files by using an editing program such as Windows Media File Editor. They can also open the files in a program that imports Windows Media files, such as Windows Movie Maker or Producer.

Archiving Files from a Live Broadcast

After editing the files, the technicians copy them to a final archive location. The Media department can add links to these files from the Media Guide site.

If you expect files to receive heavy play, you can save network bandwidth by scheduling playback through a broadcast publishing point by using multicast streaming. For example, if the program is 25 minutes, you can schedule it to play repeatedly on the hour and half-hour. That way end users know they can tune in at 2:30 PM, for example, and catch the beginning of the program. This technique is very useful in an international company, like Fabrikam, in which end users may be tuning in at various hours of the day, depending on the local time zone.

To accomplish the scheduling, you can simply stand by the server snap-in and restart the publishing point manually. You can also experiment with techniques like adding blank material or a still image to the end of the program so that the Windows Media file is exactly 30 minutes long. You can do this with an advanced editing program. Then add the digital media file to a playlist, set the list to loop, and start the publishing point on the hour or half-hour.

A more advanced solution would be to create a scheduling program by using the Windows Media Services SDK. The program could enable a technician to attach start times to publishing points, and the start times would be triggered by the system clock.

Building a Windows Media Road Kit

When the Fabrikam staff brainstormed ideas for doing live productions, it immediately became clear that not all productions would take place in the ideal studio environment. Some system would be needed for encoding on location. The Media department already had road kit packages that they could use to handle remote live-to-tape production, such as major company-wide meetings and product launches.

Figure 18.8 shows an example of a production road kit used for Microsoft in-house production. The road kit consists of one or more rugged shipping cases containing equipment that is mounted and wired in racks. The cases can be shipped in vans across town or via air freight to another city or country. When the cases arrive, technicians simply attach wheels, roll them into position, open the cases, attach power and external inputs and outputs, and they are ready to record.

Figure 18.8 A road kit for on-location video production.

To handle remote encoding, the Media department will build an encoder road kit. Figure 18.9 shows a similar encoder road kit built by the Microsoft in-house production department. Figure 18.10 shows the back of the same road kit.

Figure 18.9 An encoding road kit for on-location Windows Media-based production.

The road kit begins with a road case, custom built by a company such as Anvil or Flight Form. The inside of the case is lined with thick padding, and the 19" equipment rack is securely attached. The case shown here is set on a furniture dolly, but you can find cases with detachable wheels.

All equipment in the case is either securely mounted to the equipment rack or attached firmly to the interior of the case. Even the wiring is attached to the metal structure with plastic wire wraps. The system contains the following components:

- Keyboard and LCD monitor on a shelf. The monitor folds flat on top of the keyboard and slides back into the case for shipping.

- Two encoding computers. Each has a 2 GHz CPU, 256 of RAM, and a 40 GB hard drive. Both computers contain video capture cards and NICs, and run Windows XP Professional. Windows Media Encoder 9 Series and an audio and video output splitting program or plug-in is also installed. The computers are not rack mounted, but strapped securely to rack-mounted shelves.

- Distribution amplifiers. Audio and video DAs are mounted below the computers.

- Network Switch. Provides an ideal network connection for both computers, with no packet loss and low jitter. The switch will be 100 BT run in full duplex mode.

- Power panel. A rack-mounted panel that provides one master power switch and outlets.

- Connection panel. Provides audio and video inputs and outputs and network connectors.

Figure 18.10 Connections on the rear of the encoding road kit.

The program video and audio outputs from a switcher, camera, or VCR are plugged into the connection panel, and the DAs split the signals to the computers. An extra audio and video output from the DA is fed back to another connector on the panel so the signals can be connected to other devices, such as VCRs and public address systems.

You can use the standard encoder session files created for the control room encoders in the remote encoders as well. To prepare for live production, load a session file into each encoder, and configure the sources on two publishing points. A live remote production procedes the same as a studio production. If a server administrator is logged on to the remote encoders, Windows Media Services Administrator for the Web can be opened on one of the encoding computers to control the publishing point remotely. You can also use push encoding to configure and control a publishing point. For more information about the push method, see the Connecting the Encoder and Server sidebar.

Another way users at Fabrikam will be able to produce content is with the Producer mini-studio. In the next chapter, we will see how the Fabrikam team builds a mini-studio. We will also learn how users can turn their PowerPoint presentations into Microsoft Producer projects, which end users can view on demand over the corporate intranet.

Connecting the Encoder and Server

In order to host a live stream from an encoder on a Windows Media server, a connection must be established between the two computers over an IP network. Windows Media 9 Series supports two ways to do that: the "pull" method and the "push" method.

With the pull method, the server establishes the connection. (Examples in this book have all used the pull method.) A port number (such as 8080) is assigned to the encoder, and the server publishing point is configured to source from the encoder by using its IP address or domain name and the port number (for example, http://EncodingComputer:8080). Typically, the publishing point is created and started by a server administrator, and then the encoder is started.

The pull method is used most often because it will work in most network situations. For example, it can be used when you want to connect a server that is behind a corporate firewall to an encoder that is on the other side of the firewall, such as on the Internet.

With the push method, the encoder initiates the connection. The name of the Windows Media server, the port number that the server uses for the HTTP protocol, and the name of an existing or new publishing point are entered in the encoder. On the server, a publishing point can be created with Push:* entered as the source. If a new name is entered on the encoder, a new publishing point will be

Connecting the Encoder and Server   *(continued)*

created on the server. The encoder can also be configured to start the publishing point and remove it when the session is finished.

Using the push method, a server administrator is not required to configure a publishing point. Any properly configured encoder can establish a connection with the server. One use of the push method would be to establish a connection between an encoder that is behind a corporate firewall and a server on the Internet.

When creating a live stream destined for multicast delivery, you must use an existing publishing point for which the WMS Multicast Data Writer plug-in has been enabled. You can use the Multicast Announcement Wizard in the encoder to generate the announcement and multicast information files. Then you can copy the files to a location from which end users can access the files and stream the multicast, such as a Web server.

In order to create or remove publishing points, the user who is logged on to the encoding computer must have create access permissions (at both the server and publishing point level) through the WMS Publishing Points ACL Authorization plug-in on the Windows Media server. Also, the WMS HTTP Server Control Protocol plug-in must be enabled on the server, and must be configured with the port number used to configure the encoder. (The port number does not have to be entered if the user logged on to the encoding computer has access permissions to the Windows Media Services service through DCOM.)

For more information, see Windows Media Encoder 9 Series Help.

19

Phase II: Microsoft Producer Mini-studio

In phase II of the Windows Media deployment, the Fabrikam Media and IT departments expand on the on-demand streaming system created in phase I. In the previous chapter, they added live encoding capability to the studio and built an encoder road kit. In this chapter, the staff will make it easy for users to take their PowerPoint presentations online with Microsoft Producer and a Producer mini-studio.

Using Microsoft Producer Presentations

At Fabrikam, like many corporations, people use PowerPoint slides to help them present information. To make more efficient use of their time, and reach more viewers, presenters can record their presentations with Producer. Then individuals and groups can view the recordings of the presentations.

To convert a live PowerPoint presentation to a form that can be viewed on-demand, a video camera is used to record the presenter giving the presentation. Then the slides and other digital media, such as Web pages and images, are synchronized to the recording. When an end user plays back the presentation, the slides play in synchronization with the video in a presentation page displayed in a Web browser, as shown in figure 19.1.

In this example, the presentation page includes video and audio of the presenter, the PowerPoint slides, and a clickable table of contents that allows users to skip to different parts of a presentation. A presenter can choose from a number of preconfigured templates in Producer, and can include additional Web pages, links, and images. Producer provides a presenter with a simple, yet powerful, way to build on-demand presentations, and then helps the presenter coordinate, package, and publish all the elements.

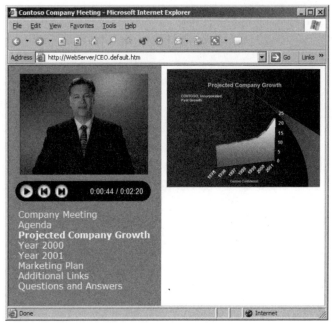

Figure 19.1   Producer presentations can be displayed in a Web browser.

To help users record their presentations, the Fabrikam staff will build a self-service Producer mini-studio. They will also provide users with Producer and the information they need to convert their presentations. The Media department decided a small investment in a Producer mini-studio would enable employees to make better use of their time. The studio would, therefore, save the company money in the long run.

Users capture video and audio for presentations in several ways:

■   Record presentations directly into Producer using audio and video capture cards.

■   Record to videotape, and later capture the recording with Producer.

■   Capture with another utility, such as Microsoft VidCap32, and then import the file into Producer.

The mini-studio will provide tools and instructions for using Producer to capture live content to a Windows Media file. Users can then synchronize the slides with the file manually, edit all the presentation elements, and create and publish a final presentation with Producer.

In the Fabrikam scenario, the final presentation can be published directly from Producer to the Media Guide SharePoint Portal Server site. Because SharePoint makes use of the metadata provided by Producer, end users will be able to locate the presentation by searching for particular keywords or browsing the site.

In the first part of this chapter, we will see how Fabrikam builds the mini-studio. In the second half, we will see the process of recording, synchronizing, saving, and publishing a presentation. The Fabrikam Media department will create a very detailed explanation of this process and make it available to company employees.

Building the Mini-studio

In planning the studio, the Fabrikam staff must weigh cost against benefit. The studio will not generate money for the company directly, but using it and Microsoft Producer will save the company money that might otherwise be spent on transportation, lodging, loss of productivity, and other expenses related to face-to-face presentations. By recording the presentation, employees can view it at their convenience, rather than organizing their time and travel around a meeting. The presentation can reach more viewers worldwide, and can save the company money, time, and resources.

Fabrikam will create a studio that is easy to use, even for employees who know nothing about producing videos. They need a space that is large enough to hold the presenter, a desk, the camera, and other recording equipment using a layout similar to the one shown in figure 19.2.

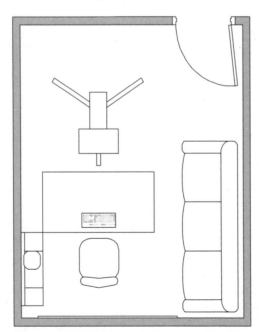

Figure 19.2 The layout of a simple Producer mini-studio.

With this layout, the presenter controls the entire recording process while sitting at the desk. He faces the camera across the desk, and uses the keyboard and mouse to control the capture and what he sees in the teleprompter. A low side table to the presenter's left holds the audio mixer and processor. The sofa is not necessary for recording a presentation. However, it is not a bad idea to keep in mind that others may be involved, so the space should be large enough to accommodate several people, even though only one will be on camera.

The Fabrikam staff will first select an appropriate room for the mini-studio, then they will prepare the space. After the studio space is completed, they will bring in the equipment and wire it.

Selecting the Mini-studio Space

In this scenario, there is no need to build a special studio. For example, an enclosed office can provide an adequate space. In selecting the space, there are some things to consider. For video, you need a space in which you can control the light. Fabrikam will be using small studio lights that provide the correct type and amount of light. You need to be able to eliminate other sources of light, such as overhead fluorescent lights and outdoor light. You also need to eliminate potential distractions for the presenter, such as people walking by. An interior, windowless room would be ideal.

For audio, you need a space in which you have control over the sound that gets recorded. Ideally, the end user should hear only the presenter. Anything else, such as machines, people talking, air conditioning, and birds singing, is distracting. You also want to be able to eliminate sound reflections, which can make the presenter sound like she is in a restroom or warehouse. A carpeted office space with some acoustic tile will help. The best way to test a potential space is to simply stand in it and listen. If you hear elevator motors, heavy office conversation, outside traffic, or any other sound, there is a good chance that it will be picked up by the microphone.

The perfect studio for recording sound has very thick walls for eliminating external sound. Professional audio studios are actually constructed on floating floors. All walls, the ceiling, and the floor are acoustically isolated from the external building and the ground so no external sound, including very low-frequency sounds from traffic and airplanes, gets transferred into the space. There are also no parallel surfaces, so sound cannot bounce between two wall planes. The surfaces are also softened with acoustical material to stop sound from reflecting.

Fabrikam finds the ideal space in an interior office that was used for storage. The space is 10 feet by 12 feet, with a dropped acoustic-tile ceiling. The floor is carpeted and, with the door closed, no external light gets in. Except for the occasional hallway meeting and some air conditioning noise, the room is quiet.

Preparing the Mini-studio Space

The Fabrikam studio space comes with carpeting and a dropped ceiling that absorbs some of the reflected sound. However, there are several other sound issues that need to be addressed.

Ventilation Noise

The sound of air rushing through ventilation ducts is so ubiquitous that you may have learned to tune it out. However, microphones pick up this sound with as much clarity as the presenter, and it is not easy to eliminate. HVAC airflow is a full-spectrum sound, meaning that it contains sound of all frequencies—high hissing to low rumbling. The best way to eliminate it is to turn off the source, but this is not always possible in an office environment. It would also not be advisable because the enclosed studio could become uncomfortably hot when filled with people and video lights.

The best solution for dealing with the sound of rushing air coming through air ducts is to baffle or deaden the sound. The noise is caused by air being forced through and over surfaces. You can eliminate some noise by removing the air diffuser, so the air flows straight and unimpeded into the room. You can also hire an HVAC contractor to lengthen the inflow duct so that it can be bent into two or three loops to baffle and slow the air. A baffle box can also be built to cover the return duct. It should include a section of ducting that contains sound-absorption material.

Hard Surfaces

The office space is small and all the surfaces are parallel. Except for the soft floor and acoustic ceiling panels, conditions are near perfect for creating standing waves and reflections. A standing wave occurs when a sound wave gets trapped between two parallel surfaces that are the same distance apart as the length of the wave. The result is an increase in volume of sounds at that frequency.

To help eliminate some standing waves and reflections, you can add thick sound absorption material to the walls. You can hang sound baffles that contain fiberglass insulation covered by a cloth like burlap. A better solution is to cover the walls with sound panels, such as the ones used in the compression suite in chapter 15. The panels are made from a foam material that is easy to apply and cut to fit around objects. Figure 19.3 shows the uneven surface of the panel, which serves to baffle or diffuse the sound waves. You cannot eliminate every hard, reflective surface. The goal is to cover at least one side of a parallel pair.

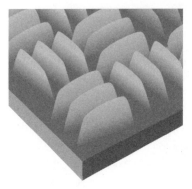

Figure 19.3 Wavy surfaces of sound panels help reduce standing waves.

Noisy Equipment

As part of preparing the space, the Fabrikam staff needs to create a sound-dampened area or enclosure where the encoding computer can be located. They could use an enclosed rack like the one in the compression suite. The only problem with a rack is that it takes up space in an already crowded room. Also, the computer does not need to be in the room. Fabrikam takes a tip from the design of the studio control room and locates the computer in an adjacent office. All they need is a hole in the wall to route cables for the mouse, keyboard, monitor, audio, and video.

People Sounds

Fabrikam adds an "on-air" light next to the studio door in the hall to eliminate one important source of noise. The light is wired to a switch on the desk. The switch can also be wired to the studio lights. Prior to recording, the presenter merely flips the switch on. Lights, such as the one illustrated in figure 19.4, are available from a number of broadcast suppliers.

Figure 19.4 On-air lights remind colleagues that a recording is in progress.

Outfitting the Studio

In keeping with the quality standard established by the Media department, Fabrikam will use professional or semi-professional equipment that produces broadcast-quality video and audio, and is well constructed so that it can withstand heavy use. The following list describes the equipment and where it will be located.

Video-related Equipment

The following video equipment is used in the mini-studio:

■ Camcorder. A semi-professional digital camcorder that provides high-quality video and professional features. The one used by Fabrikam includes three CCDs (Charge-Coupled Devices), sometimes called chips, for converting light into an electrical signal. With three CCDs, the camcorder is capable of recording sharper pictures that have truer colors. Canon, Sony, and JVC are among the companies that make three-chip camcorders.

■ Tripod. A professional tripod from a company such as Sachler or Vinten that is lightweight, but capable of holding a camera and teleprompter.

■ Teleprompter. A teleprompter enables presenters to view images on a monitor while looking straight into the camera lens. It appears to viewers as if the presenter is looking directly at the camera even though the presenter is actually looking at the monitor image reflected on a piece of glass. The image the presenter chooses to view can be a script, a rundown, notes, PowerPoint slides, or anything else. Figure 19.5 shows how a teleprompter works.

Teleprompters from companies such as Mirror Image and QTV use lightweight, LCD-based monitors. A teleprompter makes it easier for the presenter, who does not have to constantly refer to notes off-screen, and it makes for a more compelling presentation for the viewer.

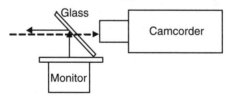

Figure 19.5   A schematic view of teleprompter operation.

■ Backdrop. A single color or textured backdrop attaches to the wall or hangs from the ceiling behind the presenter. It could even be painted on the wall. Blue, neutral gray, or a shade of brown works best. Stay away from red. Backdrops are available from studio supply companies.

Additional, optional equipment includes a videotape deck and scan converter that can be provided if you want to offer the user more production devices. Users can capture content from the tape. If they want to display the video from a laptop, for example, the scan converter can be used to match the video output to the studio's monitor and teleprompter.

After video from other sources is captured, the end user can edit it with the video of the presentation in Producer. Also, a small video monitor can be placed on the desk, so presenters can position themselves and check video quality before recording. Keep in mind, however, that the more devices and options you offer users, the more "how to" information you will have to provide.

Figure 19.6 shows part of a mini-studio configuration similar to the one Fabrikam is building. The figure shows the part that faces the presenter. The teleprompter (draped in black cloth) sits in front of the camcorder. Both are mounted on a tripod. A flat-panel computer monitor is positioned below the teleprompter. The video monitor and optional VCRs are placed to one side. Note that, in a studio, the only part that has to look good is the part the camera will see.

Figure 19.6   The video recording installation in a Producer mini-studio.

Audio-related Equipment

Here are some examples of audio equipment commonly used in a Producer mini-studio:

- Lavalier microphone. A lavalier typically comes with assorted clips that enable a presenter to quickly attach the microphone to a tie or blouse. Of all the microphones, a lavalier provides the most foolproof way to capture high-quality sound. Lavaliers are available from a variety of companies, such as Sony, Sennheiser, and Shure. A lavalier with a clip-on attachment is shown in figure 19.7.

Figure 19.7   Example of a lavalier microphone.

- Audio processor. An audio processor changes the audio signal in some way. The type of processor Fabrikam will use in the mini-studio adjusts the audio level automatically, so the volume is even and does not cause distortion. This type of processor is called a compressor/limiter. Companies such as Symterix and Rane offer specialized compressor/limiters called voice processors, which provide additional tools for working with vocal sound.

  A high-quality audio processor is often a complex device designed for use by an experienced audio engineer. For a self-service mini-studio, you can have the processor adjusted in advance, and then locate it where users cannot easily customize the settings. Several products come with a number of factory presets and enable users to save custom settings.

- Audio mixer. If you are offering the user only one microphone, you will not need a mixer. However, if you want to offer multiple microphones and the ability to copy from tapes, you can use a mixer similar to the small mixer used in the compression suite built in chapter 15.

- Speakers and headphones. The user will require some means of listening to audio that has been recorded. Studio monitors like the ones used in the compression suite would be a good choice. Often, a high-quality pair of computer speakers or headphones is adequate.

Lighting Equipment

The goal of lighting in Fabrikam's self-service studio is to create a pleasant, soft, even light that will work for just about any presenter. The lighting will be pre-configured and ready to go. All the presenter has to do is turn the lights on with one switch.

The most popular video production lighting instruments use incandescent lamps, such as quartz halogen lamps because they output adequate light for video recording, take up little space, and the color temperature of the lamp does not drift over time. (Color temperature indicates the color of a light source: incandescent light has a more reddish color temperature than sunlight, for example.)

The Fabrikam studio, however, will use fluorescent lights because they last longer and run cooler than incandescent lights. The cooler light will enable the studio to use less air conditioning, which will help lower the background noise in the room. Fluorescent lights also provide a very flat, soft light, meaning the light level is even, without harsh shadows. The fluorescents that Fabrikam will be using are brighter and produce a more even light than the ones commonly used in overhead office fixtures, and they produce light with the correct color temperature.

To give the set an even light, the Fabrikam staff will place fluorescent lamps, such as those from Lowell or Kino Flo, on either side of the camera. They will also place a backlight above the backdrop; this light is focused down on the back of the presenter's head. Backlights create a rim of light on the subject's hair that helps separate the image of the presenter from the background. The Fabrikam design will use a small, 200-watt quartz halogen light. However, a fluorescent light will work if there is enough space for it. Figure 19.8 shows the approximate placement of the lights.

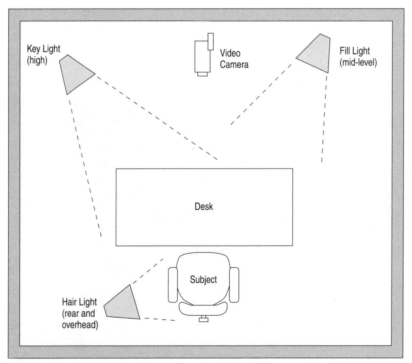

Figure 19.8   Placement of lights in the Producer mini-studio.

The lights will hang from pipes running between the two side walls so there is less clutter on the floor. You can use floor stands if you are unable to hang the lights. Light stands, mounting hardware, and complete kits can be purchased from video production or photography equipment suppliers.

Building the Production Workstation

The production workstation computer should meet the recommended system requirements for Microsoft Producer. A computer similar to the one used in the compression
suite would work fine. Make sure the CPU, memory and other specifications are ample
for capturing directly to a Windows Media file with a frame size of 320 × 240 or less.

The workstation used in the Fabrikam scenario will include the following additional
hardware and software:

■   Flat panel display. Because a flat panel display requires less desk space, it can
     be located near the camera lens sight line, so it can be used in addition to the
     teleprompter. The display will be used primarily for working with the com-
     puter: starting and stopping the encoder, playing back recordings, setting up
     notes for the teleprompter, and so forth.

■   Dual-output display card. Two display adapters or a video card with dual-output
     options can be used to feed the desk monitor and the teleprompter monitor.
     With dual displays, a presenter can arrange what she sees on the teleprompter
     and desktop monitor by simply dragging documents and program windows
     between them.

■   Video capture. A video capture card is used to capture audio and video. The
     card should provide both analog and digital inputs, so the camcorder can be
     plugged into the IEEE 1394 digital connection for direct transfers, and into
     the S-video connector when capturing live to the computer. The composite
     connection could also be used to connect a VCR, for example.

■   IEEE-1394 hub. If a cable longer than 15 feet is required to reach the com-
     puter in the adjacent office, a hub can be used to bridge two cables.

■   Software. Producer and Microsoft Office programs, such as PowerPoint and
     Word, running on Windows XP Professional. The Office programs can be
     used by presenters for organizing their scripts and slides.

■   Network Interface Card (NIC). The workstation will be connected to the
     corporate network so presenters will be able to access material on other
     computers. They will also be able to copy finished projects to another work-
     station or publish them directly to the Media Guide site.

Wiring the Studio

The diagram in figure 19.9 shows how Fabrikam's Producer mini-studio is wired.

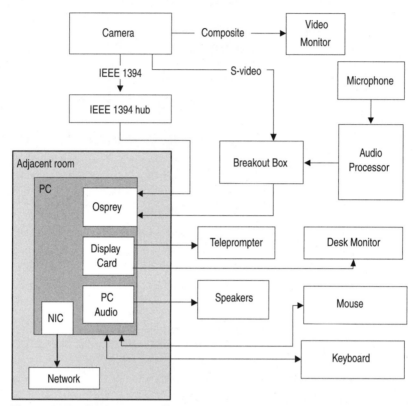

Figure 19.9 Equipment configuration and wiring of the Producer mini-studio.

The camcorder composite video output is connected to the small video monitor; S-video output is connected to the video card breakout box, if available; and the IEEE 1394 signal is connected to the capture card. The lavalier microphone is connected through the audio processor to the breakout box. If multiple microphones or sources are available, the microphones and sources would go through a mixer first. Typically, the user will record a presentation using the Capture Wizard in Producer. In that case, the S-video and video card analog audio inputs are used. The user can play back a presentation in Producer, view video on the flat-panel monitor, and hear audio through the computer speakers.

One output of the display card is connected to the desktop monitor, the other to the teleprompter monitor. Mouse and keyboard are connected using extension cables, and the corporate network is connected to the NIC.

The wiring can be varied for different situations. For example, it might make more sense to record to videotape, and then capture only the selected take to the computer. In that case, audio from the processor can be split or connected directly to the camcorder line inputs. Then the selected take can be transferred to the computer digitally through the IEEE 1394 cable.

The Fabrikam mini-studio is designed for users who have little experience running video equipment, so rewiring the studio is not promoted by the Media department. If a new configuration is requested by a customer, an engineer from the department will make the actual changes.

Creating a Presentation with Microsoft Producer

After installing the self-service studio, Fabrikam needs to provide detailed information about how to use it. They have designed ease of use into the setup. Now to make using the studio as foolproof as possible, they will intentionally limit the user's options to one simple, preferred method for capturing, editing, and playing back a presentation. Then they will carefully document the steps and test the process to make sure everything works as expected. They will also make sure troubleshooting issues are covered as completely as possible.

Of course, there are many things users can do with the camcorder, computer, audio processors, and the other components, but recording a user's garage band or editing home movies will not be allowed as options. Users will know that the studio can be used for the following tasks:

- Recording a PowerPoint presentation.

- Editing and synchronizing the recorded presentation.

- Packaging and publishing the final project.

If a user needs to create a product that is outside the scope of these tasks, she can contact the Media department and a producer will work with her to complete the project.

In this section, we go through the entire process of creating a Producer presentation. Fabrikam will provide instructions like these for their mini-studio users. We will start with the assumption that everything is connected as shown in figure 19.9.

Recording a PowerPoint Presentation

Open Producer and start the **New Presentation Wizard** from the **File** menu. Enter the following settings in the **New Presentation Wizard** and **Capture Wizard**:

- **Presentation Template, Scheme, and Information**. Choose the layout template for a presentation and enter metadata information, such as title and description. The default presentation template includes audio, video, and slides.

- **Import Slides and Still Images**. Enter the path to the PowerPoint presentation file, which has a .ppt extension. The project can be accessed on any computer on the corporate network, such as a presenter's personal computer, a SharePoint team site, a floppy disk, or a CD.

- **Import or Capture Video and Audio**. Click **Capture** and the **Capture Wizard** opens.

- **Capture Options**. Capture video with audio, and use the recommended settings. The correct capture devices should be chosen and properly configured by default. On the **Choose Capture Devices** page of the **Capture Wizard**, make sure the camcorder image displays. Also make sure audio from the lavalier microphone is selected and that the audio input level is correct.

After the project is configured the **Capture Video and Audio** page of the wizard is displayed:

1. Click the **Capture** button when you are ready to begin recording.

2. Click **Stop** when you are finished, and enter a name and path for the new video file.

3. Repeat the previous two steps as many times as necessary until you get a good take of the presentation. You can save each take separately, or overwrite the previous take with a new one.

After you have successfully recorded a take, you will return to the New Presentation Wizard and enter the following information:

- **Import or Capture Video and Audio**. Enter the path of the file you just recorded.

- **Synchronize Presentation**. Select **Yes** to synchronize the slides after they have been imported.

The PowerPoint slides and the video just recorded are imported into the Producer project, added to the timeline, and the **Synchronize Slides** dialog box opens.

Synchronizing and Editing the Recorded Presentation

The **New Presentation Wizard** guides you through the process of creating a project and capturing video for the presentation. Then the **Synchronize Slides** dialog box enables you to manually add slide changes so they are synchronized with the video.

Many users will want to retake a recording, add other images and effects, edit a project, or do something else that breaks the flow of the wizards. If the studio schedule is tight, you can suggest that they spend studio time capturing the presentation and roughly synchronizing the slides, and then complete the project later, outside the studio. For example, the presentation can be recorded in the studio, and then the project can be copied to the presenter's computer and finished there. If the presenter does not have the time or expertise to finish the project, the project can be handed over to a producer or assistant.

In Producer, to synchronize the PowerPoint slides to the newly captured video manually, do the following:

1. In the **Synchronize Slides** dialog box, select **Set slide timing**.

2. Click the **Play** button.

3. Click the button below the playback controls to display a new slide (with the **Next Slide** button) or start the next effect (with the **Next Effect** button). The button changes depending on what action occurs next in the PowerPoint presentation. The button will not be enabled until the current action is finished. For example, if a transition effect lasts 10 seconds, you cannot start the next action until the transition ends.

4. After setting the slide timing, click **Preview slide timing**, and then click the **Play** button to play the video back with the slide changes.

5. If timing looks good, click **Finish** to update the slide timings on the timeline. To redo the slide timings, repeat steps 1 through 3.

After you finish the wizards, you can change the timing of the presentation elements on the timeline that runs across the bottom of the Producer window. You can change when a video or audio clip begins or ends by dragging the left or right borders of the clip. You can change the duration of a static item such as a slide or HTML by dragging the right border to the left or right. To change the start time of a clip within the presentation, click anywhere within the clip and drag it.

You can also add transitions and effects to the video, import more media elements, such as different video clips or Web pages, and edit a video clip. For more information about working with the timeline, see chapter 21. For more information about Producer, see the Microsoft Producer Help.

After you have arranged the slides, video, and other elements on the timeline, save the project. If you open the folder where you just saved the Producer project, you will notice that it contains several folders and a project file with an .MSProducer file name extension. Producer uses a non-destructive editing technique. Unlike film editing, where you physically and permanently cut the film, nondestructive editing enables you to make as many edit changes as you want without changing the original digital media. All those folders hold the original digital media elements. The only thing that changes is the project file. As you play back the timeline, you are playing portions of the original digital media along with the edit decisions you have made on the timeline and saved in the project file.

After you have finished editing and want to publish the presentation, Producer encodes the video and audio content on the timeline into a new video file (or files), and also creates copies of source files used in the presentation.

Packaging and Publishing the Final Project

During the publishing process, Producer uses information in the project file to automatically assemble a new, edited Windows Media Video file, which is encoded at the bit rate specified in the Publish Wizard. Producer also converts and compresses image files to the selected bit rate, and then creates a final project Web page, associated project files, and a folder containing the digital media files required to display the presentation. Producer then provides several ways to publish this set of presentation components to your computer, a CD, another computer on your network, or a Web folder.

After elements have been added to a timeline and the project has been saved, you can do one of the following:

- Continue to edit the project. You work with the elements on the timeline.

- Package the project. Producer automatically packages the project, so that it can be edited on another computer, such as your desktop computer.

- Publish the project. Producer automatically encodes the final Windows Media file, converts the PowerPoint project, and creates the files that display the presentation in a Web browser.

Packaging the Project

When packaging a project, Producer copies all the elements of the project into a compressed project archive file with an .MSProducerZ file name extension. To package a project, do the following:

1. On the **File** menu, click **Pack and Go**.

2. Enter a location for the project archive file.

The file is created. You can then copy the file to another computer, open the project archive in Producer, and then continue working on the project.

Publishing the Project

When it comes time to publish a project, the Publish Wizard is used. Producer uses the same basic process regardless of whether it publishes to the local computer, a CD, a network location, or a Web folder. This section will describe publishing to Web folders, because that is how the Fabrikam Media department will make the presentations available in the Media Guide. The process is similar for publishing to any other location.

Typically, after a Fabrikam user finishes a project, the project is repacked and sent to the Media department. A producer in the Media department then checks the project for errors and production quality. The producer then publishes it to the Media Guide. At another company, a completely different review process might be required before a presentation is released companywide. A SharePoint staging site can be created for a work in progress, which would be accessible only to a review team, the presenter, and others who are working on the project.

One useful feature of Producer is its ability to publish directly to SharePoint Portal Server. The moment the files have finished copying to the server, they can be accessed by users through the Media Guide. If the user has entered metadata in the project, such as title and descriptive text, the information is searchable from within the Media Guide.

At Fabrikam, when a project is published to the Media Guide site, the presentation Web pages and images will be copied to SharePoint Portal Server, and the Windows Media files will be copied to a location on the Windows Media server. The Publish Wizard in Microsoft Producer handles all of the linking automatically. All the user has to do is specify where the files should go.

To publish a project to the SharePoint Portal Server site, do the following:

1. On the **File** menu, click **Publish Presentation**.

2. In the **Publish Wizard**, click **Web server**, and then, in the drop-down list, click **Add a new Web server**.

3. On the **Internet or Intranet Host Settings** page, provide the following information:

   - In the **Friendly host name** box, type a name for this publishing profile. In the future, this name will appear in the drop-down box on the previous page of the wizard.

   - In the **Publish Web files to** box, type **the location** of the Web folder in the format http://*PortalServer*/*Workspace*/*Documents*. *PortalServer* is the name of the server running SharePoint Portal Server, *Workspace* refers to the workspace on the server to which files can be copied, and *Documents* is the Web folder the presentation files are stored in. The Web files in your presentation are copied to this location.

   - In the **Playback presentation address (optional)** box, type the intranet location from which the presentation will be played back (for example, *http://PortalServer/Workspace/Documents*).

   - Select the **Publish Windows Media files to** check box, and then type the shared network location to which the Windows Media files will be copied; for example *Mediaserver**Wwwroot**Sharedfolder*. You can also specify the URL in the format http://*Mediaserver*/*Alias* if IIS on the Windows Media server has Web Distributed Authoring and Versioning

(WebDAV) enabled. It was automatically enabled on the Web server when SharePoint was installed.

- In the **Playback address for Windows Media files** box, type the publishing point on the Windows Media server from which the Windows Media files will be played back (for example, mms://Mediaserver/Alias).

- If you have enabled Web discussions on the specified server, select the **Discussion server address** check box. A discussion server can be used if a presentation is part of a collaborative team effort or was designed to initiate a discussion.

- In the **Discussion server address** box, type the name of the Web discussion server (for example, http://Discussionserver).

4.   Complete the **Publish Wizard**.

When you click **Finish** on the last page of the wizard, Producer creates a finished video file, compresses image files, creates all the associated Web elements, and links the files. At the end of the process, you should test playback of the presentation to make sure the links and paths are correct. After a project has been published, end users can play the presentation by opening the default Web page in Internet Explorer.

In the next chapter, the Fabrikam IT department installs and configures Windows Media servers in remote locations so that end users anywhere in the company can stream on-demand content to their computer desktops.

20

Phase II: Remote Server Deployment

At this point, the Fabrikam staff has built and upgraded its facilities to enable producers and users to create content for streaming over the intranet. They also implemented a Web-based Media Guide to help users find content. The Fabrikam IT department installed Windows Media server farms at headquarters so on-demand content and limited live content can be streamed locally. In this chapter, the IT department installs servers in remote locations. These servers will enable users anywhere on the corporate network to stream content.

In this phase of deployment, a Windows Media server will also be installed in the company's perimeter network (also known as a DMZ), located at headquarters in Toronto. The perimeter network server will provide streaming media content to Fabrikam partners on the extranet: those users outside the firewall who connect through the Internet. Installation of this server is very similar to that of an intranet server, except that it will not use network load balancing. Also, tighter security measures will be used, which include two firewalls to protect the server and to prevent unauthorized access to the internal corporate network.

In the networking industry, many new systems for managing bandwidth and content have emerged. Internet users want speed and reliability, and they want their experience with digital media on the Web to be the same as their experience with television, DVDs, and CDs. They have little patience for low-quality video and network problems. They just want it all to work.

Intranet users have the same demands. Windows Media can use the existing network infrastructure to provide enterprise users with a high-quality streaming media experience. But streaming media places heavy demands on the intranet. To maintain the health of the network and support client needs, a system is needed that both manages bandwidth and provides a way to manage streaming media content. Fabrikam achieves both goals by decentralizing the hosting of content through the use of remote servers.

Managing Bandwidth Usage

You only need one Windows Media server to stream content over an IP network. If streaming media usage were very low in the company (only one or two concurrent, low-bit-rate streams), a Fabrikam employee in Düsseldorf could stream content from one Toronto server. The only negative impact would occur on low-bandwidth WANs. Most of the network and the server could easily handle the load. In fact, if this was the expected usage, the company could simply stream from their Web servers.

However, this will not be the case. A server and network can handle many users accessing static Web content such as Web pages and images because data is sent in bursts and large chunks. Streaming media content, on the other hand, requires that data be sent in smaller chunks, and over extended, continuous periods. For example, a user streaming a 100 Kbps stream for 30 minutes will require that much network bandwidth for that amount of time. If 1,000 users want to stream content, such as a live unicast broadcast, a 100 Mbps network will be completely consumed for 30 minutes—assuming there is no other traffic at all on the network, which is rarely the case.

Network bandwidth is by far the most important issue for streaming media. All streaming media tools, protocols, servers, encoders, and players are focused on delivering the best user experience while managing bandwidth usage. For example, an encoder reduces the bit rate of content and packages it to be sent over a network. A media server manages bandwidth to reduce impact on the network and to deliver a high-quality user experience. Protocols like UDP reduce bandwidth usage. You can stream from a Web server, but Windows Media Services works with Windows Media Player to provide much more sophisticated bandwidth management and a better end user experience.

Streaming media producers, developers, and IT professionals must balance quality with bit rate—getting the playback quality as high as possible while keeping the bit rate as low as possible.

It helps to view deploying a streaming media system as deploying a bandwidth management system. The job is not just getting pictures and sound from one place to another; it is also delivering digital media content reliably while balancing bandwidth usage and playback quality. To that end, companies continue searching for improvements in techniques and technologies for creating, delivering, and playing digital media. One of the most effective techniques available today involves decentralizing the hosting of content by placing multiple servers as close to users as possible. This technique is sometimes called "edge serving."

Using Edge Servers to Manage Bandwidth

In a typical enterprise intranet, maximum concurrencies for clients streaming on-demand content range from 8 to 15 percent of the user population. Therefore, if a network segment has 1,000 users, you can assume that about 80 to 150 users will be streaming unicast content concurrently. If the average bit rate of streaming media content is 100 Kbps, bandwidth usage will be 8 to 15 Mbps. On a 100-Mbps network, this is a reasonable amount of streaming activity, considering that 8 to 15 Mbps of bandwidth usage does not apply to the entire network, but is concentrated on the network segments nearest the servers. In other words, bandwidth usage decreases as the data paths fan out from the servers.

Using these figures as a rough guide, think about what would happen on the Fabrikam network with different server solutions. First, let's look at a simple network in which users stream from one centralized server.

In figure 20.1, you can see that the network segments nearest to the server can become very congested when all users connect to one server. Also, low- to mid-bandwidth WAN connections can be easily consumed with streaming media traffic. A centralized server may work for static content or in situations where the amount of streaming traffic is low, but this topology becomes too congested when there are many concurrent connections.

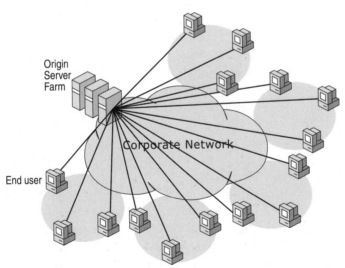

Figure 20.1   Centralized network topologies cause congestion around the media server.

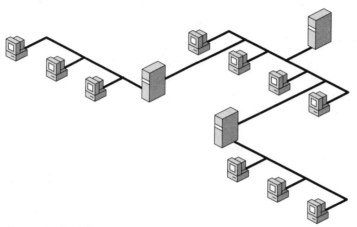

Figure 20.2 Edge servers reduce congestion by moving content closer to users.

In figure 20.2, the company added edge servers to the remote sites, and implemented a bandwidth-management system. In this managed-bandwidth scenario, instead of all clients streaming from one origin server farm, clients stream from the edge server that is closest to them. Bandwidth is managed on the segments nearest the origin servers and across the entire network, including all WANs.

By adding remote servers and a bandwidth-management system, the company has decentralized server activity so bandwidth usage is spread out evenly across the network. With edge serving, network bandwidth no longer dictates the quality of the end user experience. By decentralizing the distribution of streams, you can offer a higher-quality user experience without having to install a higher-bandwidth infrastructure. To handle an increase in user demand, you can simply add more edge servers.

Streaming broadcast content can place more load on a network than on-demand content because there is more likely to be a higher number of concurrent connections for a live event. Fabrikam plans to use multicast for broadcasting live streams. Multicast solves the network load problem because many users can stream multicast content with little increase in bandwidth usage.

However, there will be areas of the network that cannot be configured for multicast because they are served by routers that cannot be multicast-enabled or are on token-ring segments. Also, remote users connecting over dial-up or Internet connections may not be able to receive multicast packets. To solve these problems, the remote servers can be configured to distribute or rebroadcast a unicast stream. This is called "stream splitting." The server makes one connection to the origin server or another distribution server, and then splits or duplicates the stream to multiple clients that connect locally. By splitting the live stream, the remote server helps to minimize bandwidth usage on the network segments leading to the origin server.

Managing Content

Bandwidth management using edge servers means getting the content closer to the end user. Content management means knowing what content you have on your servers, and making sure that it is the right content. You can do that manually by making lists in a spreadsheet, and manually copying files to edge servers, or you can automate the process with a content management system.

One way to automate the management of on-demand content is to use a system that regularly replicates content from the origin server to all remote servers. The advantage of such a system is that users everywhere in the company will have quick access to any content, and bandwidth usage on the core infrastructure is minimized. Replication can be scheduled to occur at times when network usage is low, such as at night or during weekends. However, not all content is needed at all locations. For example, programs created specifically for a Toronto-based audience might not need to be available on a server in Rotterdam. Therefore, a system of selective replication could greatly decrease the time and bandwidth needed for the process, as well as the storage requirements on the remote servers.

One way to implement selective replication is to manually decide which files should be replicated. However, this process can be time and resource intensive. Besides, how do you make those selection decisions? For example, there might be one employee in Rotterdam who must view the Toronto video. A better solution might be to automate the selection process with cache/proxy servers.

If remote servers have cache/proxy functionality, you do not need to replicate or push content to the servers. Cache/proxy servers automatically cache content that end users request. If a request is made for content that is available in the cache, the cache/proxy server streams the file locally. Otherwise, it streams the file from the origin server, sending the stream to the end user while caching a copy. A cache/proxy server also checks to make sure the local file is current (or "fresh") before streaming it. Only files that are used locally need to be cached. And by caching only the content that is requested, bandwidth usage on the core network infrastructure is minimized.

One problem of automatic, on-demand caching is that an end user may not choose the best time to request some content that must be streamed from the origin server. For example, an end user may decide to play a stream over a WAN connection when the network is at peak usage. Also, incomplete or partial caches may occur when an end user views only part of a long file or skips to different sections of a file. To remedy this situation, a cache/proxy server can cache the file in a stream that is independent of the stream being sent to the end user.

The best solution for managing content, therefore, is a combination of these concepts. With a complete content management solution, you can choose how to control when content is sent from the origin server. The following items summarize the on-demand content-management solutions and how they might work together:

Automated Replication

With automated replication, you configure a content management system to automatically prestuff files based on your estimation of client usage. Prestuffing is the process of moving content to a cache/proxy server's cache before it is requested by an end user. You can select which files are replicated and at what time replication occurs. You can also select which servers will receive the files.

For example, you could schedule a Europe-specific video file for replication to all European servers at 2:00 AM GMT. Based on your estimation, the European data centers will then be prepared for the expected high demand of the content.

Cache/proxy Functionality

If content is not available on a remote server, the server's cache/proxy functionality handles the streaming and caching of the file from the origin server when an end user requests it. For example, an end user in New York might want to view the Europe-specific program, which has not been replicated to his local server.

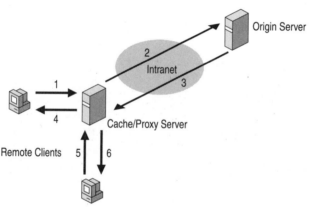

Figure 20.3 Steps of the cache/proxy process.

Figure 20.3 shows how the cache/proxy process works. The steps of the process occur in this order:

1. Client makes a request for content on the origin server. The request is intercepted by the local cache/proxy server, which checks for the content in the local cache.

2. If the content is not found in the local cache, the cache/proxy server transfers the request to the origin server.

3. The origin server streams the content to the cache/proxy server.

4. The cache/proxy server stores the content in the cache and streams the content to the client.

5. A second client makes a request for the same content on the origin server. Again, the request is intercepted by the local cache/proxy server.

6. The cache/proxy server checks for the content in the local cache. If content is available and fresh, the cache/proxy server streams the content locally.

Manual Delivery

In cases where automated replication and cache/proxy functionality are not the best ways to get content closer to the user, you can fall back on manually prestuffing files. For example, you may need to disable cache/proxy functionality on specific remote servers to restrict streaming over slow WANs. However, there may be times when end users in these areas need to view files that have not been automatically replicated. In cases like these, you can implement a system through which users can request content. For example, an end user in New York can request the Europe-specific program. A system administrator or an automated system can then copy the file to the New York server manually or add it to the files to be replicated automatically overnight.

The following summarizes broadcast content management solutions:

Multicast Delivery

In the ideal enterprise network, all end users would receive live programming through multicast delivery. With multicast, one stream serves multiple users, so bandwidth usage is as low as possible. Bandwidth usage is further restricted to only those network paths on which clients request the stream. For example, 10 end users in Düsseldorf will require the same network bandwidth as 500 users. If there are no clients receiving the multicast stream in Düsseldorf, the stream will not be present on the network and, therefore, no bandwidth will be used. For more details on multicast delivery, see chapter 22.

Unicast Distribution

The goal of the Fabrikam deployment is to use multicast delivery on as much of the network as possible. However, if network devices such as firewalls and switches block multicast packets, they can use unicast distribution to stream through the devices, and then use multicast delivery on the other side. Figure 20.4 shows how this works.

Any broadcast publishing point that is configured for multicast delivery can also be enabled for unicast delivery. To set up unicast distribution, publishing points on one or more remote Windows Media servers are configured to source from the origin server or another distribution server using unicast. Then the remote publishing points rebroadcast the stream using multicast delivery. By leap-frogging areas of the network that do not pass multicast packets, you can avoid having to upgrade or redesign those areas.

You can also use multicast distribution, in which you source from a multicast stream and rebroadcast it as unicast streams.

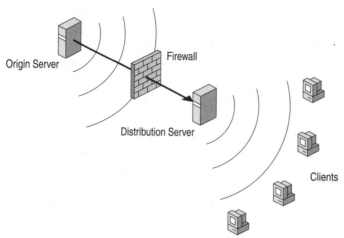

Figure 20.4 Using unicast distribution for multicast delivery through a firewall.

Automatic Stream Splitting

In areas of the network that are not multicast enabled, you can use stream-splitting. Unicast distribution and stream-splitting do roughly the same thing: one stream feeds multiple clients. The differences have to do with how the methods are implemented and how the stream is delivered to the clients. Figure 20.5 shows how stream splitting works:

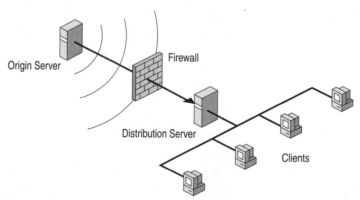

Figure 20.5 Using stream-splitting with a cache/proxy server.

Where multicast or unicast distribution is accomplished using a broadcast publishing point on a Windows Media server, stream-splitting is accomplished with a cache/proxy server. The advantage is that cache/proxy servers handle stream-splitting automatically, unlike the distribution method in which publishing points need to be created and configured manually. However, a disadvantage of stream-splitting is that clients receive streams through a unicast connection. Therefore, stream-splitting should only be used on network segments that cannot pass multicast traffic, but have the bandwidth to handle multiple unicast streams. For example, cache/proxy servers can be used to split live streams to remote users connected using Remote Access Service (RAS).

Scheduled Delivery

This method combines many of the advantages of on-demand and live delivery. With scheduled delivery, a Windows Media file that would typically be played on demand by an end user is instead broadcast on a publishing point. To view the file, end users tune in at scheduled times. Because multicast can be used for scheduled delivery, more users can view the content concurrently and receive a better user experience with less impact on network bandwidth.

Directing the Client to Content

An edge server solution has two components. The first component involves getting the content closer to the user. The second component involves getting the user to the content. You can do that by redirecting user requests for content on an origin server to a remote or cache/proxy server. After intercepting a request, the cache/proxy server handles the request by streaming content from its cache, streaming and caching content from the origin server, or by splitting a live stream from the origin server.

There are three ways to direct or redirect a client request to an edge server:

Directing the User Manually

If the edge server is not a proxy server, an end user simply enters the URL of the edge server in Windows Media Player. This would be the case if the remote server is simply another Windows Media server connected to the origin server. This might be a good solution in a small company with only a few remote locations. You could manually replicate all files, the file structure, and publishing points from the origin server to all remote servers. Then an end user could connect directly to the remote server. For example, if the URL of some content on the origin server was rtsp://Origin/File.wmv, a remote user would enter the URL rtsp://RemoteServer/File.wmv to access that content.

To make the manual method easier for users, you can include the URL in a Windows Media metafile. For example, you could create a metafile Chicago.asx through which Chicago users could access the file from their remote server. The URL of the file could be something like rtsp://ChicagoWMS1/File.wmv.

You could also create a system that automates the generation of custom metafiles. For example, you could develop an ASP page that returns custom metafiles based on a user's IP address.

Configuring Proxy Settings

If the edge server is a proxy server, an administrator can configure proxy settings in Windows Media Player. This method is commonly referred to as the forward proxy method for redirection. Figure 20.6 shows the proxy settings in Windows Media Player.

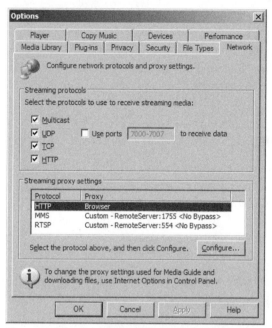

Figure 20.6   Configuring Player proxy settings to access a specific proxy server.

After an end user has added a proxy server and port to a protocol, all requests made using that protocol are sent to the proxy server. For example, if a user requests rtsp:// Origin/File.wmv, the Player will send the request to RemoteServer on port 554.

The Enterprise Deployment Pack for Windows Media Player can be used to create a custom installation package for the Player. When creating the package, proxy settings can be specified so every installation of the Player is preconfigured with the correct settings.

Transparent Proxy

At Fabrikam, the cache/proxy servers support the transparent proxy of client requests. This means that all client requests for streaming content at a remote site are automatically sent through the proxy server, regardless of the URL entered by an end user or the proxy settings specified in Windows Media Player.

With the transparent proxy method, the Player and other applications do not require any configuration to use a cache/proxy server. This makes edge serving easier for end users and IT personnel. After transparent proxy has been set up, all redirection is handled using one method, which is controlled by the IT department. For example, an end user cannot mistakenly configure the wrong proxy server in his Player or request content from the wrong remote server.

The easiest way to enable transparent proxy is to assign IP address ranges to remote clients based on location. Then use a system that redirects client requests based on IP address. A layer 4 or layer 7 switch, Web Cache Communication Protocol (WCCP) routers, or policy-based routing can be used to redirect requests. Because the devices work on the application layer, they can redirect the connections within the network and cache/proxy devices transparently to the user and Web application. For more information about the layers of the Open System Interconnection (OSI) model, see the OSI model sidebar in chapter 22.

In the Fabrikam scenario, the IT department will be deploying a decentralized system that delivers streaming media using transparent proxies, that manages bandwidth, and that enables them to manage content. The system also provides feedback that can help Fabrikam understand the health of the system, the quality of the user experience, and details of streaming media usage on the company intranet.

Content Delivery Networks

Fabrikam is essentially building a Content Delivery Network (CDN) for an enterprise. (This type of network is sometimes called an eCDN.) The CDN concept has become popular as a way of describing a decentralized system for delivering content over the Internet.

Service providers such as Akamai and Network Appliance offer services, applications, and hardware to help companies host their content on the Internet. Some providers manufacture the hardware or software in addition to offering a hosting service—a complete CDN solution. The solution can include an array of edge servers located throughout the world, or content management systems that move the content to the edge servers and provide usage feedback. An Internet radio station, for example, can simply send its encoded signal to a CDN, which can then handle all the distribution. Users simply access the URL of a streaming site, and CDN software automatically redirects the client to the edge server that will provide the best playback quality. For more information about CDNs, see chapter 13.

Following the success of CDNs on the Internet, several companies packaged their services and devices for use on private intranets run by medium-to-large enterprises. With these devices and the associated software, you can create an eCDN that delivers Windows Media-based streaming content—as well as Web content and other multimedia content—on an intranet. Many of the appliances are standalone devices that you simply install, configure once, and then manage remotely.

An eCDN system helps companies manage content and bandwidth by providing components for storage, content distribution, intelligent delivery, and reporting, as shown in figure 20.7. Most eCDN solutions are flexible and scalable. You can put together the components to deliver streaming media content over just about any type and size of IP network. The infrastructure of an enterprise network often presents the most challenges for upgrading an intranet for streaming. Edge servers and an eCDN system for managing content can help you work around the challenges.

An eCDN system enables both push and pull approaches to content management. IT personnel can push or prestuff content to the remote sites that they feel will receive a high number of hits. Users can also pull content from the origin server if the content is not available in the remote cache.

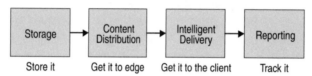

Figure 20.7 Components of an eCDN system.

An eCDN system consists of the following components:

- Storage. A file server or storage device that can hold large amounts of data, and then access it quickly and reliably over sustained periods. It must also be capable of streaming the data to a number of clients concurrently. Storage solutions include:

  - Direct Attached Storage (DAS), such as hard drives attached directly to a server.

  - Network Attached Storage (NAS), which are servers that only provide file storage.

  - Storage Area Network (SAN), which provide high-speed, private networks of shared storage devices.

  - Redundant Array of Independent Disks (RAID), which are arrays of hard drives that can provide various levels of storage-access speed and fault tolerance.

- Content Distribution. Computers, appliances, and software that manage content distribution from origin servers to edge servers.

- Intelligent Delivery. Many CDNs use software that enables "intelligent delivery" of content. For example, if an end user in New York uses the Internet to request a video stream from an origin server in Oslo, the CDN software automatically locates the content on the edge server that will provide the best connection and stream quality. It can also provide a type of load-balancing function so that the closest server with the lowest number of concurrent users and the most available bandwidth is used.

■ Reporting. A single Windows Media server creates daily usage logs, providing a detailed view of client activity. In an eCDN system, many servers are used, with each creating its own usage logs. An important component of a complete eCDN system is automatic collection and compilation of usage logs, as well as tools for creating reports from the data. The usage logs and reports can provide important performance and usage information. IT staff can ascertain the health of the system and pinpoint trouble spots, and content producers can learn how to improve their programming to better meet the needs of viewers.

Edge serving and content-management solutions provide exciting areas of growth for the streaming media industry. Instead of an independent, centralized point of origin for content that relies heavily on a solid, immoveable infrastructure, the eCDN approach views the network as one dynamic organism that can change and grow.

Visualizing the Fabrikam eCDN

Though many products and solutions can be used, the Fabrikam eCDN will be based on remote servers running Windows Media Services and a cache/proxy plug-in. The cache/proxy plug-ins can be created by using the Windows Media Services SDK. The plug-in works directly with the server, and can be administered from the Windows Media Services snap-in or Windows Media Services Administrator for the Web.

Because the cache/proxy plug-in works with an existing server, Fabrikam will have the flexibility of using the same Windows Media server to host on-demand content, live content, and playlists, to distribute streams from other servers, and to perform the functions of a cache/proxy server. For example, an edge server in Mexico City that is configured with a cache/proxy plug-in can proxy client requests, cache content, and host content produced locally. If it were not possible to receive a multicast stream from Toronto, the edge server could also be configured for unicast distribution or stream-splitting.

The Fabrikam cache/proxy plug-in is based on the sample provided with the Windows Media Services SDK. The SDK provides developers with the tools and information to build custom plug-ins or complete content management and distribution systems. You may choose a solution that uses the cache/proxy plug-in architecture or any other edge server solution, but the basic concepts still apply.

The Fabrikam eCDN will enable the company to manage on-demand and live content.

To manage on-demand content, the Fabrikam staff must know which files exist on all remote servers, and they must make sure the sites have the correct content. Technicians can find out which files exist on a remote server by either opening the remote server WMRoot folder in Windows Explorer, or by viewing the **Source** tab of the server's default publishing point. They can see which files exist in remote caches by using the content management solution. If producers know that a file is likely to receive a high number of hits, they can prestuff the file on all remote sites. Alternatively, they can rely on the cache/proxy plug-in to cache files as they are requested.

To manage live streams, the goal is to make sure all sites can receive a broadcast. The plan is to have the majority of the network multicast-enabled, so most users will be able to connect to a broadcast with a multicast stream originating from Toronto. On areas of the network that cannot handle multicast traffic, Fabrikam will use unicast distribution or stream splitting. When a large number of concurrent hits are expected for some on-demand content, scheduled delivery can be used.

The following summarizes the strategies that Fabrikam will use to manage content:

■   Pull content. Content management is handled automatically with a cache/proxy plug-in.

■   Push content. Certain content is prestuffed on remote servers. Third-party tools are available to handle the automatic replication of files, system management, usage reporting, and other tasks. Fabrikam can also simply push on-demand files manually.

■   Broadcast multicast. The majority of sites receive broadcasts with a multicast connection. To make multicast delivery viable, Fabrikam first needs to make sure that most of their network devices can pass multicast traffic. Routers and switches must have multicasting enabled. Devices that cannot be enabled, such as simple hubs, may need to be replaced.

■   Unicast distribution. At remote sites and certain areas of the network that cannot receive multicast packets, unicast distribution is used. To distribute a stream, the remote server can connect directly to the origin server farm by using the RTSP protocol, which supports the resending of packets. RTSP supports both TCP and UDP protocols. If TCP is used, data reception is guaranteed. With UDP, the data is not guaranteed, but packets can be resent.

■   Stream-splitting. At remote sites and areas of the network where multicast packets cannot be received, stream-splitting is used. The cache/proxy plug-in that is installed for the remote servers at these sites will intercept requests from users, and then establish a connection with the origin server. The remote server delivers a unicast stream to the first client and any additional clients that request the content, but will not need to establish any additional streams with the origin server.

■ Scheduled delivery. Windows Media files that are expected to receive a large number of concurrent hits can be broadcast on a schedule. The broadcast can be looped, or scheduled to start at regular times. Scheduled delivery can be nearly as convenient for end users as on-demand delivery because you can broadcast the content continuously. For example, you can start a 30-minute program at 2:00 PM and set it to loop. An end user can then view the program from the beginning by tuning in at the hour or thirty minutes after the hour.

Building the eCDN Components

Now that you have an understanding of decentralized networks and eCDNs, we can see how Fabrikam builds the components for delivering content on the corporate network. The rest of this chapter covers the following implementation topics:

■ Installing and running the cache/proxy plug-in. This also includes configuring and then testing the plug-in on the bench. The plug-in will enable content-management strategies such as pulling content and stream-splitting.

■ Setting up unicast distribution. Walks through the process of creating a distribution publishing point that delivers a multicast stream.

■ Creating a system for pushing content. Describes some ideas for creating a system that makes it easy to push content to many servers.

Using the Sample Cache/proxy Plug-in

The cache/proxy plug-in you use may have a different installation procedure and configuration, but the concepts will be similar. For testing cache/proxy functionality, you can use the sample provided with the Windows Media Services SDK. Keep in mind that the sample was designed as a starting point for developers to create complete cache/proxy solutions, and is not recommended for deployment in its current state.

To use the sample, first install the SDK from the link on the companion CD. After installing the SDK, you will need to use Microsoft Visual C# .NET or Visual Studio .NET to build the plug-in files from the sample C# project. The project file for the cache/proxy plug-in is installed by default in %systemdrive%\WMSDK\WMServices9\Samples\CacheProxy\Csharp\CacheProxyPluginSample.sln. Follow the procedure in the SDK for building and registering the C# Cache Proxy Plug-in Sample on your computer.

To use the plug-in on another computer, copy all the files that were created in the %systemroot%\System32\Windows Media\Server folder, and use the command-line tool Regasm.exe to register the DLL files. The DLL files must be registered on the server for the plug-in to work.

After the plug-in has been registered, restart Windows Media Services. Open the Windows Media Services snap-in. To restart the service, click the server in the console tree, and then, on the **Action** menu, click **Stop**. After you see the server has stopped, click **Start**. When the service is restarted, it will add the cache/proxy plug-in.

To configure the cache/proxy plug-in, do the following:

1. With the Windows Media Services snap-in open, expand the server, and then expand **Cache/Proxy Management**.

    The **Cache/Proxy Management** node in the console tree, which had previously been empty, now contains additional items for monitoring and configuring the plug-in. The plug-in you use may have a different set of configurable parameters, and a different way of organizing them.

    The basic functions of a plug-in can be broken down into two areas: the functions it performs when end users access on-demand content, and the functions it performs when end users access a broadcast publishing point. In a typical plug-in, **Cache/Proxy Management** contains two items that correspond to these functions. The main on-demand function of a cache/proxy plug-in is the automatic caching of end user requests, as described previously. The main broadcast function is stream splitting.

    Figure 20.8 shows **Cache/Proxy Management** with the sample cache/proxy plug-in installed.

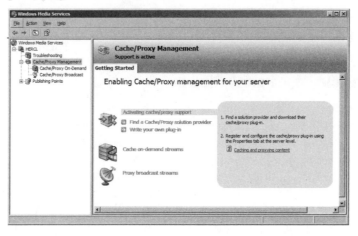

Figure 20.8 Managing the sample cache/proxy plug-in.

2. Enable cache/proxy management. Click the server name in the console tree, and open **Properties** for the server. Click **Cache/Proxy Management** in

the **Category** list, click the cache/proxy plug-in in the list, and then click the **Enable** button.

Properties for the plug-in might contain global parameters that you can view and modify. In the sample plug-in, you can change how Windows Media Services loads the plug-in: in-process or out-of-process. Typically a cache/proxy plug-in runs in the same process as the server (in-process).

3. Allow new unicast connections. Click **Cache/Proxy On-Demand** and, on the **Monitor** tab, click **Allow new unicast connections**. Do the same for **Cache/Proxy Broadcast**. By default, your plug-in might be configured to deny new connections for security purposes.

To help you visualize how a cache/proxy plug-in works in Windows Media Services, you can think of the cache/proxy items in the console tree the same way you think of publishing points. A publishing point acts as an interface between the end user and the content, and has plug-ins and properties that enable you to modify how content is sourced and delivered. The **Cache/Proxy Management** items perform similar functions.

As you can see in figure 20.9, the tabs in the details pane of each node look similar to the tabs for publishing points. The difference is that a cache/proxy plug-in will have no tabs for **Source**, **Advertising**, and **Announce** because those details do not apply. However, you can apply plug-ins, properties, and limits to **Cache/Proxy Management** as you would to a publishing point. For example, you could apply logging, add authentication, and add authorization to cache/proxy requests. You can also monitor cache/proxy usage.

With this in mind, you can see how Windows Media Services and a cache/proxy plug-in work together to provide a variety of services in one container. For example, the server represented in figure 20.9 acts as a cache/proxy server, and hosts on-demand content and broadcasts.

Enabling Cache/proxy Support on Origin Servers

Before a cache/proxy plug-in can cache content or split streams, those properties must be enabled on the publishing points of the origin servers.

For on-demand publishing points, caching options are set in the **General** category of the **Properties** tab. You can also set cache expiration in the **Cache/Proxy** category. This setting attaches an expiration time to files that are cached by a cache/proxy server. Before a cache/proxy server plays content from its cache, it checks the expiration value to determine whether the content is fresh. If the expiration time has passed, the cache/proxy server checks the content on the origin server. If the content has not changed, the cache/proxy server streams the file from its cache. Otherwise it streams fresh content from the origin server.

For broadcast publishing points, stream-splitting options are set in the **General** category of the **Properties** tab. In the **Cache/Proxy** category of the publishing point, you can also set an expiration policy.

Windows Media Services provides the ability to enable or disable cache/proxy support because many users, especially those on the Internet, do not want their content cached or broadcasts split. For example, a site offering copyrighted material can disable caching if the owners do not want the content to be stored by a cache/proxy server.

Testing Cache/proxy Functionality

To test the cache/proxy plug-in, the Fabrikam technicians will configure proxy settings in Windows Media Player. Once they have determined that the cache/proxy plug-in works as expected, a layer-4 switch can be added to the system. This switch will be configured to transparently send all client requests for Windows Media content to the cache/proxy plug-in.

To test the cache/proxy plug-in, the technicians connect the cache/proxy server to a network that provides access to another Windows Media server. This network also includes a client that can connect to the servers. They will perform the test on the bench in an isolated environment.

Once the test network has been built and configured, the technicians follow these steps to configure the Player:

1. On the client, open Windows Media Player.

2. On the **Tools** menu, click **Options**, and then the **Network** tab.

3. In the **Streaming Settings** area, click the **MMS** protocol, and then click **Configure**.

4. Select **Use the following proxy server**, and enter the address of the cache/proxy server and the port number for the protocol. Within a corporate intranet, the address is usually the name of the remote server, for example WMRemote01. The port for the MMS protocol is 1755.

5. Repeat step 4 for the **RTSP** protocol, using port 554. If the technicians have configured the origin and remote servers for HTTP streaming, they would repeat step 4 for that protocol.

6. Enter the URL of some on-demand content on the origin server, such as rtsp://WMOriginFarm/Test.wmv.

After entering the URL, the Player connects to the cache/proxy plug-in on the remote server (WMRemote01). If the content is not cached, the cache/proxy plug-in requests the content from the origin server. The technicians can see what is going on by viewing the default publishing point **Monitor** tab of the origin servers and the **Cache/ Proxy On-Demand Monitor** tab of the remote server.

Assuming no other clients are accessing the servers, the first time users play the content, the **Monitor** tabs will show one client connection on each server: the end user connected to the **Cache/Proxy On-Demand** part of the plug-in on the remote server, and the remote server connected to the default publishing point on one of the origin servers. After users stop the stream, the cache/proxy plug-in continues streaming until the entire file is copied to the cache.

Figure 20.9 shows the on-demand **Monitor** tab on the cache/proxy server with one client connected receiving a 46 Kbps stream. Figure 20.10 shows the **Monitor** tab of the default publishing point on the origin server with the cache/proxy server connected receiving the stream.

Figure 20.9   Usage information is displayed for the cache/proxy server.

The next time a technician attempts to access the content, the cache/proxy plug-in plays it from the cache. The technician should see only one client connection to the remote server, and no connections to the origin server farm. He can check the remote server to see the cached file.

Figure 20.10   Usage information displayed for the origin server.

The last step is to configure Windows Media Player on one or more additional computers, as in steps 4 and 5. Then, the technicians can enter the URL of a broadcast publishing point. For example, they could use the sample broadcast playlist that is installed with Windows Media server, rtsp://WMOriginServer01/Sample_Broadcast.

After a technician enters the URL, Windows Media Player connects to the cache/proxy plug-in on the remote server. The plug-in handles the request as a broadcast request. If the plug-in is not currently streaming the broadcast, it requests the stream from the origin server. In this scenario, all broadcasts use multicast streaming, so the origin server that is designated as the broadcast server (WMOriginServer01) is accessed directly rather than through the load-balancing cluster address. The technicians can see what is going on by viewing the **Cache/Proxy Broadcast Monitor** tab and the Sample_Broadcast publishing point **Monitor** tab. With one client connected, they should see one client on both **Monitor** tabs.

Now they can connect the additional Players that have been configured. The cache/proxy plug-in will split the stream to the clients. The **Cache/Proxy Broadcast Monitor** tab should reflect the total number of clients connected, but the origin server **Monitor** tab should still show one connection.

Adding a Layer 4 Switch

Details of configuring layer 4 switches are outside the scope of this book because every switch is different. The basic function of the switch is to intercept all traffic destined for the WANs of Fabrikam's remote sites and send the traffic to a cache/proxy server. You have seen that a cache/proxy server is composed of a Windows Media server and cache/proxy plug-in, but cache/proxy servers and cache appliances come in many sizes and shapes. Most handle both streaming media and Web page requests.

Figure 20.11 shows how a layer 4 switch fits in to the remote site topology. Typically a layer 4 switch would operate in a transparent proxy scenario by reading the contents of URL requests, and then redirecting the client to the local cache. If you were to use a cache/proxy appliance that handled both streaming media and Web content, the switch would redirect all requests for these types of content.

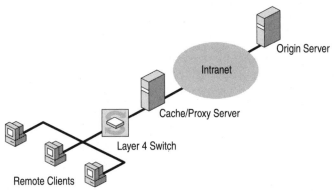

Figure 20.11   Using a layer 4 switch in the network.

You can test configuration of the switch by configuring Windows Media Player to not use a proxy. Then enter the URL of an item or publishing point on the origin server. The request should be redirected to the remote server.

Setting up Unicast Distribution

To enable unicast distribution, the Fabrikam technicians create a broadcast publishing point on a remote server that sources from the broadcast publishing point on the origin server. Then they configure the remote publishing point for multicast delivery. End users normally connect to the multicast stream from the origin publishing point. However, broadcast publishing points that are configured for multicast can also deliver unicast streams.

When you distribute from a broadcast publishing point, clients connect by using unicast streaming, which means that they can take advantage of packet resending and error detection for a higher-quality stream. You could also configure distribution in the opposite way, by sourcing from a multicast stream and distributing unicast streams through stream-splitting. The same basic steps apply in either case.

Unicast distribution is enabled in two steps. First, create a broadcast publishing point on the remote computer, then configure it for multicast delivery.

Creating a Broadcast Publishing Point for Distribution

On the remote server, the technicians add a new publishing point using the advanced method, entering the following information:

- For **Publishing point type**, select **Broadcast**.

- For **Publishing point name**, type the name of the remote publishing point. It can be the same as the publishing point name on the origin server, but you may want to avoid possible confusion by customizing the name to match the name of the server (for example, RemMCast01).

- For **Location of content**, type the unicast URL of the publishing point (for example, rtsp://WMOrigin01/MCast01). Or, if you want to source from the multicast stream, type "mcast://", followed by the location of the multicast information file for the publishing point (for example, mcast:// C:\Temp2\Mult01.nsc). The path must reference a file on the local drive or a network share.

The technicians make sure the origin server publishing point is set to allow new unicast connections so that the publishing point will continue to send a multicast stream while accepting unicast connections. The server can deliver unicast streams as soon as the publishing point has been created and the **Allow new unicast connections** option has been enabled.

To rebroadcast the stream using multicast delivery, the technicians would need to create a multicast information file and announcement file.

Configuring Multicast Delivery

To enable multicast delivery on the new publishing point, the Fabrikam technicians do the following:

1. On the **Announce** tab of the new remote publishing point, run the **Multicast Announcement Wizard**.

2. Click **Yes** on the message asking whether to enable the WMS Multicast Data Writer plug-in.

3. In the wizard, enter the following information:

   - Create a multicast information file (.nsc) and an announcement file (.asx).

- Add stream format by typing the URL of the origin server publishing point (for example rtsp://WMOrigin01/MCast01).

- Enter a path to save the two files. These metafiles are typically hosted on a Web server so they can be accessed easily by end users (for example, \\WebServer\Inetpub\Wwwroot\RemMCast01.asx and \\WebServer\Inetpub\Wwwroot\RemMCast01.nsc).

- Enter the URL of the .nsc file. For example, the URL on a Web server might be http://WebServer/RemMCast01.nsc.

4. Start the publishing point.

At this point a technician can open Windows Media Player and enter the URL of the .asx file (for example, http://WebServer/RemMCast01.asx). She will not see any client connections on either publishing point because multicast clients do not connect to a server, and distribution publishing points do not show up as clients on the origin server.

Push Content Setup

A cache/proxy plug-in maintains its own cache file structure. This is typical of most cache devices. By using a proprietary system, a cache device or server can handle requests much faster and with less processing overhead. Instead of storing files in a hierarchical system of folders, a cache typically stores all files in one folder, gives each file a unique name, and maintains an index that links a file to a URL. The index is a database that also includes expiration information. Here is how it would work:

1. A user requests a file with a URL such as rtsp://WMServer/File.wmv.

2. The cache/proxy plug-in intercepts the request and looks for the file in its cache file system.

3. If the file is found in the cache and is not expired, the file is streamed. Otherwise, the cache/proxy plug-in requests a new stream from the origin server.

In order to push content to the cache, you cannot simply copy files to a folder. The cache/proxy plug-in or other cache device must initiate the prestuffing process so that the content can be properly entered into the caching system database. The Windows Media Services SDK sample does not support prestuffing. However, a complete cache/proxy plug-in solution that pushes content can be created with the SDK.

To push content, a content management program initiates the Prestuff method from a central location. For example, the prestuffing program can run in Toronto and remotely control the cache/proxy plug-ins at one or more remote sites. The technician can enter the source files to be prestuffed, along with the destinations for the files. Then the program can begin prestuffing the files. A complete third-party content management system or appliance should make the process of prestuffing easy, and should include the ability to cache Web content such as Web pages, image files, and script.

With the installation of the remote servers, Fabrikam has completed the second phase of its Windows Media deployment. Live and on-demand content can be created, and end users throughout the enterprise can stream content. In the last phase, we will see how Fabrikam creates a series of training videos, enables multicast streaming throughout the network, and explores ways to create client usage reports.

21

Phase III: Producing a Training Series

In chapter 20, Fabrikam completed the second phase of its Windows Media deployment. The company can now create on-demand content and stream it to any computer connected to the corporate network. Limited live streaming can also be done, but not on a large scale until the network is multicast enabled (which is described in the next chapter).

The first task Fabrikam will undertake in phase III is the production of an interactive online training course.

In this chapter, we will follow the process as the Fabrikam Media department works with the Training department to produce a series of courses. After the courses are produced, they will be published to a site built on SharePoint Portal Server, like the Media Guide site. On the Fabrikam employee online training site, employees will be able to quickly register for a class or course, and then immediately stream the course to their computers. The Training department can then develop a system for tracking student progress using feedback forms, such as online tests, and monitoring attendance using reports gleaned from client usage logs—although those tasks are beyond the scope of this book.

Producing an online training course follows the same process as producing, implementing, or deploying anything else. In film and video production, the names of the processes might be different from those used in networking, for example, but the meaning is the same.

On-demand digital media content is produced in the following stages:

1. Create a concept, which is similar to a vision statement for a film or video.

2. Develop the concept into a blueprint for production. It can be in the form of a script, rundown, or outline.

3. Plan, budget, and schedule production (pre-production).

4. Shoot or record the audio and video segments that will make up the finished production.

5. Edit the audio and video segments, add graphics, transitions, and effects, and then create the final product (post-production).

6. Make the product available to the end user or audience.

At the completion of each step, there is a product, such as a script, a plan, or video segments, that will be used in the next step.

The process for producing a broadcast is similar. However, because the production is live, there are no post-production and distribution steps unless the live production is to be made available on-demand. For example, you could broadcast a live presentation, such as a live class with an interactive question and answer session, and then edit a recording of the presentation for viewing on-demand. In general, because a live production cannot be edited as it is being presented, more time and resources are spent in the planning stages to help ensure that production goes smoothly.

In this chapter, however, we will focus on the production of on-demand content. Typically, it is easier to produce on-demand content than a live production. In addition, the results are often better for the amount of production resources involved, because with a live production you only get one chance. For example, two people can produce a polished on-demand video of a CEO report to the company. The same report, if broadcast, can require a great deal more preparation, testing, and resources to make sure the production takes place without problems.

Developing the Training Series Concept

A concept is a quick summary of a proposed movie. A good concept statement makes it clear to everyone involved exactly what the project is about: producers and managers know what they will be investing in, co-workers know what they will be working on, and an audience or end user knows what the point of the project is and what they should be taking away from the experience.

A concept can also be thought of as a vision statement for a production. In a corporate video, there is a direct connection between the speaker in the video and the viewer. The speaker wants the viewer to do or understand something. In advertising, this is known as a "call to action." To create a concept for a corporate video, then, the Fabrikam producers need to include or imply in it a call to action.

A concept should describe the video content you want to create, not how or why you want to create it. For example, the statement "describe how to use a lathe safely," is a better concept than, "show employees using a lathe correctly," or "keep insurance costs down." These other statements can be included in the video, but they are not necessarily part of the core concept.

The concept of a video may seem obvious, but if it is not stated clearly from the beginning, you may discover later that the production has veered off course. It is easier to establish a clear concept early on than to re-edit a video multiple times because every team member has a different idea of what the video is about. A concept provides a base for creating a script, and then shooting the video and editing the pieces into a final presentation.

At Fabrikam, production of the online series was motivated by a desire to save training resources and reach more employees. From this high-level motivating factor, we can watch the actual work needed to accomplish this goal. That brings us to specific products that can be created and concepts for individual courses or presentations.

A complete concept can contain as much detail as necessary, but it is important that, regardless of the amount of detail, you should be able to boil a concept down to one simple statement. The Training department decides to create a four-part series related to shop-floor safety. The concepts for the four videos are:

- Describe how to use a lathe safely.

- Describe the use of safety equipment and apparel.

- Describe how to keep work areas free of hazards.

- Describe the role of safety teams and how to form one.

Your concepts can include different language. For example, you might want to make the call to action more apparent. However, the important thing is to have one core concept for a video that everyone understands, including the viewer.

Developing a Production Blueprint

With a clear concept established, the blueprint for the production can be created. A production blueprint describes the audio and video the audience will experience. It does not include items such as reasons for creating the video or plans for how the video should be completed. In this stage of the production process, a writer or producer takes the concept and turns it into a finished plan. Once this production plan is approved by all parties, it becomes the blueprint for the rest of the production process. Good planning at this stage will reduce the number of changes needed later.

A production blueprint can take many forms. However, the following blueprint is typically used:

- Script. A detailed description of what the audience will see and hear. Scripts are often preferred by producers because they are easier and less expensive to shoot and edit. The producer knows exactly what the video will require, so planning, budgeting, and scheduling can be done more accurately.

■   Rundown. A summarized chronological description of what the audience will see and hear. Rundowns are more often used in producing a live event, such as a company meeting or training. A rundown must supply enough information for the production to be organized around it.

Other forms can also be used, such as outlines, lists, or simply an existing PowerPoint presentation. Video is time-based, as opposed to a graphic, which is static. Therefore, a blueprint should list and describe events chronologically. The more you can plan up front, the better the production is likely to progress.

Writing Scripts

If you know exactly what you want to say and show, you can create a script. Typically a script includes every spoken word, a description of the video that goes with the words, and descriptions of any extra audio, such as music and sound effects. A script can also include comments for the director or editor, such as how you would like to transition from one scene or event to another, or the type of visual effect you would like to use.

The television-style script is used often for corporate videos. This style typically consists of a video column on the left and an audio column on the right, as in the following example:

Video	Audio
Worker dumps oily rag	Narrator (VO): Oily rags and spent tubes of lubricant must be disposed of in special hazardous waste containers.
DISSOLVE to worker emptying container	At the end of each shift, the containers are emptied...
DISSOLVE to worker dumping rags in hazmat barrel	And the contents transported to hazmat stations, located throughout the factory.
Narrator in studio	Narrator (On-camera): It is important that hazardous waste be disposed of properly—important for the company, and important for the environment.

Shorthand terms are used in writing scripts. A *shot* is a section of video that begins when the camera starts running and ends when the camera stops. *VO* stands for voice-over, indicating that the narrator is not seen. *Dissolve* is a type of transition in which one shot fades out as another fades in. There are many books that provide information about the terms used in scriptwriting and about production in general, including *Microsoft Windows Movie Maker Handbook* (Microsoft Press, 2000).

As previously mentioned, a good script can save production time and resources. A producer can plan and schedule the production to run more efficiently because the script explains exactly what to shoot and how long a shot needs to be. A complete script is particularly important if a video contains shots from a number of different locations. For example, a script can help estimate the running time of the narration, so you will know how much narration needs to be shot and where, and what supporting (or "b-roll") shots need to be filmed. With this information, you can more accurately schedule time for equipment, facilities, crew, and talent (the narrator).

Creating a Rundown

A rundown is a detailed list of events that make up a video. As mentioned previously, a rundown is more often used when shooting a live event, which will either be broadcast live or recorded live to tape and made available on demand. Rundowns are also used in broadcast news in addition to a script.

Rundowns are easier to create than scripts, and many speakers prefer to work from rundown-style notes rather than a script. However, a disadvantage of a rundown is that important details may not be included. Rundowns can take many forms, and usually contain columns to help organize the information. You can even create a combination rundown and script that contains scripted segments and notes.

The Training department decides to go with a rundown because they will be recording video of instructors who base their lectures on notes added to PowerPoint slides. The following example shows the rundown of a portion of one of the videos.

Visual Support	Notes
Slide 5 – Organizing a team	Internal resources available: HR, Health & Safety department, etc. Team leader action items
Video: "Team Building"	6:24
Slide 6 – Team members	Stills of teams How leader chooses members What to look for Who should not be included
Slide 7 – Scheduling meetings	How many, how long During work or after work Keeping consistent
Slide 8 – Meeting agenda	Focus on problem solving Action items and results

Rundowns should be uncomplicated and easy for anyone to understand. This sample rundown basically describes chronologically what happens when an instructor gives a live lecture. Because the on-demand courses are just standard presentations that will be converted to Producer presentations, this style of rundown will probably be sufficient.

After the instructor finishes slide 5, he introduces a video. The Fabrikam producers will capture the video to a file and edit it into the presentation. Also, during Slide 6, the instructor would like to insert still images. The producers will convert the images to JPEG format and insert them over the video of the instructor when they edit this part of the video.

The rundown does not show details such as the content of the slides and how long the instructor plans to talk about each slide. However, considering the style of the video, these details should not cause a problem in post-production. The Fabrikam staff just needs to make sure they bring enough tape to record the lecture. They also might want to note when the lecturer changes slides, so they will be able to insert the images in the correct places.

Pre-production

With the script or rundown in hand, you can begin pre-production. During this phase, you define how to turn the blueprint into a final product. The goal of pre-production is to make sure time and resources are used most efficiently during the next two phases, production and post-production. To accomplish that, make lists of items to purchase or rent, personnel who need to be hired or scheduled, equipment needed for shooting and editing, and other elements that are required for the video. For example, the Fabrikam producer needs to make sure the editor has the "Team Building" video and images, in addition to the videotape of the lecture and the slides.

In the Fabrikam training videos, the production style and plan are fairly straightforward. The Media department crew will shoot the lectures the same way they have been shooting lectures and meetings for years.

Things to consider in a production include the following:

- A production plan for how the production, post-production, and distribution will be accomplished. A production plan can be a formal document, or a simple list of action items discussed and agreed upon in a meeting.

    In creating a plan, it may be necessary to visit (or "scout") the locations you plan to shoot in order to make sure they are appropriate for your needs. In Fabrikam's case, the lectures will be recorded in a company classroom. The tape will then be captured and edited with other elements into final videos. Then PowerPoint slides will be synchronized in Producer, and a final presentation will be rendered and published to the Training Web site. The final presentation will also include a short quiz. The quiz will use a feedback Web page that, when submitted, will enter information into a Training department student database.

- A list of personnel involved in the videos. The list includes training personnel who will provide information and approve the final presentations, Media department personnel who will produce and edit the presentations, and people who will operate the camera and VTR. For more information about roles in a production, see chapter 18.

- Technical items needed for the production, including the recording equipment (camera, VTR, and so forth), facilities (edit suite), locations (classroom), expendables for shooting and editing (videotape, batteries), and rentals (a truck to haul the equipment).

- Art elements used in the production. The elements that must be obtained or created, including sets, special lighting equipment, props, music, sound design, and effects. In Fabrikam's case, the Training department must create the PowerPoint slides and quiz Web page.

- A schedule that indicates when production and post-production will take place, and the personnel, technical, and special considerations for each location. Remember to include time for setting up and putting away the equipment and sets, and travel time.

- Budget. Typically, the production phase is the most expensive part of creating a video, because it takes the most time and requires the most personnel and equipment. When putting together a budget, consider all the items in this list, especially personnel, technical, and design. For example, you might schedule four hours to shoot a class, which includes setting up, shooting, putting the equipment away, and traveling. From this, you can calculate the cost of the two contractors and any equipment that must be rented. There also may be special considerations, such as a charge for parking, or paying for meals.

- Any special considerations. This is where a producer must stretch her imagination and attempt to envision every possible facet of the production. Special considerations can include presenters who need to be picked up at the airport, special permits to shoot and park vans, or a VIP's special needs.

  You may also need legal releases when shooting off-site. If you are shooting employees on your company's property, permissions may be easy to come by. However, when you plan to include non-employees and locations outside your company in your video, be aware that you may be required to obtain legal releases to do so.

To shoot the training classes, one camera will be used. A lecture can be over an hour in length, so the audio and video must be recorded on a separate videotape recorder (VTR) since the digital Betacam camcorder can hold only enough tape to record up to 30 minutes. A second operator will run the VTR and monitor the recording process. Audio of the lecturer will be recorded using a wireless lavalier microphone.

Production

In the production phase, you capture audio and video to videotape or a digital media file. You follow the production plan and shoot or create elements that will be assembled in editing. Everything must eventually be digitized into files, including video of the four presentations and other shots that support the presentation, like graphics and video from other sources. PowerPoint slides are also created during production.

A production session, as well as the process of recording with a camera, is often referred to as a "shoot" or "shooting." In the Fabrikam production, the producer allotted four hours to shoot each one-hour class. On the day of the shoot, the two-person crew arrives one hour before the class and sets up the following components:

- Camera. The producer gave the crew a plan describing where the instructor would be, and where the camera should be to shoot the best angle of the presenter. The camera operator places the tripod at that location, mounts the camera, and runs cables to a power strip and the VTR.

- VTR. The crew places the VTR near the camera, and runs cables for the power, camera, external video monitor, and microphone. The crew can now view the camera output on the monitor.

- Lighting. Typically, video production lights are used to boost and even out the light level so the image captured by the camera is clear and pleasing to the eye. The Fabrikam crew will simply add a backlight so the image of the presenter does not blend in with the background. To set up the lights, a crew person stands in as the presenter, while the other crew person checks the image on the monitor and adjusts the lighting. For more information about backlighting, see chapter 19.

- Audio. The wireless lavalier microphone system consists of the microphone, the transmitter pack, and the receiver, which is plugged into the VTR. Prior to production, transmitter batteries are tested, the system is set up, and the receiver antenna is positioned for best reception.

All systems are tested prior to shooting, including the camera, VTR, and audio. During the shoot, the camera operator focuses the presenter in the video frame, and pivots (or pans) the camera horizontally to keep the presenter framed as he moves. The camera operator does not need to focus on the projected slides because they will be added later using Microsoft Producer. The VTR operator monitors the recording and adjusts the audio.

Post-production

After all the elements for a segment have been shot, created, or acquired, the editor can digitize them and begin the editing process. During the pre-production phase, the editor was brought in to the process so that he could learn about the production plan and provide input. Then the editor developed an approach for editing the segments based on the plan and the script or rundown.

The final product will be streamed to end users on the company's intranet and must include audio and video of the presenter synchronized to PowerPoint slides, some still images, and edited video from an outside source. A number of editing tools and processes could be used to assemble the production. However, because the final product must include PowerPoint slides, Fabrikam decides to save a step and edit the video using Microsoft Producer. With Producer, they can also add the slides and publish the finished presentation to the Training department's Web site.

Distribution

After a video or project has been finished, it can be distributed. Distribution of a major motion picture is very complex and entails the sale, duplication, and delivery of thousands of film prints to theaters. Distribution of the Fabrikam project, on the other hand, is about as easy as it gets. All they have to do is publish the project in Producer, and then promote the course online and in e-mail.

When the Fabrikam producers publish a project, Producer compresses and encodes a Windows Media file of the audio and video, and then packages it with other files that include the PowerPoint slides, table of contents, the quiz and contact pages, and templates pages. Then Producer copies the package of files to the Training site, which is actually another workspace of the SharePoint Portal Server that hosts the Media Guide site. For more information about how to create an SharePoint workspace and dashboard, see chapter 16.

Using Microsoft Producer

After capturing the video elements and copying the still images and PowerPoint presentation to a location that can be accessed by the Producer workstation, the Fabrikam staff can begin building the project. One Producer project is created for each of the four presentations.

The following procedure is an example of how the editor at Fabrikam will assemble and edit a Producer presentation. Before starting this process, the editor will need the following digital media elements:

- Video of the presenter. Video captured as a digital media file in any of the supported formats, such as WMV or AVI.

- Existing "Team Building" video.

- JPEG images of safety teams. These are small JPEG image files that will be edited with the video.

- PowerPoint presentation. This is the PowerPoint presentation originally used by the presenter to give the training course.

- HTML page containing contact information. A simple Web page containing a name and e-mail address.

- Feedback HTML page containing the quiz. Another Web page that provides form elements for completing a short quiz.

Before assembling the presentation, the editor makes sure he is familiar with the script or rundown. Then he follows this process to complete the Producer presentation:

1. Import. Use the **Import** command to add the digital media elements to the Producer project:

2. Add the first Producer template to the timeline. A template defines the layout and appearance of elements on the final presentation Web page. The template will contain pre-defined areas for the video, PowerPoint slides, a table of contents, and a small area for the contact HTML. The Fabrikam project will use the **Standard Video (240x180) – Fixed Slides and HTML** template provided with Producer, but a custom template could be created.

3. Add the contact HTML page to the HTML track.

4. Add the presenter video to the timeline. The video can be edited, if necessary, to remove mistakes and long pauses. Also, the beginning and end of the video can be edited and fade transitions added.

5. Add the "Team Building" video to the timeline. The editor will split the presenter video at the point where he wants to add "Team Building," and then drag the clip to that point on the timeline.

6. Smooth out the edits. Wherever the editor removes a pause or mistake, there will be a noticeable jump in the presenter video. He can smooth out some of the *jump-cuts* by adding a short fade transition at that point. Figure 21.1 shows a short fade transition on the timeline.

After removing a section of video, drag the incoming clip on the right over the top of the outgoing clip on the left. The area where the two clips overlap is converted into a fade transition by default.

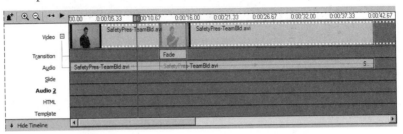

Figure 21.1   Adding a short fade transition to the presentation.

7.   Move audio and add stills. In one part of the video, the editor wants to show four JPEG still images, while the audio track of the presenter continues. To do that, he first moves the audio of the section to the **Audio 2** track on the timeline. Then he can add the images to the **Video** track. Figure 21.2 shows the presenter audio moved to the **Audio 2** track and still images added to the timeline. For more details about inserting video only and still images on the timeline, see the Video Inserts in Producer sidebar in this chapter.

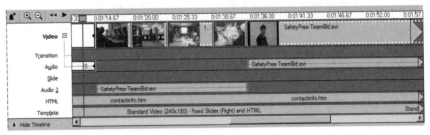

Figure 21.2   Adding images to the timeline.

8.   After the video has been edited, drag the PowerPoint presentation to the timeline, and then use the **Synchronize** command to manually add slide-change cues to the **Slide** track. You can manually adjust the timing directly on the timeline the same way you adjust video edit timing. Figure 21.3 shows the timeline after slides have been synchronized.

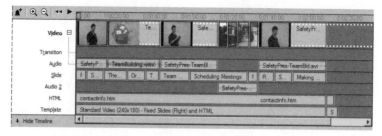

Figure 21.3   Synchronizing slides and video on the timeline.

9.   At the end of the video, add the quiz Web page. First add a new template to the end of the presentation: Standard Audio – Resizable HTML. Then, add the Web page at the same point on the **HTML** track. When the video ends, the presentation will switch to the new template, and the quiz page will appear as in figure 21.4, enabling the end user to fill in the form and submit it.

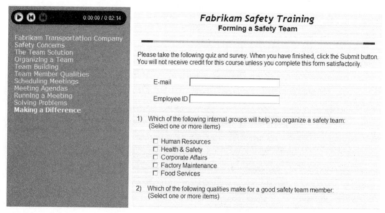

Figure 21.4   The quiz HTML page in Fabrikam's training presentation.

10.   When editing is complete, use the **Publish Wizard**. Producer encodes the final Windows Media files and creates the Web pages and folder. Then it copies the Web pages to the training site, and copies the Windows Media file to the Windows Media server. Figure 21.5 shows all the elements displayed in the finished presentation.

If your presentation requires many complex edits, you may want to use an advanced video editing tool, and then import the edited file into Producer to add slides. However, for most business presentations, Producer can save you the extra step. For more details about using Producer, see chapter 19, or the book *Creating Dynamic Presentations with Streaming Media* (Microsoft Press, 2002).

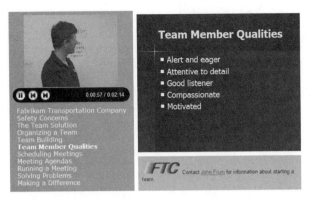

Figure 21.5   The completed Fabrikam Producer presentation in a Web browser.

Video Inserts in Producer

Producer provides a way for you to cut to a video shot or still image, while continuing the audio track from the previous shot. For example, in the Fabrikam scenario, when the presenter talks about safety violations in the factory, the editor can cut to video shot in the factory that illustrates the point. In video editing, this type of edit—replacing the video, while continuing the audio—is called a "video insert." Figure 21.6 shows a portion of a timeline with a video-only insert.

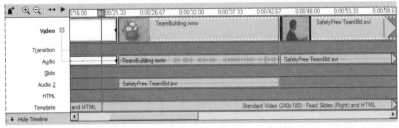

Figure 21.6   A video insert plays video over the audio from another clip.

In this description, we will refer to the video clip of the presenter that contains synchronized video and audio as the *sync* clip. We will refer to the clip we want to add as the *insert* clip.

In Producer, you insert content by moving the section of a sync clip that you want to insert video over to the **Audio 2** track, and then adding the insert clip to the **Video** track. When you add video to the **Audio 2** track, only the audio portion of the clip plays, but the video remains with the clip. If you move the clip back to the **Video** track, the video plays again.

(continued)

Video Inserts in Producer   *(continued)*

To insert a video-only clip, do the following:

1. Prepare the insert clip. For example, you can add the unedited video to a blank area of the timeline, and use the **Split** command to edit the clip you want to insert.

2. Split the sync clip at the point where you want to add the insert clip.

3. Right-click the portion of the sync clip to the right of the split and drag it to the **Audio 2** track. Make sure the beginning of the clip snaps to the end of the previous clip on the **Video** track. When you drop the clip, select **Move**.

4. Add the insert clip to the **Video** track, making sure that it snaps to the end of the sync clip.

5. Use the frame locator buttons on the video viewer to locate the last frame of the insert clip.

6. Select the **Audio 2** track, and split the sync clip.

7. Right-click the portion of the sync clip to the right of the split and drag it back to the **Video** track. Make sure it snaps to the end of the insert clip. When you drop the clip, select **Move**.

8. If the insert clip contains audio you do not want, right-click the clip and click **Mute**.

Playing the Presentation

The following process describes what will happen when an end user accesses a course on the training site:

1. End users link to the training site. The link can be placed on the Media Guide site or on other internal sites, or links can be sent in e-mail messages. For example, after the safety courses are finished, the Safety department can send e-mail to factory managers describing the safety initiative and how employees can take the course online.

2. End users search for the course. The Training site can take advantage of all the features available to SharePoint Portal Server users, such as the search

engine, dashboards, and Web parts. The original Media Guide contains a Training category. After the Training site is in place, all content from the Media Guide portal will be moved to Training.

3.   A course link on the Training site actually points to a sign-up ASP page. After the form is submitted successfully, the link to the presentation is returned to the end-user's browser, and the course loads and plays.

4.   The end user can view the course from beginning to end, pause playback, or use the table of contents to jump forward or back to a different section. By default, slide start times are used as table of contents entries.

5.   At the end of the Producer presentation, the quiz page is displayed. The page can be an ASP page that checks the answers, and only awards credit for the course if the answers are correct, or it can be a HTML page that simply transfers results to a database.

6.   Results of the quiz page are added to the database entry started in step 3. This provides a degree of certainty that an end user has actually taken a course. You, of course, can add further measures to ensure compliance.

The Training and Media departments follow these procedures to produce the four videos in the series and distribute them to employees. Later when usage reports become available to customers, training planners can review details of client usage to help them create more effective online courses. They can also review usage logs to see how much of a course is viewed by an end user. The system that the two departments develop will be an extension of their existing employee education and training programs. For example, the new online series will be part of the same offerings and have the same certification management.

In the next chapter, the IT department finishes the task of enabling the network for multicast. After the network infrastructure has been enabled, the company can begin large-scale broadcasting to every computer in the company connected to the network.

22

Phase III: Multicast-enabled Network

In chapter 20, the Fabrikam Media and Training departments produced a series of training videos to kick off the company-wide deployment of Windows Media. The company can now deliver on-demand streaming media to every desktop and computer-equipped meeting room. It can also deliver broadcast content on a limited basis using unicast delivery. After performing the steps outlined in this chapter, the company will have full capability to deliver broadcast content to every computer on the corporate network.

The key to delivering broadcast content to every desktop is a multicast-enabled network. As mentioned previously, unicast delivery is not the best solution for delivering hundreds or thousands of concurrent streams. For example, 5,000 clients receiving a 100-Kbps unicast stream would require a network infrastructure capable of handling a 500-Mbps load. The same number of clients receiving a multicast stream would require a maximum bandwidth of only 100 Kbps. Edge servers help the unicast bandwidth problem by distributing content closer to end users. However, the current number of cache/proxy servers deployed by the company would not be able to handle the expected broadcast load if unicast was the only method of delivery.

Multicast is by far the most bandwidth-efficient method currently available for delivering a broadcast to large numbers of end users in an enterprise. But one impediment to multicast delivery is the ability of the network infrastructure to handle multicast traffic. It is not a matter of bandwidth or computing horsepower because one multicast stream can easily feed every client in the company with no more bandwidth or server usage than one unicast stream. In order to use multicast on a network, the routers, switches, other network devices, and subnetworks must be configured to handle multicast traffic. Once the network is multicast-enabled and solutions have been implemented on network segments that cannot be enabled, multicast delivery can begin. If the system is configured properly, clients everywhere in the company can either join or subscribe to the multicast group and receive the broadcast.

In this chapter, we describe how Fabrikam enables multicasting on their enterprise network. It would be impossible to describe how to enable every network because each enterprise network is unique. The Fabrikam network is fairly typical for a mid-sized company, and includes modern networking equipment. Many networks have both new and older equipment, and contain a collage of operating systems and hardware.

There are certain minimum requirements for a network to handle multicast traffic. If parts of your network do not meet these requirements, you can either upgrade those parts or work around those areas. Chapter 20 described some common solutions for existing networks. You can, for example, add a cache/proxy server and use unicast stream splitting or multicast distribution to leap over troublesome areas.

To understand the concepts in this chapter, it helps to be familiar with the Open System Interconnection (OSI) Reference Model that defines a networking framework for implementing IP protocols. For more information, see the sidebar, The OSI Model. You should also be familiar with how the protocol layers work together to convey data. Before jumping right into enabling the network, you need to understand the basics of a multicast system.

The OSI Model

The Open System Interconnection (OSI) Reference Model defines seven layers that describe how applications running on network-aware devices communicate with each other. The model is generic and applies to all network types, not just TCP/IP; and to all media types, not just Ethernet.

- Layer 1 is the Physical Layer. It defines the physical and electrical characteristics of the network. The NIC in a computer and the interfaces on routers all run at this level because they send strings of ones and zeros through the cables.

- Layer 2 is known as the Data Link Layer. It defines the access strategy for sharing the physical medium, including data link and media access issues. Protocols such as PPP, SLIP, and HDLC operate at this layer.

- Layer 3 is the Network Layer. It provides a means for communicating open systems to establish, maintain, and terminate network connections. The IP protocol operate at this layer, and so do some routing protocols. All the routers in a network operate at this layer.

The OSI Model   *(continued)*

- Layer 4 is the Transport Layer, and is where TCP operates. The standard says that "The Transport Layer relieves the Session Layer (Layer 5) of the burden of ensuring data reliability and integrity." It is at this layer that, should a packet fail to arrive (perhaps due to misrouting, or because it was dropped by a busy router), it will be retransmitted when the sending party fails to receive an acknowledgement from the device with which it is communicating. The more powerful routing protocols also operate here. OSPF and BGP, for example, are implemented as protocols directly over IP.

- Layer 5 is the Session Layer. It provides for two communicating presentation entities to exchange data with each other. E-commerce uses this layer for shopping baskets, which are placed on a Web server and are not load balanced in order to preserve the content of the session.

- Layer 6 is the Presentation Layer. This is where application data is either packed or unpacked, ready for use by the running application. Protocol conversions, encryption/decryption, and graphics expansion all take place here.

- Layer 7 is the Application Layer. This is where end user and application protocols operate, such as telnet, FTP, and mail (POP3 and SMTP).

Devices that communicate across networks use the OSI seven layer model as follows: An application forms a packet of data to be sent; this takes place at layer 7. As the packet descends the layers, also known as the stack, it is wrapped in headers and trailers, as required by the various protocols. Having reached layer 1, it is transmitted as a frame across the medium in use. When the packet reaches device B, it moves up the stack. The networkdevice strips off the appropriate headers and trailers, delivering just the data to the application.

Multicast Communication

Unicast is a one-to-one communication model; multicast is a one-to-many model. Unicast is used to create an individual connection through which data can be sent reliably between two hosts; Multicast is used to send data to many hosts at one time without a direct connection. The notion of a networking system, in which there is no direct communication between server and client—a broadcast model of networking—is not a natural extension of modern networks, specifically IP networks.

Multicasting was created many years ago to enable host computers to communicate in groups, called multicast groups. For example, four end users could connect to a multicast group, and send and receive text messages that would be read by all the users in the group. Today this sort of communication is most often handled with a unicast solution, such as an instant messenger system in which a number of users connect to a chat server. Collaboration is made possible by the chat server, and each user connects to the server using a unicast protocol. Multicast today is used primarily for one-to-many communication, such as broadcasting streaming media. Applications can also use multicasting for file distribution, pre-stuffing data to caches, and sending messages between systems.

In the unicast model, communication is initiated by a client. The content sits on a server until a client requests it. In the multicast model, the server sends the stream regardless of whether there is a client to accept it because there is no communication between client and server. In the unicast model, a client reaches a server using the server's IP and MAC addresses. In the multicast model, a client makes a request to join a multicast group, using the group address. Instead of addressing an IP packet to a specific client, the server addresses multicast packets to a multicast group. And instead of a client sending a request directly to a server, a client sends a request to join a multicast group, which is received and handled by routers and switches in the network.

To distribute multicast traffic on a network, network infrastructure devices such as routers and switches exchange information by using a system of communication protocols. The information enables the devices to set up distribution paths for the multicast packets. In order for a network to handle multicast, therefore, the devices must be configured to use the protocols.

There are several types of one-to-many communication models reflecting the improvements made over the years. Since Fabrikam will be configuring a new system, we do not need to dwell on understanding the history of multicasting. But it is helpful to understand how a simple one-to-many system works.

IP Broadcasting

Unicast is the basic one-to-one communication model. IP broadcast, on the other hand, is the basic one-to-many communication model. IP broadcast should not be confused with broadcast in Windows Media. Windows Media live streams can be broadcast to many clients using the unicast or multicast model, but not IP broadcast. In IP broadcast, the server sends IP packets that reach every part of the network. Routers block broadcast traffic, so the scope is limited to a local subnet. Figure 22.1 shows an IP broadcast.

The problem with IP broadcast is that it does not scale well. If it were possible to configure all routers to pass IP broadcast traffic, the packets would flood the network. Even if only three users requested the packets, the traffic would still consume bandwidth on all segments of the network. Imagine a network using many low-bandwidth WANs, and then adding a number of IP broadcast streams. Imagine the multitude of bandwidth and collision problems if you were to attempt this on the Internet. A simple IP broadcast solution is fine on a small network. However, as you increase the number of clients, the scope of the broadcast, or the number of concurrent broadcasts, the solution quickly becomes impractical.

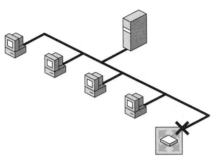

Figure 22.1   An example of IP broadcasting.

In the multicast model, a stream is restricted to only those paths where it is requested by clients. This traffic control is handled primarily by routers and switches, using a system of messages and timers. In the multicast system, routers and switches do not pass multicast traffic until a request is received from a client.

The key to understanding multicast is having a clear picture of the messages that network components send to each other in order to add or delete distribution paths. In this chapter we will focus on the system implemented at Fabrikam. The system uses Internet Group Management Protocol version 2 (IGMPv2) to send messages between the client (the computer requesting a stream) and the router. It also uses the Protocol Independent Multicast-Sparse Mode version 2 (PIM-SMv2) to direct multicast traffic between routers. There is no communication between the source or server and a network device, because it is the client request that initiates the routing of the multicast packets.

Communication Between Clients and Routers

Routers that connect directly to clients are sometimes called leaf or last-hop routers because they are on the ends of network branches. IGMP is the protocol used for communication between a client and the leaf router. In IGMPv2, there are three types of messages:

- Membership Query. Sent by a router to determine whether any clients are members of a multicast group.

- Membership Report. Sent by a client if it receives a query message and is a member of a group. A client also sends a membership report to initially join a group.

- Leave Group. Sent by a client when an end user closes the multicast stream on the Player.

447

When a leaf router receives a membership report, it begins a process to locate and route the stream to the client. After it starts forwarding multicast traffic, it periodically queries all clients on the interface. If no clients return a membership report, the router terminates the traffic and initiates a process to stop (or "prune") traffic from other routers. If the router receives a Leave Group message from a client, it will immediately query all clients on the interface and terminate the stream if it gets no response within a specified time.

As long as a router receives periodic membership reports, it forwards the stream on one or more of its interfaces regardless of whether the stream is being received by one client or 1,000 clients. In PIM-SMv2, the multicast state of the router depends on the messages it receives, both from other routers and from clients.

In IGMPv2, the Membership Report message contains only the address of the multicast group the client is requesting. The client has no routing information about the source of the multicast, just as the source has no information about the clients who want the stream. It is up to the routing system to determine how to locate the multicast source or stream and forward the packets to the client.

Communication Between Routers and Switches

A router is a layer 3 device, which means it reads the IP address of packets. By reading IP addresses, it determines which packets are multicast packets, and on which interfaces to route the traffic. A switch, on the other hand, is a layer 2 device, which means it reads the Ethernet or MAC addresses of frames, which are encapsulated packets. MAC addresses do not provide enough information for routing multicast traffic, so when a switch, hub, or repeater receives a multicast packet, it forwards the packet to all ports. This is sometimes called "flooding" the ports.

Without a system for controlling the flow of traffic through a switch, much of the gains made with router control would be lost. For example, a subnet containing 150 clients would be flooded with a multicast stream, even if only one client requested the stream. The solution that many switches use today is called "IGMP snooping." Switches that have this feature are able to read the IP headers of packets in order to separate IGMP messages from other multicast packets. With this information, the switch can forward multicast traffic to only those ports on which an IGMP membership report was received. Most switches that offer the feature can also remove the connection when an IGMP Leave Group message is received.

Cisco routers and switches can be configured to use the Cisco Group Membership Protocol (CGMP), which relieves the switch from the task of reading IP headers. When a CGMP-configured router receives an IGMP Membership Report from a client, the router sends a CGMP message to the switch. The switch then forwards multicast packets only to that port.

After the source computer has delivered packets to its leaf router and the client has requested the packets from its leaf router, the routers that make up the infrastructure of the network send and receive messages to locate and forward the traffic to the client.

Communication Between Routers

When a router receives either an IGMP membership request from a client or a multicast packet from a source, it starts communicating with other routers by sending and receiving messages. Fabrikam will use PIM to route multicast traffic. This protocol can be implemented in either *dense* or *sparse* mode. Fabrikam will use sparse mode (PIM-SMv2), in which all requests for a multicast group are sent through a router designated as a Rendezvous Point (RP). Figure 22.2 shows an RP in a network. A network can have multiple RPs that can each handle multiple multicast groups. However, there is normally only one active RP for each multicast group address.

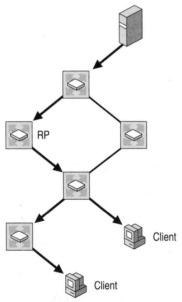

Figure 22.2   A Rendezvous Point (RP) in a multicast-enabled network.

The alternative to using RPs is for clients to reference a multicast from its source. Source-based routing is used in dense mode, which is not used as often because it is based on a "flood and prune" model. In this model, the network is first flooded with multicast traffic, and then pruned back on those branches that have no clients requesting the multicast. As you might imagine, flooding areas with multicast packets is not an efficient method for managing bandwidth. Also with dense mode, routers must maintain more state information, which requires more memory and processing.

In sparse mode, no multicast traffic is forwarded until a client requests a stream. Then the stream is routed through the RP to the client. Forwarding of multicast packets can be handled quickly and there is no flooding.

Dense and sparse modes produce what are commonly called *source trees* and *shared trees*, respectively. These trees create multiple, branch-like paths that lead away from the source or RP to multiple clients. A router can be assigned as the RP statically or by using a dynamic method that provides redundancy in the event an RP router should fail. Fabrikam will use the static method.

In order to get the packets from here to there, a complex system of messages and timers is used to open and close paths. The object of the routing mechanism is to provide a high-quality user experience and make the most efficient use of network resources and bandwidth. The following points describe the router messages that apply to PIM-SMv2 with a static RP:

- Hello. A router periodically sends a hello message to neighboring routers to confirm the presence and status of the router.

- Register. When a leaf router receives multicast packets from a source, it sends a register packet to the RP. This initiates the process of creating a path for the source stream to the RP. Register packets are unicast packets that encapsulate the multicast packet.

- Register-stop. The RP sends a register-stop packet back to the source leaf router to stop sending register packets.

- Join/Prune. A join message causes an upstream router to route packets from a multicast group on the interface on which the join was received. A prune message causes an upstream router to stop sending the multicast group out of the interface. Joins and prunes are initiated when a leaf router receives a Membership Report or Leave Group message from a client.

- Bootstrap. A message from the selected bootstrap router (BSR), which is used to announce the presence and location of the RP to all routers. The bootstrap system was developed for PIM-SMv2. Many multicast systems still use the Auto-RP method of dynamically assigning RPs that was developed by Cisco for PIM-SMv1. If Auto-RP is used, a message similar to the bootstrap message is used to announce the presence of an RP.

- Assert. Determines a designated forwarding router for a multi-access network. This method eliminates the situation where a router receives the same multicast packet from multiple routers connected to different interfaces.

When a leaf router receives an IGMP membership report from a client or a multicast packet from a source, it initiates the process of forwarding the multicast stream to the receiving clients by routing the stream through the RP. When a leaf router receives a Membership Report, it sends a join message to the RP, which then begins sending the multicast stream out the interface that the message was received on.

Completing the Multicasting System

This section provides an overview of the processes used to send and receive a multicast stream. The source, a Windows Media server, generates and sends the multicast IP packets. The client, Windows Media Player, receives and renders the packets. All of the routing of the packets is handled by messages and timers. The messages provide or request information, and the timers wait for responses.

Note that the term "aware" is a shorthand description of what happens when a router processes and stores information received from other routers. For example, when router A receives a hello message from router B, we say that router A is now aware of B.

Figure 22.3 shows a portion of a shared tree containing clients, a server generating a stream, the routers and switches that create the path for the stream, and the RP through which hundreds or thousands of clients can receive the stream.

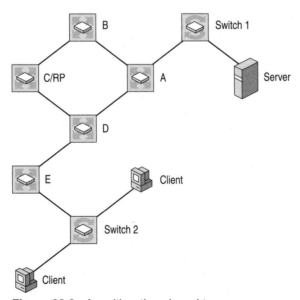

Figure 22.3   A multicasting shared tree.

Configuration and Operation of the Network

The following steps describe how the protocols and messages work together to deliver a multicast stream to a client. Some parts of the process require user intervention; other parts are handled automatically by computers and other devices. The devices are usually configured through a command-line interface.

The process begins with configuring a router as the RP:

1. Statically assign router C as the RP. When assigning an RP statically, all routers in the PIM domain (for example all routers in the Fabrikam intranet) must be configured with the same RP address. Using the router configuration tool, assign the role of RP to router C, and configure the RP to handle distribution of multicast streams of one multicast group address, a range of addresses, or all addresses.

2. Disable automatic RP assignment. Most routers have systems for dynamically and automatically assigning RPs, using either the Auto-RP system or a router assigned as the BSR. If either dynamic RP system is not explicitly disabled, it might preempt static assignment.

With a broadcast publishing point configured for multicast, the following steps (shown in figure 22.4) describe what happens after the broadcast publishing is started and before a client has requested the stream.

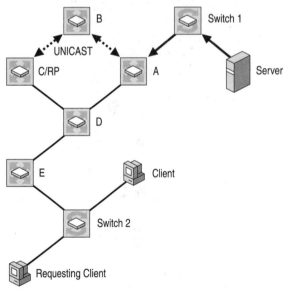

Figure 22.4   Requesting a multicast stream.

1.   The source, a Windows Media server, sends packets containing streaming content and a multicast group address.

2.   Switch 1 uses IGMP traffic snooping to read the IP header of multicast packets. Because the packets do not contain an IGMP message and no IGMP requests have been received from other ports for the multicast, the switch sends the multicast traffic to the router A serial port only. Without IGMP traffic snooping, the switch would flood multicast traffic to all ports. Notice that the source does not join a multicast group or even communicate with any external network device in sparse mode.

3.   Router A becomes aware that the multicast packets from switch 1 contain a multicast group address assigned to the RP. It was already aware of the RP after router C was statically configured.

4.   Router A forwards a PIM-SMv2 Register packet to the RP. The Register packet is a multicast packet encapsulated in a unicast packet. Because it is sent via unicast, the packet will contain the IP address of the router A interface, and router A will receive acknowledgement of its receipt by the RP.

5.   When the RP receives the message, it extracts the multicast packet. At this point, no downstream clients have requested the stream, so the RP sends a Register stop message to router A. The RP does nothing further until a join request comes from a client.

  All routers, including the RP, maintain an outgoing interface list (oilist) that contains those interfaces that have received requests for traffic from a multicast group. At this point, there are no entries in the oilist.

6.   Router A receives the Register stop message and does not route the multicast packets.

The two pieces of information a router or client can use to locate a multicast group are the source IP address and the multicast group address, often seen in the form (S,G). If dense mode is used, all routers and clients need to send and maintain (S,G) state information. In a sparse mode shared tree, the client and all routers except the RP need only maintain group address state information or (*,G). At this point, the RP has (S,G) information, but no multicast packets will be forwarded until a client makes a request to join the group.

The process shown in figure 22.5 describes what happens when a client requests a multicast stream.

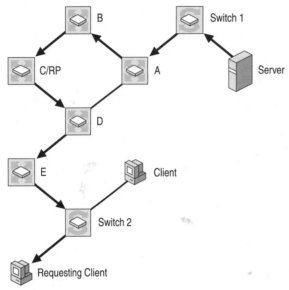

Figure 22.5 A client requests a multicast stream.

1. When the client requests a multicast stream, it sends an IGMP membership report containing only the multicast group address (*,G).

2. Switch 2 uses IGMP traffic snooping to map the traffic to the client port only, and it sends the IGMP membership report on to router E.

3. Router E is aware of the RP and the multicast groups the RP handles, so router E adds the request to its oilist and sends a join request upstream toward the RP.

4. Router D receives the request, adds the request to its oilist, and passes it on to router C, the RP.

5. Router C adds the request to its oilist, and then forwards the multicast packets on the shared tree toward router E. Remember, the register process gave the RP awareness of the location of the source.

6. With the addition of the join request to its oilist, router A has state for the multicast group, and begins forwarding the multicast packets through the routers to the client.

7. In addition to the multicast packets, router E receives the source address from the RP and begins rerouting the multicast stream through the most direct route back to the source. The shared tree path is not always the shortest path back to the source, and is, therefore, not the most efficient use of network resources and bandwidth. A shorter path provides less latency and a higher-quality end user experience. PIM-SMv2 solves this problem by providing a

system for routers to automatically switch over from the shared tree to the shortest path tree (SPT). In SPT switchover, a leaf router uses the source address to locate the most the direct route. If the RP is the most direct route, it takes no action. In this scenario, however, router D locates a more direct route to router A, as illustrated in figure 22.6.

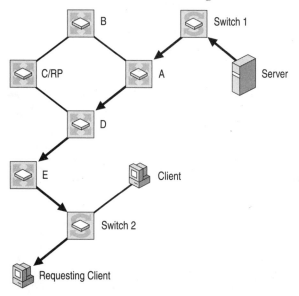

Figure 22.6 Locating the shortest path tree in a multicast network.

8. After router D switches, it sends a prune message back to the RP. With no clients requesting the multicast group, the path from router D through the RP is removed, along with the entries in the oilists of the associated routers.

9. Router E forwards the stream to switch 2, which has been configured by the IGMP membership report to map the stream only to the client port that requested the stream.

10. The client receives the stream and begins rendering the packets.

When a client stops a multicast stream, the following messages are sent:

1. The client sends an IGMP leave group message.

2. Switch 2 stops multicast packets from being forwarded to the client port and passes the IGMP leave message to router E.

3. All routers prune their downstream paths and forward the message upstream, removing the request from their oilists. As long as the source continues streaming, packets will appear at the router A interface leading to the source, but they will not be forwarded until another join request is received.

Source-Specific Multicasting

The Fabrikam network will be configured for PIM-SMv2. However, there is an improved system called PIM Source-Specific Multicast (PIM-SSM), to which Fabrikam can upgrade later. Most enterprises use PIM-SMv2, and more support is available for it. However, Windows Media 9 Series supports PIM-SSM, and it is becoming increasingly available for most routers.

PIM-SSM simplifies the multicast process and provides a better experience for end users. Basically, instead of going through an RP and receiving a stream over a shared tree, the client is aware of the source IP address and sends an IGMPv3 membership report that contains (S,G) information. The SSM-enabled leaf routers then initiate a process that builds a shortest path tree (SPT). PIM-SSM uses the PIM-SMv2 functionality to create the SPT without an RP. There is no longer the notion of an RP and all the messages and procedures associated with it. With PIM-SSM, the path between client and source is known as a channel.

The following steps outline the PIM-SSM process using the network in the previous figures:

1. The client initiates the process by sending an IGMPv3 Membership Report to router E. Note that the switch performs IGMP traffic snooping as with PIM-SM. In IGMPv3, the report contains the source address as well as the multicast group address.

2. Router E uses the source address to locate and forward a join message to router A directly.

3. The message initiates the building of a source tree. In an actual network, there may be a number of routers between the client and source. Each receives the join message and maintains an (S,G) state.

4. Multicast packets are forwarded from the source to the client.

A disadvantage of PIM-SSM is that a network may not be fully enabled. Routers need to be upgraded to handle PIM-SSM and IGMPv3, and switches, clients, and sources need to be able to create and read IGMPv3 messages. Attempting to deploy a system that contained a mixture of PIM-SM and PIM-SSM multicast traffic would probably lead to confusion and errors.

Windows Media Multicast Support

Fabrikam already tested multicast using the closed LAN (see chapter 17). The technicians configured a broadcast publishing point for multicast streaming, and then used Windows Media Player on the client computer to connect to the stream. When the publishing point was started, the switch connected to the server flooded the stream to all ports. If the switch had supported CGMP or IGMP traffic snooping, the multicast stream would not have been sent to a port until the switch received a membership request from a client.

Windows Media Services—or any multicast source for that matter—does not need to maintain any sort of state because multicast is a connectionless protocol. The server merely sends the packets, which contain the digital media content and the multicast group address.

A client running Windows Media Player 9 Series does not maintain a connection state either. The Player sends a request for the stream, and then plays the packets as they arrive. The devices that maintain state and are involved with actively routing and moving multicast traffic are the routers and switches, as you have seen.

To enable the routers and switches to create states and route packets, the Player sends messages and the server sends IP multicast packets. From the Player and server points of view, you configure a multicast broadcast as follows:

1. Configure a broadcast publishing point for multicast by enabling the WMS Multicast Data Writer plug-in. The data writer converts the source stream into a stream of multicast packets.

2. Create a multicast information (.nsc) file and an announcement (.asx) file. When you finish the configuration, the data writer is configured with the multicast group address. The .nsc file contains stream format information, the IP address of the source, and the multicast group address. The .asx file contains the URL of the .nsc file.

   The live stream from Windows Media Encoder is a common source for a broadcast publishing point configured for multicast. For more information about configuring the encoder and server, see chapter 18.

3. An end user enters the URL of the .asx file in the Player.

4. The Player downloads the .asx file, and then downloads the .nsc file.

5. The Player uses the following information in the .nsc file:

   ■ Stream format. The Player loads and configures codecs to decode and display audio and video.

   ■ Multicast IP address. The IP multicast group address is used to create an IGMPv2 Membership Report. There are other elements such as time-to-live (TTL), which is used by routers for distributing the stream, and the port number on which the multicast is streamed.

   ■ Log URL (optional). The URL of a multicast logging program, which runs on a Web server and receives client usage information when a user ends a multicast session.

   ■ Unicast rollover address (optional). The unicast URL of the publishing point.

6. The Player sends the Membership Report, which is received by the leaf router.

7. The leaf router uses the multicast group address to create a shared tree through an RP.

When an end user stops the Player, the following events occur:

1. The Player sends an IGMP leave message to the leaf router.

2. The router receives the message. If there are no more Player requests for the stream on that router, the router sends a prune message upstream.

3. The prune message is used by upstream routers to stop routing the stream to the router.

4. The Player sends logging information to the URL specified as the LogURL in the .nsc file.

Building the Multicast Network Infrastructure

There are several ways to configure a network for multicasting, depending on the type of routing you plan to use. The method Fabrikam chose provides a high-quality end user experience and an efficient use of network resources. This method can be implemented with readily available equipment and has been tested and used successfully in enterprise environments.

There are a number of companies that manufacturer appropriate hardware and software for implementing multicast, including Cisco, Extreme, and Foundry. However, the basic concepts apply regardless of the hardware you choose. The following list summarizes the protocols and configurations that are used in the Fabrikam scenario, and describes alternatives for each:

IGMPv2 Client/Router Communication

Enables the client to initiate the routing of a multicast stream and leave the multicast. Supports PIM-SMv2.

IGMPv1 is less efficient because it does not support Leave Group messages. Without a Leave Group message, the only way that a router detects whether an end user has closed a Player is by sending query messages and waiting for a response. The path leading to the client is therefore filled with multicast packets until the process times out. IGMPv3 supports PIM-SSM, which is an improved multicast routing system that eliminates the need for an RP. IGMPv3 is supported by Windows Media 9 Series.

IGMP Snooping

Enables switches to restrict the forwarding of multicast packets to only those ports where an IGMP request has been received.

If you are using Cisco routers and switches, you can use the Cisco CGMP protocol, which requires less processing by switches. If a switch does not provide layer 3 snooping support, multicast streaming is still viable if it is restricted to small networks or network segments.

PIM-SMv2

Provides for efficient use of network resources and bandwidth by not forwarding multicast packets until a client request is received. With SPT switchover enabled, routers automatically create the shortest path between the source and clients.

In the future, Fabrikam may upgrade to PIM-SSM. PIM dense mode can be easier to set up than PIM sparse mode, but it is less efficient because it uses the flood-and-prune method. This mode and the original multicast routing protocol, Distance Vector Multicast Routing Protocol (DVMRP), are no longer preferred by most users because of their inefficient use of network resources and bandwidth.

Static RP

Multicast traffic is routed through an RP that has been assigned manually. Dynamic RP systems (such as Auto-RP) in which RPs are automatically and dynamically assigned can make multicast traffic handling easier on networks that carry many multicast groups. To implement dynamic RP, candidate RPs and BSRs are chosen. The BSRs will map multicast groups to RPs. In the Fabrikam scenario, one statically assigned RP can easily handle the predicted multicast traffic.

Multicast Network Configuration

Details of configuring hardware are outside the scope of this book, but we will explore the basics that are common to most switches and routers. The following list describes those areas that will need to be configured to support a multicast system such as the one at Fabrikam.

Routers

Configure router interfaces that will enable multicast distribution in the areas of the network that have been targeted. The following list describes typical settings:

- Multicast support. Unlike switches, routers do not forward multicast traffic by default, so you need to enable multicast support.

- Routing mode. Select the routing mode that you will use, such as PIM-SMv2.

- RP selection. Fabrikam will statically assign one router as the RP for all multicast traffic.

■   SPT-Switchover. Enabling and configuring switchover causes a leaf router to automatically switch a client from a shared tree to a shortest path source tree. Fabrikam will configure the switchover to occur immediately.

Switches

Configure switches with the following typical settings:

■   Multicast traffic forwarding. Most switches forward all multicast traffic by default.

■   Layer 3 snooping. Most modern switches offer some method for forwarding multicast traffic to only those ports from which a group Membership Report has been received, and the system is often enabled by default.

Testing the Multicast Network

The easiest way to test the multicast system is to start a multicast-enabled broadcast publishing point, and then attempt to connect to the stream from players around the network. When you do so, enable the **Deny new unicast connections** option on the publishing point and do not enable unicast rollover. This will force clients to connect to the multicast stream only. You can also select only the multicast streaming protocol on the **Network** tab of the **Options** dialog box in Windows Media Player.

Because multicast is connectionless, there is no way to check whether clients can receive a multicast stream other than attempting to open a stream on the client. Multicasting is similar to television broadcasting in that respect. The only way to receive feedback from a client is to enable multicast logging. With logging enabled, clients send usage information to a logging URL on a Web server when the end user closes the stream.

For detailed information about the activity on a given router or interface, you can run debug or display commands. By monitoring debug information, you can see every message sent and command executed on the interface. For example, the following sample debug output is from a router.

```
09:41:16: PIM: Received v2 Hello on Serial1 from 172.161.4.1
09:41:16: PIM: Received v2 Hello on Serial0 from 172.161.3.12
09:41:16: PIM: Send v2 Hello on Serial0
09:41:16: PIM: Send v2 Hello on Serial1
09:42:03: PIM: Received v2 Join/Prune on Serial1 from 172.161.4.1
09:42:03: PIM: Join-list (*,224.3.5.45) RP 172.161.2.2, RPT-bit set,
WC-bit set, S-bit set
```

In the last two lines of the debug output, a join request is received on the Serial1 interface, and the join is implemented and added to the oilist.

You can also use the command-line tool Mcast.exe, available in the Windows 2000 Server Resource Kit. You can use Mcast.exe to send multicast packets or listen for multicast packets sent to a multicast group address in order to test multicast connectivity between hosts on a network. You could do the same thing with a server and Player. However, Mcast.exe can be faster and easier to use when you simply want to check connectivity. For example, you could configure Mcast.exe on one host to send 10 packets with a given source and group address, and then configure Mcast.exe on a second host to listen for the packets and print the results on the screen.

After the switches and routers have been multicast-enabled, configured for IGMPv2 and PIM-SMv2, and the system has been tested to make sure multicast traffic is forwarded as expected, the system will be able to stream multicast broadcasts across the company. All the Fabrikam technicians have to do is configure a broadcast publishing point for multicast and begin streaming. The leaf router connected to the source will automatically register the stream with the RP, and end users will be able to receive the broadcast on their Players.

With the network multicast-enabled, the Fabrikam streaming media system is fully prepared to deliver on-demand and broadcast content to every desktop, conference room, and resource center computer in the company. In the next chapter, we explore ways to compile usage logs into reports that can be used for planning content creation and making improvements to the network.

23

Phase III: Usage Reports and Feedback

In chapter 21, the Fabrikam Media and Training departments produced a series of training videos to kick off the company-wide deployment of Windows Media, thus enabling delivery of on-demand streaming media and unicast broadcasts to every desktop and meeting room that is computer equipped.

But because Fabrikam's current network infrastructure is not capable of delivering the broadcast through unicast to all of the employees who might request it, Fabrikam, in chapter 22, implemented multicast on their network. Streaming via multicast makes more efficient use of their available network bandwidth because it delivers only one stream to many clients. Multicast streaming is also a viable alternative to transporting people to one location for large company meetings, classroom instruction, and new product briefings.

Now that the system has been running for about a month, Fabrikam is ready for the last task in the deployment of their Windows Media solution: designing and implementing a reporting system. Fabrikam management has asked the IT department to create a report to answer the following questions:

- How many employees have used streaming media since the rollout?

- How much of the content selected was actually viewed?

- How much buffering did employees experience while viewing?

- What was the overall quality of the stream?

- How did employees feel about using streaming media versus other online learning tools?

To find the answers to these questions, a system is needed to do the following:

- Collect and aggregate client usage data on a daily, weekly, and monthly basis to illustrate content usage. The goal is to ascertain the popularity of various content files and broadcasts. This information can then be used to aid in program design, to show customers how their programs are doing, and to justify production expenses.

- Compile the data into key statistics that illustrate client usage, errors, and system health. The goal is to see where system improvements are needed in order to better serve end users and protect the network.

- Collect user feedback from the Media Guide site. This information can be used for data trends found in the client usage data or to provide subjective analysis of the data.

Most of the answers that Fabrikam needs are already part of the log files created by Windows Media Services logging plug-ins. However, collecting subjective data about the content requires a custom solution.

Collecting the Data

Windows Media Services has built-in data-collection and reporting capabilities and makes use of other data collection features in Windows Server 2003. Here are some of the reporting options that are provided by default:

Windows Media Performance Monitor reports

These reports use performance counters that are available at both the server and publishing point level of your Windows Media servers. Performance Monitor can be used for real-time monitoring and historical reporting purposes.

WMS Unicast Client Usage Logs

These are log files that are created by the WMS Client Logging plug-in. These logs can be created for either an entire server or an individual publishing point.

WMS Multicast Client Usage Logs

These are log files that are created by the Multicast and Advertisement Logging Agent which is an ISAPI plug-in that can be used with IIS 6.0 to report on multicast client usage.

WMS Cache/proxy Server Logs

These are log files that are created by the WMS Client Logging plug-in on a cache/proxy server. These log files can be retained on the cache/proxy server or sent to the origin server.

Using Performance Monitor Reports

Performance Monitor uses a set of specialized counters for real-time reporting. These counters collect data that is similar to what is reported in the Windows Media log files, so comparing the two could be informative.

Windows Media Services provides two sets of performance counters that you can use to monitor Windows Media servers and publishing points. To access these counters from your Windows Media server, navigate the console tree and click the server or publishing point that you want to monitor. In the details pane, click the **Monitor** tab, click the **Performance Monitor** button at the bottom of the screen, and then add or remove counters from the monitor to suit your specific needs. Figure 23.1 shows the **Performance Monitor** button, which is indicated by a rectangular outline.

Figure 23.1   Click the **Performance Monitor** button to view reports.

Because they want an historical report of streaming activity, the Fabrikam technicians choose the following counters for their report:

- **Total Connected Players**. This statistic reports how many users connected to the server or publishing point.

- **Total UDP Resend Requests**. This statistic reports the number of times a client has requested that the server resend packets because they were not received. Resend requests can be high when the server cannot send UDP packets reliably or if network overload is preventing packets from being delivered.

- **Total Stream Errors**. This statistic reports how many errors, such as dropped packets, occurred during streaming. A high number can indicate poor stream quality.

- **Total Stream Denials**. This statistic reports the number of stream data packets discarded by the server. Discarding occurs when the CPU cannot keep up with the demand for data. This typically occurs in conjunction with late reads and can indicate too much network or disk traffic.

Many other counters for both the server and publishing point are available as well. For example, these counters are useful for diagnosing problems on a server:

- **%Processor Time**. This is the percentage of CPU time that is used to execute non-idle threads. If the server is consistently at a level of 85 percent or higher, then it may indicate the need for a faster CPU.

- **Current Late Read Rate**. This is a disk read operation that takes significantly longer than expected to complete. If this number is greater than 0, then it may indicate that the disk drive is too slow for the load.

- **Current Late Send Rate**. This is a disk write operation that indicates when the server is unable to send out data at the rate that is expected. A sustained late send rate could mean that you need faster or additional CPUs.

- **Total UDP Resends Sent**. This should be similar in number to **UDP Resend Requests**. If this number is significantly lower than **UDP Resend Requests**, then it may indicate that the server load is too high.

See appendix B for a complete list of Windows Media performance counters that are available for both the server and publishing points.

Once you have selected the counters you want to use, it is easy to create a Performance Monitor report. To create the report, open Windows Media Performance Monitor, and then click **View Report**. The report is displayed and can be printed. The total counters were used by Fabrikam because this is an overall historical report; current and peak counters may be added if they are of interest.

Using Log File Data

Windows Media Services logging plug-ins are used to collect statistics about the server's operation. A logging plug-in can write logging statistics to a text file, or to a named pipe if you are using Microsoft SQL Server to collect data. There will be separate log files for unicasts, multicasts, and cache/proxy servers.

Reporting Data About Unicasts

Clients that connect to unicast content from your Windows Media server report their logging statistics back to the Windows Media server that hosted the publishing point to which they connected. To collect this data, the WMS Client Logging plug-in must be enabled on your Windows Media server. The logging plug-in can be used to log information about the activity of the entire server, or it can be enabled on a specific publishing point on the server. The server and publishing point logs work in conjunction to give you the entire picture of the unicast activity on your server.

Reporting Data About Multicasts

Because clients that connect to a multicast do not connect to the Windows Media server, they do not have a means to report back to that server. However, if you are using IIS Web services to host your multicast information file and announcement files or if you have saved these files to a network share, you can use the Multicast and Advertisement Logging Agent to collect limited usage data from multicast clients.

The Multicast and Advertisement Logging Agent is an optional subcomponent of Windows Media Services and is not installed by default. To install this component on your IIS server, do the following:

1. Click **Start**, click **Control Panel**, click **Add or Remove Programs**, and then select **Add/Remove Windows Components**.

2. When the Windows Components Wizard opens, select **Windows Media Services**, and then click **Details**.

3. Select **Multicast and Advertisement Logging Agent** from the list of available subcomponents.

4. Click **OK** to install the agent on the server.

The Multicast and Advertisement Logging Agent should be installed on your IIS server and not your Windows Media server. Therefore, when using the Multicast and Advertisement Logging Agent on an IIS server, it is not necessary to install the other three Windows Media Services subcomponents (Windows Media Services, Windows Media Services Administrator for the Web, and Windows Media Services snap-in).

Reporting Data from Cache/Proxy and Distribution Servers

When you use a cache/proxy or distribution server to distribute content, you have additional unicast logging choices. The WMS Client Logging plug-in enables you to choose whether to have cache/proxy servers forward client logs to the origin server. If the logs are not forwarded, then they are retained on the cache/proxy server. Fabrikam wants to collect all of its logs on the origin server, so they elect to enable this feature by following these steps:

1. Select the cache/proxy server from the console tree.

2. In the details pane, click **Properties**, and then click **Logging**.

3. Right-click the **WMS Client Logging plug-in**, and then click **Properties**.

4. Click the **Log Entries** tab, and then select the **Sessions played from a player cache or a cache/proxy server** check box.

Distribution servers only report information about their connection to the origin server and are not able to forward client connection statistics. The WMS Client Logging plug-in can be enabled on the distribution server and collect client logging data about the clients that connect to it, but that information must be correlated with the logging information from the origin server to get the entire picture of the client activity supported by the origin server.

When analyzing the logging data from the origin server, you can expect to see the following information:

- A single log entry for each connection from the distribution server to the origin server, regardless of the number of clients connected simultaneously to the distribution server.

- A log entry for the cache/proxy server client.

- A log entry for caching the content on the cache/proxy server, plus all the logs from clients that streamed the content from the cache/proxy server.

For a complete list of fields reported in Windows Media log files, see appendix C.

Creating an Activity Snapshot

Having identified all of the different log files that are available, and having selected those that they will use, Fabrikam needed a quick and easy way to consolidate all of the log files from the servers into a cohesive report. The solution? A script file.

Parselog.js is a simple script file that runs from a command window and shows how Windows Media Services log files can be processed to generate detailed information about the usage of your server. You can use the script to parse individual log files from unicast, multicast, or cache/proxy servers, or you can specify a directory that contains all of the log files and let the script aggregate the results into the report. The script file can be used with log files from both Windows Media Services 4.1 and Windows Media Services 9 Series, so if you have both types of media servers in your enterprise, you can compare statistics between them.

If you are using the script with a directory of log files, it identifies Windows Media Services log files by the first three characters of the file name, and will use any appropriate files that have names starting with WMS. This is the default naming scheme used by the logging plug-ins.

Parselog.js provides summary information such as reception statistics, types of client operating systems, and URL hits sorted in three different ways: by total hits, by unique client hits, and alphabetically.

Parselog.js is available on the CD provided with this book.

Using the Parselog.js Script with Log Files

Follow these steps to run the Parselog.js script on log files created by Windows Media Services:

1.   Place the Parselog.js file on a computer that has log files you want to analyze.

2. Open the command window on the computer.

3. In the command window, change directories to the location of the Parselog.js file. For example, Fabrikam created a special folder off the root drive named Logs, so they typed "cd c:\Logs" at the command prompt.

4. Run the script by typing the command "cscript Parselog.js", and then specifying the parameters you want to use.

   Parselog.js uses the following command-line syntax:

```
cscript Parselog.js [[/url:sortorder] [/ip:sortorder] [/summary]]
input_file
```

Command-line parameters supported by the Parselog.js script are described in the following table:

Parameter	Description
/url:*sortorder*	Organizes the detail section of the report by the number of client requests per publishing point connection URL.
/ip:*sortorder*	Organizes the detail section of the report by the client IP addresses.
sortorder	Defines the way in which the detail information is displayed. Type one of the following characters to specify the sort order you want: t = Total Hits a = Alphanumeric u = Unique client requests
/summary	Specifies that the report should only display summary statistics.
input_file	Specifies what data the script should parse. The input must be specified as a path. The path can be to an individual log file or to a directory that contains multiple log files. If the path contains spaces, make sure to enclose the path in quotation marks.

For example, Fabrikam wants the report to be sorted by the number of client requests and wants to include all of the log files in their log file folder, so they type the following at the command prompt:

```
cscript Parselog.js /url:u c:\LogFiles.log
```

Figure 23.2 shows an example that was generated by using this tool on Fabrikam's log files:

```
*****************************************************************
Summary of records from:
        Tue Nov 19 16:10:51 PST 2002 to Tue Nov 19 20:03:18 PST 2002

Total Log Entries: 279

Unique Clients: 2
Unique URLs: 14
Max Simultaneous Clients: 2

Total Server Packets Sent:      57753
Total Packets Received:         57748
Total Packets Recovered ECC:    0 (0.00% of total sent)
Total Packets Recovered Resent: 0 (0.00% of total sent)
Average Reception Quality:      99.99% (Min: 99.54% <--> Max: 100.00%)

Total Cache Playback:           0 (0.00% of total entries)

Client OS Information:
        99.64%  --  Windows_2000 5.0.0.2195
        0.36%   --  Windows_.Net_Server 5.2.0.3718

Client Status Information:
        100.00% --  200
*****************************************************************

Total Hits      Unique Hits(*)    URL
---------       -------------     ----------------------
2               2                 /welcome1.asf
3               1                 /acos_WMA2_5k8khzM.wma
3               1                 /drm_1min.asf
22              1                 /22ksbr2min.asf
50              1                 /22ksbr1min.asf
13              1                 /56k2min.wma
26              1                 /56k1min.wma
13              1                 /mp3-128kbps-120s.mp3
26              1                 /funky.mp3
21              1                 /mbr28k56k100k2min.asf
42              1                 /mbr28k56k100k1min.asf
48              1                 /bpp2
10              1                 /bpp
1               1                 /dpp/d1/22ksbr1min.asf

Total Hits(*)   Unique Hits       URL
-----------     ----------        ----------------------
278             13                10.194.23.53
1               1                 10.194.22.181
```

Figure 23.2   Summary report produced by ParseLog.js.

Analyzing Log Files by Using a Database

The script Fabrikam used to create the activity snapshot does not allow them to do any further analysis of the data in the log files. For more advanced reporting, it is recommended that you store your log file in a database. Storing the file in a database will allow you to track trends, perform historical analysis, and answer follow-up questions. Fabrikam decided to use the server log files for weekly activity snapshots, and to save publishing point logs to a database for monthly reports on content popularity.

Once the files are in the database, they can use the information in the log files to ascertain the following information about the usage reports:

■ For each piece of content streamed, on average how long did users stay connected?

This number can be attained by grouping the statistics by their s-contentpath value and then calculating the average of the x-duration field for each group. Comparing this value against the known length of content can also provide a percentage value as to how much of the content users received before disconnecting from the stream.

- For each publishing point, how much time was spent buffering content?

    This number can be attained by grouping the statistics by their cs-uri-stem value and then summing the value of the c-totalbuffertime field for each group. This provides a measure of how stable the stream was between the clients and the server.

- For each client, how many stream errors were encountered?

    This number can be attained by sorting statistics on the c-playerid value, and then summing the value of the c-pkts-lost-client for each group. This value shows how many data packets were lost that could not be recovered through error correction or resend requests. This statistic can be a good predictor of client satisfaction with the service.

Collecting User Feedback

Fabrikam also needs to reflect the subjective user experience with the new streaming media system in their usage reports. There are different methods for collecting user feedback, and Fabrikam decided to use a combination of methods to get the best cross-section of data during the pilot program.

For the unicast content, each publishing point is assigned a wrapper playlist that introduces the content. At the end of the content, the playlist redirects the user to a Web form where they can record their opinions about the content.

The Media Guide Web site provides a feedback link that can be used at any time to provide opinions about the streaming program to the administrator, either through e-mail or through the survey site.

The statistics gathered this way will provide context for the information collected from the log files and performance counter analysis, and will provide important direction for development of the streaming media program within Fabrikam.

Part V

Appendixes

Appendix A

SMIL Reference

This appendix provides an overview of the Synchronized Multimedia Integration Language (SMIL) 2.0 elements and attributes used to create server-side playlists. Server-side playlists can be created in a text editor, such as Microsoft Notepad, or with Windows Media Playlist Editor, which you can install from the companion CD. A finished script file is saved with a .wsx file name extension, and then assigned or copied to a publishing point on a Windows Media server, where it can be accessed by end users. If you use the Playlist Editor, the settings you make in the editor are automatically transformed to a SMIL script when you save them to a file. For more information about creating server-side playlists, see Windows Media Services Help.

Playlist Construction

A playlist file is made up of seven basic Extensible Markup Language (XML) elements:

- **smil**
- **media**
- **seq**
- **switch**
- **excl**
- **priorityClass**
- **clientData**

An element can either define or control the behavior of one or more other elements. By arranging elements and setting values for their corresponding attributes, you can determine the playback and presentation structure of a playlist.

The organization of playlist elements defines a playlist's control structure. For example, if you open a playlist in a text editor, you will notice that some playlist elements are enclosed within other playlist elements. Elements that contain other playlist elements are known as parent elements. A parent element controls the behavior of all child elements within it.

Six of the seven basic playlist elements act as parent elements: **smil**, **seq**, **excl**, **media**, **priorityClass**, and **switch**. The **seq** and **excl** elements act as time containers, meaning that they control the timing of child elements. The **priorityClass** and **switch** elements act as control containers, meaning that they control the interaction of child elements.

In a playlist, the **smil** element is the document root, meaning that it is the parent of all the other elements in the playlist. In the following example, a **seq** element is the child of the **smil** element. The **seq** element contains **media** and **clientData** elements, which are modified by **src** and **title** attributes, respectively. The **wsx** element preceding the **smil** element is used to identify the version of the server-side SMIL syntax being used.

```
<?wsx version='1.0'?>
<smil>
    <seq>
        <media src="file1.wmv">
            <clientData title="My File #1"/>
        </media>
        <media src="file2.wmv">
            <clientData title="My File #2"/>
        </media>
        <media src="file3.wmv">
            <clientData title="My File #3"/>
        </media>
        <media src="File4.wmv"/>
            <clientData title="My File #4"/>
        </media>
    </seq>
</smil>
```

Elements

The following section provides descriptions of each of the playlist elements.

smil
Identifies child elements as a playlist based upon the SMIL standard. The **smil** element is the root element of the playlist file. Additionally, a **smil** element has the same function as a **seq** element, meaning that its child elements are played sequentially.

media
Contains a digital media source, such as files on a local computer, streams from a remote computer running Windows Media Encoder or Windows Media Services, other playlist files, ASP pages on Web servers, or digital media files on third-party storage systems.

Attributes of a **media** element provide the locations of digital media sources and can specify how the digital media content plays back or is presented to the client. A **media** element can refer to any digital media source that can be accessed by a data source plug-in and parsed by a media or playlist parser plug-in.

seq

Specifies that child elements play sequentially, from the first element to the last. The **seq** element is a time-container element.

switch

Specifies alternative **media** elements that can be used if one or more of the current **media** elements fails. The **switch** element is useful for implementing content rollover in a server-side playlist. To identify a valid element that can be successfully accessed and streamed, the server evaluates the child elements within the **switch** element in the order they are listed. When the server identifies and streams a valid element, the other elements within the **switch** element are ignored. After the selected element stops streaming, the server continues to stream the portion of the playlist after the **switch** element.

excl

Specifies that child elements play back according to their timing attributes. Use an **excl** element if you want to control when child elements begin based on variable criteria. For example, a child element can be triggered by using either a programmatic event or a **begin** attribute that explicitly specifies a start time. Unlike child elements of a **seq** element, which play in order once the **seq** element has been activated, the child elements of an **excl** element do not play unless they are started explicitly. An **excl** element is often used in conjunction with **priorityClass** elements.

priorityClass

Controls how child **media** elements interrupt playback of their peer elements. If you simply want to configure one element to interrupt playback of another, you can use an **excl** or **seq** element with a **begin** attribute set to start one element while another element is playing. The **priorityClass** element, however, enables you to specify whether the interrupted element stops, pauses, or can never be interrupted. If a **media** element is set to pause when interrupted, it will continue to stream from the point at which it was paused when the element that interrupted it ends. If it is set to stop, it will not stream when the element that interrupted it ends.

Using the **priorityClass** element, you can also specify whether an interruption is deferred until the current **media** element finishes or is ignored altogether. Furthermore, the child elements in a **priorityClass** element and the **priorityClass** elements contained within an **excl** element container are prioritized by the order in which they are listed in the playlist. The ability to adjust the priority further enables you to control the behavior of child elements.

clientData

Specifies descriptive text, banner images, and logging information for the parent element. Descriptive text, such as artist name and track title, is then displayed in Windows Media Player 9 Series or a player that uses the Windows Media Player 9 Series ActiveX control. Using the **clientData** element, you can also display banner images, associated hyperlinks, and ToolTip text.

You can insert a **clientData** element anywhere in a playlist. It can be a child of any element except another **clientData** element. The information it contains is sent to the client when the **clientData** element becomes active.

Attributes

Attributes are categorized into four functional groups: media definition, metadata information, synchronization, and timing.

Media Definition Attributes

Attributes in this group define an element.

id

Specifies a name for an element so that it can be referenced by another element in a playlist. You can use the **id** attribute to add an identifier to any element, but it is most useful for identifying **media** elements. The **id** attribute is used to identify an element as a SyncBase for timing and synchronization purposes.

mediaName

Specifies a name for a **media** element. The server uses the **mediaName** attribute to log data, and the **mediaName** attribute value overrides name information sent to clients. This attribute is useful if you are using log files for reporting or if you want to prevent users from seeing the names of your servers and the paths to your content.

noSkip

Specifies whether the next, rewind, fast forward, pause, and seek functions are enabled in Windows Media Player when a **media** element plays. You can use this attribute to prevent users from skipping a **media** element, such as an advertisement.

role

Specifies a purpose or type for a **media** element. This attribute enables you to create custom categories for digital media sources, such as music, bumper, promo, or public service announcement. The WMS Client Logging plug-in uses the value specified in the **role** attribute to populate the **cs-media-role** field.

src

Identifies the content source of a **media** element using a URL, Universal Naming Convention (UNC) path, or absolute path. The source can be any type of digital media content or file as long as there is an enabled data source plug-in that can access the content and a media parser or playlist parser plug-in that can parse the content.

In general, any stream that can be assigned as the source of a publishing point is a valid value for the **src** attribute. By default, you can specify any of the following sources for a media element:

- A Windows Media file

- A JPEG image file

- An MP3 audio file

- An encoder stream

- A stream or file from a remote Windows Media server

- A stream or file from a local publishing point

- A playlist file

Metadata Information Attributes

Attributes in this group are used with the **clientData** element to specify information that is sent to the client.

album

Specifies the album name associated with a single **media** element or a collection of **media** elements. An **album** attribute value is included in the content description list that is sent to the client. Windows Media Player displays the **album** attribute value when the **media** element or elements are played.

artist

Specifies an artist name for a single **media** element or collection of **media** elements. An **artist** attribute value is included in the content description list that is sent to the client. Windows Media Player displays the **artist** attribute value when the **media** element or elements are played.

author

Specifies a content creator name for a single **media** element or collection of **media** elements. An **author** attribute value is included in the content description list that is sent to the client. Windows Media Player displays the value when the **media** element or elements are played.

bannerURL

Typically used with the **bannerInfoURL** and **bannerAbstract** attributes to add a banner image to the Windows Media Player interface. The **bannerURL** attribute value is the URL of a banner image file.

bannerAbstract

Typically used with the **bannerURL** and **bannerInfoURL** attributes to add ToolTip information to a banner image displayed in Windows Media Player. The **bannerAbstract** attribute value provides the text information displayed when a user pauses the mouse pointer on the banner image.

bannerInfoURL

Typically used with the **bannerURL** and **bannerAbstract** attributes to add a hyperlink to a banner image displayed in Windows Media Player. You can use the **bannerInfoURL** attribute to provide users with a link to a Web page that is associated with one or more **media** elements. For example, the Web page may provide users with more information about the content source or an advertiser.

copyright

Specifies copyright information for a **media** element or collection of **media** elements. A **copyright** attribute value is included in the content description list that is sent to the client. Windows Media Player displays the value when the **media** element or elements are played.

genre

Specifies a genre type for a **media** element or collection of **media** elements. A **genre** attribute value is included in the content description list that is sent to the client. Windows Media Player displays the value when the **media** element or elements are played.

logURL

Specifies a URL to which a client sends logging information. In addition to the unicast and multicast logging capabilities included with Windows Media Services, the **logURL** attribute enables each **clientData** element to direct logging information to other locations on the network. By using the **logURL** attribute within a **clientData** element, usage information about the elements contained within the **clientData** element is sent by the client to a logging program that either displays the data, integrates it into a database, or saves it as a file. Logging data is sent once for each address specified in the **logURL** attribute.

title

Specifies a content title for a **media** element or collection of **media** elements. A **title** attribute value is included in the content description list that is sent to the client. Windows Media Player displays the value when the **media** element or elements are played.

Synchronization Attributes

Attributes in this group control playback of **media** elements contained in a **priorityClass** element.

higher

Specifies the behavior of the **media** elements within a **priorityClass** element when they are interrupted by **media** elements of a higher **priorityClass**. A **higher** attribute can have the following values:

- **Pause** specifies that the **media** element pauses when its playback is interrupted by a **media** element that has a higher priority. The interrupted **media** element resumes playback when the higher-priority element ends.

- **Stop** specifies that the **media** element stops when playback is interrupted by a **media** element that has a higher priority. The interrupted element does not resume playback.

lower

Specifies the behavior of the **media** elements within a **priorityClass** element when they are interrupted by **media** elements of a lower **priorityClass**. A **lower** attribute can have the following values:

- **Defer** specifies that an attempt by a lower-priority **media** element to interrupt playback is deferred. Playback of the interrupting **media** element begins when the higher-priority **media** element ends.

- **Never** specifies that an attempt by a lower-priority **media** element to interrupt playback is denied. The interrupting **media** element does not play.

peers

Specifies the behavior of a **media** element within a **priorityClass** element when its playback is interrupted by another **media** element in the same **priorityClass** (called a peer). A **peers** attribute can have the following values:

- **Pause** specifies that the **media** element pauses when its playback is interrupted by a peer **media** element. The interrupted **media** element resumes playback when the peer ends.

- **Stop** specifies that the **media** element stops when its playback is interrupted by a peer **media** element. Playback does not resume. This is the default value for **media** elements contained within an **excl** or **priorityClass** element.

- **Defer** specifies that an attempt by a **media** element to interrupt playback of a peer is deferred. Playback begins when the **peer** element ends.

- **Never** specifies that an attempt by a **media** element to interrupt playback of a **peer** element is denied. The interrupting element does not play.

Timing Attributes

A timing attribute defines the aspects of an element's behavior that relate to time and sequence. For example, the timing value assigned to a **begin** attribute defines when an element starts playing; while the timing value assigned to a **clipEnd** attribute defines when a **media** element ends. If an attribute has no assigned value, the default value is used.

Timing values are specified as either clock values or as events. An event value consists of the **id** attribute value of the trigger element followed by a period (.) and the attribute of the trigger element on which the timing is based. For example, a **begin** attribute value of Advert1.begin means that an element is set to begin playing when the **media** element Advert1 starts; a **begin** value of 0s means the **media** element starts playing immediately.

begin

Specifies the timing value used to start or activate an element. The **begin** attribute is most useful for activating elements in **excl** or **priorityClass** elements. Unlike the immediate children of **seq** or **smil** containers, child elements of an **excl** or **priorityClass** element have no default start time, and will therefore not start without a **begin** attribute value.

clipBegin

Specifies the point in a **media** element source at which playback begins.

clipEnd

Specifies the end point for a **media** element.

dur

Specifies the length of time that an element plays.

end

Specifies the timing value at which an element stops streaming data and ends. By default, the **end** attribute value is the natural end of the element.

endSync

Specifies the following end values for an element in an **excl** element:

- **First** specifies that the **excl** element ends after the first active child element ends.

- **All** specifies that the **excl** element ends after all child elements that have a resolved **begin** attribute value end. Elements with an unresolved **begin** attribute value will prevent the **excl** element from ending because the duration cannot be determined.

- **Id-value** specifies that the **excl** element ends when the child element with the specifed **id** attribute value ends.

- **Last** specifies that the **excl** element ends when the last active child element with a resolved and definite **begin** attribute value ends. If there are no children with a resolved **begin** attribute value, the **excl** element ends immediately.

repeatCount

Specifies how many times an element plays sequentially. For example, a **repeatCount** attribute value of 2 means an element plays twice (repeating once). You can use this attribute to repeat a **media** element or a time container element, such as a **seq** or **excl** element. A value of "indefinite" specifies that the element repeats indefinitely.

repeatDur

Specifies the length of time that an element repeats before stopping. For example, a **media** element that is five seconds long with a **repeatDur** attribute value of 20s plays four times and then stops. If an element is still playing when the **repeatDur** attribute value ends, the element stops, even if it has not repeated. Thus, when it has a specified **repeatDur** attribute value, an element may repeat many times, repeat for a fractional number of times, never repeat, or play for a shorter time than its duration. You can use this attribute to repeat a **media** element or a time container element, such as a **seq** or **excl** element.

syncEvent

Specifies an element in a wrapper playlist that is activated by a broadcast playlist element. For example, the **syncEvent** attribute can be used to switch from a broadcast to a wrapper element, and then switch back to the live broadcast.

Appendix B

Windows Media Performance Counters

Windows Media Performance Monitor includes numerous performance counters that you can use to monitor the health of your streaming media system. Some counters are available for the server, some for publishing points, and some for both. The following table lists the performance counters in alphabetical order and indicates whether it is available for servers or publishing points.

Counter	Description	Server	Publishing Point
Current Cache Downloads	The number of concurrent streams being downloaded to the memory area of the cache/proxy server.	✓	
Current Connected Players	The current number of players with unicast connections to the server. This number does not include distribution server connections.	✓	✓
Current Connection Queue Length	The current number of connection requests that are pending on the server from both players and distribution servers.	✓	
Current Connection Rate	The current number of clients per second that are connecting to the server.	✓	
Current File Read Rate	The current rate, in kilobits per second (Kbps), at which data packets are read from a file.	✓	✓
Current Incoming Bandwidth	The current bandwidth, in Kbps, allocated for streams from other servers.	✓	
Current Late Read Rate	The current number of data packets per second that take longer than 400 milliseconds to read from the file system.	✓	✓
Current Late Send Rate	The current number of packets that are sent out 0.5 seconds or more after the marked send time.	✓	

(continued)

Counter	Description	Server	Publishing Point
Current Outgoing Distribution Allocated Bandwidth	The current bandwidth, in Kbps, allocated for streams to distribution servers.	✓	✓
Current Outgoing Distribution Connections	The current number of distribution servers that are connected to this server.	✓	✓
Current Outgoing Distribution Send Rate	The current rate, in Kbps, at which data packets are being streamed to distribution servers.	✓	
Current Player Allocated Bandwidth	The current amount of bandwidth, in Kbps, that is allocated for all streams to players.	✓	✓
Current Player Send Rate	The current rate, in Kbps, at which data packets are being streamed to players.	✓	
Current Stream Error Rate	The current number of errors per second due to dropped packets.	✓	✓
Current Streaming HTTP Players	The current number of players that are being streamed data through the HTTP protocol. This does not include players that are stopped or paused.	✓	✓
Current Streaming MMS Players	The current number of players that are being streamed data through the MMS protocol. This does not include players that are stopped or paused.	✓	✓
Current Streaming Players	The current number of players that are being streamed data across all protocols. This does not include players that are stopped or paused.	✓	✓
Current Streaming RTSP Players	The current number of players that are being streamed data through the RTSP protocol. This does not include players that are stopped or paused.	✓	✓
Current UDP Resend Requests Rate	The current number of requests for UDP resends per second received from clients.	✓	
Current UDP Resends Sent Rate	The current number of UDP resends per second sent to clients.	✓	
Peak Connected Players	The peak number of players that have connected since the last time the counter was reset.	✓	✓
Peak Outgoing Distribution Allocated Bandwidth	The peak bandwidth, in Kbps, allocated for all streams to distribution servers that have connected since the last time the counter was reset.	✓	✓
Peak Outgoing Distribution Connections	The peak number of distribution servers that have connected since the last time the counter was reset.	✓	✓

(continued)

Counter	Description	Server	Publishing Point
Peak Outgoing Distribution Send Rate	The peak rate, in Kbps, at which data was streamed to distribution servers since the last time the counter was reset.	✓	
Peak Player Allocated Bandwidth	The peak bandwidth, in Kbps, that has been allocated for all streams to players since the last time the counter was reset.	✓	✓
Peak Player Send Rate	The peak rate, in Kbps, at which data was streamed to players since the last time the counter was reset.	✓	
Peak Streaming Players	The peak number of players that have been streamed data concurrently since the last time the counter was reset.	✓	✓
Total Advertisements	The total number of advertisements that have been streamed from playlists since the last time the counter was reset.	✓	✓
Total Connected Players	The total number of players that have connected to the server since the last time the counter was reset.	✓	✓
Total File Bytes Read	The total number of bytes read from files by the server since the last time the counter was reset.		✓
Total Late Reads	The total number of times that the server required more than 400 milliseconds to read data from the file system since the last time the counter was reset.	✓	✓
Total Late Sends	The total number of times the server sent out data packets 0.5 seconds or more after the marked send time since the last time the counter was reset.	✓	
Total Outgoing Distribution Bytes Sent	The total number of bytes streamed to all distribution servers since the last time the counter was reset.	✓	✓
Total Outgoing Distribution Connections	The total number of distribution servers that have connected to the server or publishing point since the last time the counter was reset.	✓	✓
Total Player Bytes Sent	The total number of bytes streamed to all players since the last time the counter was reset.	✓	✓
Total Server Uptime	The elapsed time, in seconds, that the Windows Media Services service has been running since it was last started.	✓	
Total Stream Denials	The total number of times the server refused to send a requested stream to a client since the last time the counter was reset. This includes denials that occurred due to failure to be authorized or authenticated, as well as denials that occurred because limits were exceeded.	✓	✓
Total Stream Errors	The total number of stream errors due to dropped packets since the last time the counter was reset.	✓	✓

(continued)

Counter	Description	Server	Publishing Point
Total Stream Terminations	The total number of streams that were terminated due to inactivity or errors since the last time the counter was reset. This includes terminations that occurred because player inactivity and timeout limits were exceeded, as well as terminations due to events such as late reads.	✓	✓
Total Streaming Players	The total number of players that have been streamed data since the last time the counter was reset.	✓	✓
Total UDP Resend Requests	The total number of requests for UDP resends received from clients since the last time the counter was reset.	✓	
Total UDP Resends Sent	The total number of UDP resends sent to clients since the last time the counter was reset.	✓	

Appendix C

Log Fields

The following list identifies all of the fields that can be reported in all of the Windows Media log files, and whether they are used to report data from unicast clients, multicast clients, or both.

c-ip
Description: The source Internet Protocol (IP) address of the connected socket. This may be the IP address of a proxy server or firewall.
Sample value: 157.56.219.146
Client data reported: Unicast, multicast

date
Description: Date when a client connected (in international date format).
Sample value: 2001-04-19
Client data reported: Unicast, multicast

time
Description: Time when the client connected. The time format is either in Coordinated Universal Time (UTC) or local time, depending on how the logging plug-in is configured.
Sample value: 15:30:30
Client data reported: Unicast, multicast

c-dns
Description: Used when you want to use version 4.1 scripts to analyze Windows Media 9 Series logs.
Client data reported: Unicast, multicast

cs-uri-stem
Description: The path (requested URL without the schema, host, port number, and question mark) to the content that was requested. See **cs-url** for the full URL. Note that this represents a change from Windows Media Services version 4.1, in which this field contained the full URL.
Sample value: /test/sample.wmv or /broadcast
Client data reported: Unicast, multicast

c-starttime

Description: Time stamp (in seconds, no fractions) indicating the point in the stream when the client started to render content. For live broadcasts, this field is set to 0.
Sample value: 39
Client data reported: Unicast, multicast

x-duration

Description: Length of time (in seconds) of the data received by the client. For Player log entries, the value does not include buffered data. For distribution server log entries, the value includes all time spent receiving data, including any buffering.
Sample value: 31
Client data reported: Unicast, multicast

rate

Description: The rate at which data is sent from the server to the client. Possible values are shown in the following table:

Value	Description
0.5	Half the real-time rate.
1	Real-time rate.
2	Twice as fast as the real-time rate.
5	Fast forward.
-5	Fast rewind.

If you are using Fast Streaming, these values could be considerably higher or lower depending on the content and the available bandwidth.
Sample value: 1
Client data reported: Unicast, multicast

c-status

Description: Codes that describe client status. Possible codes are shown in the following table:

Value	Description
200	The connection was successful.
210	The client reconnected (after first disconnecting).
400	The requested URL was invalid.
401	The client was denied access.

(continued)

Value	Description
404	The requested content was not found.
408	The client failed to submit a log because the client disconnected.
420	The client was disconnected and attempted to reconnect, but failed.
500	The Windows Media server encountered an internal error and stopped streaming.

For the code value of 420, the client will then connect again starting a new session. This code reflects the client's statistics when it was originally disconnected. For each log entry with this code, there should be a 408 code that has the same session ID.

Sample value: 200

Client data reported: Unicast, multicast

c-playerid

Description: Globally unique identifier (GUID) of the client. For Player log entries, if the Player is configured to not send unique identification information to content providers, the value is: {3300AD50-2C39-46c0-AE0A-xxxxxxxxxxxxx}, where xxxxxxxxxxxxx is the session ID of the client. For distribution server log entries, this value is always a series of zeroes.

Sample value: {c579d042-cecc-11d1-bb31-00a0c9603954}

Client data reported: Unicast, multicast

c-playerversion

Description: For Player log entries, this field represents the version number of the Player. For distribution server log entries, this field represents the version number of the distribution server.

Sample value: 6.2.5.415

Client data reported: Unicast, multicast

c-playerlanguage

Description: Language and country/region code of the Player.

Sample value: en-US

Client data reported: Unicast, multicast

cs(User-Agent)

Description: Used to determine whether the embedded Player is a version 6.4 Player with a Windows Media 9 Series wrapper or a legacy 6.4 Player. The tag used to identify a Windows Media 9 Series wrapper is WMPDXM.

Sample value: Mozilla/4.0_(compatible;_MSIE_4.01;_Windows_98)

Client data reported: Unicast

cs(Referer)

Description: URL to the Web page in which the Player was embedded (if it was embedded). If this is unknown, this field is blank.
Sample value: http://www.example.microsoft.com
Client data reported: Unicast

c-hostexe

Description: For Player log entries, the host program (.exe) that was run. For example, a Web page in a browser, a Microsoft Visual Basic-based application, or a standalone Player. For distribution server log entries, the name of the distribution server's service program (.exe) that was run.
Sample value: iexplore.exe, vb.exe, mplayer2.exe, WMServer.exe
Client data reported: Unicast, multicast

c-hostexever

Description: Host program (.exe) version number.
Sample value: 4.70.1215
Client data reported: Unicast, multicast

c-os

Description: Client operating system.
Sample value: Windows_NT
Client data reported: Unicast, multicast

c-osversion

Description: Version number of the client operating system.
Sample value: 4.0.0.1381
Client data reported: Unicast, multicast

c-cpu

Description: Client CPU type.
Sample value: Pentium
Client data reported: Unicast, multicast

filelength

Description: Length of the digital media file (in seconds). This value is 0 for a stream delivered from a broadcast publishing point.
Sample value: 60
Client data reported: Unicast

filesize

Description: Size of the digital media file (in bytes). This value is 0 for a stream delivered from a broadcast publishing point.
Sample value: 86000
Client data reported: Unicast

avgbandwidth

Description: Average bandwidth (in bits per second) at which the client was connected to the server. The value is calculated across the entire duration of the connection.
Sample value: 24300
Client data reported: Unicast, multicast

protocol

Description: Actual protocol used to access the content (may differ from the protocol requested by the client). A value of "Cache" indicates that a client played the content from its disk-based cache. A value of "asfm" indicates that the content was delivered using multicast transmission.
Sample value: MMST
Client data reported: Unicast, multicast

transport

Description: Transport protocol used to stream content. Multicast content is always streamed using UDP.
Sample value: UDP, TCP
Client data reported: Unicast, multicast

audiocodec

Description: For Player log entries, the audio codecs used to encode the audio streams that the client accessed. If multiple codecs were used, the values are delimited by semicolons. This field contains a hyphen (-) in distribution server log entries.
Sample value: Microsoft_Audio_Codec
Client data reported: Unicast, multicast

videocodec

Description: For Player log entries, the video codecs used to encode the video streams that the client accessed. If multiple codecs were used, the values are delimited by semicolons. This field contains a hyphen (-) in distribution server log entries.
Sample value: Microsoft_MPEG-4_Video_Codec_V2
Client data reported: Unicast, multicast

channelURL

Description: URL to the multicast information file. This field contains a hyphen (-) in a client receiving content as a unicast stream unless the unicast stream is a result of a unicast rollover from a multicast stream.

Sample value: http://www.example.microsoft.com/channel.nsc

Client data reported: Unicast, multicast

sc-bytes

Description: Total number of bytes that the server sent to the client. The value does not include any overhead that is added by the network stack. However, protocols such as MMS, RTSP, and HTTP may introduce some overhead. Therefore, the same content streamed using different protocols may result in different values. This field contains a hyphen (-) in propagated cache/proxy logs and in multicast log files.

Sample value: 30000

Client data reported: Unicast

c-bytes

Description: Number of bytes received by the client from the server. The value does not include any overhead that is added by the network stack. However, protocols such as MMS, RTSP, and HTTP may introduce some overhead. Therefore, the same content streamed using different protocols may result in different values. If **c-bytes** and **sc-bytes** are not identical, packet loss occurred.

Sample value: 28583

Client data reported: Unicast, multicast

s-pkts-sent

Description: Number of content packets sent by the server to a connected client. The value does not include TCP or UDP packets. This field contains a hyphen (-) in propagated cache/proxy logs and in multicast log files.

Sample value: 55

Client data reported: Unicast

c-pkts-received

Description: Number of packets from the server (**s-pkts-sent**) that are received correctly by the client on the first try. Packets that are not received correctly on the first try can be recovered if they are resent through the UDP protocol. Packets that are not recovered through UDP resend are considered lost. You can recover these packets if error correction is enabled. The value does not include TCP or UDP packets.

Sample value: 50

Client data reported: Unicast, multicast

c-pkts-lost-client

Description: Packets lost during transmission from server to client that were not recovered at the client layer through error correction or at the network layer through UDP resends. These packets are sent by the Windows Media server, but never played by the client. The value does not include TCP or UDP packets.

Sample value: 5

Client data reported: Unicast, multicast

c-pkts-lost-net

Description: Number of packets lost on the network layer. You can recover these packets if error correction is enabled. The value does not include TCP or UDP packets.

Sample value: 2

Client data reported: Unicast, multicast

c-pkts-lost-cont-net

Description: Maximum number of continuously lost packets on the network layer during transmission from server to client. If the value is high, the network conditions were bad, with long periods of time during which the client received no packets. The value does not include TCP or UDP packets.

Sample value: 2

Client data reported: Unicast, multicast

c-resendreqs

Description: Number of client requests to receive new packets. This field contains a 0 unless the client is using UDP resend.

Sample value: 5

Client data reported: Unicast, multicast

c-pkts-recovered-ECC

Description: Packets lost in the network (**c-pkts-lost-net**) that were repaired and recovered at the client layer because error correction was enabled. Error correction is the only means of packet recovery for multicast streams. Packets repaired and recovered at the client layer are equal to the difference between **c-pkts-lost-net** and **c-pkts-lost-client**. The value does not include TCP or UDP packets.

Sample value: 3

Client data reported: Unicast, multicast

c-pkts-recovered-resent

Description: Number of packets recovered because they were resent through UDP. The value does not include TCP or UDP packets. This field contains a 0 unless the client is using UDP resend.

Sample value: 5
Client data reported: Unicast, multicast

c-buffercount
Description: Number of times the client buffered while playing the stream.
Sample value: 4
Client data reported: Unicast, multicast

c-totalbuffertime
Description: Time (in seconds) the client used to buffer the stream. If the client buffers more than once before a log entry is generated, **c-totalbuffertime** is the total amount of time the client spent buffering.
Sample value: 6
Client data reported: Unicast, multicast

c-quality
Description: The lowest level of stream quality reported by the Player during the playback of the stream.
Sample value: 96
Client data reported: Unicast, multicast

s-ip
Description: IP address of the server that received the log file. For multicast log files, this value will be the IP address of the Web server on which Wmsiislog.dll is installed.
Sample value: 224.24.41.189
Client data reported: Unicast, multicast

s-dns
Description: Domain Name System (DNS) name of the server that received the log file. This field contains a hyphen (-) in multicast log files.
Sample value: media.server.contoso.com
Client data reported: Unicast

s-totalclients
Description: Number of clients connected to the server (but not necessarily streaming) at the time the event was logged. This field contains a hyphen (-) in propagated cache/ proxy logs and in multicast log files.
Sample value: 20
Client data reported: Unicast

s-cpu-util

Description: Average load on the server processor (0 to 100 percent). If multiple processors exist, this value is the average for all processors. This field contains a hyphen (-) in propagated cache/proxy logs and in multicast log files.
Sample value: 40
Client data reported: Unicast

cs-username

Description: The user name the client provided during authentication. This field contains a value only if authorization and authentication plug-ins are enabled. If an anonymous authentication method is used, this field will contain a hyphen (-).
Sample value: JSmith
Client data reported: Unicast

s-sessionid

Description: A session identifier the server uses to track a stream session. This is important for tracking multiple log entries to the same session. Note that if Windows Media Player version 6.4 received content over HTTP, the **s-sessionid** value will change for each log entry, even if the entries are for the same session.
Sample value: 123456
Client data reported: Unicast

s-contentpath

Description: The actual content that streamed. A plug-in may resolve a requested path to another path. If the client was redirected, this field represents the location to which the client was redirected.
Sample value: file://C:\WMPub\WMRoot\Encoder_ad.wmv or http://www.example.microsoft.com/speech.wma
Client data reported: Unicast

cs-url

Description: The actual URL requested by the client. For multicast clients, this value is the multicast IP address and port. However, Windows Media Player 9 Series and the Windows Media Player 9 Series ActiveX control multicast clients submit the multicast IP address and port, followed by the IP address of the network interface from which the server broadcasts the multicast.
Sample value: mms://example.microsoft.com/mycontent.wmv, asfm://206.73.118. 254:26502 or (for Windows Media Player 9 Series) asfm://multicast IP address:port/ Server IP address
Client data reported: Unicast, multicast

cs-media-name

Description: The **media** element the client was receiving if the client was receiving content from a playlist. The value is derived from the **mediaName** attribute of the playlist media element. If the **mediaName** attribute is not present, the value in this field is derived from the file name value. This field is blank if the client was not receiving content from a playlist. Alternatively, this entry can be specified in the announcement file in order to classify logs according to user or content.

Sample value: /ads/MyAd2.asf

Client data reported: Unicast

c-max-bandwidth

Description: The maximum bandwidth rate (in bits per second) of the client. This value can be used to determine whether clients have the capacity for higher-bandwidth content. The value recorded for this field can be of the following types:

- A valid number of bits per second (bps) reported from the client, such as 38400.

- An undetermined amount, logged as 0.

- A very large amount that cannot be accurately measured, but is greater than 1,000,000 bps and less than 1,000,000,000 bps, logged as a hyphen (-).

- A hyphen (-), when a file is being played from the local cache and no bandwidth is used.

Sample value: 384000

Client data reported: Unicast, multicast

cs-media-role

Description: A user-defined value that identifies the role of a **media** element in a playlist. Typically, this field is used to enable advertisement logging. If the **media** element does not have a **role** attribute, or if the client was not receiving content from a playlist, this field is blank. Alternatively, this entry can be specified in the announcement file in order to classify logs according to user or content.

Sample value: Ad

Client data reported: Unicast

s-proxied

Description: Indicates whether the client connected through a cache/proxy server. A value of 0 indicates no cache/proxy server was involved. A value of 1 indicates a cache/proxy server was involved.

Sample value: 1

Client data reported: Unicast

Appendix D

Windows Media Metafile Elements

This appendix provides an overview of the elements used to create client-side playlists in Windows Media metafiles. Client-side playlists can be created with a text editor, such as Microsoft Notepad. Announcement files, which are simplified playlists containing only one media element, can be created using the **Announcement Wizard** in the Windows Media Services MMC snap-in.

Metafiles are saved with one of three file name extensions depending on the primary type of content referenced in the metafile:

- .asx for mixed content
- .wax for audio content
- .wvx for video content

Finished metafiles are typically distributed on a Web site. For more information about creating client-side playlists, see the Windows Media Player SDK.

Windows Media metafiles are based on XML syntax and can be encoded in ANSI or UNICODE (UTF-8) format. They are made up of various elements with their associated tags and attributes. The following script is an example of metafile syntax used in a client-side playlist:

```
<ASX  VERSION="3.0">
    <TITLE>Example Windows Media Player Show</TITLE>

    <ENTRY>
        <TITLE>Example Clip</TITLE>
        <REF HREF="http://example.microsoft.com/media.asf" />
    </ENTRY>

    <ENTRY>
        <TITLE>Another Clip</TITLE>
        <REF HREF="http://example.microsoft.com/more_media.asf" />
    </ENTRY>
</ASX>
```

The following provides short descriptions of each element:

ABSTRACT   Text that describes the associated ASX, BANNER, or ENTRY element.

ASX   Defines a file as a Windows Media metafile.

AUTHOR   The name of the author of a media clip or a Windows Media metafile.

BANNER   Specifies the URL of an image file that appears in the display panel of Windows Media Player.

BASE   Specifies a string that is appended to the front of URLs sent to the client.

Comments   Specifies the XML syntax for comments (<!--...-->).

COPYRIGHT   Copyright text for an ASX or ENTRY element.

DURATION   Specifies the length of time Windows Media Player renders a stream.

ENDMARKER   Specifies a marker at which Windows Media Player stops rendering a stream.

ENTRY   Specifies the path for a digital media stream.

ENTRYREF   Links to the ENTRY elements in an external Windows Media metafile that has an .asx, .wax, .wvx, or .wmx file name extension.

EVENT   Defines a behavior or action taken by Windows Media Player when it receives a script command labeled as an event.

LOGURL   Instructs the Player to submit any log data to the specified URL.

MOREINFO   Specifies the URL of a Web site, e-mail address, or script command associated with a show, clip, or banner.

PARAM   Specifies the value of a custom parameter associated with a clip.

PREVIEWDURATION   Specifies the length of time a clip is played in preview mode.

REF   Specifies the URL of a piece of digital media content.

REPEAT   Specifies the number of times Windows Media Player repeats one or more ENTRY or ENTRYREF elements.

SKIN   Specifies the URL of an embedded skin.

STARTMARKER   Specifies a marker at which Windows Media Player starts rendering the stream.

STARTTIME   Specifies a time at which Windows Media Player will start rendering the stream.

TITLE   The title of an ASX or ENTRY element.

Glossary

Symbols

.asx   The file name extension of an announcement file. This extension is also used to indicate a client-side playlist.

.nsc   The file name extension of a multicast information file.

.prx   The file name extension of a profile.

.wma   The file name extension of an audio file in Windows Media Format. The audio content of the file is encoded with the Windows Media Audio codec.

.wme   The file name extension for a Windows Media Encoder session file.

.wms   The file name extension for a Windows Media Player skin definition file.

.wmv   The file name extension of a video file in Windows Media Format. The video content of the file is encoded with the Windows Media Video codec.

.wmz   The file name extension of a Windows Media Player skin file, which is made up of a skin definition file and its supporting graphic files.

.wsx   The file name extension of a server-side playlist.

A

access control list (ACL)   A list of security protections that applies to either an entire object, a set of the object's properties, or an individual property of an object.

ACL   See definition for: *access control list (ACL)*

Advanced Systems Format (ASF)   An extensible container format designed to store synchronized multimedia data.

analog   The traditional format in which audio and video are transmitted by using a wave or analog signal. An analog signal may not work with digital speakers; computers use digital signals.

announcement   A Windows Media metafile that gives a player the information needed to receive content. Announcement files contain Extensible Markup Language (XML) scripts.

aspect ratio   The ratio of the width of an image to its height.

attribute   A name-value data pair.

Audio Video Interleaved (AVI)   A multimedia file format for storing sound and moving pictures in Resource Interchange File Format (RIFF).

authentication   The process of verifying that an entity or object is who or what it claims to be. For example, a user name and password may be used to authenticate a user. See also: *authorization*

authorization   The process of granting access to protected resources. See also: *authentication*

AVI   See definition for: *Audio Video Interleaved (AVI)*

B

bandwidth   A network's capacity for transferring an amount of data in a given time.

bit rate   The number of bits transferred per second.

broadband   A transmission medium designed for high-speed data transfers over long distances. Cable modem services and DSL are examples of broadband networks.

broadcast   A method by which a client receives a stream. During a broadcast connection, clients cannot control the stream. This is the opposite of an on-demand presentation.

broadcast publishing point   A type of publishing point that streams content to multiple users at once, similar to a television broadcast. Content streamed from a broadcast publishing point can be delivered as a multicast or unicast stream.

buffer   An area of computer memory reserved for temporarily holding data before that data is used on the receiving computer. Buffering protects against the interruption of data flow.

bumper advertisements   Advertising content that is played before and after the primary content. See also: *interstitial advertisement*, *wrapper playlist*

C

cache   A temporary data storage location, or the process of storing data temporarily. A cache is typically used for quick data access.

cache/proxy server   A server running Windows Media Services for which a cache/proxy plug-in has been enabled, allowing the server to provide cache and proxy support to another Windows Media server.

caption   Text that accompanies images or videos, either as a supplemental description or a transcript of spoken words.

capture   To record audio, video, or still images as digital data in a file.

capture device   Hardware that transfers audio and video from an external source, such as a VCR or camcorder, to a computer.

CBR   See definition for: *constant bit rate (CBR)*

challenge   In Windows Media Rights Manager, a request for a license. A challenge contains information about the consumer's computer, a list of requested rights, and other information about the content, including the content header and key ID.

codec   An abbreviation for compressor/decompressor. Software or hardware used to compress and decompress digital media.

compression   A process for removing redundant data from a digital media file or stream to reduce its size or the bandwidth used.

configuration file   A text file used by Windows Media Encoding Script that specifies the content to be encoded and the command-line options to be invoked.

connection speed   The maximum rate, in bits per second, at which data can be transferred between a network and a computer or device.

constant bit rate (CBR)   A characteristic of a data stream in which the bit rate remains nearly uniform for the duration of the stream. See also: *variable bit rate (VBR)*

consumer   In Windows Media Rights Manager, a person who acquires Windows Media files and requests licenses to play them.

content   Audio, video, images, text, or any other information that is contained in a digital media file or stream.

content owner   The person or organization that controls access to protected content.

content provider   The person or organization that distributes Windows Media files (for example, a record, movie, or streaming media company). The content provider may also be the content owner.

content revocation   In Windows Media Rights Manager, a process by which content owners or content packagers can disable licenses for their own packaged files.

cookie   A block of data placed by the server on a client computer that identifies the client for future connections.

D

DACL   See definition for: *discretionary access control list (DACL)*

decrypt   To convert encrypted content back into its original form.

deinterlace   To combine the interlaced fields in a video frame so that, during playback, the lines of the video frame are painted sequentially. See also: *interlace*

delta frame   A video frame that contains only the changes from the previous frame. In contrast, a key frame contains all the data necessary to construct that frame.

digital rights management (DRM)   A technology that provides a persistent level of protection to digital content by encrypting it with a cryptographic key. Authorized recipients (or end users) must acquire a license in order to unlock and consume the content.

discretionary access control list (DACL)   The part of an object's security descriptor that grants or denies specific users and groups permission to access the object. Only the owner of an object can change permissions granted or denied in a DACL; access to the object is thus at the owner's discretion.

distribution server   A server running Windows Media Services that publishes content received from another streaming source, such as an encoder or another Windows Media server.

download   To transfer a file over a network in response to a request from the device that receives the data. Downloaded content is kept on the receiving device for playback on demand. In contrast, streamed content is played as it is delivered.

DRM   See definition for: *digital rights management (DRM)*

dynamic range   The difference (in decibels) between the quietest and loudest sounds in a single piece of audio content.

E

element   A fundamental syntactic unit in markup languages, such as HTML or XML. Elements are delimited by start tags and end tags.

encode   To convert audio and video content to a specified digital format.

encoder   A technology that converts live or prerecorded audio and video content to a specified digital format. Typically, content is compressed during encoding. Windows Media Encoder is an example of an encoder.

encrypt   To programmatically disguise content to hide its substance.

error correction   In Windows Media Player, a process to ensure that digital audio data is read from the CD-ROM drive accurately during playback or copying. Using error correction can prevent undesirable noises that are not part of the original material.

event   An automatic notification of a user action or a change in state that can be recognized by an object and responded to programmatically.

Extensible Markup Language (XML)   A markup language that provides a format for describing structured data. XML is a World Wide Web Consortium (W3C) specification, and is a subset of Standard Generalized Markup Language (SGML).

F

Fast Streaming   A method of delivering content that combines downloading and streaming to use the available network bandwidth in the most effective manner.

file format   The structure or organization of data in a file. File format is usually indicated by the file name extension.

file name extension   A set of characters added to the end of a file name that identifies the file type or format.

file type   A description of the content or format of a file. File type is usually indicated by the file name extension.

firewall   A combination of hardware and software that enforces a boundary between two or more networks and prevents unauthorized access to a private network.

frame   One of many sequential images that make up video.

frame rate   The number of video frames displayed per second. Higher frame rates generally produce smoother movement in the picture.

H

HDCD   See definition for: *High Definition Compatible Digital (HDCD)*

header   A part of the file structure that contains information required by an application to decompress and render the content. In Windows Media Rights Manager, the header in a protected file also contains information required to get a license.

High Definition Compatible Digital (HDCD)   A patented encode/decode process that improves the quality of all forms of digital audio recording and playback by increasing resolution and reducing distortion that occurs during analog-to-digital (A/D) and digital-to-analog (D/A) conversion, digital processing, and digital filtering.

HTTP   See definition for: *Hypertext Transfer Protocol (HTTP)*

Hypertext Transfer Protocol (HTTP)   The Internet protocol used to deliver information over the World Wide Web.

I

IEEE 1394   See definition for: *Institute of Electrical and Electronics Engineers (IEEE) 1394*

IGMP   See definition for: *Internet Group Management Protocol (IGMP)*

Institute of Electrical and Electronics Engineers (IEEE) 1394   A high-speed serial bus standard that provides enhanced computer connectivity for a wide range of devices, including consumer electronics audio/video (A/V) appliances, storage peripherals, other computers, and portable devices.

intelligent streaming   In Windows Media, a type of streaming that detects network conditions and adjusts the properties of a video or audio stream to maximize quality.

interlace   To display a video frame in two fields. One field contains the even lines of the frame, the other field contains the odd lines. During playback, the lines in one field are displayed first, then the lines in the second field are displayed.

Internet Group Management Protocol (IGMP)   A protocol used by IP hosts to report their multicast group memberships to neighboring multicast routers.

Internet Protocol version 6 (IPv6)   A revised version of the Internet Protocol (IP) designed to address growth on the Internet. Improvements include a 128-bit IP address size, expanded routing capabilities, and support for authentication and privacy.

interstitial advertisement   An advertisement that appears between pieces of content. When one piece of content finishes playing, the ad appears before the next piece of content plays. See also: *wrapper playlist*

inverse telecine   The process that removes the frames that were added when 24-fps film was converted to 30-fps video.

IPv6   See definition for: *Internet Protocol version 6 (IPv6)*

K

key   A piece of data that is required to unlock a packaged Windows Media file. This key is included in a separate license.

key frame   A video frame containing all the data needed to construct an image without reference to previous frames.

L

latency   The delay that occurs while data is processed or delivered.

letterbox   A video display format in which black bars appear above and below the video image while it is played. The letterbox format maintains the original aspect ratio of an image when it is displayed in a window with a different aspect ratio.

license   Data attached to protected content that describes how the content can be used.

license acquisition   The process of obtaining a license to play a packaged Windows Media file. The player attempts to obtain a license from a license acquisition URL, which is specified in the Windows Media file.

license acquisition URL   The URL that points to the first Web page that appears in the license acquisition process. A license acquisition URL is included in each packaged Windows Media file; when a consumer tries to play a Windows Media file that is not licensed, the player opens the license acquisition URL to acquire a license.

license issuer   The person or organization that uses the Windows Media Rights Manager SDK to issue licenses for packaged Windows Media files, for example, a license clearing house.

license key seed   A shared secret value that is used to generate keys to encrypt Windows Media files.

license management   A feature of the Windows Media Rights Manager SDK that enables consumers to back up the licenses for their Windows Media files and restore them to the same computer or to different computers. The restoration process is managed by Microsoft License Management Service, which limits the number of times a license can be restored to prevent fraud.

license store   An area on a computer where licenses are stored.

licensed file   A Windows Media file that has an associated license restricting the playing of that file. The restrictions stated in the license vary depending on the license creator.

licensing server   A computer that runs Windows Media License Service and issues licenses.

load balancing   A technique used for scaling the performance of a server-based program by distributing client requests across multiple servers.

log   To record actions that take place on a computer.

loop   To repeat a stream continuously.

lossless compression   A process for compressing data in which information is arranged in a more concise form and restored to its original state upon decompression.

lossy compression   A process for compressing data in which information deemed unnecessary is removed and cannot be recovered upon decompression. Typically used with audio and visual data in which a slight degradation of quality is acceptable.

M

marker   A text string that is associated with a designated time in Windows Media-based content. Markers often denote convenient points to begin playback, such as the start of a new scene.

MBR   See definition for: *multiple bit rate (MBR)*

media element A content item that is streamed from a server-side playlist. This can be a file, a stream from an encoder, a remote stream, another playlist file, or a Windows Media file on a Web server.

metadata Information about digital media content such as the artist, title, album, producer, and so forth. Also known as media information or tags.

Microsoft Media Server (MMS) protocol A proprietary protocol using User Datagram Protocol (UDP) or Transmission Control Protocol (TCP) to deliver content as a unicast stream.

MMS protocol See definition for: *Microsoft Media Server (MMS) protocol*

multicast A content delivery method in which a single stream is transmitted from a media server to multiple clients. The clients have no connection with the server. Instead, the server sends a single copy of the stream across the network to multicast-enabled routers, which replicate the data. Clients can then receive the stream by monitoring a specific multicast IP address and port.

multicast-enabled network A network that has routers that can interpret Class D IP addresses.

multichannel audio An audio reproduction system that processes several, typically more than two, channels of sound. For example, 5.1 multichannel audio refers to a surround sound system in which there are five primary channels and a subwoofer channel.

multiple bit rate (MBR) A characteristic of a data stream in which the same content is encoded at several different bit rates in order to optimize content delivery.

N

National Television Standards Committee (NTSC) The dominant television standard in the United States and Japan. NTSC delivers 30 interlaced frames per second at 525 lines of resolution.

NTSC See definition for: *National Television Standards Committee (NTSC)*

O

on-demand publishing point A type of publishing point that streams content to clients by request. Content streamed from an on-demand publishing point is always delivered as a unicast stream.

one-pass encoding An encoding method in which content is analyzed and compressed in the same pass through the encoder.

origin server A Windows Media server from which content is published.

P

packaged Windows Media file   A Windows Media file encrypted with a key, which consumers cannot play unless they have a key provided by a license. A packaged Windows Media file is produced by and protected through the implementation of digital rights management using the Windows Media Rights Manager SDK or a program based on the Microsoft Windows Media Format SDK.

packaging   The process that protects and signs a Windows Media file, producing a packaged Windows Media file. The packaging process includes generating or specifying a key, generating and signing the content header, and then encrypting the Windows Media file with this information.

packaging server   A computer used for packaging Windows Media files.

packet   A unit of information transmitted as a whole from one device to another on a network.

PAL   See definition for: *Phase Alternating Line (PAL)*

parse   To break input into smaller chunks so that a program can act upon the information.

PCM   See definition for: *pulse code modulation (PCM)*

Phase Alternating Line (PAL)   The dominant television standard in Europe and China. PAL delivers 25 interlaced frames per second at 625 lines of resolution.

pixel format   The size and arrangement of pixel color components. The format is specified by the total number of bits used per pixel and the number of bits used to store the red, green, blue, and alpha components of the color of the pixel.

player   A client program or control that receives digital media content streamed from a server or played from local files. Windows Media Player is an example of a player.

playlist   In Windows Media, a list of digital media content that is interpreted and rendered by a player.

plug-in   An auxiliary software component that extends or enhances the features of other software.

port   A connection point in a computer through which a peripheral device or another computer can communicate.

portable device   A mobile electronic device that can exchange files or other data with a computer or device. Examples of portable devices include Pocket PCs, portable digital music players, and Smartphones.

postroll   To extend the amount of encoded video by a specified number of frames.

preroll   To capture or play a number of video frames or a portion of audio data before encoding or rendering begins, in order to allow the source device to stabilize. Also used as a noun to describe the portion of the data to be prerolled.

private key   The secret half of a public/private key pair used in cryptography. Private keys are typically used to encrypt a symmetric session key, digitally sign a message, or decrypt a message that has been encrypted with the corresponding public key.

profile   In Windows Media Encoder, a group of settings that match content type and bit rate with appropriate audio and video codecs.

Profile Editor   A tool provided with Windows Media Encoder that creates and edits the encoding profiles.

protect   To encrypt files with a key and add information such as the license acquisition URL.

protocol   A set of formats and procedures that enable computers to exchange information.

protocol rollover   A procedure that enables switching from one protocol to another when a Windows Media server fails to make a connection using a particular protocol.

proxy server   A server located on a network between client software, such as a Web browser, and another server. It intercepts all requests to the server to determine whether it can fulfill them itself. If not, it forwards the request to another server.

public key   The non-secret half of a public/private key pair used in cryptography. Public keys are typically used to encrypt sessions, files, and messages, which are then decrypted using the corresponding private key.

publishing point   An organized memory location that translates a client request for content into the physical path on the Windows Media server hosting the content. A publishing point essentially acts as a redirector.

pull   To deliver data to a client only upon client request.

pulse code modulation (PCM)   A technique for digitizing audio into an uncompressed format by assigning a value to the amplitude of the signal at fixed intervals.

push   To deliver data to a client without a client request for the data.

R

Real Time Streaming Protocol (RTSP)   An Internet protocol that delivers real-time, live, or stored audio and video streams over a network.

registration   In Windows Media Rights Manager, the process in which a consumer enters information to acquire a license, such as an e-mail address.

render   To display video, audio, or text content from a file or stream using a software program, such as Windows Media Player.

repacketization   The process by which the server breaks down existing data packets and reassembles them into different-sized data packets for distribution to clients.

revocation list   A list that contains all the application certificates of those player applications known to be damaged or corrupted. This list is included in licenses and then is stored on consumers' computers by the digital rights management (DRM) component of the player application.

RGB   A color model that describes color information in terms of the red (R), green (G), and blue (B) intensities that make up the color.

RTSP   See definition for: *Real Time Streaming Protocol (RTSP)*

S

SACL   See definition for: *system access control list (SACL)*

sampling   The process of measuring the amplitude of an analog signal at regular intervals for the purpose of converting the signal into a digital format.

sampling rate   The frequency of sampling. The higher the sampling rate (that is, the more samples taken per unit of time), the more closely the digitized result resembles the original.

script commands   Named data that is associated with a designated time in Windows Media-based content. The data can be used by players to perform a specific action such as displaying a Web page.

SDMI   See definition for: *Secure Digital Music Initiative (SDMI)*

Secure Digital Music Initiative (SDMI)   An organization that sets standards for secure digital music. One of the main goals of SDMI is to create a framework for the secure playing, storing, and distribution of digital music.

sign   To bind an identity, such as a network login, hardware ID, or certificate, to a message, file, or other piece of digitally encoded information.

silent delivery   To deliver licenses without the consumer being aware of the process. A server running Windows Media License Service can issue a license without prompting the consumer.

Simple Network Management Protocol (SNMP)   A network protocol used to manage TCP/IP networks. In Windows, the SNMP service is used to provide status information about a host on a TCP/IP network.

skin   A user interface that provides an alternative appearance and customized functionality for software such as Windows Media Player.

skin definition file   An XML document that specifies the elements in a skin, along with their relationships and functionality. A skin definition file has a .wms file name extension.

skin mode   An operational state of Windows Media Player in which its user interface is displayed as a skin.

SMIL   See definition for: *Synchronized Multimedia Integration Language (SMIL)*

SNMP   See definition for: *Simple Network Management Protocol (SNMP)*

source   Audio and video content that can be captured and encoded from devices installed on your computer or from a file.

stream   Digital media that is in the process of being delivered in a continuous flow across a network.

stream format   The properties of a stream, such as the codecs used, frame rate, and frame size. A player uses stream format information to decode a stream.

stream format file   A file used by a player to decode a multicast stream.

stream thinning   The process of lowering the frame rate of source video to reduce the bandwidth required for streaming to be lower than or equal to the available client bandwidth. If necessary, the video portion of the stream may stop streaming and only the audio portion streamed.

streaming   A method of delivering digital media across a network in a continuous flow. The digital media is played by client software as it is received. Typically, streaming makes it unnecessary for users to download a file before playing it.

Synchronized Multimedia Integration Language (SMIL)   An XML-based language being developed by the World Wide Web Consortium (W3C) that enables Web developers to divide content into separate streams (audio, video, text, and images), send them to a client computer, and then have them displayed as a single stream. This separation reduces the time required for transmission over the Internet.

system access control list (SACL)   A list that represents part of an object's security descriptor that specifies which events (such as logon attempts and file access) are to be audited per user or group.

system profile   The default, predefined templates that contain the necessary technical details for encoding a particular piece of content.

T

TCP   See definition for: *Transmission Control Protocol (TCP)*

telecine   The film-to-video conversion system that adds frames to video to compensate for the differences in frame rates between film and video.

time code   A digital signal applied to a stream. The signal assigns a number to every frame of video, representing hours, minutes, seconds, and frames.

time-to-live (TTL) The number of routers through which a multicast stream can pass before a router stops forwarding the stream.

Transmission Control Protocol (TCP) The protocol within TCP/IP that governs the breakup of data messages into packets to be sent through IP, and the reassembly and verification of the complete messages from packets received by IP.

TTL See definition for: *time-to-live (TTL)*

two-pass encoding An encoding method in which content is analyzed in one pass through the encoder, after which compression is applied in the second pass.

U

UDP See definition for: *User Datagram Protocol (UDP)*

UDP resend An error correction method that allows the client to request that the server retransmit lost data packets.

UNC See definition for: *Universal Naming Convention (UNC)*

unicast A method used by media servers for providing content to connected clients in which each client receives a discrete stream. No other client has access to that stream.

unicast rollover Redirection of a client to a unicast stream in the event the client cannot access the multicast stream.

Universal Naming Convention (UNC) The full name of a resource on a network. It conforms to the \\servername\sharename syntax, where servername is the name of the server and sharename is the name of the shared resource. UNC names of directories or files can also include the directory path under the share name, with the following syntax: \\servername\sharename\directory\filename.

User Datagram Protocol (UDP) A connectionless transport protocol in the TCP/IP protocol stack that is used in cases where some packet loss is acceptable, for example, with digital media streams.

V

variable bit rate (VBR) A characteristic of a data stream in which the bit rate fluctuates, depending upon the complexity of the data.

VBR See definition for: *variable bit rate (VBR)*

visualization In Windows Media Player, a graphical display that changes in response to the audio signal.

W

Windows Media Audio codec   A codec used to compress and decompress audio streams.

Windows Media file   A file containing audio, video, or script data that is stored in Windows Media Format. Depending on their content and purpose, Windows Media files use a variety of file name extensions, such as: .wma, .wme, .wms, .wmv, .wmx, .wmz, or .wvx.

Windows Media Format   The format used by the Windows Media platform (or another product that incorporates a licensed Windows Media technology) to author, store, edit, distribute, stream, or play timeline-based content.

Windows Media metafile   A file that provides information about Windows Media files and their presentation. File name extensions for Windows Media metafiles include .asx, .wax, .wvx, .wmx, and .nsc.

Windows Media Screen codec   A codec used to compress and decompress sequences of screen images.

Windows Media server   A server on which Windows Media Services has been installed.

Windows Media Services   A service that enables content to be streamed over the Internet or an intranet.

Windows Media Video codec   A codec used to compress and decompress video streams.

wrapper playlist   A Windows Media metafile that places additional content at the beginning or end of a stream. Examples of this content include welcome messages, goodbye messages, advertisements, and station branding.

X

XML   See definition for: *Extensible Markup Language (XML)*

Y

YUV   A color model that describes color information in terms of its brightness (luminance, or Y), and color (chrominance, or U and V).

Index

Bill Birney

Bill has been creating content for more than 35 years. He started out in radio as a disc jockey, then gained broad experience in many fields, including television, music, audio production, film, corporate communications, and software. During his career, he has worked as a scriptwriter, composer, producer, director, video editor, sound designer, and creative director. Bill was a developmental editor and co-author of the book *Inside Windows Media* (Que, 1999), and was most recently co-author of the *Windows Movie Maker Handbook* (Microsoft Press, 2000).

Tricia Gill

Tricia began her career as a newspaper reporter before moving into technical communication. Over the past 18 years, she has written about a range of topics including hydroelectric power plants, pet food drives, passenger jets, public school programs, and computer software. While at Microsoft, Tricia has written online Help for Microsoft Site Server and Windows Media Encoder, assisted with the user interface design of Microsoft Commerce Server, and written numerous Web articles and white papers about Windows Media Technologies.

Get a **Free**
e-mail newsletter, updates,
special offers, links to related books,
and more when you

register on line!

Register your Microsoft Press® title on our Web site and you'll get a FREE subscription to our e-mail newsletter, *Microsoft Press Book Connections*. You'll find out about newly released and upcoming books and learning tools, online events, software downloads, special offers and coupons for Microsoft Press customers, and information about major Microsoft® product releases. You can also read useful additional information about all the titles we publish, such as detailed book descriptions, tables of contents and indexes, sample chapters, links to related books and book series, author biographies, and reviews by other customers.

Registration is easy. Just visit this Web page and fill in your information:

http://www.microsoft.com/mspress/register

Microsoft®

MICROSOFT LICENSE AGREEMENT

Book Companion CD

IMPORTANT—READ CAREFULLY: This Microsoft End-User License Agreement ("EULA") is a legal agreement between you (either an individual or an entity) and Microsoft Corporation for the Microsoft product identified above, which includes computer software and may include associated media, printed materials, and "online" or electronic documentation ("SOFTWARE PRODUCT"). Any component included within the SOFTWARE PRODUCT that is accompanied by a separate End-User License Agreement shall be governed by such agreement and not the terms set forth below. By installing, copying, or otherwise using the SOFTWARE PRODUCT, you agree to be bound by the terms of this EULA. If you do not agree to the terms of this EULA, you are not authorized to install, copy, or otherwise use the SOFTWARE PRODUCT; you may, however, return the SOFTWARE PRODUCT, along with all printed materials and other items that form a part of the Microsoft product that includes the SOFTWARE PRODUCT, to the place you obtained them for a full refund.

SOFTWARE PRODUCT LICENSE

The SOFTWARE PRODUCT is protected by United States copyright laws and international copyright treaties, as well as other intellectual property laws and treaties. The SOFTWARE PRODUCT is licensed, not sold.

1. **GRANT OF LICENSE.** This EULA grants you the following rights:

   a. **Software Product.** You may install and use one copy of the SOFTWARE PRODUCT on a single computer. The primary user of the computer on which the SOFTWARE PRODUCT is installed may make a second copy for his or her exclusive use on a portable computer.

   b. **Storage/Network Use.** You may also store or install a copy of the SOFTWARE PRODUCT on a storage device, such as a network server, used only to install or run the SOFTWARE PRODUCT on your other computers over an internal network; however, you must acquire and dedicate a license for each separate computer on which the SOFTWARE PRODUCT is installed or run from the storage device. A license for the SOFTWARE PRODUCT may not be shared or used concurrently on different computers.

   c. **License Pak.** If you have acquired this EULA in a Microsoft License Pak, you may make the number of additional copies of the computer software portion of the SOFTWARE PRODUCT authorized on the printed copy of this EULA, and you may use each copy in the manner specified above. You are also entitled to make a corresponding number of secondary copies for portable computer use as specified above.

   d. **Sample Code.** Solely with respect to portions, if any, of the SOFTWARE PRODUCT that are identified within the SOFTWARE PRODUCT as sample code (the "SAMPLE CODE"):

      i. **Use and Modification.** Microsoft grants you the right to use and modify the source code version of the SAMPLE CODE, *provided* you comply with subsection (d)(iii) below. You may not distribute the SAMPLE CODE, or any modified version of the SAMPLE CODE, in source code form.

      ii. **Redistributable Files.** Provided you comply with subsection (d)(iii) below, Microsoft grants you a nonexclusive, royalty-free right to reproduce and distribute the object code version of the SAMPLE CODE and of any modified SAMPLE CODE, other than SAMPLE CODE, or any modified version thereof, designated as not redistributable in the Readme file that forms a part of the SOFTWARE PRODUCT (the "Non-Redistributable Sample Code"). All SAMPLE CODE other than the Non-Redistributable Sample Code is collectively referred to as the "REDISTRIBUTABLES."

      iii. **Redistribution Requirements.** If you redistribute the REDISTRIBUTABLES, you agree to: (i) distribute the REDISTRIBUTABLES in object code form only in conjunction with and as a part of your software application product; (ii) not use Microsoft's name, logo, or trademarks to market your software application product; (iii) include a valid copyright notice on your software application product; (iv) indemnify, hold harmless, and defend Microsoft from and against any claims or lawsuits, including attorney's fees, that arise or result from the use or distribution of your software application product; and (v) not permit further distribution of the REDISTRIBUTABLES by your end user. Contact Microsoft for the applicable royalties due and other licensing terms for all other uses and/or distribution of the REDISTRIBUTABLES.

2. **DESCRIPTION OF OTHER RIGHTS AND LIMITATIONS.**

   - **Limitations on Reverse Engineering, Decompilation, and Disassembly.** You may not reverse engineer, decompile, or disassemble the SOFTWARE PRODUCT, except and only to the extent that such activity is expressly permitted by applicable law notwithstanding this limitation.

   - **Separation of Components.** The SOFTWARE PRODUCT is licensed as a single product. Its component parts may not be separated for use on more than one computer.

   - **Rental.** You may not rent, lease, or lend the SOFTWARE PRODUCT.

- **Support Services.** Microsoft may, but is not obligated to, provide you with support services related to the SOFTWARE PRODUCT ("Support Services"). Use of Support Services is governed by the Microsoft policies and programs described in the user manual, in "online" documentation, and/or in other Microsoft-provided materials. Any supplemental software code provided to you as part of the Support Services shall be considered part of the SOFTWARE PRODUCT and subject to the terms and conditions of this EULA. With respect to technical information you provide to Microsoft as part of the Support Services, Microsoft may use such information for its business purposes, including for product support and development. Microsoft will not utilize such technical information in a form that personally identifies you.

- **Software Transfer.** You may permanently transfer all of your rights under this EULA, provided you retain no copies, you transfer all of the SOFTWARE PRODUCT (including all component parts, the media and printed materials, any upgrades, this EULA, and, if applicable, the Certificate of Authenticity), **and** the recipient agrees to the terms of this EULA.

- **Termination.** Without prejudice to any other rights, Microsoft may terminate this EULA if you fail to comply with the terms and conditions of this EULA. In such event, you must destroy all copies of the SOFTWARE PRODUCT and all of its component parts.

3. **COPYRIGHT.** All title and copyrights in and to the SOFTWARE PRODUCT (including but not limited to any images, photographs, animations, video, audio, music, text, SAMPLE CODE, REDISTRIBUTABLES, and "applets" incorporated into the SOFTWARE PRODUCT) and any copies of the SOFTWARE PRODUCT are owned by Microsoft or its suppliers. The SOFT-WARE PRODUCT is protected by copyright laws and international treaty provisions. Therefore, you must treat the SOFTWARE PRODUCT like any other copyrighted material **except** that you may install the SOFTWARE PRODUCT on a single computer provided you keep the original solely for backup or archival purposes. You may not copy the printed materials accompanying the SOFTWARE PRODUCT.

4. **U.S. GOVERNMENT RESTRICTED RIGHTS.** The SOFTWARE PRODUCT and documentation are provided with RESTRICTED RIGHTS. Use, duplication, or disclosure by the Government is subject to restrictions as set forth in subparagraph (c)(1)(ii) of the Rights in Technical Data and Computer Software clause at DFARS 252.227-7013 or subparagraphs (c)(1) and (2) of the Commercial Computer Software—Restricted Rights at 48 CFR 52.227-19, as applicable. Manufacturer is Microsoft Corporation/One Microsoft Way/Redmond, WA 98052-6399.

5. **EXPORT RESTRICTIONS.** You agree that you will not export or re-export the SOFTWARE PRODUCT, any part thereof, or any process or service that is the direct product of the SOFTWARE PRODUCT (the foregoing collectively referred to as the "Restricted Components"), to any country, person, entity, or end user subject to U.S. export restrictions. You specifically agree not to export or re-export any of the Restricted Components (i) to any country to which the U.S. has embargoed or restricted the export of goods or services, which currently include, but are not necessarily limited to, Cuba, Iran, Iraq, Libya, North Korea, Sudan, and Syria, or to any national of any such country, wherever located, who intends to transmit or transport the Restricted Components back to such country; (ii) to any end user who you know or have reason to know will utilize the Restricted Components in the design, development, or production of nuclear, chemical, or biological weapons; or (iii) to any end user who has been prohibited from participating in U.S. export transactions by any federal agency of the U.S. government. You warrant and represent that neither the BXA nor any other U.S. federal agency has suspended, revoked, or denied your export privileges.

DISCLAIMER OF WARRANTY

NO WARRANTIES OR CONDITIONS. MICROSOFT EXPRESSLY DISCLAIMS ANY WARRANTY OR CONDITION FOR THE SOFTWARE PRODUCT. THE SOFTWARE PRODUCT AND ANY RELATED DOCUMENTATION ARE PROVIDED "AS IS" WITHOUT WARRANTY OR CONDITION OF ANY KIND, EITHER EXPRESS OR IMPLIED, INCLUDING, WITHOUT LIMITA-TION, THE IMPLIED WARRANTIES OF MERCHANTABILITY, FITNESS FOR A PARTICULAR PURPOSE, OR NONINFRINGEMENT. THE ENTIRE RISK ARISING OUT OF USE OR PERFORMANCE OF THE SOFTWARE PRODUCT REMAINS WITH YOU.

LIMITATION OF LIABILITY. TO THE MAXIMUM EXTENT PERMITTED BY APPLICABLE LAW, IN NO EVENT SHALL MICROSOFT OR ITS SUPPLIERS BE LIABLE FOR ANY SPECIAL, INCIDENTAL, INDIRECT, OR CONSEQUENTIAL DAM-AGES WHATSOEVER (INCLUDING, WITHOUT LIMITATION, DAMAGES FOR LOSS OF BUSINESS PROFITS, BUSINESS INTERRUPTION, LOSS OF BUSINESS INFORMATION, OR ANY OTHER PECUNIARY LOSS) ARISING OUT OF THE USE OF OR INABILITY TO USE THE SOFTWARE PRODUCT OR THE PROVISION OF OR FAILURE TO PROVIDE SUPPORT SERVICES, EVEN IF MICROSOFT HAS BEEN ADVISED OF THE POSSIBILITY OF SUCH DAMAGES. IN ANY CASE, MICROSOFT'S ENTIRE LIABILITY UNDER ANY PROVISION OF THIS EULA SHALL BE LIMITED TO THE GREATER OF THE AMOUNT ACTUALLY PAID BY YOU FOR THE SOFTWARE PRODUCT OR US$5.00; PROVIDED, HOWEVER, IF YOU HAVE ENTERED INTO A MICROSOFT SUPPORT SERVICES AGREEMENT, MICROSOFT'S ENTIRE LIABILITY REGARDING SUPPORT SERVICES SHALL BE GOVERNED BY THE TERMS OF THAT AGREEMENT. BECAUSE SOME STATES AND JURISDICTIONS DO NOT ALLOW THE EXCLUSION OR LIMITATION OF LIABILITY, THE ABOVE LIMITATION MAY NOT APPLY TO YOU.

MISCELLANEOUS

This EULA is governed by the laws of the State of Washington USA, except and only to the extent that applicable law mandates governing law of a different jurisdiction.

Should you have any questions concerning this EULA, or if you desire to contact Microsoft for any reason, please contact the Microsoft subsidiary serving your country, or write: Microsoft Sales Information Center/One Microsoft Way/Redmond, WA 98052-6399.